PERSPECTIVES ON WOMEN'S ARCHIVES

EDITED BY TANYA ZANISH-BELCHER WITH ANKE VOSS

SOCIETY OF
American
Archivists

CHICAGO

Society of American Archivists
www.archivists.org

Printed in the United States of America.

Graphic design by Sweeney Design, kasween@sbcglobal.net.

Library of Congress Cataloging-in-Publication Data
  Perspectives on women's archives / edited by Tanya Zanish-Belcher, with Anke Voss.
    pages cm
  Includes index.
  ISBN 978-1-931666-47-3
  1. Women—History—Archives. 2. Women—History—Sources. 3. Feminism—History—Archives.
  4. Feminism—History—Sources. I. Zanish-Belcher, Tanya.
  HQ1150.P475 2013
  305.4—dc23
                          2013027198

Acknowledgments

THE WOMEN'S ARCHIVES READER HAS BEEN LONG IN THE MAKING, AND
MANY HANDS HAVE BEEN INVOLVED IN ITS CONCEPTUALIZATION AND
CREATION. Special thanks are due to Teresa Brinati, director of publishing
for the Society of American Archivists, as well as the SAA Publications
Board and its chair, Dr. Peter Wosh. We would also like to thank the blind
reviewers who worked on behalf of the Publications Board and provided
excellent recommendations for this volume.

Many people have contributed to the successful completion of this
book in a variety of ways, and we would especially like to recognize and
thank Tom Connors, Amy Cooper Cary, David Gregory, Kathryn Jacob,
Karen Jefferson, Kären M. Mason, L. Rebecca Johnson-Melvin, Joanne
Kazcmarek, Doris Malkmus, Eva Moseley, Elizabeth Myers, Kathryn Neal,
Sherrill Redmon, Margery Sly, Laura Sullivan, Susan Tucker, Kate Theimer,
and Kelly Wooten. Special thanks are due to the Iowa State University
Library, the ISU Center for Excellence in the Arts and Humanities, and
the ISU Women's Studies Program for their support of this project.

TANYA ZANISH-BELCHER WITH ANKE VOSS

Table of Contents

Introduction

TANYA ZANISH-BELCHER AND ANKE VOSS

THE HISTORY OF WOMEN'S ARCHIVES AND THE COLLECTING OF WOMEN'S RECORDS REFLECT THE LARGER CULTURAL AND SOCIETAL DEVELOPMENTS OCCURRING IN AMERICAN HISTORY OVER THE PAST FEW CENTURIES. The act of writing documents and organizing archives is a powerful act of creation, and women have used both processes to connect their communities and enhance their identities as women. The original goal for this reader was to collect, and present with appropriate context and background, all previously published archival literature on women's archives and collections (at both national and international levels) in a single volume. As we reviewed the literature for seminal studies, however, we found a dearth of broad scholarship related to our topic. While early articles focused on the important issues of finding and listing collections, they provided little interpretation, analysis, or reflection. Furthermore, there were major gaps in the historical record of archival practice, so our concept of a retrospective reader had to be expanded to include solicited articles in neglected areas. We identified many core topics still needing to be explored, but realized that a single reader could never adequately address all of them. Thus, this reader is only a beginning and is not intended to be definitive. The essays in this volume pose questions that remain to be answered in future scholarship on women's archives and women's collections. We hope that others will take up this challenge.

When Margaret Rossiter was writing *American Women in Science: Struggles and Strategies to 1940,* published in 1981, she "worried whether there would be enough sources."[1] By the end, she realized there was more content than she could ever capture in one volume. The articles in this reader illustrate a similar point: while women's collections may be difficult to locate, on closer examination, the amount of material can be overwhelming. This reader is organized into four sections along the following lines: "Reclaiming Our Past"; "Locating Women in the Archives"; "Documenting Women's Experiences"; and "Conclusion." The reader begins and ends with articles by historian Gerda Lerner, the first written in the 1970s when the field of women's history was just emerging. In the second article, written a half-century later, she reflects upon a mature field of women's history and explores the desirability of a more holistic history. The development of women's archives owes much to the historians who pioneered the study of women's history; one of our themes concerns the diverging paths that women's historians and archivists have traveled over the past fifty years.

Early Development of Women's Archives and the Link with Historians

Many of the issues and challenges in developing theoretical frameworks for women's archives lie in Gerda Lerner's scholarly work and the work of other historians during the resurgence of women's history in the 1960s and 1970s. These early pioneers, including Lerner, Anne Firor Scott, Carroll Smith-Rosenberg, and others, blazed a trail for a new women's history. As Smith-Rosenberg said, this new history was a "product of complex interaction between the political perspective of the contemporary women's movement and the methodology and focus of the New Social History."[2] One could not have happened without the other, and the imperative in these early years was to locate much-needed sources and to develop a "compensatory" history to demonstrate the value of women's activities. The essays in this reader represent and reflect many aspects of the development of women's history in the mid-to-late twentieth century: a need to find and locate sources on women; a sense of identity empowering the creation of women's archives and preserving women's collections; efforts to document the unique female experience; and finally, a vision for the future focusing on the whole of human experience, while not losing the unique experiences that make us who we are.

Main Themes

Certainly, the need for a complete synthesis of the historical experiences of women (in addition to that of other underdocumented groups based on race, class, and role) should be a major goal for archivists and historians alike. There are additional important themes in the essays that follow, ranging from the role of the archivist, to the need for greater diversity in our collecting and scholarship, to women's archives and what their creation has meant psychologically for women. However, we would like to spend some time examining what we consider to be several major issues for women's collections, as they also raise significant issues for the archives profession as a whole.

First, there is a need for renewed collaboration and partnership with historians of women's history, women's history librarians, and women's studies faculty. At several critical junctures, women's historians, collaborating with archivists, fostered efforts to collect and survey sources on women. As the archives profession has continued to evolve, its emphasis on information management (both analog and electronic), and the nesting of archives training within library science programs, has diminished the role of the historical narrative in archives training and perhaps within the profession as a whole.[3] While a degree in public history is still an acceptable path to the profession, it has been somewhat sidelined. Archivists may work with individual faculty on the uses of primary sources, but we need to forge new relationships and networks with other groups of users. How do we accomplish this? We need to explore ways to connect, whether by participating in each other's conferences, sharing via newsletters or blogs, or raising awareness of each other's work. We need to emphasize potential collaborations through a variety of activities, including conferences such as the Berkshire Conference on Women's History, and jointly sponsored grant proposals such as the National Endowment for the Humanities grant that funded *Women's History Sources: A Guide to Archives and Manuscript Collections in the United States* (1979). We can focus on sharing information through sites such as Women and Social Movements, International, which includes a column on newly available collections and other news items.[4] We also need to better communicate with others in the archival profession about the gendered aspects of recordkeeping and focus on its broader meanings for archival work. We must be mindful of other potential collaborators with similar goals and interests throughout our communities, particularly those working in culture and heritage.

Second, we must recognize and confront the many challenges related to the accessibility of women's collections. Access, or the lack thereof, has been a major issue for women's collections for the past fifty years or more. There are many missing sources that may exist, but cannot be found due to lack of description or poor care, or their being housed outside mainstream repositories. The lives and experiences of women have long been cloaked in what is considered "private life," and documenting this hidden or inner life has been problematic. How does one capture sexuality, spirituality, and the sometimes mundane experience of everyday existence? Oral history provides a partial solution. But even more broadly, beyond creating and collecting material, we need to explore issues of intellectual control and access, such as descriptive practices that can either promote or hinder the discovery of these collections by our public.

For many, technology is a panacea for archives, both for creating and sharing access to primary materials and experiences. Archivists can now share what we know and can find new tools to better fit the needs of the user. Not only does technology enable archivists to provide access to our collections, it also allows any individual or organization to create records and share them widely with the public. Private narratives are becoming public through social media and reaching audiences well beyond the lone scholar diligently researching in a traditional reading room. But with all these opportunities, technology also presents many barriers. Digitizing and digital preservation still require the intellectual process of selection and present the added challenge of maintaining and refreshing a variety of electronic formats. Are we merely repeating many of the mistakes made in the past by once again emphasizing the management of institutional records as opposed to what may be considered gendered memory-making? As archivists, do we spend too much time training or learning about the tools of the trade rather than considering the more complex issues and implications related to what we can and should be collecting? We are destined to lose many records due to technological constraints and other limitations. The important question remains: how do the records we leave behind reflect our society? Archivists invest significant time and resources into those records we consider "integral" and "important," do we not? There will be haves and have-nots, but how will this impact the documentation of women? The difficulty and costs of comprehensive digital preservation of traditional electronic records and social media are simply too high at this particular point in time. This is not just about storage costs, but time and commitment too. Those institutions and individuals with resources will determine the majority of what is to be saved of the archival record.[5]

Which brings us to our third major theme—the development of community archives and the rise of the citizen archivist. Local grassroots groups have always played a role in collecting the papers of women, even when the early focus was on the importance of national collecting for the Schlesinger Library for the History of Women and the Sophia Smith collections. Grassroots and regional efforts in collecting, such as those described in Mary Caldera's and Danelle Moon's essays in this volume, demonstrate that this work is still a significant source of identity and power. This activism is especially important for groups operating outside of the mainstream; however, there may sometimes be a cost. Mere passion or an emotional connection to collecting and saving may not overcome a lack of professional training or adequate facilities for preserving the materials permanently. Furthermore, women's participation in online and virtual communities also raises the question—what is local? How do you determine what is of historical value in this new global community, and how do you extract it from an overwhelming amount of information? Does the online aspect of the virtual community erase context and meaning? Who is going to collect this? Who is responsible? We are participating in an environment where we are not the only recordkeepers. But who then will select, appraise, and preserve these records and make them available for future use? This raises major questions about the roles and the responsibilities of archivists. Are we still relevant? How does what we do distinguish us from others? How will the tools archivists currently use apply to the future development of women's archives? We have raised many more questions than we can possibly answer, but we hope we have also inspired new conversations about the value and worth of women's collections and the value of the archival profession as a whole.

Reader Overview

The first section of this reader, "Reclaiming Our Past," provides a starting point for any consideration of women's collections and archives during the late twentieth century and encompasses several examples of early scholarship from this time period. These articles illustrate the origins of a woman-centered history which developed steadily through the decades following the emergence of the modern women's movement in the 1960s. Key components for archives include efforts to locate sources for women's history, the belief that archives should actively collect and preserve women's history sources, and a growing sense of the significance of the female experience in history. The theme "my experience matters" motivated an activist concept of archives throughout this period and is echoed throughout this reader.

Gerda Lerner was one of the pioneers of women's history, proffering an early challenge to the patriarchal organization of the historical record. Her 1975 article presents aspects of the developmental stages of women's history. Though historians such as Mary Ritter Beard had blazed a trail in writing about women's experiences decades before the advent of the modern women's movement, their work was largely ignored. Anke Voss identifies a number of ideas in Beard's work, such as the impact on self-identity that comes of having one's history valued and preserved. Voss describes Beard's proactive work in creating archives even though Beard herself was a historian, not an archivist, and notes the important role played by universities in documenting the experience of women and serving both as repositories for documentation and centers for research.

The next two articles represent an important perspective that has frequently been overlooked: the experience of African American women. Deborah Gray White and Audrey McCluskey explore themes common to many articles in this reader—African American women feeling undervalued and invisible as they confronted initial resistance to the importance of their experiences, compounded by the difficulties scholars faced in locating sources either due to poor indexing of existing collections or the failure of archivists to collect sources on African American women. McCluskey's article discusses the desire of African American women in the 1970s to write their own history as opposed to having their experience presented through the prism of others. Throughout the latter half of the twentieth century, oral history provided such a means and opportunity, and proved its value in documenting experiences missing from the written record. Historians again played an important role in locating sources and driving documentation projects; Darlene Clark Hine coordinated the Black Women in the Middle West project to record oral histories and preserve papers of African American women. Gerda Lerner and other historians collaborating with archivists played an integral role in conceptualizing and bringing about *Women's History Sources: A Guide to Archives and Manuscript Collections in the United States*, which, edited by Andrea Hinding, eventually became known as the "Hinding Guide."

The Women's History Sources Survey, the run-up to the publication, and its importance in locating women's collections in the United States cannot be overestimated. Kären Mason provides a much-needed review of its inception and how it was accomplished. Eleven thousand repositories were surveyed in a gargantuan effort by archivists, fieldworkers, and local guardians of the historical record throughout the United States. *Women's History Sources* demonstrated that sources by and about women did indeed exist, but that there were many groups and topics about which few records had been preserved or described, most notably women of color. The guide also illustrated the difficulty in defining what women's collections were and demonstrated the limitations of printed guides that could not easily be updated. However, the "Hinding Guide" serves as an archival snapshot of the late 1970s and is an invaluable resource still used by researchers and scholars today. There have been many calls to update *Women's History Sources*, but the tremendous resources and effort required to do so have proved too daunting.

This section closes with a work by Eva Moseley published in *The American Archivist* in 1980. Written the year after *Women's History Sources* was published, it discussed the challenges of documenting farming, the working class, the poor, and women more generally. Moseley indicated how limited the early efforts to gather sources on women were, but what an important start had been made.

The second section of the reader addresses the importance and urgency of locating collections and proving the value of the female experience. Countering the establishment argument that not enough sources were available, many efforts were made to locate potential sources throughout the country. One result of these joint efforts by archivists and feminists was the creation of women's archives in many locations, particularly in the 1990s. But, in addition to locating collections in mainstream repositories and creating woman-centered archives, efforts were also made to creatively reexamine family papers as sources for the presence of women, to record oral histories documenting little-known aspects of women's lives and work, and to gather records documenting gendered experiences. In 2000, Kären Mason and Tanya Zanish-Belcher, as curators of women's archives, began to notice the burgeoning number of similar collections throughout the United States. They analyze the philosophical question of whether women's archives should exist, a topic previously raised by Eva Moseley in the 1970s. Would the day ever come when there was no need for women's archives? Mason and Zanish-Belcher conclude that while we may question the existence of identity-based archives, women's archives have a greater meaning than the collections they house. Their very existence confers weight on the value of women's history, increases the demand for sources, and offers the important opportunity to promote and enhance the study of women's history.

The role of women in the process of memory formation and record-keeping is analyzed in an essay by Susan Tucker, who examines this theme through the lens of family history. She describes the proactive ways women have created memories for the next generation, whether by oral stories, embroidery, or scrapbooking. The documentation of women is oftentimes hiding in plain sight, and Fernanda Perrone discusses one example of this by focusing on the uniquely female experience of women religious. She notes that while these archives consist of first-rate sources, many times they are overlooked, possibly since they are considered outside the mainstream. She also acknowledges the difficulties and challenges of documenting the inner life of spirituality, providing access to these sources, and their long-term chances for survival.

Mary Caldera describes the development of community-based archives resulting from activism in the lesbian, gay, bisexual, and transgender (LGBT) community, a topic that bears great relevance for the current archives profession. In her essay, she details the strengths of archives that are created and cared for by activist groups, which in many ways parallel the archives created and maintained by small, local historical societies. While the passion and dedication of such individuals cannot be matched, the lack of archival education and training and (in the case of LGBT collections in particular) thorny privacy issues present challenges to the long-term viability of these collections and their survival in local communities. On the other hand, the mere creation of these collections has raised awareness among archivists and the general public of this important history and of the role one's history plays in identity formation.

Tanya Zanish-Belcher closes this section with a review of papers and records relating to human reproduction. The article addresses the surprising fact that a unique experience shared by the entire human population is rarely discussed or documented, which leads to a conceptual challenge for archivists and researchers attempting to collect, locate, or even think about these records. She argues for documentation strategies and creative approaches to collecting, sharing, interpreting, and preserving this unique aspect of the human experience.

The reader's third section details specific efforts toward the process of documenting women's experiences. Mason and Zanish-Belcher again explore issues relating to woman-centered recordkeeping. Expanding on their previous work, they examine a broad range of issues, including collection development, research use, and the omnipresent role of oral history. They argue that women's archives have been at the forefront in creatively and diligently documenting women's lives and experiences. Taronda Spencer explores the unique and special role that Historically Black Colleges and Universities (HBCUs) have played in documenting African American women. Her article reveals a deep and vast array of collections yet to be mined for historical research.

Those who work with women's collections often recognize special opportunities for building connections with communities and donors. Janice Ruth pragmatically describes collaborative in-house efforts to more effectively share the Library of Congress women's collections with the public. Her essay describes the continued importance of good cataloging, the creation of subject guides, and the utilization of new technologies and partnerships as well as outreach through public symposia. Danelle Moon's essay on the importance of regional collecting looks at early efforts focused on the national level, then shifts to the regional level for a more in-depth documentation project on second wave feminism. She contends that her project is important both for the history of San José *and* for a broader history of women and concludes, like Mason, that removing documents from their area of origin separates them from their context. Finally, Virginia Corvid examines a modern, distinctly gendered method of documenting the personal and political in her essay on the archival role of zines. Zines are a creative and proactive way to share experiences, whereby the private becomes public. This unique and fragile format is not widely collected, but it offers an alternative means of documenting women that can be especially valuable for offering the perspectives of young women.

The concluding section of the reader examines the state of women's history, archives, and collections at the end of the first decade of the twenty-first century. In her article "Holistic History," Lerner reviews both her career and the current state of women's history. She sees scholars focusing on the "differences" between women—especially race, ethnicity, gender, and sexuality. She argues that "to interpret the female past from a female-centered point of view demands that we question and redefine the values by which we order historical data."[6] She contends that while progress has certainly been made, women have not "seized the space where we rightfully belong." There are still many "periods, regions, and groups that remain underdocumented and uninterpreted."[7] Only by fully collecting and documenting the vastness of the female (and male) experience can we hope to attain a fully integrated perspective of the past. A holistic history is still an ideal, a goal for which many archivists and historians are still striving.

In the reader's final essay, Beth Myers offers a concluding review of the essays in this volume, touching on many of the current issues in women's archives and women's collections, with an eye turned toward the future. She states, and we concur, that archivists need to be better at collecting, surveying, and describing. She echoes issues raised in our introduction—from the culpability of archivists, to the importance of technology as a tool, and the new and growing role of the citizen archivist. Archivists for women's collections can further develop our efforts at inclusivity and serve as much-needed role models for the entire profession. As archivists, while we may struggle with the day-to-day challenges of preserving the historical record, we must also be cognizant of the broader stream of history that society's recordkeeping reflects.

Special thanks to Kären Mason, University of Iowa,
for her contributions to this introduction.

NOTES

[1] Margaret Rossiter, preface to *Women Scientists in America: Struggles and Strategies to 1940* (Baltimore: Johns Hopkins Press, 1982), xi.

[2] Carroll Smith-Rosenberg, "The New Woman and the New History," *Feminist Studies, Inc.* 3, nos. 1–2 (1975): 186.

[3] For more on this issue, see Francis X. Blouin Jr. and William G. Rosenberg, *Processing the Past: Contesting Authority in History and the Archives* (New York: Oxford University Press, 2011).

[4] *Women and Social Movements in the United States, 1600–2000* is coedited by Kathryn Kish Sklar and Thomas Dublin, http://womhist.alexanderstreet.com/journal.htm, accessed 9 November 2012. See also Sklar and Dublin, "Creating Meaning in a Sea of Information: The Women and Social Movement Sites" (Spring 2012), in *Writing History in the Digital Age*, ed. Jack Dougherty and Kristen Nawrotzki, http://writinghistory.trincollege.edu/data/sklar-dublin-2012-spring, accessed 9 November 2012.

[5] Andrew Flinn discusses these issues in detail in "An Attack on Professionalism and Scholarship? Democratising Archives and the Production of Knowledge," *Ariadne* 62 (January 2010), http://www.ariadne.ac.uk/issue62, accessed 4 September 2012.

[6] Gerda Lerner, "Holistic History: Challenges and Possibilities," in *Living with History/Making Social Change* (Chapel Hill: University of North Carolina, 2009), 24.

[7] Lerner, "Holistic History," 25.

Reclaiming Our Past

CHAPTER 1

Placing Women in History: Definitions and Challenges

GERDA LERNER

IN THE BRIEF SPAN OF FIVE YEARS IN WHICH AMERICAN HISTORIANS HAVE
BEGUN TO DEVELOP WOMEN'S HISTORY AS AN INDEPENDENT FIELD, THEY
HAVE SOUGHT TO FIND A CONCEPTUAL FRAMEWORK AND A METHODOL-
OGY APPROPRIATE TO THE TASK.

The first level at which historians, trained in traditional history,
approach women's history is by writing the history of "women worthies"
or "compensatory history."[1] Who are the women missing from history?
Who are the women of achievement and what did they achieve? The
resulting history of "notable women" does not tell us much about those
activities in which most women engaged, nor does it tell us about the significance of women's activities to society as a whole. The history of notable
women is the history of exceptional, even deviant women, and does not
describe the experience and history of the mass of women. This insight
is a refinement of an awareness of class differences in history: women of
different classes have different historical experiences. To comprehend the
full complexity of society at a given stage of its development, it is essential
to take account of such differences.

Women also have a different experience with respect to consciousness, depending on whether their work, their expression, their activity is
male-defined or woman-oriented. Women, like men, are indoctrinated

in a male-defined value system and conduct their lives accordingly. Thus, colonial and early nineteenth-century female reformers directed their activities into channels that were merely an extension of their domestic concerns and traditional roles. They taught school and cared for the poor, the sick, the aged. As their consciousness developed, they turned their attention toward the needs of women. Becoming woman-oriented, they began to "uplift" prostitutes, to organize women for abolition or temperance, and to upgrade female education, but only to equip women better for their traditional roles. Only at a later stage, growing out of the recognition of the separate interests of women as a group, and of their subordinate place in society, did their consciousness become woman-defined. Feminist thought starts at this level and encompasses the active assertion of the rights and grievances of women. These various stages of female consciousness need to be considered in historical analysis.

The next level of conceptualizing women's history has been "contribution history": describing women's contribution to, their status in, and their oppression by male-defined society. Under this category we find a variety of questions being asked: what have women contributed to abolition, to reform, to the Progressive movement, to the labor movement, to the New Deal? The movement in question stands in the foreground of inquiry; women made a "contribution" to it; the contribution is judged first of all with respect to its effect on that movement and secondly by standards appropriate to men.

The ways in which women were aided and affected by the work of these "great women," the ways in which they themselves grew into feminist awareness, are ignored. Jane Addams's enormous contribution in creating a supporting female network and new structures for living are subordinated to her role as a Progressive, or to an interpretation that regards her as merely representative of a group of frustrated college-trained women with no place to go. In other words, a deviant from male-defined norms. Margaret Sanger is seen merely as the founder of the birth control movement, not as a woman raising a revolutionary challenge to the centuries-old practice by which the bodies and lives of women are dominated and ruled by man-made laws. In the labor movement, women are described as "also there" or as problems. Their essential role on behalf of themselves and of other women is seldom considered a central theme in writing their history. Women are the outgroup, Simone de Beauvoir's "other."

Another set of questions concern oppression and its opposite, the struggle for women's rights. Who oppressed women and how were they oppressed? How did they respond to such oppression?

Such questions have yielded detailed and very valuable accounts of economic or social oppression, and of the various organizational, political ways in which women as a group have fought such oppression. Judging from the results, it is clear that to ask the question—why and how were women victimized—has its usefulness. We learn what society or individuals or classes of people have done to women, and we learn how women themselves have reacted to conditions imposed upon them. While inferior status and oppressive restraints were no doubt aspects of women's historical experience, and should be so recorded, the limitation of this approach is that it makes it appear either that women were largely passive or that, at the most, they reacted to male pressures or to the restraints of patriarchal society. Such inquiry fails to elicit the positive and essential way in which women have functioned in history. Mary Beard was the first to point out that the ongoing and continuing contribution of women to the development of human culture cannot be found by treating them only as victims of oppression.[2] I have in my own work learned that it is far more useful to deal with this question as one aspect of women's history, but never to regard it as the *central* aspect of women's history. Essentially, treating women as victims of oppression once again places them in a male-defined conceptual framework: oppressed, victimized by standards and values established by men. The true history of women is the history of their ongoing functioning in that male-defined world, *on their own terms.* The question of oppression does not elicit that story and is therefore a tool of limited usefulness to the historian.

A major focus of women's history has been on women's-rights struggles, especially the winning of suffrage, on organizational and institutional history of the women's movements, and on its leaders. These, again, are important aspects of women's history, but they cannot and should not be its central concern.

Some recent literature has dealt with marriage and divorce, with educational opportunities, and with the economic struggles of working women. Much recent work has been concerned with the image of women and "woman's sphere," with the educational ideals of society, with the values to which women are indoctrinated, and with gender role acculturation as seen in historical perspective. A separate field of study has examined the ideals, values, and prescriptions concerning sexuality, especially female sexuality. Ron Walters and Ben Barker-Benfield have tended to confirm traditional stereotypes concerning Victorian sexuality, the double standard, and the subordinate position of women. Much of this material is based on the study of such readily available sources as sermons, educational tracts, women's magazines, and medical textbooks. The pitfall in such interpretation, as Carl Degler has pointed out in his recent perceptive article, is the tendency to confuse prescriptive literature with actual behavior. In fact, what we are learning from most of these monographs is not what women did, felt, or experienced, but what men in the past thought women should do. Charles Rosenberg, Carroll Smith-Rosenberg, and Carl Degler have shown how to approach the same material and interpret it from the new perspective of women's history.[3] They have sharply distinguished between prescription and behavior, between myth and reality.

Other attempts to deduce women's status from popular literature and ideology demonstrate similar difficulties. Barbara Welter, in an early and highly influential article, found the emergence of "the cult of true womanhood" in sermons and periodicals of the Jacksonian era. Many historians, feminists among them, have deduced from this that Victorian ideals of woman's place pervaded the society and were representative of its realities. More detailed analysis reveals that this mass media concern with woman's domesticity was, in fact, a response to the opposite trend in society.[4] Lower-class women were entering the factories, middle-class women were discontented with their accustomed roles, and the family, as an institution, was experiencing turmoil and crisis. Idealization is very

frequently a defensive ideology and an expression of tension within society. To use ideology as a measure of the shifting status of women, it must
be set against a careful analysis of social structure, economic conditions,
institutional changes, and popular values. With this caution, society's attitudes toward women and toward gender role indoctrination can be usefully analyzed as manifestations of a shifting value system and of tensions
within patriarchal society.

"Contribution" history is an important stage in the creation of a true
history of women. The monographic work that such inquiries produce
is essential to the development of more complex and sophisticated questions, but it is well to keep the limitations of such inquiry in mind. When
all is said and done, what we have mostly done in writing contribution
history is to describe what men in the past told women to do and what
men in the past thought women should be. This is just another way of
saying that historians of women's history have so far used a traditional
conceptual framework. Essentially, they have applied questions from traditional history to women and tried to fit women's past into the empty
spaces of historical scholarship. The limitation of such work is that it deals
with women in male-defined society and tries to fit them into the categories and value systems that consider *man* the measure of significance.
Perhaps it would be useful to refer to this level of work as "transitional
women's history," seeing it as an inevitable step in the development of new
criteria and concepts.

Another methdological question that arises frequently concerns the
connection between women's history and other recently emerging fields.
Why is women's history not simply an aspect of "good" social history? Are
women not part of the anonymous in history? Are they not oppressed the
same way as racial or class or ethnic groups have been oppressed? Are
they not marginal and akin in most respects to minorities? The answers
to these questions are not simple. It is obvious that there has already been
rich cross-fertilization between the new social history and women's history, but it has not been nor should it be a case of subsuming women's
history under the larger and already respectable field of social history.

Yes, women are part of the anonymous in history, but unlike them, they are also and always have been part of the ruling elite. They are oppressed, but not quite like either racial or ethnic groups, though some of them are. They are subordinate and exploited, but not quite like lower classes, though some of them are. We have not yet really solved the problems of definition, but it can be suggested that the key to understanding women's history is in accepting —painful though that may be—that it is the history of the *majority* of mankind. Women are essentially different from all the above categories, because they are the majority now and always have been at least half of mankind, and because their subjection to patriarchal institutions antedates all other oppression and has outlasted all economic and social changes in recorded history.

Social history methodology is very useful for women's history, but it must be placed within a different conceptual framework. For example, historians working in family history ask a great many questions pertaining to women, but family history is not in itself women's history. It is no longer sufficient to view women mainly as members of families. Family history has neglected by and large to deal with unmarried and widowed women. In its applications to specific monographic studies, such as the work of Philip Greven, family history has been used to describe the relationships of fathers and sons and the property arrangements between them.[5] The relationships of fathers to daughters and mothers to their children have been ignored. The complex family-support patterns, for example, whereby the work and wages of daughters are used to support the education of brothers and to maintain aged parents, while that of sons is not so used, have been ignored.

Another way in which family history has been interpreted within the context of patriarchal assumptions is by using a vaguely defined "domestic power" of women, power within the family, as a measure of the societal status of women. In a methodologically highly sophisticated article, Daniel Scott Smith discovers in the nineteenth century the rise of something called "domestic feminism," expressed in a lowered birth rate from which he deduces an increasing control by women over their reproductive lives.[6] One might, from similar figures, as easily deduce a desire on the part of men to curb their offspring due to the demands of a developing industrial system for a more highly educated labor force, hence for fewer children per family. Demographic data can indeed tell us something about female as well as male status in society, but only in the context of an economic and sociological analysis. Further, the status of women within the family is something quite different and distinct from their status in the society in general.

I learned in studying the history of black women and the black family that relatively high status for women within the family does not signify "matriarchy" or "power for women," since black women are not only members of families, but persons functioning in a larger society. The status of persons is determined not in one area of their functioning, such as within the family, but in several. The decisive historical fact about women is that the areas of their functioning, not only their status *within* those areas, have been determined by men. The effect on the consciousness of women has been pervasive. It is one of the decisive aspects of their history, and any analysis that does not take this complexity into consideration must be inadequate.

Then there is the impact of demographic techniques, the study of large aggregates of anonymous people by computer technology based on census data, public documents, property records. Demographic techniques have led to insights that are very useful for women's history. They have yielded revealing data on fertility fluctuations, on changes in illegitimacy patterns and sex ratios, and aggregate studies of life cycles. The latter work has been done very successfully by Joseph Kett, Robert Wells, Peter Laslett, and Kenneth Keniston.[7] The field has in the United States been largely dominated by male historians, mostly through self-imposed sex-role stereotyping by women historians who have shared a prejudice against the computer and statistics. However, a group of younger scholars, trained in demographic techniques, have begun to research and publish material concerning working-class women. Alice Harris, Virginia McLaughlin, Judith and Daniel Walkowitz, Susan Kleinberg, and Tamara Hareven are among those who have elicited woman-oriented interpretations from aggregate data.[8] They have demonstrated that social history can be enriched by combining cliometrics with sophisticated humanistic and feminist interpretations. They have added "gender" as a factor for analysis to such familiar concepts as class, race, and ethnicity.

The compensatory questions raised by women's history specialists are proving interesting and valuable in a variety of fields. It is perfectly understandable that after centuries of neglect of the role of women in history, compensatory questions and those concerning women's contribution will and must be asked. In the process of answering such questions, it is important to keep in mind the inevitable limitation of the answers they yield. Not the least of these limitations is that this approach tends to separate the work and activities of women from those of men, even where they were essentially connected. As yet, synthesis is lacking. For example, the rich history of the abolition movement has been told as though women played a marginal, auxiliary, and at times mainly disruptive role in it. Yet female antislavery societies outnumbered male societies; women abolitionists largely financed the movement with their fundraising activities, did much of the work of propaganda writing in and distribution of newspapers and magazines. The enormous political significance of women-organized petition campaigns remains unrecorded. Most important, no historical work has as yet taken the organizational work of female abolitionists seriously as an integral part of the antislavery movement.

Slowly, as the field has matured, historians of women's history have become dissatisfied with old questions and old methods, and have come up with new ways of approaching historical material. They have, for example, begun to ask about the actual experience of women in the past. This is obviously different from a description of the condition of women written from the perspective of male sources and leads one to the use of women's letters, diaries, autobiographies, and oral history sources. This shift from male-oriented to female-oriented consciousness is most important and leads to challenging new interpretations.

Historians of women's history have studied female sexuality and its regulation from the female point of view, making imaginative use of such sources as medical textbooks, diaries, and case histories of hospital patients. Questions concerning women's experience have led to studies of birth control, as it affects women and as an issue expressing cultural and symbolic values; of the physical conditions to which women are prone, such as menarche and pregnancy and women's ailments; of customs, attitudes, and fashions affecting women's health and women's life experience. Historians are now exploring the impact of female bonding, of female friendship and homosexual relations, and the experience of women in groups, such as women in utopian communities, in women's clubs, and in settlement houses. There has been an interest in the possibility that women's century-long preoccupation with birth and with the care of the sick and dying have led to some specific female rituals.[9]

Women's history has already presented a challenge to some basic assumptions historians make. While most historians are aware of the fact that their findings are not value-free and are trained to check their biases by a variety of methods, they are as yet quite unaware of their own sexist bias and, more importantly, of the sexist bias that pervades the value system, the culture, and the very language within which they work.

Women's history presents a challenge to the periodization of traditional history. The periods in which basic changes occur in society and that historians have commonly regarded as turning points for all historical development, are not necessarily the same for men as for women. This is not surprising when we consider that the traditional time frame in history has been derived from political history. Women have been the one group in history longest excluded from political power as they have, by and large, been excluded from military decision making. Thus the irrelevance of periodization based on military and political developments to their historical experience should have been predictable.

Both Renate Bridenthal and Joan Kelly-Gadol confirm that the history of women demands different periodization than does political history.[10] Neither the Renaissance, it appears, nor the period during which woman suffrage was won, were periods in which women experienced an advance in their status. Recent work of American historians of women's history, such as Linda Kerber's work on the American Revolution and my own work, confirms this conclusion. For example, neither during nor after the American Revolution nor in the age of Jackson did women share the historical experience of men. On the contrary, they experienced in both periods status loss, a restriction of options as to occupations and role choices, and certainly in Jacksonian America, there were restrictions imposed upon their sexuality, at least in prescriptive behavior. If one applies to both of these cases the kind of sophisticated and detailed analysis Kelly-Gadol attempts—that is, differentiations between women of different classes and comparisons between the status of men of a given class and women of that class—one finds the picture further complicated. Status loss in one area—social production—may be offset by status gain in another—access to education.

What kind of periodization might be substituted for the periodization of traditional history for it to be applicable to women? The answer depends largely on the conceptual framework in which the historian works. Many historians of women's history, in their search for a unifying framework, have tended to use the Marxist or neo-Marxist model supplied by Juliet Mitchell and recently elaborated by Sheila Rowbotham.[11] The important fact, says Mitchell, that distinguished the past of women from that of men is precisely that until very recently sexuality and reproduction were inevitably linked for women, while they were not so linked for men. Similarly, childbearing and child rearing were inevitably linked for women and still are so linked. Women's freedom depends on breaking those links. Using Mitchell's categories, we can and should ask of each historical period: what happened to the link between sexuality and reproduction? What happened to the link between childbearing and child rearing? Important changes in the status of women occur when it becomes possible through the availability of birth control information and technology to sever sexuality from inevitable motherhood. However, it may be the case that it is not the availability and distribution of birth control information and technology so much as the level of medical and health care that are the determinants of change. That is, when infant mortality decreases, so that raising every child to adulthood becomes the normal expectation of parents, family size declines.

The above case illustrates the difficulty that has vexed historians of women's history in trying to locate a periodization more appropriate to women. Working in different fields and specialities, many historians have observed that the transition from agricultural to industrializing society and then again the transition to fully developed industrial society entails important changes affecting women and the family. Changes in relations of production affect women's status as family members and as workers. Later, shifts in the mode of production affect the kinds of occupations women can enter and their status within them. Major shifts in health care and technological development, related to industrialization, also affect the lives of women. It is not too difficult to discern such patterns and to conclude that there must be a causal relationship between changes in the mode of production and the status of women. Here, the Marxist model seems to offer an immediately satisfying solution, especially if, following Mitchell, "sexuality" as a factor is added to such factors as class. But in the case of women, just as in the case of racial castes, ideology and prescription internalized by both women and men seem to be as much causative factors as are material changes in production relations. Does the entry of lower-class women into industrial production really bring them closer to "liberation"? In the absence of institutional changes such as the right to abortion and safe contraception, altered child-rearing arrangements, and varied options for sexual expression, changes in economic relations may become oppressive. Unless such changes are accompanied by changes in consciousness, which in turn result in institutional changes, they do not favorably affect the lives of women.

Is smaller family size the result of "domestic freedom" of choice exercised by women, the freedom of choice exercised by men, or the ideologically buttressed coercion of institutions in the service of an economic class? Is it liberating for women, for men, or for corporations? This raises another difficult question: what about the relationship of upper-class to lower-class women? To what extent is the relative advance in the status of upper-class women predicated on the status loss of lower-class women? Examples of this are the liberation of the middle-class American housewife in the mid-nineteenth century through the availability of cheap black or immigrant domestic workers; the liberation of the twentieth-century housewife from incessant drudgery in the home through agricultural stoop labor and the food-processing industry, both employing low paid female workers.

Is periodization then dependent as much on class as on gender? This question is just one of several that challenge the universalist assumptions of all previous historical categories. I cannot provide an answer, but I think the questions themselves point us in the right direction.

It appears to me that all conceptual models of history hitherto developed have only limited usefulness for women's history, since all are based on the assumptions of a patriarchal ordering of values. The structural-functionalist framework leaves out class and sex factors, the traditional Marxist framework leaves out sex and race factors as essentials, admitting them only as marginal factors. Mitchell's neo-Marxist model includes these, but slights ideas, values, and psychological factors. Still, her four-structures model and the refinements of it proposed by Bridenthal are excellent additions to the conceptual working tools of the historian of women's history. They should be tried out, discussed, refined. But they are not, in my opinion, the whole answer.

Kelly-Gadol offers the useful suggestion that attitudes toward sexuality should be studied in each historical period. She considers the constraints upon women's sexuality imposed by society a useful measure of women's true status. This approach would necessitate comparisons between pre-scribed behavior for women and men as well as indications of their actual sexual behavior at any given time. This challenging method can be used with great effectiveness for certain periods of history and especially for upper- and middle-class women. I doubt that it can be usefully employed as a general criterion, because of the difficulty of finding substantiating evidence, especially as it pertains to lower classes.

I raised the question of a conceptual framework for dealing with women's history in 1969,[12] reasoning from the assumption that women were a subgroup in history. Not caste, nor class, nor race quite fits the model for describing us. I have now come to the conclusion that the idea that women are some kind of a subgroup or particular is wrong. It will not do—there are just too many of us. No single framework, no single factor, four-factor, or eight-factor explanation can serve to contain all that the history of women is. Picture, if you can, an attempt to organize the history of men by using four factors. It will not work; neither will it work for women.

Women are and always have been at least half of mankind and most of the time have been the majority of mankind. Their culturally determined and psychologically internalized marginality seems to be what makes their historical experience essentially different from that of men. But men have defined their experience as history and have left women out. At this time, as during earlier periods of feminist activity, women are urged to fit into the empty spaces, assuming their traditional marginal, "subgroup" status. But the truth is that history, as written and perceived up to now, is the history of a minority, who may well turn out to be the "subgroup." To write a new history worthy of the name, we will have to recognize that no single methodology and conceptual framework can fit the complexities of the historical experience of all women.

The first stage of "transitional history" may be to add some new categories to the general categories by which historians organize their material: sexuality, reproduction, the link between childbearing and child rearing; role indoctrination; sexual values and myths; female consciousness. Further, all of these need to be analyzed, taking factors of race, class, ethnicity, and, possibly, religion into consideration. What we have here is not a single framework for dealing with women in history, but new questions to all of universal history.

The next stage may be to explore the possibility that what we call women's history may actually be the study of a separate women's culture. Such a culture would include not only the separate occupations, status, experiences, and rituals of women but also their consciousness, which internalizes patriarchal assumptions. In some cases, it would include the tensions created in that culture between the prescribed patriarchal assumptions and women's efforts to attain autonomy and emancipation.

The questions asked about the past of women may demand interdisciplinary approaches. They also may demand broadly conceived group research projects that end up giving functional answers; answers that deal not with slices of a given time or society or period, but that instead deal with a functioning organism, a functioning whole, the society in which both men and women live.

A following stage may develop a synthesis: a history of the dialectic, the tensions between the two cultures, male and female. Such a synthesis could be based on close comparative study of given periods in which the historical experience of men is compared to that of women, their tensions and interactions being as much the subject of study as their differences. Only after a series of such detailed studies can we hope to find the parameters by which to define the new universal history. My guess is that no one conceptual framework will fit so complex a subject.

Methods are tools for analysis—some of us will stick with one tool, some of us will reach for different tools as we need them. For women, the problem really is that we must acquire not only the confidence needed for using tools, but for making new ones to fit our needs. We should do so relying on our learned skills and our rational scepticism of handed-down doctrine. The recognition that we had been denied our history came to many of us as a staggering flash of insight, which altered our consciousness irretrievably. We have come a long way since then. The next step is to face, once and for all and with all its complex consequences, that women are the majority of mankind and have been essential to the making of history. Thus, all history as we now know it, is merely prehistory. Only a new history firmly based on this recognition and equally concerned with men, women, the establishment and the passing away of patriarchy, can lay claim to being a truly universal history.

NOTES

This article was originally published in *Feminist Studies* 3, nos. 1–2 (1975): 5–14. In an earlier version, this article was presented at the panel "Effects of Women's History upon Traditional Concepts of Historiography" at the Second Berkshire Conference on the History of Women, Cambridge, MA, 25–27 October 1974. It was, in revised form, presented as a paper at the Sarah Lawrence College Workshop-Symposium, 15 March 1975. I have greatly benefited from discussion with my copanelists Renate Bridenthal and Joan Kelly-Gadol, and from the comments and critiques of audience participants at both conferences.

[1] For the term "women worthies," I am indebted to Natalie Zemon Davis, Stanford University. For the terms "compensatory history" and "contribution history," I am indebted to Mari Jo Buhle, Ann G. Gordon, and Nancy Schrom, "Women in American Society: An Historical Contribution," *Radical America* 5, no. 4 (1971): 3–66.

[2] Mary Beard, *Woman as Force in History* (New York: Collier Books, 1972). See also a further discussion of this question in Gerda Lerner, "New Approaches for the Study of Women in American History," *Journal of Social History* 3, no. 1 (1969): 53–62. Also available in Bobbs-Merrill, reprint, number H432.

[3] Ronald G. Walters, ed., *Primers for Prudery* (Englewood Cliffs, NJ: Prentice-Hall, 1974); Ben Barker-Benfield, "The Spermatic Economy: A Nineteenth Century View of Sexuality," *Feminist Studies* 1, no. 1 (1972): 45–74; Carl Degler, "What Ought To Be and What Was: Women's Sexuality in the Nineteenth Century," *American Historical Review* 79, no. 5 (1974): 1467–90. For a different approach, see also Carroll Smith-Rosenberg and Charles Rosenberg, "The Female Animal: Medical and Biological Views of Women in Nineteenth Century America," *Journal of American History* 60, no. 2 (1973): 332–56; Carroll Smith-Rosenberg, "The Hysterical Woman: Some Reflections on Sex Roles and Role Conflict in 19th Century America," *Social Research* 39, no. 4 (1972): 652–78; Charles Rosenberg, "Sexuality, Class and Role," *American Quarterly* 25, no. 2 (1973): 131–53.

[4] Barbara Welter, "The Cult of True Womanhood, 1820–1860," *American Quarterly* 18, no. 2 (1966): 151–57; Gerda Lerner, "The Lady and the Mill Girl: Changes in the Status of Women in the Age of Jackson," *Midcontinent American Studies Journal* 10, no. 1 (1969): 5–15.

[5] Philip J. Greven Jr., *Four Generations: Population, Land and Family in Colonial Andover, Massachusetts* (Ithaca: Cornell University Press, 1970). For a good sampling of recent work in family history, see Michael Gordon, ed., *The*

American Family in Social-Historical Perspective (New York: St. Martin's Press, 1973).

[6] Daniel Scott Smith, "Family Limitation, Sexual Control and Domestic Feminism in Victorian America," *Feminist Studies* 1, nos. 3–4 (1973): 40–57.

[7] See *Journal of Interdisciplinary History* 2, no. 2 (1971) for articles by Joseph Kett, Robert Wells, Peter Laslett, and Kenneth Keniston.

[8] Virginia Yans McLaughlin, "Patterns of Work and Family Organization: Buffalo's Italians," ibid., 219–314; Tamara Hareven, "The History of the Family as an Interdisciplinary Field," ibid.; 399–414; Susan Kleinberg, University of California San Diego, "Women's Work: The Lives of Working Class Women in Pittsburgh, 1870–1900" (unpublished paper); and Alice Harris, Sarah Lawrence College, "Problems of Class and Culture in Organizing Women Workers, 1900–1920" (unpublished paper).

[9] For a good overview of this work, see the papers of the Second Berkshire Conference on the History of Women, Radcliffe College, 1974, some of which are published in this issue and in *Feminist Studies* 3, nos. 3–4. See especially, Carroll Smith-Rosenberg, "The New Woman and the New History."

[10] See forthcoming papers by Bridenthal and Kelly-Gadol in *Feminist Studies* 3, nos. 3–4 (1975).

[11] Juliet Mitchell, *Woman's Estate* (New York: Pantheon Books, 1972); Sheila Rowbotham, *Woman's Consciousness, Man's World* (Baltimore: Penguin Books, 1973); Rowbotham, *Women, Resistance and Revolution* (New York: Pantheon Books, 1972).

[12] Gerda Lerner, "New Approaches to the Study of Women in American History," *Journal of Social History* 3, no. 1 (1969): 53–62.

CHAPTER 2

"No Documents—No History": Mary Ritter Beard and the Early History of Women's Archives

ANKE VOSS-HUBBARD

Without knowledge of women in history as actual history, dead women are sheer ghosts to living women—and to men.[1]

—MARY RITTER BEARD

ABSTRACT

The 1930s marked an important moment in the history of the national preservation effort in the United States. While the establishment of the National Archives ensured the preservation of the public record, a quest to salvage the record of women's role in civilization was just beginning. Historian Mary Ritter Beard made a commitment to the promotion of women's archives throughout the next decades. After she failed to establish a World Center for Women's Archives at the dawn of the Second World War, Beard sought her dream in institutions of higher learning, inspiring many colleges and universities to collect source materials by and about women. Smith College made the greatest commitment to support a women's archives on its campus. Beginning in the early 1940s, Mary Beard nurtured a close relationship with an ardent supporter of such an archives at Smith College, Margaret Storrs Grierson, the collection's director from 1942 through 1965. The tireless efforts of these two women provided the foundation for what has evolved into one of the most widely recognized women's collections in the United States.

THROUGHOUT HER CAREER, HISTORIAN MARY RITTER BEARD (1876–1958) CALLED ON ARCHIVISTS, EDUCATORS, AND HISTORIANS TO PRESERVE, TEACH, AND EXAMINE THE CONTRIBUTIONS OF WOMEN IN BUILDING OUR CIVILIZATION. According to historian Nancy F. Cott, Beard believed that women had always been "comakers of civilization side by side with men" and that "documenting their past shared leadership would help to cement it into contemporary reality."[2] Beard's unflagging commitment to these goals eventually inspired Margaret Storrs Grierson, the founding archivist of the Sophia Smith Collection at Smith College, to rally the administration and the alumnae of this women's college to support a collection of primary source materials in women's history. The story of Beard's involvement in founding this collection illuminates her lasting contribution to the study of women and her important place in the development of women's archives in America.

Beard, of course, was not the only historian to recognize the value of primary source materials to historical research and the urgency of preserving those records. Beginning in the late 1800s, historian J. Franklin Jameson led the campaign for a national archives from his position at the American Historical Association (AHA) and the Department of Historical Research at the Carnegie Institute. Jameson and others spent many years seeking support for an archives to preserve federal government records. Although they had had some presidential support in the past, Jameson and his assistants watched numerous legislative efforts to establish a national archives fail in the first two decades of the twentieth century. Finally, a bill passed both houses of Congress, and in May 1926, President Calvin Coolidge signed a bill that authorized funding for an archives building; it took Congress almost another decade, however, to establish a program with "broad authority to preserve and care for the archives of the federal government."[3]

With the passage of the National Archives Act of 1934, the United States Congress established an agency to direct a national preservation effort. During the 1930s and 1940s, repositories dramatically increased their efforts to collect unpublished source materials. The growth of special collections was especially visible at numerous academic libraries. According to William L. Joyce, "[a]s research became a primary university objective[,] . . . scholarship was institutionalized and professionalized."[4] To Beard's dismay, however, the efforts of libraries to collect primary sources rarely included materials related to women's history.

The Beginning of a Quest for Women's Archives

Just as Jameson's goal appeared to have been achieved, Mary Beard's quest to establish a women's archives began. In 1935, Beard initiated plans to establish a center for the preservation and study of primary source materials about women. Suzanne Hildenbrand has pointed out that Beard's achievements "encouraged many individuals and institutions to preserve materials [by and about women] that might otherwise have been lost."[5] Beard's work on behalf of women's archives was part of a broad movement to establish women's collections in the decades before and after the Second World War. Her idea for a world center was one of the earliest such efforts.

By the early 1930s, Beard had made clear her particular interest in women's history. Mary Beard and her husband, historian Charles Beard, had written several (now well-known) history textbooks, including *American Citizenship* (1914) and *The Rise of American Civilization* (1927). The true nature of the Beards' partnership seems destined to remain a mystery because none of their correspondence with each other survives. It is clear, however, that Mary Beard's role in these collaborative works was barely acknowledged by her contemporaries. Her scholarly reputation rested instead on her voluminous work on the history of women, most notably her magnum opus, *Woman as Force in History: A Study in Traditions and Realities.*[6]

Beard continued to publish articles and books on women's history, even as she devoted considerable attention and energy to promoting women's archives and a university curriculum that would use primary sources to teach women about their past. Since both archivists and historians had in the past considered materials on women to be historically insignificant, the curator of the women's collection at Radcliffe College was not surprised that they "did not immediately or happily begin to record new ideas and activities of women." But women in the archival and historical professions were instrumental in calling for a new recognition of women's archives.[7]

Mary Beard's interest in preserving sources on women's history was ignited by a disagreement with some basic premises of the women's movement in the early twentieth century. Beard sparked controversy in the suffrage movement in the 1930s when she rejected the idea that women had been subjugated throughout history and called for a reexamination of documentary evidence to prove her thesis.

Beard believed women had always been partners with men in the making of history. She explained in an address that when "we trace the lives and labors of women up through the countless centuries, we find women always playing a realistic and dynamic function, or role, in society."[8] In a fundamental challenge to feminist thought of that time, she argued that women and men shared equally wherever "operations are carried on efficiently for the care and protection of life, or where this fundamental cultural responsibility is discarded in the pursuit of self-interest."[9] As Beard saw it, women were equally responsible for defining the values of the society.

This formulation, according to historian Barbara Turoff, led to Beard's belief that "only when women learned of their historical significance would they regain self-confidence."[10] Without that knowledge, "modern women have little chance to fulfill their potential."[11] Although she praised Arthur Schlesinger's 1922 appeal for historians to consider women's contributions to history, she had little regard for historians who focused on the contemporary battle for woman suffrage while ignoring Schlesinger's plea to integrate women into history. In Beard's view, most scholarship continued to approach women's history from the "conventional view of women as negligible or nothing or helplessly subject to men."[12]

Although her rejection of the mainstream feminist thought remained controversial, Beard's call to widen the field of historical inquiry inspired many.[13] Beard realized that historians needed to examine more documentary evidence before they could examine and incorporate women's contributions to civilization into books and curricula. According to Nancy Cott, Beard believed that libraries and archives contained the materials that would illustrate women's integral role. In Beard's aim to "widen the frames of history to the women as they were in past actuality," Cott argues, "documents were her eyepiece, . . . [for] only on documents could a new vision rest." In a great irony, however, Beard herself never viewed her own papers as a source for the study of women.[14]

The World Center for Women's Archives

Beard's quest to collect and examine the documentary evidence of women began in earnest in 1935, when Hungarian-born pacifist-feminist Rosika Schwimmer approached her with the idea of establishing the World Center for Women's Archives (WCWA). Schwimmer was primarily concerned that "the facts of women's struggle and achievement" to bring peace to the world be preserved, an idea illustrated in her statement on "A Feminist-Pacifist Archive." Although Schwimmer's goal was limited to documenting women's role in the peace movement, Beard's was wider. From the outset, she believed the WCWA should expand to collect materials about women's various activities, functioning as both an archives and an education center for the study of women. As Beard stated in a letter to prospective sponsors in 1935: "[W]e want more than shelves filled with records. It is our idea to make this center a vital educational plant in which the culture represented by the archives will receive the attention at present given in 'seats of higher learning' to the culture of men alone."[15]

The WCWA had its first organizational board meeting in New York on 15 October 1935. In addition to appointing a board of directors as the main decision-making body, attendees of the inaugural meeting voted to invite well-known women sponsors to serve in advisory capacities. From the beginning, the WCWA was torn by internal strife over the center's mission and focus. As Schwimmer and others considered a collaboration with the New York Public Library, the Library of Congress, or some other institution, Beard voiced strong opposition, successfully arguing that such a union would undermine the WCWA's organizational independence and "again take women off the record." Beard later expressed these sentiments in a letter to Sue Bailey Thurman, a member of the Negro Women's Archives Committee of the WCWA, which was calling for a separate black

women's archives: "Many women and men deny the validity of a separate archive for women. I maintain that only by dramatizing women can
women be recognized as equally important with men."[16]

Beard gathered numerous sponsors, "women of the kind who would
really push [WCWA] along to realization," and their involvement again
altered the immediate goals of the organization. Women friends such as
Carrie Chapman Catt, Jane Addams, and Elizabeth Cady Stanton's daughter Harriet Stanton Blatch offered valuable support for an archives that
would preserve women's history. The scope of Beard's project broadened,
reflecting the wide array of backgrounds and occupations of the women
lending their assistance. Much to the distress of Rosika Schwimmer,
Beard's expansive vision of the WCWA's mission no longer was that of
a center focusing solely on women in peace movements.[17] In 1936,
Schwimmer resigned from the center's board of directors in frustration.
Schwimmer's dream for a collection devoted to her and other women's
role in the struggle for peace would be realized, however, in 1942, at the
New York Public Library.[18]

The WCWA finally gathered an operational fund, with endorsements
from such prominent women as Eleanor Roosevelt and Frances Perkins
and support from Fannie Hurst, Inez Haynes Irwin, Georgia O'Keeffe,
and Alice Paul. It was officially launched on 15 December 1937, at the
Biltmore Hotel in New York City. A pamphlet, bearing the center's motto,
"No documents, No history," which had been coined by French historian
Fustel de Coulanges, also stated the WCWA's purpose:

> To make a systematic search for undeposited source materials deal-
> ing with women's lives and activities, interests and ideas, as mem-
> bers of society everywhere. . . . To reproduce important materials,
> already deposited elsewhere, by means of microfilm and other
> modern processes. . . . To encourage recognition of women as
> co-makers of history.[19]

Despite wide publicity and initial support from prominent individuals, the WCWA never received the financial support it needed to
meet its far-reaching goals. Disagreements among its leadership about

racial issues further weakened the WCWA. Mary Beard had asked Mary McLeod Bethune, founder and president of the National Council of Negro Women (NCNW), for her organization's assistance in promoting African American women's history. In 1938, Bethune was invited to chair the Negro Women's Archives Committee because of her advocacy of African American women's history dating back to the mid-1920s.[20] Although she declined, Bethune and the NCNW worked with the WCWA the following year. African American women soon concluded, however, that the WCWA's commitment to promoting their efforts was tentative at best. No African American women ever served on the board of directors, only two were asked to become sponsors, and expenditures for their committee's fieldwork was minimal.[21]

Frustrated both by a lack of solidarity among the members about these and other issues and by her inability to solve the project's financial woes, Mary Beard finally resigned from the board of the WCWA. In June 1940, in a letter to the members of the board of directors, she wrote, "Unless strong new blood can be transfused into our movement's management, neither my continuous service nor any other service, old or new, will carry us further toward our goal. . . . I will not go on soliciting archives when there is no real push for money."[22] The center's demise in 1940, shortly after Beard's resignation, was blamed on the outbreak of the Second World War and the inability of any organization not involved in the war effort to raise funds. In private, however, Beard expressed a different view: "I don't like to hide behind the idea that we are a casualty of war because I think we are hiding our own inefficiency."[23]

Although unable to build a permanent future for itself, the WCWA had nevertheless, during its five years of existence, publicized Beard's ideas for the preservation of women's history. The center had received numerous pledges from women, and its preliminary work in soliciting women to donate or deposit their papers in an archives center later proved to be invaluable. Moreover, through the efforts of numerous state volunteers, the center had identified historical records about women in private hands, historical societies, universities, and other archives. Among many other activities, it had promoted exhibits of women's collections at the Library of Congress and the National Archives. From its offices in Washington and New York, the center compiled and distributed lists of secondary sources essential to the study of women, served as a clearing house for information about women at other institutions, and furnished information for a series of radio talks on women in American society. Beard also convinced Ellen Woodward, an officer of the Federal Works Project's Historical Records Survey, "to instruct the field workers . . . to make a note of women's records when they found them. The note was to take the form of a 'WH' in the margin." Although Woodward gave the instructions and the reporting took place, Beard recalled that Woodward's superiors "were exceedingly cross and said it had no place in the reports."[24]

In part because of Mary Beard's early work with the WCWA, several colleges and universities, most notably Radcliffe College and Smith College, began collecting source materials for the study of women's history.[25] After these collections took shape in the early 1940s, a number of other institutions throughout the country launched additional projects in an effort to document, preserve, and provide better access to sources on women's history.[26] Beard gained recognition among librarians and college presidents such as Wilbur Jordan at Radcliffe College and Herbert Davis at Smith. Even before the closing of the WCWA, Beard had contacted several institutions of higher learning, "attempting to affect their curricula as well as [their] collecting policies," Cott notes. Margaret Grierson, archivist of the women's collection at Smith College from the early 1940s through the mid-1960s, also recalled that Smith "was but one of many institutions where she sowed the seed."[27]

Evidence of Beard's involvement with numerous educational institutions can be seen in correspondence in the Sophia Smith Collection and in the records of the WCWA at the Schlesinger Library. Writing to one of her supporters of the World Center, Beard reported that the librarians at Syracuse were following her advice to acquire more books and manuscripts "for this advancing education . . . so everyone associated with WCWA . . . may feel that social ideas are not all being destroyed by the sweep of war." Beard not only gave her advice to these institutions, but distributed some important source materials for the study of women.[28]

When the WCWA project folded in late 1940, many of the donated collections fell into Beard's keeping. She returned some of the books and manuscripts at the donors' requests, but she distributed others to Radcliffe College, the Institute of Women's Professional Relations, Connecticut College, Purdue University, Hunter College, Columbia's Teachers College, Barnard College, and Smith College. Despite the WCWA's demise, Beard's careful distribution of the salvaged records promoted, in the opinion of one biographer, "a concern for the preservation of women's records among educators who then attempted similar projects."[29] Although Beard had advised several college librarians on their collections' strength in women's history, her most significant involvement was with the women's archives at Radcliffe and Smith. Beard's mission for the WCWA had been to support the education of women in their history. Her enthusiasm for collections at these two institutions was grounded in her belief that, by placing an archives at a women's college, this goal could be achieved.[30]

Mary Beard and Radcliffe

Beard's involvement with Radcliffe began when the college established a Woman's Rights Collection following the donation in 1943 of the papers of alumna Maud Wood Park, a noted suffragist. Newly appointed college president Wilbur K. Jordan contacted Mary Beard for advice on improving the collection. Beard responded by expressing hope for Radcliffe's success in establishing a women's archives; she subsequently wrote numerous letters advising Jordan on how to establish such a collection. From the events that followed, however, one may conclude that despite initial enthusiasm, Radcliffe was not fully committed to the project Beard envisioned. In a letter to Margaret Grierson, Beard recalled the Radcliffe librarian's question about the scope of the intended collection. Somewhat irritated, Beard replied, "[W]here women began their distinctly human work." According to Beard, the male librarian was silent for a moment, then asked, "How many books do you think we ought to have—5000?" Beard replied, "[T]hat would make a good start."[31]

In Beard's view, the collection at Radcliffe was growing very slowly. She noted in 1945 that "President Jordan . . . seems to falter, for reasons I do not understand, in the ardent and yet practical promotion of a great women's archive at Radcliffe." What must certainly have added to Beard's frustration was that she had sent Jordan a list of women "who were interested in the WCWA and might contribute financially," and she herself contributed $1,000 to the Radcliffe project. She also gave the college the WCWA records, the Leonora Reilly Papers, the Inez Irwin Papers, and other collections. Although Beard kept abreast of progress on the project, the institution would not contact her again to promote its women's archives until 1951.[32]

In her response to Radcliffe's archivist, a disappointed Beard recalled her early support for and contribution to the project, only to "learn for the first time detail of its status at this moment." She concluded rather bluntly that she had "led many women to believe that Radcliffe was the place in the U.S. for a great collection. I have regretted that Radcliffe . . . was in no great sense apparently warranting that belief."[33]

The Start of the Smith College Project

While she was involved with the project at Radcliffe in the early 1940s, Beard had also become interested in a similar effort at Smith College. At Smith, at least one person greeted Beard's efforts with open arms. Subsequent success of the women's collection at Smith College can be attributed primarily to an "intimate, lasting friendship" that developed between Smith archivist, Margaret Grierson, and Mary Beard.[34] Their mutual admiration and shared commitment to promoting women's history is clear in their correspondence, spanning the early 1940s until Beard's death in 1958. Grierson had all the skills Beard had once recommended for director of a women's archive—a person who would need to be "a capable woman to go into the field as an interpreter, archives collector, and fundraiser." In a letter to Beard's son, Grierson noted that it was Mary Beard "who patiently led us to a clear understanding of the significance of women in history and to a clear conception of the proper nature of our research collection. It is very truly her own creation."[35]

Newly appointed Smith College president Herbert Davis first proposed the women's archives at an Alumnae Association meeting held in conjunction with commencement on 14 June 1941. Davis, who saw the archives as a literary collection of works by women writers, noted that such a collection "is yet to be found anywhere outside certain private collections . . . in addition to printed books." He also urged the founding of "an association of the friends of the Smith College Library, to support us in the gathering together such a collection. [T]hey will help bring us into contact with people having suitable books and manuscripts."[36]

Davis evidently wrote Beard soon after his address, though his letter has not survived, and she responded with characteristic enthusiasm, commending Smith College for its intention to "broaden the base of their education by supplying [students] with richer materials for discovering themselves as co-makers of history." She warned, however, that this would not be achieved unless Smith made an equally strong commitment to hiring faculty "who are wise about women as [a] historical force. I think it is not an extreme statement that at present our faculty lacks such members." Despite these notes of caution, Beard was hopeful enough to inform one of her WCWA supporters that "[President Davis] has written me about his purpose as if he really intends to make it count large in education."[37]

Within a few months of her initial contact with Smith College in August 1941, Beard offered Davis some source materials from the WCWA for Smith's collection. His acceptance of the gift and his expressed interest in preserving primary sources gave Beard "intense pleasure," and she expressed her hope "to do more and better work for you in the future."[38]

Indeed, Mary Beard periodically sent books and other printed matter relating to women's history to the Smith collection. Paradoxically, Beard considered her own manuscripts and letters of little value to historians. In response to Grierson's interest in collecting her papers, Beard admitted that she had not retained any of her own manuscripts, since she could only "regard [her] revisions as revealing to excess the fuzziness of [her] mind." She even went so far as to ask that some of her "bum speeches," donated to Smith as part of another woman's collection, be destroyed "to save my face." Unfortunately, Beard's admission that she did not save her papers was true. But her promise in the 1941 letter, "to get others to give you what I do not have to give," would nonetheless signal the beginning of Beard and Grierson's fruitful relationship.[39]

The Friends of the Smith College Library (FSCL), the organization that President Davis had envisioned would take charge of the women's archives, was formally inaugurated at an Alumnae Council session on 20 February 1942. Margaret Grierson, Smith College archivist since 1940, was appointed executive secretary of the FSCL and director of the women's collection, which was introduced as a special project of the society. In the first of her detailed annual reports for the Friends, Grierson reported that the Works of Woman Writers collection "is an appropriate project for the college which so notably enlarged the opportunity of achievement for women by first providing them an education equivalent to that offered their brothers."[40]

Although Herbert Davis had proposed the women's collection, neither he nor Grierson were certain about its intended mission after it was formally established. Davis seemed partial to making it a strictly literary collection. Grierson, however, expressed her uncertainty in a letter to Nina Browne, the college archivist she had replaced in 1940: "I think that you are right in feeling that President Davis is not clear in his own mind as to what he wants." Clearly reflecting Beard's influence to expand the collection beyond literary women, Grierson continued: "Mrs. Beard, as you know, rather hoped that we would be interested in carrying on the work of the abandoned women's archives."[41]

In the early summer of 1943, Beard invited Grierson to her home in Milford, Connecticut, to discuss "a model archive" and the steps needed to accomplish that ideal.[42] Although she later admitted having been skeptical about Beard's vision for Smith, Grierson returned exclaiming, "I am all enthusiasm!" Grierson's brief stay at Beard's home convinced her that historians had ignored women's role in shaping history. She now believed that Smith must "redefine the collection to include works about, as well as by women . . . material that records and reflects the ideas, interests, visions, endeavors and achievements of American women as a force in shaping the patterns of our national growth." Surprisingly, Davis did not seem to mind straying far from his earlier proposal for a literary collection. According to Grierson, "[H]e even suggested that we might get women to come to give talks on various aspects of women's activities."[43]

On hearing about Grierson's success in winning support for the "new" collection, Beard praised her newfound friend: "You performed a master feat. . . . Your force will play a goodly part in designing a new interpretation of women in history."[44] The prospect of a distinct women's collection, however, did not meet with enthusiasm from everyone. As Grierson noted in the Friends' annual report, at least one alumna protested a separate women's collection, saying, "Aren't women people?" Grierson responded that "[t]he purpose of the collection is certainly not to sharpen the distinction between the sexes . . . but further to diminish the distinction by gathering an imposing evidence of work of women comparable in every way to that of men."[45] To Beard, the episode was a perfect illustration of why a women's archives was needed. The alumna's question indicated that too many women needed to realize "that to be 'people' they must be recognized as such and not lost to view."[46]

In 1945, the collection was renamed the Historical Collection of Books By and About Women. It is not certain whether the name change was a direct response to Beard's suggestions. The women's collection was becoming such an important project of the Friends of the Library that, in 1945, librarian Harriet McPherson included "a special mention" of the collection, which is "devoted to material by and about women," in her annual report to the president of the college.[47]

In 1946, the women's archives was renamed the Sophia Smith Collection, in honor of Sophia Smith who had donated her fortune to found Smith College in 1870. In the FSCL annual report for 1946, Grierson wrote, "[t]he collection of material directed toward a fuller and clearer knowledge of the history of women is in line with our founder's intention" to offer women the same rigorous academic training as had always been offered to men. As one alumna, who was a friend of Grierson and a supporter of the women's collection, wrote in a college publication, the project "will prove to be one of the most significant contributions Smith College will make to the future."[48] By the end of 1947, the popularity of the women's collection among alumnae and friends of the college was growing rapidly. The Friends of the Library reported that its growing membership, now numbering more than seven hundred, was due largely to "the increasingly popular enterprise in the collection of material in the social and intellectual history of women."[49]

To ensure that women's contributions would be treated equally with those of men, Smith College decided to shelve books by and about women with the rest of the materials already in the library, thus avoiding "physical segregation of the material within the library."[50] But Beard's views were influential in the way women's works were represented in the library's catalog. Because she feared that women's materials would be invisible in a large library served by only one catalog, Beard urged the library to create a separate catalog for materials related to women stressing that such a catalog would be necessary "if research is to be handled in connection with the subject." In support of her contention, Beard invoked her own experience in researching the role women played in urban history, pointing out that she had been unable to find materials about women at the New York Public Library, which at that time had no separate catalog. One cannot measure the influence Beard had on the decision, but in 1947, the Smith library developed a separate subject card catalog of materials related to the history of women.[51]

In comparing this arrangement with the women's archives at Radcliffe, Grierson noted that "[Radcliffe's] is a physically separated collection," and in her view, "much of what is purely feminist loses its significance in segregation. . . . It is artificial to consider one sex as a world apart." Balancing the goal of a physically nonsegregated collection with the goal of ensuring the preservation of delicate materials was a dilemma that gnawed at Grierson. Her annual report of 1947 recognized that growing amounts of Smith's materials, such as "manuscript collections, correspondence, records of organizations, ephemeral printings," required special storage facilities.[52]

Grierson's detailed list of donations was growing steadily by the end of the 1940s. Beginning in 1949, her annual reports devoted separate sections to acquisitions for the Sophia Smith Collection, listing donated books and manuscripts under such headings as *literary interests, education, religion, medicine, woman's movement, antislavery*, and *foreign materials*.

The Sophia Smith Collection Matures

The seventh year of the Sophia Smith Collection coincided with Smith College's election of a new president. Knowing how unlikely it was that a woman would be appointed, Beard complained rather pointedly that "if only in the whole land there were a woman who knew enough about women to take [Herbert Davis's] place, how grand that would be!"[53] When Benjamin Fletcher Wright was named to replace Davis in 1949, Beard was hopeful that support for the women's collection at the college would continue. She had met the president-elect earlier at the home of Wilbur Jordan, Radcliffe's president, and she recalled, "Professor Wright *asked* me to tell him more about my idea of women." Unfortunately, however, Wright did not believe that a college required such a research facility, and he therefore lacked Davis's commitment to the expansion of the Sophia Smith Collection.[54] Nevertheless, after her initial disappointment with Wright, Beard told Grierson that, with or without his support, the collection's "development will proceed and be a center, as you rightly declare, for the higher education of women."[55] Grierson agreed.

By the early 1950s, Beard had begun laboring to expand the archives program at Smith College to include seminars on women's history. From the time of Wright's inauguration as Smith's president and lasting through the mid-1950s, Beard campaigned to win his support for such seminars. Although she scheduled several speaking engagements at the college and penned numerous letters to the skeptical president, her efforts were fruitless; she seemed only to annoy him with her repeated requests. In one such letter Beard asked, "Don't you think the time has come to launch a course on women in history at Smith College!" In the margin Wright noted to his secretary, "Stop these!"[56] As Margaret Grierson recalled much later, Wright did not hold the Sophia Smith Collection—and especially the idea of seminars in women's history—in high regard.[57]

But with or without the administration's support, the Sophia Smith Collection was being noticed. During the 1950s, the FSCL annual reports documented, in addition to the growing book and manuscript collection, a steady increase in the use of the source materials in the women's collection. To the dismay of its director, however, few faculty at Smith and the surrounding colleges were among those users.

Early in her involvement with the Sophia Smith Collection, Mary Beard had cautioned that the archives would succeed only if the faculty incorporated it in their teaching. If one goal of the archives was to educate women about their past, "the faculty must cooperate by setting research projects." Although Margaret Grierson recalls a few faculty members, such as Smith history professor Daniel Aaron, incorporating the collection in assignments, most faculty, especially at Amherst and other local colleges, "steered [students] away" from using the source materials in the early days.[58] The situation changed slowly, but it did change. By the late 1950s many faculty members and students at Smith, as well as a growing number of faculty members at other colleges and universities, had recognized the collection's unique holdings. Indeed, a 1959 letter from Grierson to William Beard, Mary's son, shows the degree to which the collection was altering the habits of the faculty: "[Mary Beard] would especially rejoice . . . that at least a dozen of our professors have revised their courses to include women in their fields."[59]

While more and more people were praising the Sophia Smith Collection, support from the college's administration was intermittent and unpredictable. Hence, the growth of the collection during the 1950s and 1960s continued as a result of Grierson's extensive and descriptive reports and skillful relations with potential donors. According to the current archives specialist, Maida Goodwin, Grierson was frequently more familiar with the contents of these collections than the donors themselves. In a 1948 letter to Eleanor Garrison, William Lloyd Garrison's granddaughter, Grierson rejoiced at the revelation that the Garrison family was becoming "Smith-minded" in its search for a depository. Although the initial donation was small, Grierson did not neglect to tell Garrison that "what you have given us . . . has put us more firmly on the map."[60] In view of the fact that more than one hundred document boxes containing Garrison family papers now grace the shelves, her dedication was not in vain. Responding to a description of one of her family's donations, Eleanor Garrison wrote, "[O]f course I've read and reread the report and fluffed up with pride at all honorable mentions. You certainly did full justice to the offerings."[61] As with all other acquisitions, Grierson never failed to make an extensive note of the additions to the collection in her yearly reports. Grierson later recalled that at first she had no idea what her role as executive secretary of the Friends of the Smith College Library would entail, but that she concluded the society would probably like her "to write about the collections."[62] It is also clear from her daily logs that Grierson made a point to carefully inspect every new acquisition before she reported on its contents.

Throughout Mary Beard's involvement with the collection at Smith, she had directed attention to numerous women whose papers she thought should be solicited. She also advised Grierson to take a proactive approach to collection management, filling her letters with frequent suggestions about possible donors.[63] Here, Beard was not attempting to influence the purview of the archives' holdings. Although she privately criticized Alma Lutz's biography of Elizabeth Cady Stanton, calling Lutz an "intellectual juvenile," Beard nonetheless believed Lutz's papers would be very valuable to the collection. Beard also disagreed with Margaret Sanger's method of distributing birth control to poor women, but when Grierson announced the acquisition of Sanger's papers, Beard replied that "they are among the basic materials for the study of [women]." In regard to musicologist Sophie Drinker's collection, Beard noted perceptively, "She has an extraordinary collection of books on and by women in her home—is an avid collector . . . what she will do with it before she dies or where she may will it, I wonder."[64]

Beard downplayed her role in expanding the Sophia Smith Collection, but Grierson reported growing interest among potential donors as a result of Beard's association with it. Beard's recognition among prominent women, combined with her faith in the collection, resulted in some important acquisitions over the years.[65] Even after Beard's death in 1958, a woman who had worked with her on a book about Japanese women offered her correspondence to Smith only because she recalled Beard's enthusiasm for the collection.[66]

In 1968, three years after her retirement, the trustees of the college presented Margaret Grierson with the Smith College Medal in recognition of her achievements and service. In announcing the award, President Thomas C. Mendenhall exclaimed, "Under your skillful hand the Collection was given its eventual shape and purpose: the intellectual and social history of women around the world."[67]

Grierson was too modest to accept such tributes to her achievements. As she recalled in 1992, despite her two decades of work establishing and enlarging the Sophia Smith Collection, "I was around only for the beginning, for the planting of an acorn." It was Mary Beard, she would later insist, who deserved at least part of the credit for the collection. As Grierson wrote to a donor in 1961, "I wish that [Mary Beard] might be at hand to see how her project has developed and to give continuing advice to us. I hope it is obvious to one and all, that our enterprise took shape in an earnest effort to make material some of Mary Beard's sound ideas."[68]

While academic libraries were busy collecting primary source materials, their archives supported only the research of men, in Beard's view. As she boldly stated in 1938:

> [T]here has been no systematic effort to get the story of women together in any Archive center. . . . Men preside over most libraries. They naturally think of manuscripts in terms of men. In view of these conditions, . . . the need of a special library for women's papers seems convincing.[69]

As Beard's work demonstrates, the struggle to establish women's archives had to overcome many hurdles. The historic transformation at universities and colleges in the 1930s and 1940s to professionalize and institutionalize scholarship did not include women's history. It was not until pioneers like Mary Beard recognized that only through the establishment of women's archives could women's history be thoroughly professionalized and institutionalized.

The early history of the Sophia Smith Collection also exemplifies how the development of archives often depend on the vision and toil of nonarchivists. Beard was the direct inspiration for the Smith College collection of primary source materials on women, and she encouraged such collections at numerous other institutions. As Beard stated while organizing the WCWA, "If we only accomplish the stimulation of interest and thinking in colleges and communities by our plan for a great Women's Archive, I shall believe that we have been justified in this movement."[70] Beard was fortunate to find Margaret Grierson, a knowledgeable person dedicated to preserving the evidence of women's achievements, who would make her plan a reality.

NOTES

This article was the winner of the 1994 Theodore Calvin Pease Award from the Society of American Archivists, which recognizes superior writing achievements by students of archival studies. It was originally published in *The American Archivist* 58 (Winter 1995): 16–30.

[1] "The Historical Approach to Learning About Women" (speech, Radcliffe College, 22 May 1944), Mary Ritter Beard Papers (A-9), Schlesinger Library, Radcliffe College, Cambridge, MA.

[2] Nancy F. Cott, ed., *A Woman Making History: Mary Ritter Beard Through Her Letters* (New Haven: Yale University Press, 1991), 21.

[3] Donald R. McCoy, "The Struggle to Establish a National Archives in the United States," in *Guardian of Heritage: Essays on the History of the National Archives*, ed. Timothy Walch (Washington, DC: National Archives and Records Administration, 1985), 15. See also Victor Gondos Jr., *Franklin Jameson and the Birth of the National Archives, 1906–1926* (Philadelphia: University of Pennsylvania Press, 1981), and James O'Toole, *Understanding Archives and Manuscripts,* Archival Fundamentals Series (Chicago: Society of American Archivists, 1990).

[4] William L. Joyce, "The Evolution of the Concept of Special Collections in American Research Libraries," *Rare Books and Manuscripts Librarianship* 3 (Spring 1988): 23, 25.

[5] Suzanne Hildenbrand, "Women's Collections Today," *Special Collections* 3 (Spring/Summer 1986): 2. Hildenbrand traces the growth of these collections to early twentieth-century feminists who sought to preserve the documentary record of their movement.

[6] See Cott, *A Woman Making History*, 4–19; and Beard and Beard, *American Citizenship* (New York: Macmillan, 1914); *The Rise of American Civilization*, 2 vols. (New York: Macmillan, 1927). Their other collaborative efforts include *America in Midpassage*, 2 vols. (New York: Macmillan, 1939); *The American Spirit: A Study of the Idea of Civilization in the United States* (New York: Macmillan, 1942); *A Basic History of the United States* (New York: Doubleday, 1944). A selected number of Mary Beard's publications include *On Understanding Women* (New York: Longmans, Green, 1931); and a book of essays she edited, *America Through Women's Eyes* (New York: Macmillan, 1933); and, of course, *Woman as Force in History* (New York: Macmillan, 1946).

[7] Eva Moseley, "Women in Archives: Documenting the History of Women in America," *The American Archivist* 36 (April 1973): 216. See also in that issue, Miriam Crawford, "Women in Archives: A Program for Action," 223–32; Mabel Deutrich, "Women in Archives: Ms. Versus Mr. Archivist," 171–81; Elsie Freeman Freivogel, "Women in Archives: The Status of Women in the Academic Professions," 182–202; and Joanna Schneider Zangrando, "Women in Archives: An Historian's View on the Liberation of Clio," 203–24. See also Michele F. Pacifico, "Founding Mothers: Women in the Society of American Archivists, 1936–1972," *The American Archivist* 50 (1987): 370–89.

[8] "Woman—the Pioneer," a radio broadcast in 1939, jointly sponsored by Columbia Broadcasting Systems and the Women's National Radio Committee, in *Mary Ritter Beard: A Source Book*, ed. Ann J. Lane (New York: Schocken Books, 1977), 193.

[9] Beard, Introduction, *America Through Women's Eyes*, 5.

[10] Barbara K. Turoff, *Mary Beard as Force in History* (Dayton, Ohio: Wright State University, 1979), 32.

[11] Turoff, *Mary Beard as Force in History*, 48.

[12] Mary Ritter Beard, *Woman as Force in History* (New York: 1946; reprint ed., New York: Persea Books, 1987), 59.

[13] One of the earliest discussions appears in Alma Lutz, "Women's History," *Journal of the American Association of University Women* 40 (Fall 1946): 6–8. For other selected studies, see Gerda Lerner, "New Approaches to the Study of Women in American History," *Journal of Social History* 3 (Fall 1969): 53–62, and "Placing Women in History: Definitions and Challenges," *Feminist Studies* 3 (Fall 1975): 5–14; Carroll Smith-Rosenberg, "The New Woman and the New History," *Feminist Studies*, 3 (Fall 1975): 185–98.

[14] Beard, *A Woman Making History*, 47–48. A scholar once asked to examine Beard's correspondence with Alice Paul of the Woman's Party. Beard replied that although there must have been some important documents among them, she had not kept most of her correspondence, adding, "It has not been concern for my own archives which has thrust me into the big archives business." Mary Beard to Mary Philbrook, 17 November [1936], in Beard, *A Woman Making History*, 164.

[15] Ann Kimbell Relph, "The World Center for Women's Archives, 1935–1940," *Signs* 4 (Spring 1979): 599, 601.

[16] Mary Beard to Rosika Schwimmer, 14 February 1936, in *A Woman Making History*, 148; Mary Beard to Sue Bailey Thurman, 25 March 1940, in *A Woman Making History*, 198.

[17] Mary Beard to Rosika Schwimmer, 12 May 1936, in *A Woman Making History*, 151; *A Woman Making History*, 145.

[18] Suzanne Hildenbrand and E. Wynner, "Women for Peace: The Schwimmer-Lloyd Collection of the New York Public Library," *Special Collections* 3 (Spring/Summer 1986): 37–42.

[19] World Center for Women's Archives brochure, International Organization Records, Sophia Smith Collection (SSC), Smith College, Northampton, Massachusetts.

[20] Marjorie White to Mary McLeod Bethune, 28 November 1938, Mary Beard Papers (SCH).

[21] Bettye Collier-Thomas "Towards Black Feminism: The Creation of the Bethune Museum Archives," *Special Collections* 3 (Spring/Summer 1986): 43–66.

[22] Mary Beard to the members of the Board of the World Center for Women's Archives, 26 June 1940, in Beard, *A Woman Making History*, 211–12; Mary Beard to Miriam Holden, 15 August 1940, in Beard, *A Woman Making History*, 216.

[23] Mary Beard to Miriam Holden, 10 October 1940, in Beard, *A Woman Making History*, 220.

[24] "Brief Report of the WCWA," 13 November 1939, Mary Beard Papers, SCH; Mary Beard to Margaret Grierson, 22 June 1940, Mary Beard Papers, SSC.

[25] For a brief history of these collections and their holdings, see Patricia M. King, "Forty Years of Collecting on Women: The Arthur and Elizabeth Schlesinger Library on the History of Women in America," *Radcliffe Special Collections* 3 (Spring/Summer 1986): 75–100; Mary Elizabeth Murdock, "Exploring Women's Lives: Historical and Contemporary Resources in the College Archives and the Sophia Smith Collection at Smith College," *Radcliffe Special Collections* 3 (Spring/Summer 1986): 67–74. For a discussion of special reference issues in a women's archives, see Anne Engelhart, "Remembering the Women: Manuscript Reference at the Schlesinger Library," *Reference Librarian* 13 (Fall 1985): 11–22.

[26] For studies about new sources of women's history, see Martha S. Bell, "Special Women's Collections in United States Libraries," *College and Research Libraries* 20 (May 1959): 235–42; Sandra L. Chaff, "Archives and Special Collections on Women in Medicine at the Medical College of Pennsylvania," *Bulletin of the Medical Library Association* 66 (January 1978): 55–57; R. McQuaide, "A Well-Kept Secret: The Religious Archive as a Reference Source," *Reference Librarian* 13 (Fall 1985): 137–48; Eva S. Moseley, "Sources for the 'New Women's History'," *American Archivist* 43 (Spring 1980): 180–90; Eva S. Moseley, "Women in Archives: Documenting the History of Women in America," *American Archivist* 36 (April 1973): 215–22; Mary J. Oates, "Religious Archives Undo Stereotypes about the Role of Sisters," *Catholic Library World* 63 (1991): 47–52; Sarah Pritchard, "Library of Congress Resources for the Study of Women," *Special Collections* 3 (Spring/Summer 1986): 13–36. For selected projects attempting to preserve women's history, see Ronald J. Chepsiuk and Ann Y. Evans, "Videotaping [Women's] History: The Winthrop College Archives' Experience," *American Archivist* 48 (Winter 1985): 65–68; Ruth Edmonds Hill, "The Black Women Oral History Project," *Behavioral and Social Sciences Librarian* 4 (Summer 1985): 3–14; "NOW Oral History Project at Radcliffe," *Library Journal* 115 (March 1990): 16; Diane Pederson, "The Photographic Record of the Canadian YWCA, 1890–1930: A Visual Source for Women's History," *Archivaria* 24 (Summer 1987): 10–35; and "Women's History: A Heritage of Strength and Vision," *Ohio Libraries* 2 (January/February 1989): 7.

[27] Beard, *A Woman Making History*, 118; handwritten draft from Margaret Grierson to William Beard (1959), SSC Donor Files, Smith College Archives (SCA), Northampton, Massachusetts.

[28] Mary Beard to Alice Lachmund, 7 December 1942, Mary Beard Papers, SSC. Beard's correspondence discussing these efforts can be located in the papers of

women who supported the WCWA and donated their papers to Smith College; also see WCWA records in the Mary Beard Papers, SCH.

[29] Turoff, *Mary Beard as Force in History*, 72. For the full list of institutions that received materials from the defunct WCWA, see memorandum from the World Center for Women's Archives, 25 November 1940, International Organizations Records, SSC. For a description of Beard's involvement at other colleges, see, for example, Mary Beard to Alice Lachmund, 17 August 1943, Mary Beard Papers, SSC.

[30] Beard, *A Woman Making History*, 132.

[31] Among the many letters, see Mary Beard to Wilbur Jordan, 14 January 1944, 7 June 1944, Mary Beard Papers, SCH; Mary Beard to Margaret Grierson, 28 October 1949, Mary Beard Papers, SSC.

[32] The materials donated to Radcliffe were listed in a memorandum from the WCWA, 25 November 1940; Records of International Organizations, SSC; Mary Beard to Nancy Cox-McCormack Cushman, 10 August 1945, Cushman Papers, SSC; Turoff, *Mary Beard as Force in History*, 65; Mary Beard to Wilbur Jordan, 27 June 1944, Mary Beard Papers, SCH; see Mary Beard to Nancy Cox-McCormack Cushman, 18 May 1947, Cushman Papers, and Mary Beard to Marine Leland, 6 February 1951, Mary Beard Papers, SSC.

[33] Mary Beard to Elizabeth B. Borden, 8 February 1951, Mary Beard Papers, SSC.

[34] Lane, *Mary Ritter Beard: A Source Book*, 54.

[35] Mary Beard to Wilbur Jordan, 9 January 1944, Mary Beard Papers, SCH; handwritten draft from Margaret Grierson to William Beard (1959), SSC Donor Files, SCA.

[36] Typescript of speech by President Herbert Davis, before the Alumnae Association meeting, 14 June 1941, Records of the President's Office, SCA.

[37] Mary Beard to Herbert Davis, 5 August 1941, Records of the President's Office, SCA; Mary Beard to Eva Hansl, 12 August 1941, Eva Hansl Papers, SSC.

[38] For her offer of materials from the WCWA, see Mary Beard to Herbert Davis, 24 October 1941; Mary Beard to Herbert Davis, 6 November 1941; see also 16 November 1941 and 21 November, 1941, Records of the President's Office, SCA.

[39] Mary Beard to Margaret Grierson, 7 December 1941, Mary Beard Papers, SSC; Mary Beard to Margaret Grierson, 8 November 1948, Mary Beard Papers, SSC.

[40] *Annual Report of the Friends of the Smith College Library*, March 1942, SCA.

[41] Margaret Grierson to Nina Browne, 8 April 1943, Nina Browne Papers, SCA.

[42] Mary Beard to Margaret Grierson, 1 June 1943, Mary Beard Papers, SSC.

[43] Margaret Grierson to Nina Browne, 10 July 1943, Nina Browne Papers, SCA.

[44] Mary Beard to Margaret Grierson, 27 June 1943, Mary Beard Papers, SSC.

[45] *Annual Report of the Friends of the Smith College Library*, 1943, SCA.

[46] Mary Beard to Margaret Grierson, 11 April 1943, Mary Beard Papers, SSC.

[47] *Bulletin of Smith College*, President's Report Issue, 18 December 1945, SCA.

[48] Sophia Smith envisioned the college providing new opportunities for women but said that: "It is not my design to render my sex any the less feminine but to develop as fully as may be the powers of womanhood, and furnish women with the means of usefulness, happiness, and honor, now withheld from them." The women's collection, it seemed, could play an integral part in the educational experience that Smith had hoped to provide for women. These excerpts are from the last will and testament of Sophia Smith, 8 March 1870, SCA; *Annual Report of the Friends of the Smith College Library*, 1946; the devoted friend of the women's collection was Dorothy Brush, and her article appeared in the *Smith College Quarterly* 37 (August 1946), SCA.

[49] *Annual Report of The Friends of the Smith College Library*, 1947, SCA.

[50] *Annual Report of The Friends of the Smith College Library*, 1945, SCA.

[51] Mary Beard to Margaret Grierson, 22 June 1944, Mary Beard Papers, SSC. For a more detailed description of the new catalog, see *Annual Report of the Friends of the Smith College Library*, 1947.

[52] For Grierson's comments on the arrangement of the collections, see "Consideration of Several Aspects of the Sophia Smith Collection in Comparison with the Radcliffe Women's Archives," a report by Margaret Grierson, September 1950, Records of the SCA/SSC, SCA; *Annual Report of The Friends of the Smith College Library*, 1947, SCA.

[53] Mary Beard to Dorothy Hamilton Brush, 26 January 1949, Dorothy Brush Papers, SSC.

[54] For a description of her meeting with Wright, see Mary Beard to Margaret Grierson, 19 March 1949, Mary Beard Papers, SSC. For Wright's views of the SSC, see Margaret Grierson to Eleanor Garrison, 3 December 1950, Margaret Grierson Papers, SCA.

[55] Mary Beard to Margaret Grierson, 17 February 1951, Mary Beard Papers, SSC.

[56] Mary Beard to Benjamin Fletcher Wright, 4 April 1954, Records of the SSC, SCA.

[57] Margaret Grierson to Barbara Turoff, 16 October 1979, SSC Donor Files, SCA.

[58] Mary Beard to Margaret Grierson, 6 March 1944, Mary Beard Papers, SSC; Margaret Grierson in conversation with Anke Voss-Hubbard, 5 July 1993.

[59] Margaret Grierson to William Beard, 1959, SSC Donor Files, SCA.

[60] Margaret Grierson to Eleanor Garrison, 19 November 1948, Garrison Family Papers, SSC.

[61] Eleanor Garrison to Margaret Grierson, 19 March 1950, Garrison Family Papers, SSC.

[62] Margaret Grierson in conversation with Anke Voss-Hubbard, 5 July 1993.

[63] In this letter, for example, Beard advises Grierson to contact Luther Evans at the Library of Congress for materials about the suffrage amendment, Mary Beard to Margaret Grierson, 30 July 1945. Another letter includes the name of a physician at the State Department who would be a good source for materials on Latin American countries, Mary Beard to Margaret Grierson, 14 October 1944. In another, she recommends that Grierson contact Eleanor Roosevelt to get the original copy of her speech to the WCWA, Mary Beard to Margaret Grierson, 26 October 1945. All letters are in the Mary Beard Papers, SSC.

[64] For Beard's comments on Lutz, see Mary Beard to Margaret Grierson, 6 March 1944; on Sanger, see Mary Beard to Margaret Grierson, 2 July 1946; and on Drinker, see Mary Beard to Margaret Grierson, 31 March 1950. All letters are in the Mary Beard Papers, SSC.

[65] Because of the noninterventionist stand both Beards took during the war, Mary Beard believed that "the name Beard is anathema in many, many quarters," and she expressed doubt that it "has the pull which you think it has," Mary Beard to Margaret Grierson, 6 March 1944, Mary Beard Papers, SSC. On Beard's influence, see Margaret Grierson to Nina Browne, 15 April 1944, Nina Browne Papers, SCA. In these letters, for example, Beard recommends to journalist Margery Steer and Alice Lachmund, a friend from her WCWA period, that they send their source materials to Smith, Mary Beard to Margery Steer, 28 April 1951, Margery Steer Papers; Mary Beard to Alice Lachmund, 30 March 1943, Mary Beard Papers, SSC.

[66] Ethel Weed to Margaret Grierson, 31 May 1960, SSC Donor Files, SCA.

[67] For T. C. Mendenhall's Smith College medal citation, 23 October 1968, see Margaret Grierson Papers, SCA.

[68] Margaret Grierson to Amy Hague, 17 September 1992, Margaret Grierson Papers; Margaret Grierson to Margery Steer, 4 April 1961, SSC Donor Files, SCA.

[69] Mary Beard to Elsie Yellis, 16 May 1938, Mary Beard Papers, SCH.

[70] Mary Beard to Theodore C. Blegen, 14 July 1939, Mary Beard Papers, SCH.

CHAPTER 3

Mining the Forgotten: Manuscript Sources for Black Women's History

DEBORAH GRAY WHITE

TEN YEARS AGO AN ARTICLE IN A MAJOR HISTORICAL JOURNAL ON MAN-
USCRIPT COLLECTIONS ON BLACK WOMEN WOULD HAVE BEEN UNLIKELY.
Not only was interest in doing black women's history minimal, but some
collections that exist today did not even exist then. This article, therefore, owes a debt to the emergence of Afro-American history and women's
history. It also is in debt to historians who, having researched either or
both histories, have found that in the vast body of literature generated in
the decade of the 1970s, there is a missing character—the black woman.
This is by no means a comprehensive survey of manuscript collections on
black women; it is intended rather as a point of departure for those still in
search of that missing character.

Newly discovered documents or those recently made available enable
scholars to rescue black women from their submergence and invisibility
in both Afro-American history and women's history. We are beginning to
learn, for example, that black women have always played major roles in
black protest movements, but that their motivation, styles of activism, and
objectives did not always replicate those of black men. Similarly, when
black women moved into the public arena of work and politics, they did
so under conditions distinct from those that mobilized white women and

with different strategies and goals. Our ability to understand the complex ways in which race and gender have shaped black women's lives depends on intensive work in primary sources. In many ways, however, such sources continue to elude scholars.

To understand the nature of manuscript collections on black women, one must recognize that existent records conform to fundamental aspects of black female history. Important is the fact that black people have an oral tradition sustained by almost three hundred years of illiteracy in America. Equally important, the black woman's world has been peripheral to those most likely to keep records of any kind, men and white women. Such circumstances have combined to make manuscript collections on black women scarce. They also make oral histories a very important source for the personal aspects of black female life. Indeed, some of the richest sources, the Work Projects Administration (WPA) Slave Narrative Collection, for instance, are personal oral histories. There are, of course, other kinds of records, but they are not always easy to locate. In the first place, many indexes were compiled before either blacks or black and white women became important subjects of study. Therefore, it is usually hard to identify the papers of black women or records that contain significant materials about black women. For example, the guide to the Southern Historical Collection at the University of North Carolina, Chapel Hill, is organized around the white individuals whose papers have been preserved, and although many of the papers contain information about southern black women's experiences, the 1970 guide and its 1976 supplement do not identify them. Similarly, Andrea Hinding's *Women's History Sources* is a valuable index, but it provides no means of finding the manuscripts of black women that are not coded with the terms black, Afro-American, or Negro.[1]

Along with inadequacies of indexes is the related problem that a black woman's papers are sometimes subsumed in those of the prominent male member of her family or buried in someone else's papers. For example, the papers of the Kansas City Federation of Colored Women's Clubs can be found in the Frederick Douglass Collection in the Manuscript Division of Howard University's Moorland-Spingarn Research Center. Similarly, the very interesting papers of Marchita and Pauline Lyons are in the Henry Albro Williamson Collection at the Schomburg Center for Research in Black Culture in New York City. Williamson was Pauline's son and Marchita's nephew. Marchita Lyons was the first black female teacher in Brooklyn, New York, and her papers include an unpublished autobiography. The papers of Pauline Lyons include private correspondence that describes the trials of her single parenthood in late-nineteenth-century San Francisco. These and other manuscripts were rescued by archivists sensitive to black women's history, but in the past such archivists have been rare.

Black women have also been reluctant to donate their papers to manuscript repositories. That is in part a manifestation of the black woman's perennial concern with image, a justifiable concern born of centuries of vilification. Black women's reluctance to donate personal papers also stems from the adversarial nature of the relationship that countless black women have had with many public institutions and the resultant suspicion of anyone seeking private information. Finally, black women have infrequently saved and donated papers because they have grown used to being undervalued and invisible, believing that no one is interested in them.

These circumstances help us to appreciate the efforts of the Black Women in the Middle West Project (BWMW). The brainchild of historian Darlene Clark Hine, the BWMW commissioned volunteers to uncover and collect records from black women in the Midwest. The project was originally intended to cover all five midwestern states, but guided by the advice and funding of the National Endowment for the Humanities, the BWMW collected records, oral histories, and photographs of black women only in Illinois and Indiana. It is disappointing that the General Collections form the smallest part and that they are housed in not one, but five, cooperating institutions. Yet, given the problems associated with obtaining materials from black women, the accomplishment is quite notable.

The General Collections of the BWMW Project include the papers and records of renowned individuals, ordinary citizens, local organizations, and church congregations. More significant in terms of linear feet are the files and biographical data generated by the project itself and by project participants. While these manuscripts are easier to exploit because they are all housed at the Indiana Historical Society in Indianapolis, the biographical data make for very short files. As is the case with most raw materials used in historical analysis, the project files, while invaluable now as a measure of the pulse of contemporary black female America, will become even more precious as time provides the opportunity for scrutiny in historical perspective.[2]

Donors of materials to the BWMW were encouraged to make their papers completely accessible with a minimum of restrictions; unfortunately, this does not seem to have been the case with the Black Women's Oral History Project of the Schlesinger Library at Radcliffe College in Cambridge, Massachusetts. Of the seventy-two oral histories collected between 1976 and 1981, nine are restricted and permission to see them must be obtained from the interviewee. The collection features interviews with prominent and working-class black women, and individual interviews are available through interlibrary loan. Yet, although the typescripts are easily accessible, each interview comes with stipulations sufficient to make its use nothing short of frustrating. The most common injunctions are against photocopying and quoting any part of the interview without permission of the interviewee or her designated surrogate. Since permission to quote is not always granted, one must sometimes paraphrase and thus sacrifice the original flavor of a comment. Needless to say, these restrictions reflect the previously noted reluctance of black women to share personal experiences and documents with an often-hostile public. One can understand the anxiety associated with being analyzed by even a benign or benevolent public. Nonetheless, working with these oral histories can be frustrating and can make one all the more appreciative of collections that are totally open and accessible.

The subject files of the Claude A. Barnett Papers form such a collection. Located at the Chicago Historical Society (now the Chicago History Museum), most of this collection is also available on microfilm.[3] Barnett was the founder and the director of the Associated Negro Press, and the papers describe the world of black America at the height of its separate development, before integration. The files are arranged topically within each subject, making it easy to identify files exclusively devoted to black women and their world. Correspondence, news clippings, and news releases are available on such subjects as beauty, culture, black women in the military, black sororities, the Young Women's Christian Association (YWCA), Baptist women's organizations and foreign missions, and black female authors, artists, and entertainers. The subject index at the end of the published guide is helpful in locating the correspondence of individuals within particular topic files. To use these files, one must wade through much correspondence dealing with the mechanics of publication, but the researcher will find the papers an invaluable source on many different aspects of the black woman's personal, public, and organizational life.

As a single source on a variety of black female activities in the postbellum era, the Barnett papers are probably unmatched. However, a trip to Washington, DC, gives access to several valuable resources for re-creating black women's history. The Library of Congress houses some of the papers of black female activists Mary Church Terrell and Nannie H. Burroughs. While the Library of Congress contains some of Mary McLeod Bethune's papers, the bulk of this leader's papers are found elsewhere. Administrative records relating to the founding and presidency of Bethune-Cookman College are located at the college in Daytona Beach, Florida. Bethune's records relating to the National Youth Administration are located at the National Archives in Washington, and most of the remaining papers are at the National Archives for Black Women's History, also in Washington. In the records of the National Association for the Advancement of Colored People, one also finds papers of Bethune and Terrell, along with those of novelist Jessie Fauset.

The Moorland-Spingarn Manuscript Division at Howard University in Washington, DC, has a large collection of manuscripts and oral histories of black women. Researchers should obtain the annotated "List of References to Women" compiled by Esme Bhan, because the *Guide to Processed Collections in the Manuscript Division of the Moorland-Spingarn Research Center* unfortunately does not list all of the center's holdings on black women.[4] As noted earlier, the papers of the Kansas City Federation of Colored Women's Clubs are cataloged in the Frederick Douglass Collection, yet the *Guide* contains no mention of these rare minutes or records. Compensating for other omissions in the *Guide*, the annotated list indicates single-document manuscripts, and it distinguishes a wife's or daughter's papers from those of the male on whom a collection centers. As with most collections relating to black women's history, the bulk of the relevant holdings of the Moorland-Spingarn Manuscript Division reflect a particular black woman's public activities. They also resemble other collections in that most of the files are quite small.

More personal data can be found in the oral histories that are a part of the Civil Rights Documentation Project at Howard University. An invaluable source for researchers of recent American history, the collection has oral histories of famous black women like Ella Baker and Fannie Lou Hamer, and of less renowned women like Barbara Arthur, a former member of the Black Panther Party, and Annie Devine, one of the three black candidates who challenged the election and seating of the regular Mississippi congressional delegation in 1965. The library has provided a thoughtfully compiled, nonannotated list of black female oral histories. Full annotation is available in a guide edited by Vincent J. Browne and Norma O. Leonard.[5]

Without doubt the most impressive and significant collections of manuscripts for black women's history are in Washington, DC, at the National Archives for Black Women's History and the Mary McLeod Bethune Memorial Museum, commonly known as the Bethune Archives, the only repository in the country solely devoted to the collection and preservation of materials relating to American black women. The 1979 dedication of the museum and archives was the realization of a goal set in 1940 by the National Council of Negro Women (NCNW). Consequently, the major holding of the archives is the records of the NCNW, from 1935 through 1978. The records are arranged in twenty-three series and document a wide variety of subjects. Materials include correspondence of founder Bethune and countless other women, minutes, reports, financial and membership records, NCNW publications, and over one thousand photographs.

Because the NCNW was and is an organization of organizations, the records also provide information about black women's organizations that were affiliated with the NCNW, including national sororities, church groups, and black women's business organizations. The Bethune Archives has other records, including those of the National Committee on Household Employment, the National Association of Fashion and Accessory Designers, and the Historical Annals of the Ladies' Auxiliary of the black Catholic men's organization, the Knights of Peter Claver. The Bethune Archives holds personal papers as well. The most significant are those of Polly Cowan, the white director of the Wednesdays in Mississippi Civil Rights Project of the NCNW, and Susie Green, the first black woman to be licensed as a printer.

If there is a drawback to this repository, it is that except for the NCNW records, the holdings are all unprocessed and therefore open only on a very limited basis to researchers with an appointment. The problem stems in large part from the fact that the archives has had an archivist only for intermittent periods and, as of January 1987, was without one. Consequently, researchers will experience difficulty in using the holdings for years to come. There are some bright signs, however. The Bethune Archives recently obtained the papers of the National Black Feminist Organization. Even though they probably will not be processed for some time, it is heartening to know that they will not be lost or destroyed. The archives has just initiated a restoration and preservation project to expand facilities for researchers and to protect its files. It is producing an edition of selected papers of Mary McLeod Bethune and compiling a published guide to the archives' Mary McLeod Bethune series. Thus, the future of the Bethune Archives looks better than the past and present.

The same can be said for the future of black women's history. This brief summary of a few of the manuscript collections on black women is testimony to the growing interest of both scholars and lay people in this area of American history. Further research will undoubtedly turn up records previously buried in unrelated files and in damp and dusty cellars and attics. It should also increase the sensitivity of archivists, research librarians, and indexers. In the process, black women will cease to be the missing characters in black and women's history. Black women's history will complete, as well as bind together, these two fields. In the end it will be the general field of American history that is enriched.

NOTES

This article was originally published in *The Journal of American History* 74 no. 1 (1987): 237–42.

[1] Susan Sokol Blosser and Clyde Norman Wilson Jr., eds., *The Southern Historical Collection: A Guide to Manuscripts* (Chapel Hill: University of North Carolina, 1970); Everard H. Smith III, comp., *The Southern Historical Collection: Supplementary Guide to Manuscripts, 1970–75* (Chapel Hill: University of North Carolina, 1976); Andrea Hinding, ed., *Women's History Sources: A Guide to Archives and Manuscript Collections in the United States*, 2 vols. (New York: R. R. Bowker LLC, 1979).

[2] Darlene Clark Hine et al., *The Black Women in the Middle West Project: A Comprehensive Resource Guide, Illinois and Indiana* (Indianapolis: Indiana Historical Bureau, 1986), describes the project as well as the various parts of the collection.

[3] August Meier and Elliott Rudwick, *The Claude A. Barnett Papers: The Associated Negro Press, 1918–1967; Part Three, Subject Files on Black Americans, 1918–1967* (Frederick, Md.: University Publications of America, 1986).

[4] Greta S. Wilson, comp., *Guide to Processed Collections in the Manuscript Division of the Moorland-Spingarn Research Center* (Washington, DC: Moorland-Spingarn Research Center, 1983).

[5] Vincent J. Browne and Norma O. Leonard, eds., *Bibliography of Holdings of the Civil Rights Documentation Project* (Washington, DC: Howard University, 1974).

CHAPTER 4

The Current Status of Black Women's History: Telling Our Story Ourselves

AUDREY T. McCLUSKEY

If anyone's gonna tell my story I guess it'll be me, myself.

—LANGSTON HUGHES

I AM EXTREMELY HAPPY TO BE A PART OF THIS EFFORT TO CELEBRATE AND TO RECLAIM BLACK WOMEN'S HISTORY (HERSTORY). I share your enthusiasm, pride, and even awe at the tremendous accomplishments and sweet inspiration of our African American foremothers. Our remembrance of our foremothers creates in us a common bond, a bond forged by our collective memory of their spirit and aspirations, their will to live and to fight the good fight. Whether they lived on a dirt farm in rural Mississippi or in the big house in Atlanta or migrated to Gary, Indiana, in search of a better life, they left us a legacy of commitment and struggle that is, indeed, the inspiration for the Black Women in the Middle West Project.

This, then, is a reclamation project. It is not—and the difference is important—an attempt to "discover" black women's history. Reclamation connotes a process through which black women's history will be brought out in the open and accorded the intellectual scrutiny and historical relevance it deserves. It has never been a question of whether a black women's history exists. The question has always been a political one. Why have black women been denied their rightful place in history? Bear with me.

I want to begin by reminding you of how African American women have been portrayed in history and contrast those images with the *self-portraiture* provided via written and oral sources from black women themselves. There has always been a contradiction between traditional historical portraiture of black women and self-revealed portraiture. Black women, especially during the early nineteenth century, were not considered historically relevant. They were annulled out of history primarily because they did not fit the conventional view of the nineteenth-century woman, idealized as it was. Black women were not like their Euro-American counterparts who were defined by men in terms of what they could *not* do. The term "lady" became a synonym for the restraints placed on females who needed to be constantly provided for by their male "protectors." Black women had no such protection or provision. They met the needs of their own families as well as the families of the enslavers. Black women often assumed and carried out the traditionally defined responsibilities of both male *and* female. Slavery was indeed an equal opportunity employer! Although very necessary for black survival, this duality of roles did confuse historians and sociologists: "Whatever will we do with the black woman? She is not like the white woman. Can we explain her in terms of the black man? . . . Perhaps we'd better leave her alone." So for years black women have been denied a voice in American history, although their presence was undisputed. The problem, like that of Ralph Ellison's *Invisible Man*, was that people, especially historians and academicians, have refused to see black women in their own terms.

When black women did begin to appear in history and literature, they were caricatures without depth or substance. It was easier that way. Perhaps there was a fear of what was behind the black woman's thinly veiled posture of deference. If they would have listened to the voices of these women, then they would have learned the truth. In 1852, Sojourner Truth, in her stirring and poetic "Ain't I A Woman" speech, tried to tell

them as she pleaded for a broader, less restrictive definition of what it
means to be a woman:

> I have plowed and planted and gathered into barns, and no man
> could head me, and ain't I a woman? I could work as much and eat
> as much as a man when I could get it. And bear the lash as well, and
> ain't I a woman?

It was her attempt to tell her story herself. Experience, concrete experience, as Simone de Beauvoir suggests, makes a woman a woman, not
mere biology. If they would have listened, then they would have heard
black women defining themselves as mothers, as workers, as nurturers,
as builders, as soothsayers and oracles, as participant-contributors in the
panoply of human experience. Poet Margaret Walker in *For My People*
(New Haven, Connecticut, 1942) captures this full and bountiful spirit in
her poem of homage to black foremothers entitled "Lineage":

> My grandmothers were strong.
> They followed plows and bent to toil.
> They moved through fields sowing seed.
> They touched earth and grain grew.
> They were full of sturdiness and singing.
> My grandmothers were strong.

Although victimized, black women seldom defined themselves exclusively
as victims—at least not the whining self-pitying type of victim. That atti-
tude—"I may be down, but I ain't out!"—is the stuff out of which survival
and history are made. In fact, black people made it into an art form. It is
called the blues—America's original music. The blues rejects self-pity. It
begins with self-acceptance, not self-hatred, and allows one to transcend
immediate catastrophe and thus to achieve personal salvation. Female
blues voices provide a rich source of female self-portraiture, particularly
of early semi-urban black women, that deserves further study.

Because historians have ignored or failed to make adequate use of
the evidence of self-portraiture, there have been basically three errors in
the portraiture of black women in traditional historiography. These are
1) errors of distortion, 2) errors of omission, and 3) errors of a biased

perspective. The dissatisfaction among black women with how they are depicted in history has not been measured, but their displeasure is evident to anyone who takes the time to listen. I have recorded some typical reactions of black women to these errors of scholarship:

> Girl, did you read that mess in *Time* magazine about the matriarchal black family being the cause of black juvenile delinquency? What does that mean? I've got two children to feed and clothe whether or not my man is home.

This is reaction to distortion. This is the use of so-called facts and statistics to draw dubious conclusions—and to blame the victim. The next reaction illustrates the degree to which black women have been omitted from history texts:

> Say, what? You mean to tell me that a black woman was the first woman to become a self-made millionaire in America? Why didn't I know that?

This final example is a reaction to a biased perspective in teaching about black women:

> Mama, my teacher says that activist Angela Davis is a radical communist and a criminal who wants to overthrow the U.S. government.

Distortions, omissions, and flawed perspectives are all common problems with the historical approaches used in dealing with black women's history.

The two main historical approaches to which I refer are 1) the victimization school and 2) the contributionist school. The victimization school emphasizes the brutalization of black women. It is a very popular approach. It serves to motivate and to raise our consciousness. The problem with the victimization school is that it tends to view black women as passive and as bystanders in the fight for their own freedom. This approach elevates suffering to an art form—and leads us to expect that suffering is natural for black women.

The second most popular approach to black women's history is the contributionist approach. It is very popular during Black History Week. It emphasizes the contributions that outstanding black women have made to this country. It attempts not to rethink traditional historical cant but to fill in the gaps, to give black women "a piece of the action." This emphasis is on success as defined by Euro-Americans, not blacks themselves. We may think that the mother who worked three jobs to put all of her five children through college is a success, but she would not fit into the contributionist format. These approaches are necessary and valuable, but neither gives black women a voice nor allows them to "tell their own story." They do not challenge the status quo or force us to re-evaluate the male-normative perspective of traditional teaching and research.

A third approach, an approach that I feel has the most to offer in terms of finally beginning to understand the intricacies of black women's history, is what has been called a women-centered approach to history. It is being used by less tradition-laden historians, researchers, writers, both black and white, and is playing a major role in revitalizing interest in black women's history and presence in America. This approach begins by asking the question: "What have black women done and how did they do it?" It is obviously an adaptable model for rethinking the history of all women and all minorities because it is free of Eurocentric patriarchal assumptions and biases. This approach does not ignore the oppression or victimization of women, but it does afford them the dignity of being historical actors and creators rather than passive victims.

This is the direction that I think the study of black women's culture will continue to take in the future. The result will be a more thorough, more satisfying depiction and articulation of the black female voice in traditionally white, male disciplines. Practitioners of this women-centered approach to the study of black women are social scientists as well as humanists from a variety of disciplines, such as Joyce Ladner and La Frances Rodgers-Rose in sociology; Mary Helen Washington and Barbara Smith in literary criticism; Sharon Harley, Rosalyn Terborg-Penn, Paula Giddings, and Dorothy Sterling in history, to name a few.

This effort is being helped tremendously by the current renaissance in black women's literature. Toni Morrison, Paule Marshall, Alice Walker, Toni Cade Bambara, Gloria Naylor, and others are providing the literary complement to those black foremothers who were "full of sturdiness and singing" and whose everyday experiences were larger than life, yet for them routine. The writing of these women is an act of empowerment for all women and is undoubtedly putting starch back into the increasingly limp fabric of American moral fiction.

This suggests that black women could maximize their recent gains by uniting to launch an all-out attack on the remaining vestiges of racism and sexism. By looking at history in this way, we can see that organizing efforts by black women have always been successful. Our foremothers did this back in 1896 when, provoked by a white male journalist who had the temerity to question black women's moral virtue, they convened a national meeting that resulted in the founding of the influential National Association of Colored Women's Clubs. Membership quickly reached into the tens of thousands.

This is an important time for women of color and oppressed people. We now have the means and the opportunity to rewrite herstory, to direct our own future. We must form coalitions with other like-minded groups and progressive individuals. We know that strength lies in unity and that we have the collective power to transform our world into a better, more humane, egalitarian place—a place where race and gender are human descriptors not barriers to human development. That is why this grassroots effort to collect and to preserve black women's history—to tell our story ourselves—is imperative at this historical juncture. Let me conclude by paraphrasing Mrs. Rosa Parks, whose iron resolve and sense of purpose gave birth to the civil rights movement: "If not now—when? If not us—who?" In 1985, the answers to these questions must be: "Now is the time. This is the place. And we are the women."

NOTES

This article was originally published in Darlene Clark Hine et al., *The Black Women in the Middle West Project: A Comprehensive Resource Guide, Illinois and Indiana* (Indianapolis: Indiana Historical Bureau, 1986).

CHAPTER 5

"A Grand Manuscripts Search": The Women's History Sources Survey at the University of Minnesota, 1975–1979

KÄREN M. MASON

In 1970 the status of Women's History was nonexistent. At a time when political and institutional history was the measure of significance and social history had only recently been elevated to legitimacy, the subject "women" was defined as doubly marginal. Women's History was not recognized as a legitimate field and to admit that one worked in it was considered the kiss of death professionally.

—GERDA LERNER
LIVING WITH HISTORY / MAKING SOCIAL CHANGE

IN THE LATE 1960S, THE WOMEN'S MOVEMENT EXPLODED ON THE SCENE. The movement took many forms, from formal organizations to consciousness-raising groups, childcare collectives, demonstrations, and guerilla actions. Unlike the first wave of feminism, which built slowly from

the 1840s to the 1920s and had one goal—winning the vote for women—
this second wave was a storm that came up suddenly and burst forth in
many directions; Sara Evans likened the latter movement to a tidal wave
sweeping across the nation. The Presidential Commission on the Status of
Women appointed by John F. Kennedy in 1961, and the state commissions
that followed, documented the discrimination women faced in employment, pay, legal status, and other areas. These commissions tapped into
a cohort of professional women and community activists who had experienced discrimination in their own lives. Betty Friedan's *The Feminine
Mystique*, published in 1963, struck a chord with these women and with
the college-educated women who were frustrated by societal expectations
that they be content with the roles of housewife and mother. Three years
later, Friedan helped organize the National Organization for Women
(NOW), which spread quickly across the country in state and local chapters. Within a year of the 1966 founding of NOW, more radical organizations, such as the Chicago Women's Liberation Group and the New York
Radical Women, began meeting. In 1968, radical feminists objecting to
the maternalist rhetoric of Women Strike for Peace disrupted an antiwar
demonstration in Washington, DC, bringing coffins and banners to pro-
claim "the death of traditional womanhood." That same year, members
of NOW picketed the *New York Times* to protest sex-segregated classified
ads, the National Abortion Rights Action League was formed, and radical
women protested the Miss America Pageant in New York City by throw-
ing bras, girdles, curlers, and other "objects of female torture" into a trash
can outside the pageant.[1]

Against this backdrop, women historians began to assert themselves
within the national and regional professional organizations. These women
were both scholars and activists—inspired by the civil rights movement,
the student movement, the peace movement, and the women's liberation movement—and determined to make broad changes in society. They
viewed the professional organizations as "gentlemen's clubs" that were
either indifferent to or actively hostile to women scholars and dismissive
of women's history as a subject of scholarly inquiry. Inspired by the wom-
en's movement, these historians set out to legitimize the field of women's

history and the role of women in the academy. As Berenice Carroll later recalled, "Our indignation and anger drove us, our shared labor and laughter sustained us."[2]

In the fall of 1969, Carroll, who was a peace activist and historian then teaching in the Political Science Department at the University of Illinois, circulated a petition to friends and prominent historians asking that the American Historical Association (AHA) appoint a committee on the status of women in the profession. Paul Ward, executive secretary of the AHA, was sympathetic to the request, and when the resolution was presented to the AHA council in October, the council adopted it. Recognizing that women historians should also have an independent organization, about twenty-five women met at the annual conference of the AHA in December 1969 and formed the Coordinating Committee on Women in the Historical Profession (CCWHP). Carroll has written of the CCWHP that "from the outset we saw our 'activism' for women in the profession as closely tied to scholarship in women's history." The CCWHP organized panels on teaching and research in women's history for the AHA and the Organization of American Historians (OAH), argued for those panels with program committees, and worked to get women appointed to those committees.[3] Within a few years, women's historians would enlist archivists to undertake an immense, path-breaking survey of primary sources in women's history.

Gerda Lerner, one of the modern founders of the field of women's history, believed that gaining acceptance for the field of women's history required a four-pronged approach: showing that "adequate and interesting" sources were available in women's history; producing first-rate work; training teachers and developing syllabi; and convincing administrators and colleagues that students wanted such courses. Of these, she considered identifying the sources the most critical. Scholars and graduate students interested in studying women's history were constantly told that primary sources were insufficient to support such research. But those who had done research in women's history knew that sources existed for the study of women's experience and were tired of being told otherwise.[4] The Sophia Smith Collection at Smith College and the Schlesinger Library at Radcliffe

College had been gathering women's papers for a generation, and scholars who had studied women's history knew that a wealth of sources existed beyond these repositories.

In April 1971, a group of historians who had done archival research on women met at the annual meeting of the OAH to discuss ways to make sources for women's history more accessible. Anne Firor Scott, Carl Degler, Janet Wilson James, Clarke Chambers, and Gerda Lerner decided that a survey of archival repositories' holdings on women should be undertaken.[5] The group formed an Advisory Board on the Proposal for a Guide to Women's History and began working with historian Dorothy Ross, who was then the American Historical Association's special assistant to the Committee on Women Historians and later had a distinguished career as a professor of history at Johns Hopkins University. Ross was an early champion of the women's history sources project. In December 1971, the AHA recommended the project to the American Council of Learned Societies, seeking its support for a project to create a series of guides to manuscript sources in the history of American women.[6]

Meanwhile, the five historians proposed a session on "Archival and Manuscripts Resources for the Study of Women's History" for the 1972 convention of the OAH. They asked Clarke Chambers to chair the session because he was "both a sympathetic historian, sympathetic to women's history and to Twentieth Century history" and because he was "identified with a significant archives which had women at its center. Social welfare had always had women at its center." Clarke Chambers was a 1942 graduate of Carleton College who had earned his PhD at the University of California, Berkeley, in 1950. He had taught in the History Department at the University of Minnesota since 1951 and was serving as chair of the department at this time. Chambers was a pioneer in the field of social welfare history; he had founded and served as the director of the Social Welfare History Archives at Minnesota since 1964. His own experiences seeking out sources for a new field of inquiry in "back rooms, offices, attics" and "buried in disguise in old and regular kinds of records that we are accustomed to using" made him a particularly apt choice, as he was confident that there were many historical records by and about women waiting to be discovered.[7]

Chambers turned to Andrea Hinding to help plan the OAH session. Hinding, a 1966 graduate of the University of Minnesota who earned a master's degree in history from Minnesota in 1973, had begun working at the Social Welfare History Archives as a student in 1965; by 1967, when she was just twenty-five years old, she had become the curator. The two decided to ask several people who were both archivists and historians "to show up at a session and talk a little bit about what they knew and what they'd found." But Hinding thought it would be a good idea to type up a list of collections and repositories ahead of time, because the audience wouldn't be able to catch all the information during the session. She asked the participants to send her the basic information, and Rosemary Richardson, also on staff at the Social Welfare History Archives, typed it up, creating a forty-two-page checklist of women's history sources.[8]

The response to the session indicated that there was indeed a very strong interest in women's history and the sources for studying it. The session attracted an overflow crowd of more than 150 people and had to be moved to a larger room. Those who attended received the checklist of sources on women; the checklist was later mailed to hundreds more who wrote to request copies.[9] Writing a few days after the conference to thank Joan Hoff Wilson for participating on the OAH panel and for contributing descriptions of collections for the checklist, Chambers said, "You must know what a major contribution the 'Beginning' document makes at this point in time. I regret that the disruption accompanying our move from that garrett room to the ballroom and the number of persons who just had to be heard, meant that we became pressed for time and could not spin out our thoughts with greater leisure. In my entire career in this profession I don't think I've ever faced such pressure of lack of time and surfeit of material." He said that the checklist and the ensuing discussion had provoked such great interest that before the convention ended, a small steering committee had been formed to explore ways to launch a "comprehensive effort to gather references to these kinds of sources."[10]

After the OAH conference, the Rockefeller Foundation held a two-day symposium on women's history for historians and archivists. The outcome was a set of priorities for the field of women's history, chief among them a nationwide survey of women's history sources. Clarke Chambers and Andrea Hinding were asked to draft a grant proposal seeking funding for such a survey. Writing to Paul Ward of the AHA, Anne Firor Scott explained that Chambers and Hinding "undertook this project at the behest of practically all the leading people in women's history, after their astonishing performance at the 1972 OAH, when, on about two months' notice, they put together a stunning bibliographical workshop." The "mix of archival and history expertise represented in the Social Welfare History Archives" and the willingness of the University of Minnesota to provide partial funding for the project were key factors in selecting Minnesota to undertake the survey.[11]

As Dorothy Ross prepared to leave her position with the AHA in 1972, she wrote to the advisory board about the National Endowment for the Humanities (NEH) grant process, and said that there had been "a breakthrough on the NEH front, in the form of Simone Reagor at NEH, an extremely capable young woman who wants to see more women's research projects funded" and who was to be promoted to a division directorship on July 1. Ross conveyed Reagor's suggestions to the board, saying that, in addition to being very specific about the project's timetable, personnel, and institutional ties, "The proposal should also make an extensive argument for the importance of the materials dealt with. Her experience has been that projects in women's history get turned down because the judges presuppose that the subject is just not important enough (i.e., since women in history are considered relatively unimportant to begin with)."[12]

Clarke Chambers and Andrea Hinding went to work on the proposal. In March 1973, Chambers sent a draft to the advisory board, asking for comments. He stated that they intended to add archivists to the advisory board because the project would succeed best as "a *joint* enterprise of historians and archivists at every point and at every level." Commenting on the draft proposal, Frank Evans of the National Archives and Records Service said that he hoped the omission of the national level was not intentional and urged that National Archives and Library of Congress holdings be included. He added that subject guides to holdings on black and American Indian history and science and technology were in progress at the National Archives, but none on women. (He added that he hoped it was not sexist of him to object to the term "inarticulate women" that had been used in the draft proposal.)[13] When the revised proposal went forward, it did include institutional archives as well as manuscripts repositories.

The grant application submitted to NEH on 7 May 1973 sought funds "to compile a guide to manuscripts and archival sources for the study of the history of women (of all classes, races, and regions) in the United States from the colonial period until the present. The project would survey by mail or field visit all the known repositories in the country, including national, state, and local archives; state and county historical societies; church, business, and other institutional archives." Chambers and Hinding believed that this would amount to 3,500 repositories across the United States to be surveyed.[14]

The proposal made an impassioned plea for the necessity of such a survey: "Though women have lived half of human history and though their experience has been a separate and identifiable one, biologically and culturally, scholars have given little systematic attention to women's lives. And because scholars have generally been unconcerned, the sources which support women's history have likewise been neglected or 'buried' within collections or repositories. But recently, contemporary feminism and developments in urban and minority history have reawakened interest in the study of women's past and the role women have played in society. . . . If this interest in women's history is to result in substantial scholarly work, the primary material housed in archival agencies and manuscripts repositories must be re-assessed and made known to the scholarly world."[15] Chambers and Hinding believed that one of the greatest benefits of the survey would be to "aid archivists in re-examining their holdings and providing useful criteria and definitions of needs important in accelerating acquisition of new material. The establishment of closer working relations between historians, librarians, and archivists will be another dividend."[16]

The first application to NEH was turned down, in part because the reviewers assumed that it duplicated the work of the *National Union Catalog of Manuscript Collections* (NUCMC). First published in 1959 with supplements and cumulative indexes printed in succeeding years, NUCMC contained summary descriptions of collections in manuscript repositories across the United States, drawn from information submitted by the repositories themselves. Upon learning of the NEH rejection, Frank Evans telephoned Andrea Hinding "hopping mad that NEH turned us down with a form letter" and incensed that "NEH gave the Forest History Foundation $80,000 to do for trees what we proposed to do for women's sources."[17] Chambers sought the advice of the advisory board on whether to submit a revised proposal to NEH or another foundation or just drop the project. He noted that the Social Welfare History Archives was using grant money from the Rockefeller Foundation for a preliminary survey of historical welfare sources in Minnesota and that the results might suggest other regional surveys. Janet Wilson James replied that the Minnesota survey—which would undoubtedly uncover sources on women, "proof of the pay dirt we know is there"—might serve as a model or pilot project for a series of regional surveys. She speculated that the proposal was turned down because it was considered "too big a job for the limited time now allowed for NEH projects."[18] While the size of the task may or may not have been the reason for denying the grant, James's speculation about the immensity of the undertaking was on the mark: the amount of material uncovered and the staff and time it took to complete the massive project proved to be considerably greater than anticipated. The first proposal, in fact, had the project director visiting all the nonreporting repositories to record their women's collections, a task that was ultimately given to twenty fieldworkers, each spending several months surveying repositories. Hinding later recalled that an early draft of the grant proposal requested "$65,000, three assistants, and 15 months. We might as well have requested a canoe and box lunch to cross the Atlantic Ocean."[19]

The project might have ended with the NEH rejection, but Simone Reagor called Chambers and Hinding to ask why they hadn't reapplied and invited Hinding to Washington, DC, to discuss how they might improve the next application.[20] In the revised application, submitted the following year, Chambers and Hinding were explicit about the ways in which the Women's History Sources Survey (WHSS) would differ from NUCMC. While NUCMC would serve as a model, its existence did not preclude a guide to women's sources. For one thing, many repositories did not report their holdings to NUCMC; of the estimated 3,500 manuscript repositories in the nation, only 900 had reported to NUCMC. Furthermore, public archives were not even included in NUCMC; in fact, the inclusion of archives as well as manuscripts repositories became one of the things that would later set *Women's History Sources* apart from NUCMC. Finally, a comparison of collections listed on the 1972 checklist of women's sources with the collections in NUCMC revealed that only about a third of the collections on the checklist were in NUCMC, even though those repositories had reported other holdings to NUCMC. Chambers and Hinding speculated that "by asking a different question, perhaps, a different response may have been elicited."[21] On 31 March 1975, Chambers and Hinding learned that their second grant application had been successful: the WHSS project was awarded a grant totaling $347,773 from NEH and $34,006 from the University of Minnesota. A "grand manuscripts search," as Anne Firor Scott called the survey, was underway.[22]

When the WHSS staff began work in the spring of 1975, its first task was to develop a mailing list of repositories and historical societies that might have relevant collections. Since no union list existed, staff "combed directories, published guides and scholarly works, and nooks and crannies of reference rooms to compile a list."[23] Initial estimates of the universe of repositories ranged from 3,500 to 6,000, but as the staff received lists from the American Association for State and Local History and the National Historical Publications and Records Commission (NHPRC), as well as suggestions from archivists and historians, the number kept growing; the initial mailing in 1976 went to nearly ten thousand repositories. Ultimately, eleven thousand repositories were contacted.[24]

While the work of compiling the mailing list was underway, the WHSS staff began drafting the form letters, questionnaires, and instructions for completing them, and criteria for inclusion of collections. The staff tried "to strike a balance between what they wished to know and what information—in a complex, questionnaire-ridden world—it would be possible to elicit. They stressed collegiality and cheerfulness, language as clear and direct as possible, and forms that were attractive (not 'grey') and legible—and that didn't appear, at least initially, intimidating." They solicited input from archivists on what should be included in the questionnaire and asked the University of Minnesota's Measurement Services Center to assess it.[25]

Deciding on the criteria for inclusion was no small feat. One colleague at the University of Minnesota suggested that since "women comprise half the human race, they appear 'organically' in most manuscripts collections and in the records of virtually all organizations and institutions." Should every collection then be considered a women's collection? Unwilling to open the "Pandora's box of historiographic and philosophical questions" raised by this suggestion, the WHSS staff ultimately decided on a fairly general criterion: "That the collections contain material by women or about women's lives and roles." They illustrated the criterion with examples of different kinds of collections: papers of a woman, family papers, records of women's organizations and of organizations and institutions in which women played a significant role or that significantly affected women, artificial collections assembled around a theme relating to women, and collections with "hidden" women (i.e., the title of the collection did not indicate women's presence).[26] One fieldworker spent the summer of 1975 surveying repositories in Minnesota and the Dakotas as a test of fieldwork procedures and effectiveness.[27]

In March 1976, the WHSS staff sent form letters to ten thousand repositories, asking them to return a postcard noting whether the repository held any archives or manuscripts, and, if so, whether any pertained to women. By 31 March, nearly 30 percent had returned the postcards. Hinding wrote to the advisory board that "The only truly alarming note is that large numbers of college and university archivists report having archives but insist that nothing in them pertains to women." These early responses revealed that there would be a large educational component in dealing with the repositories. Believing that a mailing that clarified the intentions of the survey would be effective, follow-up letters were sent a few weeks later to women's colleges, as well as to minority organizations and to "some non-responding institutions that staff members feared had not understood the purpose of the Survey." As the cards were returned to Minneapolis, the staff sent packets of questionnaires, instructions for completing the questionnaires, and criteria for inclusion of collections. Ultimately, the survey received nearly seven thousand responses, of which two thousand reported holdings pertaining to women. Many repositories were unable or unwilling to fill out the questionnaires; in the summer of 1976 fieldworkers were sent to survey and report the holdings of these repositories and to visit the "suspicious no's"—repositories that said they had no women's papers but more likely didn't know what was in their holdings or didn't understand what kinds of materials were of interest to the survey. Eva Moseley, curator of manuscripts at the Schlesinger Library, described the fieldworkers as "an advance party of the 'new women's history'" and said that the survey "has given everyone in the archival profession notice that women's history is here to stay." [28]

After drafting what they thought was a straightforward questionnaire with clear instructions, the staff was no doubt taken aback by some of the responses, leading Hinding to conclude that "the demand for the personal touch in dealing with respondents is much more essential than we thought."[29] Fieldworkers confirmed this. Sandra VanBurkleo, who surveyed North and South Carolina, reported that it was particularly important to send fieldworkers to smaller repositories. Larger repositories more often had a professionally trained archival staff, so "the possible gap between survey definitions and staff perceptions may be more narrow" than in smaller repositories.[30] VanBurkleo reported on visits to several women's colleges. One woman in charge of the historical records of a North Carolina college thought the Women's History Sources Survey was "just wonderful" but was intimidated by the official-looking forms; she didn't understand the terminology, and so waited for a fieldworker to arrive to describe the collections, which included grocery bags containing extensive research notes for a history of the college.[31]

In the summer of 1976, twenty fieldworkers were selected from a pool of 130 applicants from across the country. The fieldworkers attended a two-day training session in Minneapolis that dealt with such matters as "terminology, techniques, archival principles and etiquette (how to approach a cranky archivist)." The country was divided into regions, with fieldworkers assigned to each one and to the National Archives, the Federal Records Centers, and the Library of Congress. Their task was to visit repositories that did not fill out questionnaires and convince the repository staff to fill out the questionnaires; failing that, they were to survey the holdings and fill out the questionnaires themselves. Armed with lists of repositories drawn up from responses to the WHSS mailings, the fieldworkers spent the next few months visiting repositories in whatever region they had been assigned.[32] Except for the fieldworkers assigned to the National Archives and the Library of Congress, most of the fieldworkers visited a variety of repositories, large and small, public and private. They took varied approaches and had both good and bad experiences.

Responses to the survey and to the fieldworkers differed widely. While there were many instances of "friendly cooperation" on the part of professional archivists at major institutions, some were indifferent and others hostile to WHSS (and in fact to surveys in general).[33] No doubt some thought the subject matter unimportant. More often, archivists at large institutions objected to devoting staff time to the survey when they had already completed collection descriptions for NUCMC, even though they recognized that sources on women were not adequately represented therein.[34] Dee Ann Montgomery, working in the Midwest, noted that "cooperation by professional archivists was not all it could have been" and was appalled by the failure of archivists and librarians to return the mailed questionnaires. Yet some repository staff were extremely helpful: an archivist at the State Historical Society of Wisconsin worked evenings and weekends alongside Montgomery to describe the women's sources in hundreds of collections.[35]

The situation at local historical societies, college archives, and other small repositories was another story altogether. Marylynn Salmon found the collections in local historical societies in Pennsylvania so disorganized that the time spent attempting to report on them, locate biographical information, and determine inclusive dates was not worth the effort. Feeling that the materials in the smaller repositories were not nearly as rich as those in larger institutions, she decided instead to devote her energies to reporting on the larger repositories that refused to fill out the questionnaires themselves, feeling it would be a travesty to omit them.[36] Sandra VanBurkleo believed that the "minor repositories" held incredibly rich sources, but that the people in charge of them rarely understood the value of their collections; they tended to bring out clipping files and pictures of prominent or famous people. She recounts her experience at one South Carolina college: "The longer I remained and chatted, the more they remembered and found. Before I was forced to leave for lack of time, their definitions had been expanded sufficiently to allow sudden recognition of the value of an entire *attic* full of materials: complete records of the nursing school, great bulging files full of the records of doctors' wives' auxiliaries and professional groups, personal receipt books containing home remedies used by a widow who owned a plantation and treated her slaves, the records of a coroner who described in great detail how he diagnosed the illnesses and deaths of Charleston women."[37]

Phyllis Steele, the fieldworker for Iowa and Nebraska, suggested a potential barrier for learning about the sources in local repositories: locals' mistrust of the fieldworkers. Steele hypothesized that the words *social welfare* in the return address turned off some people and made them less likely to fill out questionnaires. She wrote to Hinding: "I also made one discovery this summer which is somewhat funny if looked at from the proper perspective. At least one (if not more) of your original inquiries about collections didn't get an answer because the inquiry came from an organization with the politically suspicious term 'Social Welfare' in its name! Needless to say, this reaction was at a county repository, and needless to say, I did *not* talk politics this summer. (I also started identifying myself as being from the Univ. of Minnesota, with the rest mumbled afterwards, when I found myself in towns under 50,000 in population.)" She believed that people in small towns in Iowa responded more favorably to her when they learned she was an Iowa resident.[38] Through the summer and into the fall, the fieldworkers submitted questionnaires they had completed to the staff in Minneapolis, who drafted guide entries from them. The fieldworkers visited as many repositories as they could within the allotted few months, and met again in Minneapolis for a debriefing in December 1976.

As they spread out across the country to visit repositories of all shapes and sizes, the fieldworkers were given the additional task of filling out repository assessment forms that examined the physical state of repositories as well as the knowledge and training of the staff in order to gauge the condition and needs of archival repositories nationwide. Taken together, these forms provide a remarkable snapshot of the state of archival repositories in the 1970s. One thing they pointed to was the need for education and training among those assigned to care for archival collections. Another was the dire state of the facilities in which many of the collections were housed. This information did lead to some discussion at professional conferences of how to train people in basic archival skills, but, for the most part, the repository assessment forms were not utilized; the overwhelming task of completing the book sapped the energy of the staff. Once *Women's History Sources* was published, they were ready to move on to other things.

The mechanics of the project were mind-boggling, and the sheer immensity of the undertaking sometimes threatened to overwhelm the staff. As they received the questionnaires—from repositories and from fieldworkers—the staff in Minneapolis had to take widely divergent questionnaire responses and make consistent entries for the guide. The staff took great pains to make the entries accurate and readable, and created an authority file for proper names. Their requests to fieldworkers for clarification and for further biographical information, birth and death dates, and inclusive dates of collections sometimes rankled the fieldworkers, who had worked under great time pressure, often in poor conditions, to describe collections that ranged from immense and unprocessed to intriguing but fragmentary. The completed entries were sent to the repositories to review for accuracy and interpretation. The quick turnaround time for reviewing these entries, glitches in the workflow, and the confusion caused when follow-up letters crossed in the mail with already completed questionnaires were a source of frustration for repository staff and fieldworkers alike. One fieldworker complained of the false economy of sending mail library rate. But the fieldworkers at least understood the immensity of the task of compiling the guide, whereas staff at some of the repositories saw only unreasonable demands being placed upon them. Even those who supported the project and willingly committed resources to it felt that the staff in Minneapolis didn't recognize how much time it took for a repository—large or small—to analyze its holdings and complete questionnaires. And perhaps it was difficult for the WHSS staff, zealously engaged in this exciting and groundbreaking project, to fully appreciate that for the archivists, librarians, and volunteers around the country, filling out these questionnaires was yet another task for already overburdened personnel.[39]

Taking the collection descriptions from questionnaires to published volumes was a complicated, multistep process. Entries drafted by one staff member were reviewed by another. A third checked or entered names in the authority file. Ames Sheldon Bower, the associate editor, reviewed the drafts "for format, stylistic consistency, and sense" and sent them to the indexer and to the person responsible for developing an accurate list of repository names.[40] She also wrote a style manual for the staff to follow in drafting entries, trained the staff in the style, and developed a workflow using route slips that detailed each of the many steps in the process.[41] Andrea Hinding read each entry before it was sent to the publisher.

Cognizant of the difficulty of doing historical research on women because their names often change upon marriage, the editors of WHSS took great pains to include as much information as possible about women's names. Thus, in addition to a woman's given name, they included maiden names in parentheses, husbands' names in brackets, and nicknames in quotation marks.[42] The index, nearly four hundred pages upon completion, required a great deal of checking and rechecking against the in-house authority file to verify women's names, birth and death dates, and spellings. All of this was done before the advent of desktop computers and online databases to aid in the development of mailing lists, editorial revisions, or maintenance and use of authority files. Upon publication, the index itself became a name authority, aiding not only scholars but genealogists, family historians, archivists, librarians, and others.[43]

Throughout the project that kept "growing like Topsy," it was Andrea Hinding—with the able assistance of Ames Sheldon Bower—who held everything together. Keeping the project on track as it grew past all expectations required considerable administrative skill, and Hinding possessed that. She was immersed in the day-to-day work of the project, as well as the administrative aspects of managing a grant, overseeing the budget, writing reports, and seeking additional funding. She navigated between the various groups involved in the project—fieldworkers, repository staff, the Minnesota staff, funding agencies, the publisher, advisory board, media—and not always easily. Though neither she nor Clarke Chambers anticipated the eventual scale of the project when it began, they soon recognized how momentous it would be. As the public face of the Women's History Sources Survey, she was its effective and enthusiastic promoter. There was good reason that *Women's History Sources* came to be known as "the Hinding guide."

Women's History Sources was published in 1979 in two volumes, the first consisting of 1,095 pages of collection descriptions, along with introductory material and eighteen pages of repository listings. The second volume was a 391-page index. The collection descriptions were arranged alphabetically by state, then by city, then by repository, and finally by collection title. The geographical arrangement was one of the book's strengths. A researcher reading through the entries of a particular town or state could get a sense not only of the universe of documentation on women and their activities in that locale, but of who the local women were and what they had done. *Women's History Sources* was consciously directed at a broad audience, not only graduate students and scholars, but the general public. Thus, the front matter included a section on how to use an archives, a glossary of archival terms, and a section explaining how to use the book.[44]

Reviews of *Women's History Sources* by archivists were for the most part favorable. Archivists were impressed by the number of repositories contacted and the success rate. Though she criticized the survey staff for failing to include certain collections that were listed in other guides or in the bibliographies of *Notable American Women*, Anne Kenney was impressed by the "astonishing cooperation" by repositories, noting that seven thousand of the eleven thousand repositories contacted had responded and that nearly 30 percent of them reported collections, "a figure which compares favorably with the number of institutions included in the whole history of NUCMC." Archivists lauded the fact that *Women's History Sources* included both archives and manuscripts repositories. And, though he expressed skepticism of the concept of subject guides that catered to "new trends in historical research," Richard Cox called *Women's History Sources* "an essential archival reference tool that will remain essential for years." Hinding conceded that surveys were expensive and cumbersome, but contended that in select cases they were warranted. She noted that surveys help repositories publicize their holdings and that the Women's History Sources Survey encouraged some repositories to systematically survey and create guides to their women's holdings, which they had done informally for some time in response to researcher queries.[45] Archivists tended to be critical of the concept of printed guides on special subjects, arguing that they would be outdated as soon as they were printed.[46] There was some criticism of the publisher, R. R. Bowker, for the cost of the final product—$175 for the two-volume set. But as Hinding pointed out in her final report to NEH, Bowker had invested "enormous time and money" in the project and had to sell at least one thousand copies to break even.[47]

Women's historians were enthusiastic about *Women's History Sources*. Karen Blair exclaimed that "No library should be without it." Though not an unbiased reviewer, Darlene Roth, who had been a fieldworker for the survey, called it "the essential beginning point for anyone doing primary historical research on women in America."[48] Edith Mayo of the Smithsonian's National Museum of American History offered thanks to Hinding "from those of us in Women's History who find the *Women's History Sources* invaluable in our work." But the real test of *Women's History Sources* came over the next decade as historians had a chance to use it in their research. Laurel Thatcher Ulrich wrote many years later that she owed her second project, the Pulitzer Prize–winning book *A Midwife's Tale,* to it. Before *Women's History Sources,* she had not thought to visit the Maine State Library, a repository used primarily by genealogists. *Women's History Sources* brought to her attention not only the diary of eighteenth-century Maine midwife Martha Ballard, but also "a fine collection of supporting documents" held by the library. In Ulrich's words, "For all of us [women's historians], research was made easier by the publication in 1979 of *Women's History Sources.*"[49] Elisabeth Israels Perry scoured it for sources on her research topic, required graduate students in US women's history courses to become familiar with it, and viewed it as the starting point for any serious primary research in women's history. Rima Lunin Schultz recalls "finding Hinding on the reference shelf of The Newberry Library . . . copying the pages for Illinois repositories and literally contemplating what a book would be like that had biographies of all the women identified in the archives descriptions contained in Hinding." She and the many graduate students and writers who contributed to *Women Building Chicago 1790–1990: A Biographical Dictionary* owed a great deal to *Women's History Sources.* Coming to women's history from women's studies in the mid-nineties, Tiffany Wayne was new to historical research and had no idea where to begin looking for sources. She remembers "having pencil and pad in hand and reading through the Women's History Sources, making long lists of archives I'd like to visit and returning to it when I focused my research on Massachusetts archives."[50]

Women's History Sources did have its limitations. Writing in 1988, Deborah Gray White called it a valuable resource, but faulted it for providing "no means of finding the manuscripts of black women that are not coded with the terms black, Afro-American, or Negro." A dozen years later, graduate student Julie Fairman was frustrated by the paucity of sources on nurses, one of the largest occupations of women, though in hindsight she believes that was due to the fact that nurses were invisible to historians in the 1970s because "they didn't quite fit the paradigm of liberation"; their papers just hadn't been collected yet. But Wendy Chmielewski believed that *Women's History Sources* helped pave the way for funding other archival projects on women's history and that it remains an "incredibly useful resource" thirty years later.[51] Unfortunately, students and scholars trained in the digital age are for the most part unaware of its existence.

Women's History Sources was conceived first and foremost as an access tool, a means of assisting researchers in locating sources for the study of women's history. In that aim it succeeded admirably. It opened up a world of source materials previously hidden in repositories large and small. And it provided inspiration to others to undertake surveys and create guides to women's sources, albeit on a smaller scale. As reviewers predicted, in some respects it was outdated almost as soon as it hit the shelves, for the very act of publishing such a guide inspired archivists to more actively collect women's history sources—which would of course never appear in the guide. But any printed guide is a snapshot of collections at a given time. Its static nature is a necessary limitation. Repositories are in a constant state of acquiring new materials and gaining intellectual control over previously acquired materials. No published guide can ever reflect the actual entire holdings of any single repository, let alone the entire universe of repositories. Even with current technology and the best of intentions, it is naive to think that the websites of most archives include exhaustive lists of collections. Yet it would be a mistake to focus on such shortcomings that are inherent to published guides. *Women's History Sources* functioned well as a guide to sources on women's history for many years. Kathryn Kish Sklar wrote almost a decade later that "All scholars of United States women's history are indebted to the monumental compilation, *Women's History Sources.*" Sklar noted that the guide was especially rich in organizational records; she used *Women's History Sources* as a launching point to explore the "extent and depth" of archival sources on women and progressive reform. She presumed the reader's familiarity with *Women's History Sources.*[52]

But the impact of *Women's History Sources* went far beyond its usefulness for describing particular collections or the holdings of particular repositories. First, it toppled the argument that sources on women's history were insufficient to support the field. This immense work stood as a visible testament to the existence of sources for women's history and to the struggles, achievements, and life experiences of women. It was both "a stimulus for and a reflection of an immense new interest in women's history."[53] A dozen years later, the editors of *Women in the West: A Guide to Manuscript Sources* would remark that *Women's History Sources* "proved vastly reassuring and influential" to women's history scholars who had "seriously wondered whether enough source materials existed to make in-depth research possible."[54] They wrote that the publication of *Women's History Sources* "marked a significant moment in the field [of women's history]. The guide pointed scholars to the enormous possibilities and challenges of women's history as it identified available materials, suggested new questions, and spurred research. Not only did it infuse the entire field with a new feeling of solidarity, but it also spawned many specialized imitators, of which this is one."[55]

Second, the guide inspired many archivists to reassess their holdings to reflect the presence of women and to consciously collect women's sources. As Bob McCown, archivist in the University of Iowa's Special Collections Department, remarked to fieldworker Phyllis Steele, the survey would be successful even if it were never published because it made archivists more aware of women's sources and forced them to look inside their collections to find them.[56] Martin Schmitt, curator of special collections at the University of Oregon Library, wrote to Andrea Hinding in 1978 that he had been essentially a one-man shop for thirty years and, when asked to respond to the survey, was surprised at how much material on women was hidden in the collections in his repository. Louisa Bowen, archivist for the National Board Archives Project of the Young Women's Christian Association of the USA, admitted that she was at first reluctant about describing the YWCA's collections because she knew that by definition they *all* contained materials by or about women. But she came to appreciate the task, as it gave her "the opportunity to view the holdings as a whole, and allowed me to compile some of the materials needed for a 'guide' to our holdings." According to Darlene Roth, "the project, because of its size and scope (and its staff's enthusiasm), stimulated more attention to women's records than it itself could record, spawning fresh collecting efforts, new programmatic attention to women's history, and the creation of many other inventories, finding aids, and publications at institutions around the country."[57]

Third, *Women's History Sources* brought to light a vast number of small repositories that held significant collections on women's history. As Anne Kenney wrote in a review of the guide, "For many repositories, the survey represented their first national reporting."[58] And while these repositories may never again have reported their collections or created local guides, the survey made clear that rich sources existed outside the major repositories. At the same time, the survey revealed the poor environmental conditions in which collections were housed and the lack of archival training of a large portion of those entrusted with historical records. This led some fieldworkers to conclude that local records should be given to larger institutions or regional centers that could better care for them and make them accessible to a wider audience. A few drew the opposite conclusion. After seeing how important the records were to the local community, they came to believe that the records should stay there, and that the people who cared for them should be given training in archival and preservation practices.

Fourth, *Women's History Sources* had a significant impact beyond the academic world. It resonated not only with archivists and historians but with the general public. Newspapers across the country picked up an Associated Press story about the guide after it was published. Just as important, the survey caused some custodians of historical materials to rethink their collections. The education director of the American Political Items Collectors in Walla Walla, Washington, examined its holdings and came to the realization that he had been "careless about our acquisitions of material regarding women in national politics. I must thank you for that."[59] The president of the Marshall County Historical Society, a small volunteer organization in Holly Springs, Mississippi, apologized for the delay in returning the questionnaires, which she filled out even though she wasn't sure if it was the sort of information being sought: "It all sheds light on the lives of women in our area in days gone by. To us they are very interesting, but we don't think they would be of national interest." But, she continued, even if the survey staff (whom she addressed as "Dear Sirs") decided not to use the information submitted, she thanked them for "the

experience of the questionnaire," which helped the historical society organize its collections better and even get them microfilmed. The information she sent ultimately became two entries in *Women's History Sources*:
the Kate Freeman Clark Papers and a miscellaneous collection of diaries,
correspondence, photos, club records, and land grants.[60] Perhaps the most
dramatic example of the influence of the survey occurred in the town of
Cornwall, Connecticut. While the questionnaire itself ended up in the
"round file" while the curator of the local historical society was on vaca-
tion, her subsequent survey of collections led her to conclude that "ours
has been, up to now, a MALE CHAUVINIST COMMUNITY" and that
its women had been very little involved in town politics. Spurred on by
Women's History Sources, she and other townswomen persuaded women
to join the fire department and run for elective positions.[61]

Women's History Sources opened up new avenues for research by
unearthing a vast number of hitherto unknown primary sources on
women. But it was the beginning of the journey, not the end. Collections
were missed, occupational groups overlooked, racial and ethnic groups
underreported. These omissions reflected the state of historical inquiry in
the 1970s as well as gaps in the archival record, rather than shortcomings
on the part of the survey personnel. Archival collecting and description
had yet to catch up to new interest in the fields of black, ethnic, working-
class, and women's history, and could not anticipate new areas of research.
Many archivists still considered themselves neutral arbiters of the historical record as they inherited it and shied away from the challenge to become
activist archivists. In 1980, Eva Moseley called upon her professional colleagues to recognize that history is about all sexes, races, and classes and
that archives should reflect that fact. Moseley wrote: "Most archivists and
manuscript curators don't write history. But, with the decisions we make,
especially in appraising records and papers and in describing them, we
can either promote new trends in research or throw up roadblocks in their
way."[62] Thirty years later archivists still struggle with these issues. Some
groups remain woefully underdocumented in mainstream repositories.
The reasons for this are a complex mix of bias (conscious or unconscious)

on the part of archivists, mistrust of institutional archives by potential donors of records, and the nature of records created by various groups.

Both archivists and historians have been critical of archival institutions for continuing to document those who hold power in society as this perpetuates the divide between those in power and those on the margins. But along with increased attention to documenting underrepresented groups must come greater understanding of the significance historical documents hold for the groups whose history they record. This all requires a balancing act: archivists must consciously work to create and gather documentation on groups omitted from the historical record in the past, but must also be sensitive to the desire of these groups to maintain their records—and thus their history—within their own communities. This requires archivists to be more flexible and creative in thinking about documentation. One way to do so is by forming partnerships—whether formal or informal—with community archives, and providing assistance in the form of training, professional expertise, and even archival supplies for storage of materials. In Chicago, historians, archivists, and graduate students surveyed sources for black history held within mainstream repositories and outside the archival grid in community centers, churches, and private homes. Like the Women's History Sources Survey fieldworkers, they described the materials and provided what assistance they could, but left materials where they found them.[63] While it can be difficult to leave materials in damp basements and unsecured rooms, removing documents from their place of origin also removes a source of identity and power for the members of the community. Creating digital surrogates of documents for online collections so that the originals can stay in the community is one solution, although it may raise thorny issues of who controls the materials.

Some three decades after the publication of *Women's History Sources*, where do we stand? Accessibility to collections in academic and government institutions and other large repositories has increased dramatically, thanks to online finding aids and digitized collections. But, while major institutions have increasingly placed their finding aids online, small repositories run by volunteers often lack the expertise, funding, or personnel to do so. In fact, many small repositories are probably not so different from what they were thirty-five years ago when the fieldworkers visited them. They may still lack trained personnel to process collections, let alone create finding aids for the web. While some of these custodians of historical records have been savvy enough to secure museum, library, or archives grants to upgrade their facilities, others remain in woefully inadequate buildings and spaces, their collections subject to theft or to damage from environmental factors.

It is tempting to think that all of the collections uncovered by the survey can now be discovered through online searching. But for all those described in online finding aids, many sources in local historical societies have never been described except in *Women's History Sources*. Meanwhile, researchers—ranging from students to genealogists to scholars—increasingly expect to find everything they need online. The experiences of one recent PhD in women's history spell this out in stark terms:

> Although Hinding's document guide crucially shaped scholarship in women's history throughout the 1980s and early 1990s, as [a] student conducting research in the new millennium, I had never heard of it. Trained in an era of digital databases, searchable texts, and online libraries, I never had reason to use *Women's History Sources*. Raised in an age in which access to information is taken for granted, I never learned about the exhaustive and collaborative labor that helped unearth such information from obscurity in the first place.[64]

The Internet has vaulted accessibility far beyond what was possible in 1979. But a digital divide remains, as well as a general disparity between resources in community archives and those in major institutions. If we are to fulfill the promise of *Women's History Sources* to make materials by and about women accessible regardless of where they are held, we must find creative ways of partnering with and sharing our resources with community archives through online consortia, resource guides, and the like. The Online Archive of California is a good example of how archivists at institutions with greater resources can assist smaller archives, historical societies, libraries, and museums in caring for their collections and making them accessible to a wider audience. The Washington Women's History

Consortium suggests another model. It supports a range of activities, from processing collections, placing finding aids online, and creating digital collections that bring dispersed women's history sources together online. But the consortium has also given small grants to some twenty organizations to interpret and preserve women's history at the local level.[65] In its own way, each of these initiatives helps to realize the goals of uncovering hidden histories, and as such captures the spirit of the Women's History Sources Survey. The Washington Women's History Consortium, moreover, speaks to the enduring interest in women's history and its particular meaning at the local level.

Women's History Sources revealed "an abundance of riches" in repositories large and small throughout the country. Perhaps the most important lesson of *Women's History Sources* is that the historians and archivists who made it happen were not content to accept the common wisdom that women had not created primary sources. They worked together to devise and fund a project to locate and describe systematically such sources. The staff they hired looked in closets, in attics, in basements, in the vaults of the National Archives and the Library of Congress, in storerooms of local historical societies, and in meeting rooms of women's organizations, knowing that if they looked hard enough they would find something. And everywhere they looked they found traces of women and uncovered sources useful not only for women's history but for social history. The project itself, as much as the resulting guide to women's history sources, had a profound impact on a generation of historians, archivists, and ordinary people caring for their heritage. But it was only the beginning. Historians and archivists continue to come across sources on women in unexpected places and to use oral history and other methods to document issues or groups when documentation is scarce.[66] Our challenge is to continue to work collaboratively to ensure that our archives reflect the rich diversity of society and that the sources we uncover are preserved and made known to a broad range of users. As we do so, we would do well to emulate the vision, the dedication, and the determination of the Women's History Sources Survey staff as they worked to bring to light a multitude of unknown lives and stories.

NOTES

I would like to thank Linda K. Kerber, David Klaassen, Tanya Zanish-Belcher, Anke Voss, and Matt Schaefer for their thoughtful comments on drafts of this article. I am deeply grateful to the Social Welfare History Archives for preserving the records of the grand adventure that was the Women's History Sources Survey.

[1] Gerda Lerner, *Living with History/Making Social Change* (Chapel Hill: University of North Carolina Press, 2009), 46; Sara M. Evans, *Born for Liberty: A History of Women in America* (New York: Free Press Paperbacks, 1989), 274–75; Sara M. Evans, *Tidal Wave: How Women Changed America at Century's End* (New York: Free Press, 2003), 27–28, 40; Ruth Rosen, *The World Split Open: How the Modern Women's Movement Changed America* (New York: Penguin Books, 2001), xx–xxi.

[2] Berenice Carroll, "Scholarship and Action: CCWHP and the Movements(s)," *Journal of Women's History* 6 (Fall 1994): 80.

[3] Berenice Carroll, "Three Faces of Trevia: Identity, Activism, and Intellect," in *Voices of Women Historians,* ed. Eileen Boris and Nupur Chaudhuri (Bloomington: Indiana University Press, 1999), 19–23.

[4] Lerner, *Living with History*, 47. Lerner recalls the frustrating attempts to get women's history panels accepted on national programs.

[5] Lerner, *Living with History*, 48.

[6] R. K. Webb to Gordon B. Turner, 29 December 1971, Women's History Sources Survey Records, Social Welfare History Archives, University of Minnesota (hereafter WHSS), Box 3, Folder: NEH—First application; Dorothy Ross, CV, http://history.jhu.edu/bios/_Faculty_CV/rossCV.pdf, accessed 16 February 2012.

[7] NASW Social Work Pioneers: National Association of Social Workers Foundation, "Clarke A. Chambers," http://www.naswfoundation.org/pioneers/c/chambers.html, accessed 16 February 2012; Clarke A. Chambers vita, WHSS, Box 3, Folder: NEH—First application. Andrea Hinding recalled why the group asked Chambers to chair the session in an oral history interview Chambers conducted with her in 1994. Interview with Andrea Hinding by Clarke A. Chambers, University of Minnesota (14 October 1994), 6, University of Minnesota Digital Conservancy, http://purl.umn.edu/49811. Chambers wrote in 1980: "When I began my own studies in the field of social welfare history some fifteen years ago, that was the first problem: there were no records, or very few, in traditional depositories or historical research centers. There were a few exceptions, but I was finding that the materials were buried in back rooms,

offices, attics." Clarke A. Chambers, introduction, in *Clio Was a Woman: Studies in the History of American Women,* ed. Mabel E. Deutrich and Virginia C. Purdy (Washington, DC: Howard University Press, 1980), 21.

[8] Andrea Hinding vita, WHSS, Box 3, Folder: NEH—First application.

[9] Interview with Hinding by Chambers (1994), 6; Andrea Hinding, ed., *Women's History Sources* (New York and London: R. R. Bowker Company, 1979), 1:ix; Lerner, *Living with History,* 48; Summary of application to the National Endowment for the Humanities for a grant to support a women's history sources survey, 7 May 1973, WHSS, Box 3, Folder: NEH—First application; Andrea Hinding, "Women's History Sources Survey," 10 February 1976, WHSS, Box 4, Folder: WHS Articles, Releases; Andrea Hinding and Rosemary Richardson, comp., "Archival and Manuscript Resources for the Study of Women's History: A Beginning," Social Welfare History Archives, University of Minnesota Libraries, April 1972. The session participants were Robert Asher, Mari Jo Buhle, Charlotte M. Davis , Ellen DuBois, Andrea Hinding , Mary Lynn McCree, Roberta Balstad Miller, and Joan Hoff Wilson. Hinding wrote that they had compiled the checklist because women's historians were mobbed at conferences by graduate students seeking information about where and how to locate relevant sources.

[10] Clarke Chambers to Joan Hoff Wilson, 11 April 1972, WHSS, Box 5, Folder: WHSS Advisory Board.

[11] Anne Firor Scott to Dr. Paul Ward, American Historical Association, 18 June 1974, WHSS, Box 5, Folder: WHSS—NEH correspondence; Women's History Sources Survey Final Report, 2 February 1981, WHSS, Box 3, Folder: WHSS Final Report, 1.

[12] Dorothy Ross to Advisory Board on the Proposal for a Guide to Women's History, 7 June 1972, WHSS, Box 3, Folder: NEH—First application.

[13] Clarke Chambers to Anne Firor Scott, 19 March 1973, WHSS, Box 5, Folder: WHSS Advisory Board; Frank Evans to Clarke Chambers, 28 March 1973, WHSS, Box 5, Folder: Advisory Board—Evans.

[14] Summary of application, 7 May 1973: Project description.

[15] Summary of application, 7 May 1973: Significance.

[16] Summary of application, 7 May 1973: Significance.

[17] A[ndrea] to C[larke]—summary of phone call, November 1973, WHSS, Box 1, Folder: NEH—First Application; Simone Reagor, Deputy Director, Division of Research Grants, NEH, to Clarke Chambers, 7 January 1974, WHSS, Box 3, Folder: NEH—First application.

[18] Clarke Chambers to Janet Wilson James [and six other board members], 16 November 1973, WHSS, Box 3, Folder: NEH—First application; Janet Wilson James to Clarke Chambers, 17 December 1973, WHSS, Box 3, Folder: NEH—First application.

[19] By the time it was completed, the survey had taken "five years; 20 staff members to write, edit, index, and verify names; 20 fieldworkers to survey collections in almost all 50 states; and nearly a million dollars." Andrea Hinding, "Invisible Women," *Research* (University of Minnesota, Fall 1980): 21.

[20] Interview with Hinding by Chambers (1994), 7.

[21] NEH Grant Proposal, 1975–77, WHSS, Box 3. See also Richard Cox's discussion of the importance of including both archives and manuscripts repositories: Richard Cox, "*Women's History Sources*, Women's History, and Archival Subject Guides," *Manuscripts* 33 (Spring 1981): 131.

[22] Women's History Sources Survey Final Report, 1, WHSS, Box 3, Folder: WHSS Final Report; Andrea Hinding, "An Abundance of Riches: The Women's History Sources Survey," in *Clio Was a Woman*, 29.

[23] Hinding, "Women's History Sources Survey," 10 February 1976; Hinding, "An Abundance of Riches," 24.

[24] Hinding, "An Abundance of Riches," 24; Women's History Sources Survey Final Report, 3–4.

[25] Women's History Sources Survey Final Report, 2–3.

[26] Hinding, "An Abundance of Riches," 26.

[27] Hinding, "Women's History Sources Survey," 10 February 1976.

[28] Andrea Hinding to WHSS Advisory Board, 31 March 1976, WHSS, Box 5, Folder: WHSS Advisory Board; Women's History Sources Survey Final Report, 4. In the summer of 1975, WHSS employed a University of Minnesota history graduate student, Mary Ostling, to survey repositories in Minnesota, North Dakota, and South Dakota as a trial run of fieldwork techniques. Eva Moseley, "Sources for the 'New Women's History,'" *American Archivist* 43 (Spring 1980): 180.

[29] Hinding to WHSS Advisory Board, 31 March 1976; Women's History Sources Survey Final Report, 4.

[30] Sandra F. Van Burkleo to Andrea Hinding, 19 April 1977, WHSS, Box 17, Folder: Miscellaneous fieldworker correspondence.

[31] Van Burkleo to Hinding, 19 April 1977, WHSS, Box 17, Folder: Miscellaneous fieldworker correspondence.

[32] Hinding to WHSS Advisory Board, 31 March 1976.

[33] "The large places which agreed to help with the WHSS were staffed by individuals who believed in the validity of manuscript surveys before I arrived on the scene." Marylynn Salmon report for Pennsylvania, 29 December 1976, 7, WHSS, Box 5, Folder: Fieldworker reports.

[34] Reporting on her experiences in Philadelphia, Marylynn Salmon wrote: "Given the fact that these places all had large numbers of collections to report, it would indeed have taken a staff member long hours to do the work. And there I was—a paid employee of the WHSS who might just as well do their collections as anyone else's. I could see their minds clicking away as they refused to assist me, and yes, I was annoyed. But at the same time I could not imagine leaving them out of the published guide, as other fieldworkers decided to do with similarly uncooperative repositories." Salmon report for Pennsylvania.

[35] Dee Ann Montgomery, Report, 3–4. WHSS, Box 5, Folder: Fieldworker reports.

[36] Salmon report for Pennsylvania.

[37] Van Burkleo to Hinding, 19 April 1977.

[38] Phyllis Steele to Andrea Hinding, 18 October 1976, WHSS, Box 17, Folder: Miscellaneous fieldworker correspondence.

[39] As a recent college graduate, I worked on the Women's History Sources Survey in 1977 and 1978, drafting collection descriptions from repository guides and from questionnaires. I moved to Ann Arbor in 1981 to begin my doctoral studies in history at the University of Michigan and was hired as a student assistant at the Bentley Historical Library early in 1982. I recall conversations with reference archivist Mary Jo Pugh soon after I began working at the Bentley in which she remarked that the people at WHSS never understood how much work and time it took to go through the collections to locate and describe materials about women. Author's conversation with Mary Jo Pugh, 1982.

[40] Andrea Hinding to Margaret Child, assistant director, research collections, Division of Research Grants, National Endowment for the Humanities, 7 February 1978, WHSS, Box 5, Folder: WHSS continuation.

[41] "The Life of a Batch of Questionnaires from One Repository" [by Ames Sheldon Bower], WHSS, Box 5, Folder: WHSS drafting. "Ames Sheldon Bower, assistant editor (full-time) and sine qua non of the Survey, continues routinely to perform difficult and impossible tasks without ruffling her feathers at all. She participates in managing all aspects of the Survey while supervising the editorial aspect in its entirety. She wrote an extensive style manual which has been characterized as a unique contribution to archival writing and editing; she taught

the Survey style and format to five others, only one of whom had significant writing experience, but all of whom are now producing clear and, for the most part, graceful prose." *Social Welfare History Archives Annual Report*, 1976/77, WHSS, Box 1, Folder: WHSS General Info.

[42] Hinding, *Women's History Sources*, 1:xviii. Thus, the entry for Grandma Moses reads: Moses, Anna Mary (Robertson) "Grandma" [Mrs. Thomas Salmon] (1860–1961). Hinding, *Women's History Sources*, 2:ix.

[43] Hinding, *Women's History Sources*, 2:vii.

[44] Hinding, *Women's History Sources*, 1:xv–xix.

[45] Anne R. Kenney, review of *Women's History Sources*, *American Archivist* 44 (Winter 1981): 52; Richard Cox, "*Women's History Sources*, Women's History, and Archival Subject Guides," *Manuscripts* 33 (Spring 1981): 135; Women's History Sources Final Report, 8. In the decades since *Women's History Sources* was published, there have been various discussions of updating it, either on a regional or national basis, but none has come to fruition. See, for example, Michele Aldrich's 1 September 1995 notes of a meeting held at the April 1995 Organization of American Historians, Sherrill Redmon files, Sophia Smith Collection, Smith College, and emails and meeting notes regarding a proposed Iowa–Illinois update in author's personal files, 2004–2005.

[46] As *Women's History Sources* was going to press, the new NHPRC guide was hitting the shelves. Published in 1979, it utilized new technology (Spindex), putting repository descriptions in a database that could be updated, allowing for easy reprinting of the guide. Anticipating the future of archival description and access, David Bearman was harshly critical of the technology, stating that "To plan such a program and knowingly commit ourselves to a system which prints guides but cannot be searched on-line, is folly." David Bearman, review of *Directory of Archives and Manuscripts Repositories in the United States*, *American Archivist* 42 (July 1979): 351.

[47] Women's History Sources Survey Final Report, 3; Kenney, review of *Women's History Sources*, 51–52. By 1987, Bowker had sold 1,153 sets. R. R. Bowker to Andrea Hinding, royalty statement, 30 June 1987, Sherrill Redmon files, Sophia Smith Collection, Smith College.

[48] Karen Blair, review of *Women's History Sources*, *Pacific Northwest Quarterly* 72, no. 4 (1981): 183; Darlene R. Roth, "Growing Like Topsy: Research Guides to Women's History," *Journal of American History* 70 (June 1983): 96; Edith P. Mayo to Andrea Hinding, 6 May 1981, WHSS, Box 1, Folder: WHSS—to file.

[49] Laurel Thatcher Ulrich, "Of Pens and Needles: Sources in Early American Women's History," *Journal of American History* 77 (June 1990): 200.

[50] Elisabeth Israels Perry, email to author, 21 January 2011; Rima Lunin Schultz, email to author, 21 January 2011; Rima Lunin Schultz and Adele Hast, eds., *Women Building Chicago 1790–1990: A Biographical Dictionary* (Bloomington: Indiana University Press, 2001); Tiffany K. Wayne, email to author, 23 January 2011.

[51] Deborah Gray White, "Mining the Forgotten: Manuscript Sources for Black Women's History," *Journal of American History* 74 (June 1987): 238; Julie Fairman, email to author, 21 January 2011; Wendy Chmielewski, email to author, 21 January 2011; Wendy Chmielewski, "Women's History Archives," in *Archival Information: How to Find It, How to Use It*, ed. Steven Fisher (Westport, CT: Greenwood Press, 2004).

[52] Kathryn Kish Sklar, "Organized Womanhood: Archival Sources on Women and Progressive Reform," *Journal of American History* 75 (June 1988): 176. When I arrived in Iowa in 1992 to start the Iowa Women's Archives, *Women's History Sources* was still the best, most comprehensive guide to women's sources in the state and was an invaluable resource for me.

[53] Cox, "*Women's History Sources*," 131.

[54] Susan Armitage, Helen Bannan, Katherine G. Morrissey, and Vicki L. Ruiz, eds., *Women in the West: A Guide to Manuscript Sources* (New York: Garland Publishing, 1991), xiii. In the introduction, Armitage reflected on how much had changed since the 1970s and the publication of *Women's History Sources*: "There was a time, so long ago that it now seems like the Dark Ages, when women's history scholars seriously wondered whether enough source material existed to make in-depth research possible. After all, respected male scholars repeatedly informed us that in the course of their own work, they had never found sufficient archival material on women." Ibid.

[55] Armitage et al., *Women in the West*, xiii. The process of uncovering hidden sources continued and was especially valuable in bringing to light primary sources on groups thought to be largely absent from the documentary record. See, for example, Susan J. von Salis, comp., *Revealing Documents: A Guide to African-American Manuscript Sources in the Schlesinger Library and the Radcliffe College Archives* (Boston: G.K. Hall, 1993); *Guide to African American Manuscripts in the Collection of the Virginia Historical Society* (Richmond: Virginia Historical Society, 2002).

[56] Notes from Fieldworker Debriefing, 11–12 December 1976, 4, WHSS, Box 5, Folder: Notes from Fieldworker Debriefing.

[57] Martin Schmitt to Andrea Hinding, 11 August 1978, WHSS, Box 5 [no folder]; Louisa Bowen to Andrea Hinding, 12 April 1977, WHSS, Box 1, Folder: WHSS

influence; Roth, "Growing Like Topsy: Research Guides to Women's History," 96.

[58] Kenney, review of *Women's History Sources*, 51–52.

[59] Dennis G. Fetty to Clarke A. Chambers, 18 March 1977, WHSS, Box 1, Folder: WHSS Influence; Hinding, *Women's History Sources,* 1:592.

[60] Mrs. R. L. Wyatt to Women's History Sources Survey, 1 March 1977, WHSS, Box 1, Folder: WHSS Influence.

[61] Paula V. Holmes to Andrea Hinding, undated, WHSS, Box 1, Folder: WHSS Influence.

[62] Moseley, "Sources for the 'New Women's History,'" 190.

[63] See Black Metropolis Research Consortium Survey, http://bmrcsurvey .uchicago.edu/, accessed 26 June 2013.

[64] Honor R. Sachs, "Reconstructing a Life: The Archival Challenges of Women's History," *Library Trends* 56 (Winter 2008): 653.

[65] Online Archive of California, "About OAC," http://www.oac.cdlib.org/about/, accessed 6 February 2011. Washington Women's History Consortium, http:// washingtonwomenshistory.org/, accessed 7 February 2011.

[66] See, for example, Nupur Chaudhuri, Sherry J. Katz, and Mary Elizabeth Perry, eds., *Contesting Archives: Finding Women in the Sources* (Urbana, Chicago, and Springfield, IL: University of Illinois Press, 2010) and projects such as Mujeres Latinas, an oral history project of the Iowa Women's Archives, University of Iowa Libraries, to preserve the history of Iowa Latinas, http://www.lib.uiowa .edu/iwa/mujeres/, accessed 26 June 2013.

CHAPTER 6

Sources for the
"New Women's History"

EVA S. MOSELEY

Virtually all archivists and manuscripts curators have had
some contact with members of an advance party of the "new
women's history," the fieldworkers sent into hundreds of
repositories by the Women's History Sources Survey (WHSS).
Conducted by the staff of the University of Minnesota's Social Welfare
History Archives Center and funded by the National Endowment for
the Humanities, the survey has given everyone in the archival profession
notice that women's history is here to stay.[1]

The new women's history, briefly defined, is that of all women and
their activities, achievements, and relationships, especially those not traditionally the concern of historians. That history will be of increasing
importance to archivists[2] as its practitioners approach more and more
repositories in search of the often hidden records of more or less hidden
people. Researchers will learn much about women from these records.
They will also find evidence useful in investigating two basic and intriguing questions: in what irreducible ways do men and women differ? And
how do the public and private spheres influence one another? To archivists
who share the author's interest in these issues, researchers of women's history will provide a welcome challenge, rather than an irritating distraction
from collecting and research on the big names, female or male, of history.

Carroll Smith-Rosenberg has contrasted the new women's history, which seeks to illuminate the nonpublic lives and accomplishments of elite and nonelite women, with traditional women's history, which imitates traditional history, "Great White Men," by showing that there were great women too.[3] Traditional women's history serves as a partial corrective to that of Great White Men, but it suffers from its acceptance of the values, categories, causality, and periodization of traditional men's history.[4] As Smith-Rosenberg points out, women have not figured as prominently as men in what has been considered the mainstream of historical events and change. They have constituted a tiny minority of political, military, diplomatic, and religious leaders, and few have been inventors or scientists, captains of industry, union organizers, philosophers, artists, or scholars. By concentrating on women's limited contributions to public events and trends, while ignoring the areas in which women were active and influential, traditional women's historians have defined "the majority of American women as . . . marginal to American history."[5]

Where have women been active and important? Primarily in the private world of the family; more recently in those public institutions that have assumed family functions. This is the world that social history explores, and it is social history and the contemporary women's movement, together with the exhaustion of traditional women's history, that have given the new women's history its impetus. Division of labor in the household, kinship systems, family power relationships, child rearing, marriage, divorce, sexuality, and friendship are some of the concerns of social history. Instead of concentrating on the branches of government, social history investigates such public institutions as prisons, hospitals, schools, brothels, and churches. Any or all of these might be considered in their institutional aspect by traditional historians (though usually as an afterthought). Social historians are concerned with the people who inhabit the institutions, with the people who run them, and with the interactions between the inmates and those in charge. Clearly, women form a much larger proportion of these groups than they do of the public leaders listed above.

But, just as women's history can be a version of traditional history, so social history can be pursued without including women; if this were not so, there would be no need for a new women's history. For example, a panel on family history at the 1974 SAA meeting consisted of three male speakers, and only one of two commentators was a woman.[6] The speakers' idea of a family was a succession of fathers, sons, and grandsons. The women existed only for breeding purposes; their feelings and activities were largely ignored, as were their power and influence. One of the male historians wondered how women responded to the 50 percent decline in the number of children per adult woman, from 7 in 1800 to 3.5 in 1900. The woman commentator asked a different kind of question. Why did more women remain single in the nineteenth century? Why did couples have fewer children? Was the decision made by the wife, the husband, or both, and how was it implemented? As in all new social history, the actions of nonelite, anonymous people are taken seriously by family historians, and some light is shed on how private decisions affect public life. But, evidently, few historians are willing, so far, to include women among the actors—rather than among those passively acted upon—in the historical drama.

Historians have used such public events as changes in political administrations to divide history into periods. But the impact of those events on ordinary citizens, female and male, has yet to be adequately explored. If social history reveals that the lives of most citizens remained fundamentally unchanged by events traditional historians consider crucial, it will become necessary to question the significance of the epochs those historians postulate. Richard Vann has suggested that the invention of the rubber nipple was as epoch-making for women as the invention of the Bessemer converter was for men. He proposes, in a suggestive oversimplification, that "the periodization of women's history should demonstrate the stages whereby they have emancipated themselves from the reproductive process."[7]

There are still archivists, as there are historians, not convinced that any of this new social history, female or male, is worthwhile. If we consider three variables: elite/nonelite, public/private, men/women, and ask

which of the eight possible combinations constitute "history," some scholars will still maintain that history consists primarily of the public lives of
elite men. Other combinations that have gained some acceptance are the
private lives of elite men, the public lives of a very few elite women, and
the public lives of nonelite men in groups (for example, in armies and
labor unions). But, more and more, the private lives of nonelite women
are being accepted as also the stuff of history, and increasing numbers of
researchers are asking for materials about such women.

The archivist confronted by researchers hoping to delve into the private lives of hitherto totally obscure people should be aware of the kinds of
sources that can be useful to them. There already are extensive sources for
research on middle- and upper-class women, who wrote letters and kept
diaries; these can be used in new ways. But to study women on the farm,
working-class women, and the anonymous poor, demographic sources
are essential. Census and other statistical data can help delineate the lives
of such women: the proportion of females to males and the female mortality rate for various age groups; the numbers who married, divorced,
were widowed or deserted, and at what ages; the number of children per
mother and their mortality; how many women were employed, in what
kinds of jobs, for how much pay—and so forth. Company personnel
records and reform school, prison, court, hospital, and morgue records,
when they exist and are available, will all yield useful information.[8]

Almost totally lacking for working-class women is their own comment
on their lives, in contrast to the often massive outpourings of middle- and
upper-class women. Although careful use of welfare, hospital, employment, or other case records can tell a researcher much, almost the only
way to learn what poor women felt is through oral history, which at best
reaches back only a limited number of years, and which gives a later comment on an earlier time. The difficulties in selecting subjects for such oral
histories and getting significant information from them are not generally
the concern of the archivist.[9]

The archivist can, however, keep an eye out for the occasional written record that does exist. In a newsletter issue on women, for instance,
the Archives of Labor History and Urban Affairs described a manuscript

of Matilda Robbins, remarkable less for its literary merit or its author's impact on society than for its rarity and its frankness about her state of mind.[10] The equally rare letter of an indentured servant, tenant farmer's wife, or housemaid takes on new significance in this new history. Usually buried in the individual or family papers of the masters, these documents can be brought to researchers' notice by the archivist willing to make the effort.

Much more common are reports on the poor by middle-class people: teachers, employers, reformers. For instance, the records of the earliest female reform school, the State Industrial School for Girls at Lancaster (Massachusetts), provide not only factual data about the residents but also subjective comments of the matrons.[11] These comments give an idea of the social pressures—criticism, punishment, prescription—to which the girls were subjected. The North Bennet Street Industrial School, in Boston, is not a reform school, but again there is almost no firsthand record of those who used its clubs, classes, and vocational placement office. Letters and reports of teachers, administrators, and the Board of Managers indicate the values and opportunities offered to the Italian immigrants of the neighborhood. There is only a rare and usually indirect hint of what the Italians felt about them.[12]

The Women's Trade Union League was an alliance of working-class and middle-class women. Its goals—protective legislation for women, child labor legislation, and unionization—were working-class goals. But its records are largely those of its middle-class leaders, except for those of the few working-class women, among them Mary Anderson, Leonora O'Reilly, and Agnes Nestor, whose talents made them leaders as well.[13] They provide information about values and attitudes of middle-class reformers, and perhaps about their motivation and energy levels in doing what was usually unpaid or underpaid work. Records of settlement houses and of such reform groups as the Consumers' League or the Birth Control League provide similar glimpses into the private lives and thoughts of middle-class women. Some records also provide evidence on the relations between female and male reformers.

The League of Women Voters, the General Federation of Women's Clubs, the American Association of University Women, and similar groups include only middle- and upper-class women; their records show the members in relatively impersonal stances dealing with public issues. But even these records can be useful for the new history. There are women at work here too, and their records will occasionally provide evidence of how and why some women devoted so much time and energy to certain causes; how this work complemented or conflicted with their family obligations; and how women have worked together.

Middle- and upper-class women, fewer in number than the poor, have left a much more voluminous record of their private thoughts and activities. The women's letters and diaries in individual and family collections might once have been used to throw light on the men in the family, or as data for compensatory history. Now those records can be read from a new perspective to answer questions about health; about attitudes toward sexuality and reproduction and such resulting actions as refusal to marry, more or less frequent intercourse, and abortion; about child rearing, from the point of view of both mother and daughter; about household management; about bonds among female friends and relatives; and so on. Family collections, with their multiple generations, make it possible not only to study the relations among women of various generations, but also to study in microcosm the changing patterns of marriage, child rearing, and work—household, volunteer, and paid work. Sometimes there is indirect evidence about another very large group of females: domestic servants.

Once the archivist accepts the new women's history as a legitimate field of study and therefore of collection, she[14] must not only look at present holdings with the new research needs in mind, but must try to find and acquire at least some of the kinds of records that will document this history directly. This requires a change in collecting policy and appraisal criteria. Assuming that a repository has a more or less well defined subject or geographical collecting area, only a small mental leap is needed to extend one's sights to include "ordinary" women. Once she has taken this leap, the archivist will find that acquisition methods, donor relations, and accessioning are much the same for women's papers as for men's.

Information about likely donor prospects will often appear in such printed sources as local newspapers, trade journals, union newspapers, and house organs. These leads, and especially obituaries, should be followed up with the same tact the archivist uses in dealing with all donors.[15] By means of articles, exhibits, receptions, and especially talks to women's organizations, the archivist should also actively publicize her repository among women whose papers she is hoping to collect. The talks need not be elaborate. Usually the archivist can speak off the cuff about what she does and has (perhaps showing sample manuscripts or photographs, or slides of them), and about what she wants, and why. As a result, she might acquire the records of the organization, or a promise of them; or someone in the audience may have, or know of, just such a box of family letters as has been described. For many women, as for many men, it is a source of pride that they (or their grandmothers) are suddenly a recognized part of history. An article or photo in the local newspaper when the transfer is made acknowledges a benefaction and further publicizes the repository.

Researchers are a possible source of women's papers, as they have been of men's. Researchers must know that the archivist is prepared to protect their interests (usually a matter of exclusive use for a reasonable time), but, even more, they must be made aware of the repository's interest in collecting papers of unknown women.

Female potential donors, like males, exhibit the full range of attitudes toward their papers (or those of their ancestors) and their place in history, from extreme diffidence to excessive egotism or family pride, as well as many combinations of contradictory attitudes. Like men, some women simply want the stuff out of the house, while others worry over every scrap. Probably women, accustomed to being "just" housewives or "just" schoolteachers, or to being known as their fathers' daughters or husbands' wives, tend toward greater diffidence. They, or their families, are somewhat more likely to have destroyed their papers.

If there are extant papers, the owner may question their historical value. The archivist, in trying to convince the owner that the papers are valuable, can give an honest and enthusiastic, but not too long, explanation of how the person and papers in question form an integral part of the history of a locality, organization, movement, or whatever. A simple statement such as, "Your grandmother didn't set up the mill, but without women like her it couldn't have stayed in business," is likely to be more effective than a discourse on nineteenth-century industrialism.

The potential donor may be suspicious of an "elite" or "establishment" repository. This suspicion may be disarmed by explaining the costliness of the special conditions and staff required to take care of papers adequately. A tour behind the scenes would show the potential donor that the staff are human, and how the papers will be stored, arranged, described, and used. It is best if the repository is open to the public and not just to a select few. The donor should know that she and others represented in the collection will be welcome to come and use the papers, and other papers as well.

It should go without saying that the negotiations with a seamstress, millworker, or clubwoman are conducted with the same care as those with a famous author or politician. Whatever forms and procedures the repository has should be used, the donor should be urged to answer questions about access, copying, and copyright as definitively, the papers should be stored as carefully, and their acquisition announced as enthusiastically.

As the expanding collecting interests of a repository become better known, people will begin to offer papers unsolicited, including some that the repository does not want. In deciding what to collect in these new areas, the archivist applies the usual appraisal criteria: evidentiary and informational value will determine *whether* papers should be collected; their subject or geographical emphases will be criteria for *where* they should be collected. Because the appraising archivist has adopted a different view of what constitutes history, she will apply these general criteria to acquire documentation of ordinary women's lives. Again, whatever can be said about appraisal applies to women and men, but many an appraising archivist, like many a social or family historian, needs an extra reminder that women are as much a part of history as men are.[16]

The records of virtually all women's organizations are of interest. Whenever women band together for some common purpose, the simple fact of their taking the trouble to organize indicates that their goals or activities have some general or symptomatic significance. Furthermore, the organizational records may include case records or other quantifiable data. The North Bennet Street Industrial School records, for example, include information about employment, education, health, and welfare aid for the families of day nursery pupils and clients of the vocational placement service. Information about class attendance and club membership may be trivial in itself, but significant when used with other records, such as public welfare records, to reconstruct the lives of families in immigrant neighborhoods.[17]

Even an archivist whose mission it is to document the history of an institution may need to expand the scope of the records retained. For example, a college or university archivist must clearly retain evidence of the institution's history as a provider of higher education. But the college or university is also an employer, providing maintenance and clerical work for women and men, and, for many of them, a means of being assimilated into American or urban life. Just how the institution has done this, and what it has meant in the lives of its employees, are well worth documenting. As with social service agencies, the university's personnel files may be the only extant record of the lives of these little-known people.[18]

Individual and family papers are harder to appraise than they were when the main criterion was the public (usually political, military, or literary) significance of the person or the family.[19] Travel diaries, numerous and often dull, take on new significance if they record the headaches or fainting spells suffered by a young lady on her Grand Tour of Europe, or if they illuminate the relationship she had with those who traveled with her. Researchers hoping to document changes in housework want to know which family members or servants cooked or dusted or did the laundry, how often, and how long it took. All information about domestic life— work, power, reproduction, education, and so on—can be useful. Janet Brodie, for instance, discovered that Mary Pierce Poor, the wife of Henry Varnum Poor (railroad economist, journalist, and originator of *Poor's Manual*), used symbols to note in her diaries her menstrual periods and each instance of intercourse with her husband for most of their sixty-four years of married life.[20] Such information would be equally valuable in the diaries and papers of a more obscure woman. There is clearly an intimate connection between this private information and the statistics on births per adult woman. History is richer for having both.

Mr. Poor did *not* record such private information. In general, though there are numerous exceptions, the women recorded private events and the men public events. Thanks to the new women's history we can see, for instance, that household accounts give us essential information about the American economy that statistics on industrial production or trade do not. A history of obstetrical practice from the point of view of physicians tells only part of the story. More of it can be gleaned from the account by Nancy Atwood Sprague of the birth of her daughter's child,[21] or Cyrus Taber's revelation to Allen Hamilton of his feelings when his wife died after a miscarriage.[22]

All this suggests that we should collect everything, that even the smallest bit of information about the most trivial event or feeling in the life of the most obscure person might have some research value. So it might, but we obviously cannot collect everything. What not to collect is hard to define; examples of collections the Schlesinger Library has turned down may be illustrative, though not definitive. One was a group of letters (1950s and 60s) from one woman to another discussing books she had read and the moves and meetings of otherwise unknown people. There were too few letters over too many years to make a coherent story; the other half of the correspondence had been destroyed. We suggested a local repository, where some of the people mentioned might be known, but we were pretty sure that in themselves these few letters would be meaningless anywhere.

The writer of some recent diaries had had a divorce, a nervous breakdown, and a hysterectomy, but the diaries, in the form of large, loose-leaf notebooks, had less to say about these events than about what she had for breakfast, and they were filled with long passages copied from magazines. We decided that there was not enough substance to justify the considerable space they occupy. Some older diaries, of a Harvard professor's wife, were similarly opaque. They did report when she dusted and who came to tea, but gave never a hint of her thoughts or feelings. We might have taken them for their information on housekeeping and Cambridge social life, but they were offered by a dealer, so it was not their bulk but their price that negatively outweighed their research potential.

Perhaps we were wrong in any or all of these cases. Perhaps historians and archivists a hundred years from now will be as angry at us as we are at the nineteenth-century women who, upon the death of a female relative, would collect all the letters she had written and commit them to the flames.[23] We cannot know what evidence historians a hundred years from now will want, but curators and archivists can and should discuss research needs with contemporary historians and keep in mind not only that research interests change, but also, as Herbert Finch has pointed out, that we can have some influence on them.[24]

Communication with researchers will help us not only in appraisal and collecting, but also in improving our finding aids. Papers can be lost, even in the most well-endowed repository, because of the limits of traditional description and indexing. Some years ago, for instance, Anne Farnam set up an extensive exhibit of women's papers at the Massachusetts Historical Society. Few of the items she exhibited had been listed in any finding aid; she had to follow hunches and search through a great many collections to find them. As a result of her laborious efforts the staff learned much about what they had in their care. They had not previously paid much attention to the women, presumably because no one had asked about them.

Archivists can ask about their patrons' current, and sometimes future, research interests to learn newly interesting names and subjects to point out in new finding aids. They can also encourage researchers to indicate inadequacies in description or indexing of already processed materials— inadequacies, that is, for new kinds of research.

For instance, if the aforementioned young woman touring Europe did indeed record her headaches, that collection should have a catalog entry for *Women—Health and hygiene*, as well as one for *Voyages and travels*. The young woman herself, possibly buried in a collection named for her father, brother, or husband, should find her way into the card catalog or series description, as should other women represented in the papers, including servants and other employees. It should be clear that this is a matter of expanding descriptions of collections or record groups; nothing need be lost. More information can be added in the form of additional entries in the card catalog, or an indication in the description of a manuscript collection or record group that it contains information about birth control, relations between sisters, or whatever.[25]

It is encouraging that the NHPRC's *Directory of Archives and Manuscript Repositories* uses more subject headings than did Hamer's *Guide to Archives and Manuscripts*, which it updates.[26] Finding aids (whether intra- or interrepository) with few or no subject entries reflect, and encourage, an elitist approach to history. Of course notables are indexed, and readers will look directly for Elizabeth Cady Stanton or Clara Barton, by name. But readers are not likely to know the names of domestic servants, schoolteachers, mill hands, pieceworkers, or housewives. If the new history is to take these people seriously, the papers by or about them must be pointed out by means of subject headings or being mentioned in series descriptions. The main entry for the memoir of an immigrant woman or the diary of a schoolteacher should still be the author's name. But there must also be entries for US—*Emigration and immigration* and for *Teachers*; or almost no one will be able to find the memoir or the diary.

Just as the new women's history requires that archivists add to finding aids but not substitute one kind for another, so the new women's history should be seen as adding a dimension to history, not as substituting one kind of history for another. The travel diaries filled with headaches get catalog entries for both health and travel. One can give the anonymous their due without belittling the leaders. Susan B. Anthony could not have done her work for suffrage without many women behind her; on the other hand, many of those women would have done little or nothing for suffrage without Anthony's inspiration and leadership. Anthony was not all-important, but she was important. Even as we attempt to collect and to describe adequately materials on anonymous immigrant women and on the domestic life of middle-class women, we will continue to collect and to index Anthony's letters.

Extreme views jolt us loose from comfortable old patterns of thought, but soon we must arrive at new syntheses. Carroll Smith-Rosenberg minimizes the significance of the public sphere, asserting that "women's suffrage has proved of little importance either to American politics or to American women."[27] Suffrage has perhaps not been as important as the traditional women's historians suggest, but it has made a difference. If women had not won the vote in 1920, or since, we would still be fighting for it, and in the suffrage movement, women learned to organize, to lobby, to cooperate, and to take public risks. If the vote brought about no miraculous improvement in the nation's affairs, as some suffragists had predicted it would, that is evidence that women are human like everyone else, not morally superior, and that political, social, and economic institutions are more resistant to change than the suffragists expected. In fact, we know from our own lives that who is president, what laws are passed, and whether or not the United States goes to war or annexes a piece of land do have an impact on the anonymous person's life, but they hardly begin to account for what her life is like at any historical moment. The new women's history, using papers or records about ordinary women, attempts to complete the account.

Other new information and insights can help us demote earlier points of view without discarding them altogether. Some historians believe that women have always been oppressed by men; others believe that the "oppression school" of history is wrong. But why not both? Smith-Rosenberg's valuable, pioneering research on support networks among nineteenth-century women should not blind us to the fact that women have been oppressed by men, though the oppression school, as Mary Beard warned some thirty years ago, tells a very lopsided story.[28] Oppression of women by women is another interesting issue.[29] Most obvious is the oppression of lower-class women by those of the middle and upper classes. Even among women of the same class, sisterhood has not always been the prevalent relationship, much as we might wish it were. In founding the New England Women's Club in 1869, Julia Ward Howe said, "We shall learn from contact with each other to be more just and generous to our sex." Howe used the word *sisterhood* as an ideal to work toward, not to describe what she saw around her.[30]

In revising periodization, too, a synthetic approach is most constructive. As it tries to determine what the epoch-making events for women were, the new women's history can show us how the periodization of all history might be revised. The rubber nipple was important to women, but so was the Bessemer converter; the changes steel brought about in construction, transportation, weapons, cooking utensils, and so on have affected everyone. Then again, the rubber nipple has affected men, indirectly because of the relative freedom it allowed their mothers and wives, and directly those who, like their infant sisters, had rubber nipples put into their mouths.

Women's history has been called a specialty, or even a subspecialty, of the specialty of social history. It is not a specialty. Women are not a subgroup any more than men are; nor are women, as Gregory Stiverson has called us, a "special-interest group."[31] "There are just too many of us," writes Gerda Lerner.[32] And, numbers aside, it seems impossible to believe, though many do believe it, that men's public history would have been the same no matter what women were doing. A student of unemployment between 1880 and 1930 was amazed to find how many people were unemployed how much of the time; he wondered how they managed, as they didn't earn much even when employed. But his unemployed "people" were all men; had he studied women's employment and unemployment, he might have found out how the men managed when unemployed (which is not to say that he should have studied only women's unemployment).

Most archivists and manuscript curators don't write history. But, with the decisions we make, especially in appraising records and papers and in describing them, we can either promote new trends in research or throw up roadblocks in their way. Those willing to accept the idea that "history" is about what people have done and suffered—people and not just personages, and people of all classes, races, and sexes—will find their work more significant and more exciting.

NOTES

This article was originally published in *The American Archivist* 43 (1980): 180–90.

[1] Andrea Hinding ed., *Women's History Sources: A Guide to Archives and Manuscript Collections in the United States*, 2 vols. (New York: R. R. Bowker Company, 1979).

[2] Throughout this article, the word *archivists* will be used to mean both archivists and curators.

[3] Carroll Smith-Rosenberg, "The New Woman and the New History," *Feminist Studies* 3, nos. 1–2 (1976): 186 (paper given at the 1975 SAA meeting).

[4] Gerda Lerner discussed "compensatory history" and other issues raised by women's history, in her introductory comments to the panel "Effects of Women's History upon Traditional Concepts of Historiography" at the Second Berkshire Conference on the History of Women, Radcliffe College, October 1974. Berkshire Conference papers are available at the Schlesinger Library; the call number is MC 244.

[5] Smith-Rosenberg, "The New Woman," 187.

[6] Ellen DuBois.

[7] Richard T. Vann, "Towards a Periodization of Women's History" (paper given at the Second Berkshire Conference on the History of Women; see note 4, above).

[8] See also Smith-Rosenberg, "The New Woman," 190.

[9] Whether they should be was discussed at a panel on the "activist archivist" at the 1976 SAA meeting; the papers were published in *Georgia Archive* 5, no. 1 (1977). See also F. Gerald Ham, "The Archival Edge," *American Archivist* 38 (January 1975): 5–13; and Lester J. Cappon's response, "The Archivist as Collector," *American Archivist* 39 (October 1976): 429–35.

[10] Archives of Labor History and Urban Affairs, Wayne State University, *Newsletter* 2, no. 1 (1972).

[11] These records are the property of the Commonwealth of Massachusetts but are on deposit at the Schlesinger Library, Radcliffe College.

[12] North Bennet Street Industrial School records, Schlesinger Library, call number MC 269.

[13] The Mary Anderson and Leonora O'Reilly papers are at the Schlesinger Library (A-7 and A-39, respectively); the Agnes Nestor Papers are at the Chicago Historical Society [now the Chicago History Museum].

[14] Feminine pronouns are used generically throughout this article.

[15] See Virginia R. Stewart, "A Primer on Manuscript Field Work," *Midwestern Archivist* 1, no. 2 (1976): 3–20.

[16] "Women have been a force in making all the history that has been made." Mary R. Beard, *Woman as Force in History* (New York: The Macmillan Company, 1946), vi.

[17] North Bennet Street Industrial School records, Schlesinger Library.

[18] The appraisal questions raised by modern, bulky organizational collections or record groups are the same for women's, men's, and mixed groups. The point is that the needs of the new women's history compel us to redefine "research value." Not only the leaders of important organizations, but all the members of all groups, are of interest.

[19] In fact, even the importance of a family member did not guarantee that the family papers as such would be collected. The Massachusetts Historical Society has long had the papers of Richard Henry Dana Jr., but in 1960 the numerous diaries and letters of his mother, sister, and other female relatives were still in the hands of the family. They have since been at the Schlesinger Library.

[20] Janet F. Brodie, "Fertility and Family Limitation: The Henry Varnum Poors, 1840–1880" (paper given at the Fourth Berkshire Conference on the History of Women, Mount Holyoke College, August 1978).

[21] Nancy Ann (Atwood) Sprague Papers, MC 259, 3v, Schlesinger Library, available on microfilm.

[22] Hamilton Family Papers, MC 278, 42, Schlesinger Library. This is one of the "exceptions," a man commenting on a private event, but he did so in a letter to a business associate.

[23] The author has been told that in some circles this was done routinely. This may be apocryphal, but it seems bad enough to us now if it was done at all.

[24] The author has heard, rather than read, this. C. Herbert Finch supported the notion in a private communication of 22 February 1979: "The idea of archivists influencing research trends . . . was—and still is—part of the challenge of collecting work for me."

[25] This article is not the place to discuss the form of subject headings. Let me just say that I realize that not all repositories can follow the practice of the

Schlesinger Library in changing the Library of Congress's *Women as physicians* simply to *Physicians*, as in most repositories not all the physicians are women. But I look forward to the day when the rather contemptuous Women as . . . headings are replaced by *Physicians—Men* and *Physicians—Women*.

[26] National Historical Publications and Records Commission, *Directory of Archives and Manuscript Repositories in the United States* (Washington, DC: National Archives and Records Service, 1978); and Philip M. Hamer, ed., *A Guide to Archives and Manuscripts in the United States* (New Haven: Yale University Press, 1961).

[27] Smith-Rosenberg, "The New Woman," 186.

[28] Beard, *Woman as Force in History.*

[29] And so is oppression of men by women, most notably as male infants vis-a-vis mothers or other adult females.

[30] See the records of New England Women's Club, 178, vol. 11, entry for 30 May 1869, at Schlesinger Library.

[31] Gregory A. Stiverson, "The Activist Archivist: A Conservative View," *Georgia Archive* 5, no. 1 (1977): 5.

[32] Lerner, introduction to panel, "Effects of Women's History," 11: "I started out raising the question of a conceptual framework for dealing with Women's History way back in 1969, reasoning from the assumption that women were a sub-group . . . different from any other sub-group in history. . . . I have now come to the conclusion that the idea that women are some kind of sub-group . . . is wrong. It will not do; there are just too many of us." On pp. 5–6, Lerner discusses the "oppression school" of women's history.

Locating Women
in the Archives

CHAPTER 7

A Room of One's Own: Women's Archives in the Year 2000

KÄREN M. MASON AND TANYA ZANISH-BELCHER

ABSTRACT

The number of repositories dedicated to collecting women's papers has grown substantially in the past quarter century, with no fewer than 15 established after 1990. This article analyzes that trend, arguing that activists—as well as scholars and archivists—have been at the forefront in establishing these new archives. As the fields of women's history, women's studies, and gender studies have matured, and as women's historians have broadened their vision to include diverse groups, geographic regions, and topics, significant gaps in the documentary record have become evident. Scholars, archivists, and activists have responded to that need with new collecting initiatives and new archives. The authors contend that woman-centered repositories will continue to play an important role in the archival landscape in the coming decades.

IN 1973 *AMERICAN ARCHIVIST* DEVOTED AN ENTIRE ISSUE TO THE THEME OF WOMEN IN ARCHIVES. In addition to pieces on the status of women in the profession, the issue included an article by Eva Moseley on women's collections. She focused primarily on the Schlesinger Library at Radcliffe College and on the Sophia Smith Collection at Smith College, but included discussion of a number of other women's collections. She also raised questions about the nature of separate women's collections that retain their relevance today: should women's repositories exist at all? If so, what should they collect? Should the work of documenting women's lives and activities be left to women's archives alone? Moseley suggested that women's repositories were an important step forward, but that there might come a time when separate women's collections are not needed.[1]

In the quarter century since Moseley's article, the number of repositories dedicated to collecting women's papers has grown substantially, with many established after 1990. Certainly, the growth of women's studies programs and the establishment of women's history as a legitimate field of study are a large part of the explanation for this phenomenon. But the reasons for founding women's collections are varied and come from outside the academy as often as from within. Some recent collections have been started at the request of women's studies programs, others by archivists or library directors to meet a perceived research need or to focus collecting on a neglected area. Other women's collections have been founded by benefactors offering endowments to support the establishment of women-centered archives. This article discusses some of the women's collections founded in the past decade, examines the reasons for their establishment, and considers some of the archival issues raised by the existence of such collections.

A note on definitions is in order. When we speak of "women's collections," what do we mean? In a 1986 issue of *Special Collections* devoted to women's library and archival collections, Suzanne Hildenbrand commented on the imprecision of the category:

> The definition, classification and selection of women's collections pose numerous problems. Some of these collections stand alone in separate buildings, others are the contents of a file cabinet or two in rooms used primarily for other purposes. Some consist of books that circulate with the general collection, distinguished only by a bookplate. The only guide to whether or not a collection is a women's collection is if the sponsoring institution describes it as such. Most women's materials, of course, are in general collections.[2]

For Hildenbrand, the problem was deciding which repositories to include in her survey of women's collections. The challenge of definition remains today. As the membership of the Society of American Archivists' Women's Collections Roundtable illustrates, "women's collections" can encompass freestanding buildings, endowed positions for women's studies archivists, and mainstream repositories that include women's papers as a significant collecting focus. We confine our analysis to archives that are clearly identified as women's collections, usually by the inclusion of the word "women" in their names. Our discussion highlights trends and provides examples of women's archives founded in the 1990s, but is not exhaustive.

Should Women's Repositories Exist?

The question "Should women's repositories exist?" is really two very different questions, depending on who is asking. Each has its own subtext, posing a challenge to the foundation upon which women's archives have been and continue to be built. The first form of the question challenges the notion that women merit their own repository. It views the very existence of women's archives as privileging women and, in consequence, discriminating against men. The second form of the question sees women's repositories as ghettoizing women, thereby placing women in a secondary status rather than incorporating them into the mainstream of academic study. Both concerns are important and must be addressed.

We suspect that everyone who works in a women's collection has at one time or another been asked—usually by a man, and only half in jest— "When are they going to start a men's archive?" The flip answer is that for most of history archives have been "men's archives": they have collected almost exclusively the papers of men. But a more thoughtful response is that until recently archives neglected the papers of women and non-majority groups, instead concentrating their collecting on the papers of men who held positions of power or influence in American society. As Debra Newman Ham wrote, American cultural institutions, including our archives and historical societies, have been shaped by Euro-Americans. From the colonial period on, the papers that were preserved "tended to focus on literate Euro-Americans, particularly the lives of great men, such as presidents, statesmen, and military leaders."[3] Women's archives help to redress this imbalance.

In its second form, the question "Should women's repositories exist?" speculates on the potential adverse effects of separatism: does having a separate repository for women's papers marginalize women? This parallels a debate among academics over the merits of separatism versus integration. Judy Lensink made a compelling argument for women's history remaining a separate intellectual field within mainstream academe. In essence, she contended that remaining separate can be an important intellectual tool, allowing scholars to view old subjects with fresh perspectives. Lensink warned that "A highly suspicious subtext is embedded in the ongoing call by concerned historians for 'synthesis,' in which the 'subfields' of women's and ethnic history are cajoled to reenter the confines of History writ large, to 'wrestle inside the ring'. A major strength of feminist history," she argued, "is that thinkers stand on the margins of 'the' story so as to see it as freshly as possible."[4] We believe that the separatism of women's collections likewise enriches the possibilities for collecting and for documenting groups outside the mainstream. The very notion of a women's repository frees us from some of the blinders of traditional collecting, encouraging us to think in new ways about how to document various groups and subcultures. Iowa State University's Archives of Women in Science and Engineering, for example, seeks the papers not only of prominent and successful scientists, but of those who had patchwork careers, that is, careers interrupted by the demands of family life (moving with a spouse for his job) or curtailed because of discrimination against women by colleagues or employers. This effort to document the social history of women scientists brings a new and oft-neglected dimension to the history of science.

We contend that separate women's collections are critical for two reasons. First, they provide a means of rectifying the earlier neglect of women's papers and preventing such gaps in documentation from occurring in the future. Second, they provide a vehicle to promote and enhance the study of women's history. Women's collections are established for the same reasons that other special subject repositories exist: to document an underdocumented subject or group and thus call attention to it.

Women's archives have a meaning greater than the collections they house. It is symbolically significant to have "a room of one's own," in Virginia Woolf's words, that is, a physical space set aside for women's papers, whether it be a separate building such as the Schlesinger Library at Radcliffe College, or stacks and a reading room within a university library, such as the Iowa Women's Archives at the University of Iowa.[5] Likewise, establishing a program to collect women's papers, even without a separate physical space, like the Archives of Women in Science and Engineering at Iowa State University, validates women's experiences. These tangible commitments to documenting the lives of women make it clear that women's lives and experiences are valued by society. By so doing, they encourage women who might never have thought themselves worthy of being remembered through history to donate their papers to an archives.

A Brief Look at the History of Women's Collections in the United States

The creation of repositories dedicated to collecting women's materials has gone through several phases in the twentieth century. As Anke Voss-Hubbard noted in a 1995 *American Archivist* article, the 1930s and 1940s witnessed a heightened effort on the part of the federal government and academic institutions to preserve primary sources. This concern rarely extended to materials by or about women. That work was left to feminists. According to Suzanne Hildenbrand, "the 1930s and 1940s saw a remarkable trend towards the establishment of women's collections, as veterans of the feminist campaigns of the early Twentieth century anxiously sought institutional homes for their private papers, and other materials they had collected, in a world suddenly disinterested in, or hostile to, the cause to which they had devoted their lives." Most notable was Mary Ritter Beard and Rosika Schwimmer's attempt to launch a World Center for Women's Archives in the 1930s. Their goals were to promote research on women and to ensure that a record of their campaigns for women's rights, peace, or other issues would be preserved. They hoped that the archives would also serve as an example of activism for other women. The archives foundered in 1940, but Beard had managed to interest librarians at Smith and Radcliffe in collecting women's papers. The Woman's Rights Collection at Radcliffe College and the Sophia Smith Collection at Smith College, both established in the early 1940s, ultimately grew into the premier collections of primary source material on women. The Woman's Collection of the Texas Woman's University Library was started in 1932 to collect writings by and about women in literature, the arts, and politics; in the 1970s, it acquired its first large manuscript collection and has become a major repository of the papers of women in Texas and the Southwest.[6]

Martha S. Bell's 1959 survey of special women's collections in libraries included several established in the 1940s and 1950s, such as the Afro-American Woman's Collection at Bennett College, founded in 1946, and the Willa Cather Pioneer Memorial Library in Red Cloud, Nebraska, founded in 1955. Bell defined women's collections as materials segregated from the main holdings of a library or constituting a special library in their own right. While primarily concerned with collections of published volumes, most of the thirty-eight collections on Bell's list also included manuscript materials. Bell reported that "Several excellent collections of books, files of papers, letters, journals, etc., offer scholars extensive and invaluable source material on the history of women, their contribution, collective or individual, to the social, political, and intellectual problems of their times." But as Suzanne Hildenbrand wrote, many of the collections founded prior to the 1970s "languished for decades, poorly supported and understaffed" until "[t]he upsurge of feminist consciousness . . . stimulated enormous growth and development of women's collections."[7]

As women's history emerged in the late 1960s and grew rapidly in popularity during the 1970s, scholars and archivists reluctant to accept this new field of study asserted that there were not enough primary sources to support historical research. Some archivists did take note of the increasing numbers of women's history courses and began actively soliciting women's papers.[8] Others compiled guides to their holdings on women. These guides were usually brief, typewritten, self-published lists of women's papers held by a particular repository. When the Michigan History Division published a *Bibliography of Sources Relating to Women* held by seven major repositories in the state in 1975, it listed fewer than three hundred collections. Clearly, the vast majority of primary sources by and about women in Michigan remained "hidden from history." A guide published by the State Historical Society of Wisconsin in the early 1970s took the form of a narrative essay in which the authors discussed not only specific collections, but how to locate sources by and about women buried in the society's other collections. This guide grew out of a series of classroom presentations given by the authors for a graduate women's history seminar at the University of Wisconsin.[9]

It was *Women's History Sources*, published by Bowker in 1979, that finally exploded the myth that insufficient primary sources existed to support the study of women's history. In the late 1970s, Andrea Hinding and her staff at the University of Minnesota's Social Welfare History Archives conducted this sweeping survey. They sent questionnaires to repositories around the country asking staff to describe their holdings on women. Fieldworkers followed, scouring stacks for materials on women buried within collections. The resulting guide listed more than eighteen thousand collections of personal papers, organizational records, and oral history collections in more than a thousand repositories representing all fifty states. The scope of the finished product surprised observers and participants alike, as did the realization that this guide represented only the tip of the iceberg. The impact of *Women's History Sources* was, in fact, much greater than the published guide itself. The project caused many archivists to rethink the way they organized and described their holdings, eventually bringing to light countless women's materials hidden in the papers of husbands, fathers, and sons. It could no longer be asserted accurately that there were few resources for the study of women's history.[10]

The 1970s were thus characterized by the reexamination of existing holdings for sources on women, followed by revisions of card catalogs and finding aids to reflect these discoveries. There was also a heightened effort by many repositories to collect women's papers. Some repositories compiled guides to the women's papers among their holdings, and others established discrete women's collections as a subset of their holdings. At the same time, a few distinctive new archives were established to collect the papers of groups not likely to be documented in traditional repositories. The Lesbian Herstory Archives, founded in 1974 in New York City, was staffed entirely by volunteers and housed in a private apartment. The Bethune Museum-Archives for Black Women's History, established in 1979 in Washington, DC, was the culmination of four decades of work by the Archives Committee of the National Council of Negro Women.[11]

The trend toward separate women's collections accelerated in the 1980s and 1990s. By 1989, enough archivists were involved with women's collections to support the establishment of a Women's Collections Roundtable in the Society of American Archivists.[12] Archivists sent information about their holdings to the first directory, published in 1992. These archivists represented a wide range of repositories, including distinct women's collections as well as mainstream repositories with a special collecting focus on women. By the time the third directory was published electronically in 1997, the number of entries had grown to 119 individuals and repositories. It was clear by this time not only that the Schlesinger Library and Smith College could not collect everything, but that a greater effort to document women on local, regional, and state levels was needed. The Schlesinger Library surveyed archives around the country in the early 1990s to locate local and state women's organizational records and to distribute the information to potential donors. The guide that resulted included seventy-eight repositories, reflecting the sea change that had taken place in attitudes toward women's history in the preceding quarter century.[13]

Women's Archives Blossom in the 1990s

By our count, no fewer than fifteen women's archives have opened their doors since 1990 (see appendix). Two related factors explain this flowering of women's collections in the past decade. First, as the generation that founded the women's movement of the 1960s and 1970s ages, these "second-wave" feminists have become concerned about preserving the history of the movement. Concomitantly, some are at a stage in their lives or careers in which they have significant financial resources at their disposal and can provide funding for efforts to preserve this history. Second, the maturing of women's history, women's studies, and gender studies as fields of scholarship has created a need for broader and more diverse primary source materials. Scholars, archivists, and activists have responded to that need with new collecting initiatives and archives.

The involvement of aging feminists in founding women's archives is not surprising. As Anne Firor Scott writes, "women's history in this country has developed in close relationship with women's activism and has itself affected that activism, providing the inspiration and encouragement for many efforts to broaden women's world." Along with their demands for new social, political, and economic roles, feminists of the 1960s and 1970s sought to reclaim their past by uncovering the hidden history of their foremothers. Like their feminist forebears who placed the papers of the suffrage and peace movements in archival repositories, these activists of the 1960s, 1970s, and 1980s now seek to preserve a record of their struggles as inspiration for younger women.[14]

In fact, several of the women's archives founded in the 1990s were born of the same goal that spawned the earliest women's archives in the 1930s and 1940s. That is, activist women outside universities offered endowments to support women-centered archives to preserve a record of the women's movement. The Louise Noun-Mary Louise Smith Iowa Women's Archives at the University of Iowa Libraries was founded in 1991 by two prominent Des Moines women. They were Louise Noun, an art collector, historian, and social activist, and Mary Louise Smith, who had chaired the Republican National Committee in the mid-1970s. In the 1960s, Noun had conceived the idea of a women's archive for Iowa while researching *Strong-Minded Women: The Emergence of the Woman-Suffrage Movement in Iowa* (1969). In 1991, she shared her idea with Smith, who believed the papers in such an archives would both preserve the history of women's achievements and spur young women to become involved in public life by the examples they provided. Noun sold the Frida Kahlo painting "Self-Portrait with Loose Hair" at auction in May 1991, netting $1.5 million to endow the Iowa Women's Archives at the University of Iowa. The University of Iowa Foundation then undertook a campaign to raise an additional half-million dollars for the archives, which opened in 1992.[15] Another example is the Women's Movement Archives, a component of the Women's Collections in the Georgia State University Special Collections Department. This archives was founded in 1995 when a wealthy benefactor donated her personal papers and an endowment to fund a half-time archivist. The collection documents the women's movement in Georgia, but the department also offers other women's materials. In contrast to the Iowa Women's Archives, which has its own staff, stacks, and reading room, the Georgia Women's Movement Archives is a collecting focus within the Special Collections Department at Georgia State University.

There is at least one women's archives conceived by university administrators. When Mundelein College, the last four-year women's college in Illinois, merged with Loyola University Chicago in 1991, the college wanted to maintain the women's college tradition of empowering women. To do this they established the Ann Ida Gannon Center in 1994, consisting of a women's studies program, a Heritage Room, and the Women and Leadership Archives. The archives holds the records of Mundelein College, as well as personal papers and the records of such organizations as Women-Church Convergence, Homemakers for the Equal Rights Amendment, and Deborah's Place, which operates shelters for single, homeless women in Chicago. The Women and Leadership Archives collects materials primarily in Chicago and the Midwest.[16]

With the proliferation of women's studies, women's history, and gender studies programs have come increased demands for historical documentation to support research on women. Once viewed as a passing trend, women's history is now recognized as a legitimate field of study. As its practitioners have broadened their vision to include diverse groups, geographic regions, and topics, significant gaps in the documentary record have become evident. Both scholars and archivists have taken note of these deficiencies and have responded by establishing archival programs to fill these gaps. Female faculty members have been instrumental in founding several archives in Texas and the Southwest. Examples abound. Women's history faculty took the initiative in founding a statewide project, resulting in the Nevada Women's Archives at the University of Nevada–Reno (1992) and the University of Nevada–Las Vegas (1994). The Women's Archives at the University of Houston was initiated by the University of Houston Women's Studies Program in 1996 to document Houston-area women's organizations. The Archives for Research on Women and Gender at the University of Texas at San Antonio is a joint initiative of the Special Collections and Archives Department and the Center for the Study of Women and Gender. Its mission is to make available primary source materials on women and gender in San Antonio and South Texas. The center also sponsors the electronic "Guide to Uncovering Women's History in Archival Collections" (1993).

In other cases, archivists and library directors have established women's archives to meet a perceived research need or to help focus collecting in a neglected area. The Archives of Women in Science and Engineering at the Iowa State University Library was created in 1993 in response to researcher requests for information on women engineers. The Special Collections staff analyzed the collecting scopes of repositories around the country with a science or engineering focus and found that while some university archives were collecting the papers of their women faculty in engineering and the sciences, no effort was being made to document the social history of women engineers and scientists. This new archives also supported the goals of a land-grant university and complemented its Program for Women in Science and Engineering.[17]

What Should Women's Repositories Collect?

The challenge for women's archives in the future will be to define, or refine, the collecting scope of their repositories. They must strive to document gaps in the historical record, while avoiding the mistakes of the past. They must not fall into the habit of collecting only what is easy, such as the papers of middle- and upper-class white women and the records of mainstream women's organizations. In a 1994 issue of *American Archivist* speculating on the future of archives a quarter of a century hence, Nancy Sahli suggested that

> Perhaps this is as it has always been, that the dominant culture has defined what will be preserved and transmitted to future generations. For dominant cultures have held the keys to power and to those institutions that both create and preserve the historical record. What we have been witnessing in the past thirty years, however, is the increasing diversification of that culture, accompanied by rising self-consciousness of particular groups in society, groups eager to document their own history and gain access to those bits and pieces of their history that have survived in traditional repositories.[18]

If women's repositories are to alter the archival landscape significantly, they must widen their scope, making it a priority to document hitherto neglected groups. They must promote understanding and knowledge of women from various ethnicities, classes, sexual orientations, political affiliations and beliefs, occupations, and religions. Women's archives must also work together to provide representation for historically disenfranchised groups. Archivists must reach the members of these groups, explain the repository's interest in their lives and experiences, and persuade them to donate their papers. This demands a significant commitment of time and energy on the part of staff. Collection development is a labor-intensive process. It includes publicizing the repository, networking with community leaders, public speaking, and writing to, calling, meeting, and following up with individual donors. To acquire substantial holdings rather than a few scattered collections in each area may well require a special project. Fortunately, projects to document underrepresented groups are often good candidates for grants and other forms of special funding.[19]

Archivists must also work together. The increasing number of archivists specializing in women's collections has resulted in new links between repositories and groups. Archivists at Bowling Green State University and the University of Toledo have launched a collaborative project entitled "Women in Politics in Northwest Ohio: The Historical Legacy."

> This bi-partisan, cooperative project . . . seeks to document the his-
> torical role women have played in the political culture of our region.
> The goal of the project is to collect, preserve, and make available
> records of women political leaders, women's political organizations,
> and women who have been important behind-the-scenes in politi-
> cal parties and advocacy groups.[20]

The web pages of each institution alert users, donors, and other archivists to the project and encourage would-be donors to contact the archives.

Archivists at Iowa State University, the University of Iowa, the University of Northern Iowa, and the State Historical Society of Iowa met in 1998 to discuss their efforts to document agriculture in Iowa. Afterward, each repository drafted a statement of its collecting focus and submitted it to the Special Collections Department at Iowa State. The department then created Technical Leaflet #1, "Documenting Agriculture in Iowa," which was distributed throughout the state by the Iowa State Extension Service. The meeting and the leaflet helped determine how the Iowa Women's Archives would define the parameters of its project to document rural women in Iowa in cooperation with, rather than in competition with, the other archives in the state.[21] Archivists can also work together on the national level, thanks to the Women's Collections Roundtable of the Society of American Archivists. The roundtable holds meetings annually at the SAA conference and since 1992 has periodically published a directory of individual members and institutional reposito-ries. It is an important avenue for sharing information about materials documenting the experiences of women.

As women's collections archivists consider the scope of their collect-ing, they must pay special attention to record formats that women have tended to create, such as written reminiscences, recordings of oral tradi-tions, personal scrapbooks, ephemera, and artifactual material. Archivists often regard scrapbooks as more trouble than they are worth because of their size, preservation problems, and ephemeral contents. Yet, they often contain information that would otherwise have been lost. Scrapbooks illuminate the personal memories of individuals and illustrate the con-text of women's identity and experience. Reminiscences written for family members often contain substantive historical information of interest to a wider audience. Likewise, oral histories are particularly important in documenting the lives of women who have not kept written records because they did not perceive their experiences as historically significant. In the words of Judy Lensink, "When women tell their life stories in their own words, a distinct enthusiasm, engagement, and affirmation emerges from within the dominant discourse in which ordinary women's experiences are at best perceived as a subculture. These are stories in which women are the central actors, even if their stories are camouflaged by modesty and disclaimers."[22] Indeed, the real challenge is to persuade women that their reminiscences, ephemera, and oral histories have value and interest outside their families.

Finally, women are taking advantage of new electronic technologies to preserve and disseminate these ephemeral formats. One example is the Jewish Women's Archive, which presents an alternative model for archivists attempting to document a particular subject or group. This virtual archives digitizes primary sources by or about Jewish women from across the country, leaving the originals with their owners. The value of such an endeavor is that it pulls together fragments in far-flung collections and creates an easily accessible body of primary sources. The archives will also provide resource links to repositories containing archival collections by or about Jewish women. The Jewish Women's Archive is not a project solely of professional archivists, but rather of a group of interested persons who wish to educate society about the experiences and contributions of Jewish women:

> The Jewish Women's Archive is for scholars. For activists. For mothers and daughters. For fathers and sons. For researchers, historians, and community members. For people who believe that everyone with a stake in history is a keeper of it and a partner in its transmission.[23]

Providing Access to Women's Collections

The Jewish Women's Archive skirts the boundary between collecting and access, helping archivists to think about some of the problems and possibilities in providing access to their holdings. In the past, researchers faced a number of obstacles when trying to locate women's papers. Women's materials were often not identified as such, or were "hidden" in the papers of male family members or colleagues or in organizational records.[24] As Judy Lensink noted, " . . . many lesser-known and unknown peoples' writings, particularly by women of color, are not being read because they lie obscured in historical archives. The terms, 'fragments, small collections and ephemeral writings' are signposts to unutilized women's documents."[25] Archivists' growing knowledge of women's history has resulted in better finding aids and catalog records for women's papers over the past twenty years.

Since the development of MARC-AMC in the early 1980s, the number of archival repositories cataloging their materials and submitting records to the Research Libraries Information Network (RLIN) and the Online Computer Library Center (OCLC) has increased significantly. Researchers' greater access to bibliographic utilities and their familiarity with online searching has enhanced their ability to locate relevant collections. The availability of *ArchivesUSA* in electronic form has vastly simplified the use of the *National Union Catalog of Manuscript Collections* (NUCMC) and the *National Inventory of Documentary Sources* (NIDS), providing yet another avenue of access to women's collections. The exponential growth and use of the web has also furthered access to collections while new web-based interfaces such as Endeavor and Horizon, provide a direct link from the online catalog record to individual finding aids on the web. The continuing problem of subject access is being addressed by the use of Encoded Archival Description (EAD), which holds great promise because of its powerful subject-searching capabilities and its standard for finding-aid metadata. Currently, the usefulness of EAD is limited by the small number of institutions that have the technological, financial, and staff resources to implement it.

We envision an increase in networking among archivists of women's collections and other activists, scholars, and researchers. The H-Net Women's History Listserv and the Women's Liberation Research Network are examples of this trend. Archivists will also creatively utilize the web to innovate new methods of access and interaction. Various institutions currently maintain lists of women's repositories on their websites, giving directory information, describing collecting scope, and providing links to the websites of these repositories. In addition to the electronic "Guide to Uncovering Women's History in Archival Collections" mentioned previously, there are also numerous women's history websites that link the user to sites all over the United States and the world. There will also be an international component to this process that will connect women from every continent. The recent Mapping the World of Women's Information Services project, sponsored by the International Information Centre and Archives for the Women's Movement (Amsterdam), offers electronic and book-form links to women's information resources around the globe. We imagine that all of these ideas will be expanded and furthered in the years to come.[26]

Where Do We Go from Here?

The Internet has already demonstrated its potential for improving access to archival collections. But archivists must take care not to become so infatuated with technology that they forget those who have no access to the Internet, lack the knowledge or skills to use it, or choose not to use it. Women's history grew out of a desire to recover lost voices and experiences; archivists must continue this commitment to inclusivity through outreach efforts. By making presentations, attending conferences, and producing exhibits, archivists can publicize their holdings and reaffirm their interest in documenting the lives of women from across the socioeconomic, racial, cultural, and geographic spectrum, representing a diversity of experiences and voices.

We believe that woman-centered repositories will continue to flourish and play an important role in the archival landscape. But women's repositories are not enough and they cannot do it alone. Mainstream repositories still have a responsibility to document the experiences of women and, just as importantly, provide access to their holdings by and about women. Archivists must analyze their collections to determine what information about women (and other underrepresented groups) they contain. These institutions must also have knowledge of related collections at other repositories or know how to locate such information—and inform researchers about it. In addition to providing access to these materials, archivists have a wider responsibility to educate the public about these collections and to suggest how they might be used. Archivists must also work to integrate primary sources, including resources for women's history, into K–12 and college curricula, and into community and organizational collaborative projects.[27] Sharing the historical treasures they manage by creating finding aids and websites, speaking to public groups, coordinating a History Day workshop, or producing exhibits is part of the joy of being an archivist. These activities help assure that people learn of collections, use them, and understand their cultural value.

The "rooms of their own" that have been established will be joined by others, more likely dedicated to documenting specific groups of women identified by their shared characteristics and experiences. Such archives will be established because each of these groups will need a room of its own, a place (whether physical or virtual) where its identity is affirmed by the history that has been preserved there. These repositories will accomplish the goals of providing documents for research and scholarship and will also fulfill the promise of women's history: giving women a voice.

Women's Archives in the United States: Repository	City, State	Est'd before 1970	Est'd 1970s	Est'd 1980s	Est'd 1990s
Archive of Women in Architecture of the American Institute of Architects	Washington, DC			X	
Archives for Research on Women and Gender, University of Texas at San Antonio	San Antonio, TX				X
Archives of Women in Science and Engineering, Iowa State University	Ames, IA				X
Armenian Women's Archives	Berkeley, CA				X
Brown University, Christine Dunlap Farnham Archives	Providence, RI			X	
California State University Women in Music Collection	Northridge, CA				X
Chicana-Latina Archives, UCLA	Los Angeles, CA				X
Daughters of the Republic of Texas	San Antonio, TX	X			
General Federation of Women's Clubs, Women's History and Resource Center	Washington, DC			X	
Georgia State University, Georgia Women's Collections and Georgia's Women's Movement Archives Project	Atlanta, GA				X
Hadassah Archives	New York, NY				X
History of Women in Home Economics, University of Wisconsin at Madison	Madison, WI				X
International Archive of Women in Architecture, Virginia Tech	Blacksburg, VA			X	
Iowa Women's Archives, University of Iowa Libraries	Iowa City, IA				X

Women's Archives in the United States: Repository	City, State	Est'd before 1970	Est'd 1970s	Est'd 1980s	Est'd 1990s
Jewish Women's Archive	cyberspace				X
June L. Mazer Lesbian Collection	Los Angeles, CA			X	
Lesbian Herstory Archives	New York, NY		X		
Lesbian Legacy Collection Library & Archives	Los Angeles, CA			X	
Maine Women Writers Collection University of New England, Westbrook College Campus	Portland, ME	X			
Midwest Women's Historical Collection, University of Illinois at Chicago	Chicago, IL		X		
National Archives for Black Women's History, Mary McLeod Bethune Council House	Washington, DC	X			
National Museum of Women in the Arts, Library and Resource Center	Washington, DC			X	
National Society of the Daughters of the American Revolution	Washington, DC	X			
National Women and Media Collection, Western Historical Manuscript Collection	Columbia, MO			X	
Native American Women Playwrights Archive, Miami University	Oxford, OH				X
Nevada Women's Archives, University of Nevada, Las Vegas	Las Vegas, NV				X
Nevada Women's Archives, University of Nevada, Reno	Reno, NV				X
Newcomb College Center for Research on Women, Tulane University	New Orleans, LA				X

Women's Archives in the United States: Repository	City, State	Est'd before 1970	Est'd 1970s	Est'd 1980s	Est'd 1990s
Rutgers University, Women in Public Life Archives	New Brunswick, NJ				X
Schlesinger Library on the History of Women in America, Radcliffe College	Cambridge, MA	X			
Sophia Smith Collection, Smith College	Northhampton, MA	X			
Woman's Collection, Texas Woman's University	Denton, TX	X			
Women and Leadership Archives, Loyola University	Chicago, IL				X
Women Artists Archive, Sonoma State University	Rohnert, CA				X
Women's Archives, Special Collections Department, Duke University	Chapel Hill, NC			X	
Woman's Missionary Union Archives	Birmingham, AL			X	
Women's Movement Archives	Cambridge, MA			X	
Women's Archives at Oklahoma State University	Stillwater, OK				X
Women's Archives, University of Houston	Houston, TX				X

NOTES

This article was originally published in *Archival Issues: Journal of the Midwest Archives Conference* 24, no. 1 (1999).

[1] Eva Moseley, "Documenting the History of Women in America," *American Archivist* 36 (1973): 215–22.

[2] Suzanne Hildenbrand, "Women's Collections Today," *Special Collections* 3, nos. 3–4 (1986): 7.

[3] Debra Newman Ham commentary on "Decolonizing the Body: Kinship and the Nation" by Ramón A. Gutierrez, *American Archivist* 57, no. 1 (1994): 106.

[4] Judy Nolte Lensink, "Beyond the Intellectual Meridian: Transdisciplinary Studies of Women," *Pacific Historical Review* (1992): 463–80.

[5] Virginia Woolf, *A Room of One's Own* (New York: Harcourt, Brace, and Company, 1929).

[6] Anke Voss-Hubbard, "'No Documents—No History': Mary Ritter Beard and the Early History of Women's Archives," *American Archivist* 58, no. 1 (1995): 17. (See also Mary Trigg, "To Work Together for Ends Larger than the Self: The Feminist Struggles of Mary Beard and Doris Stevens in the 1930s," *Journal of Women's History* 7, no. 2 [1995]: 52–85); Hildenbrand, "Women's Collections Today," 2; Elizabeth Snapp, "The Woman's Collection: The Texas Woman's University Library," *Special Collections*, 3, nos. 3–4 (1986): 101–14.

[7] Martha S. Bell, "Special Women's Collections in US Libraries," *College and Research Libraries* 20 (May 1959): 235–42; Hildenbrand, "Women's Collections Today," 2.

[8] At the University of Iowa, for example, archivist Robert McCown began soliciting the papers of women active in politics and of feminist organizations in the early 1970s. As a result, the university's Special Collections Department acquired substantial collections of the papers of women legislators, party cochairs, local politicians, and persons active in the women's movement, as well as records of organizations such as the Iowa Women's Political Caucus, the League of Women Voters, pro- and anti-ERA groups, and National Organization for Women chapters. These collections became the foundation of the Iowa Women's Archives' holdings when it opened in 1992.

[9] Michigan History Division, Michigan Department of State, *Bibliography of Sources Relating to Women* (Lansing, MI: Michigan Department of State, 1975). The phrase "hidden from history" comes from Sheila Rowbotham's book *Hidden from History: 300 Years of Women's Oppression and the Fight Against It* (London:

Pluto Press, 1973). James P. Danky and Eleanor McKay, "Women's History Resources at the State Historical Society of Wisconsin," 2nd ed. (Madison: The State Historical Society of Wisconsin, 1975). Danky and McKay viewed the State Historical Society of Wisconsin as unusual in the depth and breadth of its sources on women: "The recent interest in women's history has presented problems for historians that parallel those faced by many minority, urban, and working class history researchers—the lack of documentation. This shortcoming has resulted from many collecting agencies using traditional formats and gathering traditional types of items. The outcome has been a lack of materials appropriate to the research task. The State Historical Society of Wisconsin constitutes an exception to the general pattern. Since its founding nearly 130 years ago the Society has collected books, manuscripts, archival materials, pictures, and museum artifacts that detail the accomplishments and positions of women in North American society." Danky and McKay, "Women's History Resources at the State Historical Society of Wisconsin," 1. Another example of this sort of guide is Catherine E. Thompson, "A Selective Guide to Women-Related Records in the North Carolina State Archives" (Raleigh: Division of Archives and History, 1977).

[10] Andrea Hinding, ed., *Women's History Sources: A Guide to Archives and Manuscript Collections in the United States*, 2 vols. (New York: R. R. Bowker Company, 1979). Coauthor Kären Mason was a writer on the Women's History Sources staff. She recalls the constant sense of wonder and excitement felt by the project staff at the number and variety of collections the project was uncovering. The compilers of *Women in the West: A Guide to Manuscript Sources* remark that "The publication of Women's History Sources marked a significant moment in the field of [women's history.]" Whereas once it had been assumed that there was not enough source material to allow research in women's history, "[t]he guide pointed scholars to the enormous possibilities and challenges of women's history as it identified available materials, suggested new questions, and spurred research." *Women in the West: A Guide to Manuscript Sources*, ed. Susan Armitage, Helen Bannan, Katherine G. Morrisey, Vicki L. Ruiz (New York: Garland Publishing, 1991), xiii.

[11] Polly Thistlethwaite, "The Lesbian Herstory Archives: Chronicling a People and Fighting Invisibility Since 1974," *Outweek* (24 September 1989): 36–39; Brenda Marston, "Women's History Archives: Documenting Women's Lives and Women's Organizations Today," *Feminist Collections* 10, no. 1 (1988): 5–8.

[12] Personal conversation, Tanya Zanish-Belcher with Lucinda Manning, one of the founders of the SAA Women's Collections Roundtable, 5 October 1999. In its application to SAA, the Women's Collections Roundtable noted its purpose as: 1) to identify and address the concerns of archivists who are interested in or

responsible for women's collections; 2) to promote the development, preservation and cooperative acquisition of women's papers and archival collections; 3) to develop a network of interested archivists, librarians, and historians to push for increased funding and support for women's historical collections and archival projects.

[13] May Lee Tom, comp., "Directory of Repositories Collecting Records of Women's Organizations" (Cambridge, MA: Schlesinger Library, 1994). The introduction states that the objectives of the network (formed in 1988 to identify repositories interested in collecting records of local, state, or regional affiliates of national women's organizations) and the survey were to: 1) improve sharing of information about organizational archives and coordination of collecting activities among repositories; 2) help organizations find appropriate repositories for their records, and 3) provide information about the location of archives of women's organizations to potential researchers.

[14] Anne Firor Scott, "Unfinished Business," *Journal of Women's History* 8, no. 2 (1996): 118. Joan Hoff has also noted the interrelation between women's history and feminism: "Since the 1970s, women's history in the United States has been strongly rooted in the politics of women's liberation–acknowledging the need to find a collective past for the purpose of contributing to a praxis whose goal is women's autonomy and self-realization." Hoff, "Introduction: An Overview of Women's History in the United States," in *Journal of Women's History Guide to Periodical Literature*, comp. Gayle V. Fischer (Bloomington and Indianapolis: Indiana University Press, 1992), 9.

[15] For a discussion of the founding of the Iowa Women's Archives, see Kären M. Mason, "History Through Women's Eyes: The Iowa Women's Archives," *Books at Iowa* 59 (November 1993): 15–22. Also see the Iowa Women's Archives website.

[16] Valerie Browne, "Women and Leadership Archives for Women's Studies Research," *Feminist Collections* 18, no. 3 (1997): 10–11.

[17] For an article describing the Archives of Women in Science and Engineering, please see the *Women Historians of the Midwest* 28, no. 1 (1999): 4–5. Also see the Iowa State University Special Collections Department website.

[18] Nancy Sahli, commentary on "Decolonizing the Body: Kinship and the Nation," (1994): 100.

[19] The Iowa Women's Archives received corporate and foundation funding in 1995 to support a multiyear project to document the history of African American women in Iowa. Archivist Kathryn Neal, hired for the project, acquired some fifty collections for the archives during her tenure on the project. Neal also received a small grant from the University of Iowa's Cultural Affairs Committee,

which enabled her to hire a graduate student to conduct ten oral history interviews.

[20] "Women in Politics in Northwest Ohio: The Historical Legacy" was initiated by Ann Bowers (Bowling Green State University) and Barbara Floyd (University of Toledo).

[21] Iowa State University of Science and Technology, Special Collections Department, Technical Leaflet #1, "Documenting Agriculture in Iowa," ed. Tanya Zanish-Belcher (January 1999). The Iowa Women's Archives received funding in 1998–1999 from the Iowa Farm Bureau Federation and Land O'Lakes to collect the papers of Iowa's rural women. Archivist Doris Malkmus has traveled around the state publicizing the project and soliciting papers for the archives. For more in-depth discussions of documentation strategies, see Joan Warnow-Blewitt and Larry J. Hackman, "The Documentation Strategy Process: A Model and Case Study" (American Institute of Physics, 1986) and Andrea Hinding, "Creating a Concept of Documentation," *Journal of American History* 80 (June 1993): 168–78.

[22] Lensink, "Beyond the Intellectual Meridian," 472–73.

[23] From the Jewish Women's Archive website, 1999.

[24] For more discussion of this issue, see Dianne Beattie, "An Archival User Study: Researchers in the Field of Women's History," *Archivaria* 29 (Winter 1989–1990): 33–50, and Jacqueline Goggin, "The Indirect Approach: A Study of Scholarly Users of Black and Women's Organizational Records in the Library of Congress Manuscript Division," *Midwestern Archivist* 11, no. 1 (1986): 57–67.

[25] Lensink, "Beyond the Intellectual Meridian," 471.

[26] Examples of websites that link users and collections are Archival Sites for Women's Studies (George Washington University); American Women's History: A Research Guide (Middle Tennessee State University Library); Women and Gender Studies Web Sites (Yale University Library); the International Center for Research on Women; the Canadian Women's Movement Archives; and Women's International Electronic University.

[27] The Roy J. Carver Charitable Trust funded a three-year project (the Carver Trust Project) at the Iowa State University Library to integrate electronic resources into core undergraduate classes, as well as a project at the University of Iowa Libraries to create a model training program for librarians and faculty on networked information sources (TWIST/Teaching with Innovative Style and Technology Program). Archivists will need to become involved with providing selected primary resources eletronically as well as utilizing these websites to assist in documenting the learning experience.

CHAPTER 8

Tacitly the Work of Women: Personal Archives and the Public Memory of Families

SUSAN TUCKER

When the ancient Greeks called stories "geroia," when Cicero called them "fabulae aniles," and when the pictures illustrating the Contes of Perrault represented an old woman telling a story to a circle of children, they were registering the extent to which the grandmother took charge of the narrative activity of the group.

—PAUL CONNERTON, *HOW SOCIETIES REMEMBER*

In some societies, the grandmother looks to the care of the young child and, through her, contact is made with the experience, knowledge, and benefit of about a half-century earlier.

—EDWARD ALBERT SHILS, *TRADITION*

Grandmothers survive longer and relay most family annals, but male forebears are more memorialized and better remembered; women are victims of genealogical amnesia.

—DAVID LOWENTHAL, "HISTORY AND MEMORY"

*Queen Matilda I of Germany (d. 968) . . . formally discharged
her own responsibility to her granddaughter Abbess Matilda of
Quedlinburg (d. 999). On her deathbed she is said to have handed
over a roll with the names to the 13-year-old girl with the request
to pray for the souls.*

—ELISABETH VAN HOUTS,
GENDER AND MEMORY IN MEDIEVAL EUROPE

*Both my grandmothers were interested in the family and provid-
ing that history. . . . One grandmother said if I wanted to learn
anything about the family, it was in her mother's bible. Both of
the grandmothers passed down a lot of pictures, and it's really
interesting because out of the whole—on both sides, I'm the family
member that ended up with their collections. And on my father's
side, my grandmother died early. The day she died, the day before,
I was at her home . . . I was young. Twelve. And she basically said,
"Take these things, if you don't get these, you'll never get these, if
you don't take them now." And, I had to walk with it. Because she
was too sick. . . . She said, "Take these."*

—FROM AN ORAL HISTORY INTERVIEW CONDUCTED IN 2007
BY SUSAN TUCKER WITH A WOMAN BORN IN 1959

IN THESE QUOTES, THE READER WILL BE STRUCK WITH THE FAMIL-
IAR. Who has not seen a grandmother extending her role as caretaker
of children to caretaker of memory? The "genealogical amnesia" is also

commonplace since, in most cultures, female children bear the names of fathers, give up these names in marriage, often tend to male memory, and give preference to the preservation of the papers of men over the papers of women. Yet what do we know of these roles, this gendering of memory keeping? Is not, too, our unawareness of women's roles very recognizable? This essay turns to the familiar but unexplored, traditional but often tacit, roles of women as preservers of family histories—a phenomenon of cultural significance since such narratives uniformly contextualize the larger stories of human experience.[1] The first part of this essay examines what is known about women as intermediaries to memory, touching on past times and on thoughts from family historians in contemporary society. The second part brings examples that show the gendered roles influencing the transmission of family records and memories. The essay explores the complexity of gender in recordkeeping and the transformation of the roles of women in personal archives, collections themselves changing in a world of increasing gender equality built yet on ancient gender divisions.

Among the archival community, personal archives are what were once called "family papers"; as such, they were not much considered or respected before their addition to a repository. As the essays in this volume show, archivists of the past more often concerned themselves with matters of institutional archives. Yet, there is increasing acknowledgment of the need to understand the varied impulses and practices surrounding documents created prior to entry into the doors of repositories, of papers and their retention and transfer before the sill of public memory. Archivists are now pondering over the creators of records, not only in historical but also in theoretical and practical contexts. Such emerging trends have revealed the significance of the tacit recordkeeping that women have traditionally performed.

Statistics and sociological studies confirm the familiarity of women as family history keepers in North America. Since the early twentieth century, women have predominated within family history groups. Today, women generally make up from 65 to 71 percent of members of such organizations.[2] Among certified genealogists in the United States, women also outnumber men. In Utah, for example, there are fifteen professional genealogists who are women and seven who are men. In Pennsylvania, there are seven women to three men. In Louisiana and Alabama, there are four women and no men.[3] Men also enter into family history work for different reasons than do women, reasons that impact a public/private schism in recordkeeping. Men begin genealogies to pursue a dream of publication or to fill spare time, whereas women tend to begin with an idea of connecting generations.[4] Women also are more likely than men to assume roles concerned with sharing photographs and other records among family and friends.[5]

Given this background, I conducted an ethnographic study of the practices of genealogy and album making during the years 2006 to 2008.[6] I chose these two worlds of family history since the latter seemed to preserve an older form of recordkeeping, one primarily reliant on oral accounts and private records, and hence could (and did) reveal much about transmission and the base of public memory as located in personal archives.[7] The family history scrapbook, for example, is said to be "a treasure for a genealogist to behold."[8] I wanted to test how this staple of the base of knowledge about families sometimes resides outside the institutional walls of archives, and to understand what these personal compilations could tell us about gendered memory keeping.

To enlarge upon the conflation of personal archives as family papers, I defined personal archives as those papers that had remained in private hands, as many scrapbooks on family history do. But I also considered *personal archives* as a larger term than *family papers*; today's digital materials created from family records, for example, are often part of what more and more people are calling "our archives." These electronic records, and to some degree many other types of family documents, become public in increments over time. Consequently, the term *personal archives* is used today to convey a diverse body of materials that is *always* in the process of becoming public, especially via shared records of public meetings and exhibitions, or via born-digital information generated through the collaborative experience of online genealogy.

I interviewed fifty-two people for my study: twenty-six genealogists (eleven males and fifteen females) and twenty-six album makers (one male and twenty-five females). I focused on their early influences and the means by which they intended to leave records for others, but one portion of my study asked about "gatekeeping" to family history, and about the roles and gender of people who had guided their work.[9]

Women as Intermediaries of Family History, Past and Present

In 841, the Frankish noble woman Dhuoda wrote a handbook on con-duct, family, and power for her teenage son William. Separated from him in the prosperous area around Nîmes, she encouraged attention to the ancestors on his father's side: "You will find written down at the end of the chapters of this book who they were and what their names were."[10] Though Dhuoda's handbook was unusual, her emphasis on memory keep-ing was not. Memory was a process of social commemoration embedded in women's "care for the dead, prayer for the salvation of the souls of kin, and child rearing." Foremost, the mechanism of oral memory "allowed aristocratic families to use the past to legitimate their present power."[11] Dhuoda's concerns were strategic ones.

Renaissance society continued and expanded these roles for women memory keepers even as writing became more important and became also a practice denied even many noble women.[12] Still, just as the famil-iarity of the quotes at the beginning of this essay continue to remind us, and as other essays in this volume show, women (not often afforded writ-ing skills) also created and sought alternative forms of evidence and dis-semination. They used the "images and texts" that "reified the private, not the public, sphere," often meaning those materials that told of family.[13] This personal world was transmitted in quilts and other textiles, in oral accounts, and in naming patterns.

By the eighteenth century, when more women became readers and writers, particular types of written memories came to be sanctioned. Women were permitted to speak within the family *of the family*, but only "to write for private audiences," especially for one another, and thus excelled at letters and diaries.[14] One other genre allowed to women was the scrapbook that emerged as a form of memory keeping in the nineteenth century.[15] The American scrapbook holding genealogical records can be traced to family registers, especially those created in Pennsylvania and New England in the late 1700s and the early 1800s. In a place called the Ephrata Cloister, early nineteenth-century German Americans made the first of these registers, deemed today "some of the earliest and finest" genealogical art and records in the Americas.[16] Both women and men created these *fraktur* in a way that presented recordkeeping within a domestic art piece where women's names appeared alongside those of men.[17] New England schoolgirls of this era also created similar registers, watercolors, and embroideries that contained lineage information, often documenting female as well as male names.[18] The flowering of democracy, at least within the home, extended to the preservation of women's names in some form.

By 1825, when the president of the Historical Society of Pennsylvania attempted to make various changes that would represent a new, more inclusive American approach to understanding the past, these ancient roles of women as memory keepers were considered.[19] As William Rawle boldly reasoned in his argument for allowing them entry into a hitherto all male organization, women had "superior memories" and acted as "living records of oral traditions."[20] Similarly, in 1897, when a few men (who are described as "audacious") dared to bring "up the subject of opening the membership to women" within the New England Historic Genealogical Society,[21] one member offered his opinion

> that women were naturally interested in the records of family history—more so, probably, than men—and he moved that the Council consider applications from women and to pass judgment upon them on the same conditions as they applied to male applicants.[22]

The professionalism of history in the late nineteenth century brought another permutation, however, to such roles. Since all but a few very privileged women were forbidden within the domains of university graduate programs, "a symbolic and material border" came to divide all women memory keepers from the men in the academy. Male historians became accepted as "orthodox representatives of knowledge and memory,"[23] tenders to "secular national memory" in this same milieu in which modern archives, libraries, and museums also grew.[24] Women, on the other hand, remained as guardians of "sacred tribal memory." Female family historians took a different path, somewhat like what other women writers of historical fiction, biography, and travel accounts did: they "articulated liminality that worked to mark out the boundaries, spaces, and locations of femininity."[25] Male genealogists, as well, came to embody "a genre of recollection" given less prestige than academic history,[26] but women's roles were ones that built upon centuries of family memories and so became the more pronounced stereotype.[27]

Still, by the late nineteenth and the early twentieth centuries, genealogy came to offer one of the few endeavors that allowed women to transform their role as private recordkeepers into a publicly visible intellectual pursuit. An example of the leadership roles women found in family history is present in the life of Susa Young Gates, a daughter of the Latter Day Saints (LDS) leader Brigham Young. Gates established the first of the denomination's classes in genealogical methods and organized the women of the church to complete family histories and to serve as models for the way their sons should take over this work. She also pushed for adequate funding for the library in Salt Lake City, Utah. Known popularly as the Thirteenth Prophet, an unusually distinctive honor for a woman in a patriarchal church, Gates made sure that the LDS library would be open to non-Mormons—a generosity, however potentially proselytizing, which would have far-reaching influence.[28]

Other middle-class women of the late nineteenth and early twentieth centuries worked through societies such as the National Society Colonial Dames XVII Century and the Daughters of the American Revolution (DAR) to take on positions not unlike those held by Gates. These groups changed the public face of the genealogist to a woman's face and changed women's practice of private recordkeeping into a public role.[29] In particular, women played a major role in erecting monuments to commemorate the Civil War dead and also in the establishment of Memorial Day. Their efforts now figure in any number of public displays of records within libraries (including the mammoth Washington, DC, headquarters of the DAR), book groups, and prizes and scholarships for countless students.[30] For years, too, the DAR chapters across the United States compiled and published "lineage books," and multivolume sets of Bible records.[31] In addition, "Since the early 1900s local DAR units donated one copy of each of their publications to the public libraries in their jurisdiction."[32] Thus, again, women made available knowledge on family history, moving into public realms genealogical data that would otherwise have remained very obscure.

Within the National Genealogical Society (NGS, established in 1903), early presidents, with some exceptions, were men.[33] Women were the workers, rather than the leaders—or the secretaries, rather than the presidents—but here too they were *visible, public* stewards of the past. They moved easily between public and private roles, shifting legions of documents from private homes into libraries, archives, and historical societies.[34] In 2012, the NGS thirteen-person board consisted of six men and seven women, with top leadership positions all falling to women (vice president, secretary, and past president), a ratio also unusual among many organizations in the United States.[35]

Family historians themselves, though they discuss the propensity of women-dominated groups, have never studied the traditional role of women as memory keepers. Among the twenty-six genealogists I interviewed in the 2006–2008 ethnographic study, nine of the interviewees believed a family historian was more apt to be a woman, one believed a family historian was more apt to be a man, and sixteen believed this status varied. Among those who believed a woman more likely to be a family historian than a man, three were men themselves. One of these, Chuck[36] (b. 1937), discussed how he got his information from other men (his father and a male cousin). When queried about this—"Except your father kept all those records. Right?"—he replied, "He had very few. And my cousin—he had loads of stuff. But he had too much. And so, he told me, 'When I get time, I'll get my wife to copy them, I'll call you to come here pick it up.' So there again, is the woman."

For the one surveyed genealogist who thought family history more apt to be a hobby of men, her reason revolved around the issue of time. "Men have more time," said Rebecca (b. 1939). She then referred to the reading room of the local library of the Latter Day Saints. "We have three men here reading, or four men here reading and one lady." She was a Mormon herself, and in her generation particularly (born before 1950), it was male children who were encouraged to write family histories. Yet she added, "My husband doesn't like genealogy. He's not a patient person . . . but his aunt lives across the street from us. . . . And she knows his family history for him."

Family historians were interested in the question about the gender of the gatekeeper to family history. As Thomas (b. 1940) stated,

> It is one of those things, like African American history, until some-
> one asks, people who are not touched by it won't consider it. It may
> well have been a way for women to have some power and it may
> have been that they, more than the men, were just interested in
> families, in the way people were shaped in families.

Arden (b. 1940) similarly mused,

> Never crossed my mind. But then it was important to what diseases
> the family got. Say your aunt had a child who was blind, well, the
> woman remembered that when she was pregnant. She might want
> to write that down more than a man would. And then women didn't
> get the name, you know. The family history was the compensation
> prize.

As Thomas continued, "women as history keepers" are sometimes "out-side the family." He said,

> Think about who is staffing those courthouses and who is the librar-
> ian. All women. And in my case, it was the church historian. One of
> the mothers of the church did a lot of documentation. And she died
> at 101 or 102 years of age, and she had a lot of personal information
> that she gave to me.

On the other hand, as Ingrid (b. 1941) and William (b. 1966) related, the keeper of records is often determined by who remains in a particular house or a particular locale. According to Ingrid,

> In reading how to improve my genealogy process, I was reminded that my dad's first cousins and my mom's first cousins all had the same grandmother. And so, in my dad's case, since his family's home had been burned, I thought, well, I would check his cousins. And I just found a wealth of information there. And I find that most of the record groups from the immigrants that are maintained usually stay with the last family that that person is living with before they pass away.

Similarly, William explained the reasons the family recordkeeper in his father's family was his father's sister:

> Of all my dad's siblings, she didn't leave the area she grew up in. She stayed there, she married someone local, she pretty much stayed within five miles of where most of them were born. So she was the one. She knew the most family history of her generation of my dad's side.

In other words, if women do not move around the country as much as men, if they stay close to parents, it is they who inherit family papers. Yet, as Thomas said, "It depends on if a family is matriarchal or patriarchal and a lot of that depends on how many daughters, how many sons, how the money is earned if any, if there is a family home passed to the daughters or sons. So many things."

In their responses to this question about whether a gatekeeper to family history was more likely to be a man or a woman, album makers were less verbose. Uniformly all twenty-six, including one male album maker, felt women were more likely to be the keeper of family history. How did they show this belief in their albums? Ten of fifty-two heritage albums shown to me "as favorite albums" featured women ancestors as the "main character." Thirty-two featured both men and women ancestors, but began with the male. The others were created around specific subjects: the military (which for the most part meant male ancestors); material

objects such as a christening gown (male and female babies, but a tradition mediated by women) and dolls (also mediated by girls and women);
houses (of interest to both males and females); and holidays (usually more
female-dominated preparations for celebrations, but football games too
were included here).

One contemporary industry report suggests that scrapbook makers
are 98 percent female, 85 percent Caucasian, and 63 percent married with
children living at home.[37] Scrapbook making in its current incarnation—
and family history albums in particular—are often credited to a Mormon
couple, the Christensens, who gained attention at the World Conference
on Genealogy in Salt Lake City in 1980.[38] At least one journalist in the
early twenty-first century noted that scrapbook makers still are more
likely to be located in Utah—a state where family history is a part of all
religious training within the LDS Church and where women generally
have traditional roles within the family—than in other states.[39]

The most well-known scrapbook vendor, Creative Memories, was
born outside Utah, but with a religious tenor and particular stance on
women in traditional family roles somewhat like that of the Mormons.
One key element of the Creative Memories story is the recollection of
one of its founders, Rhonda Anderson, about learning scrapbooking from
her mother, a matriarchal responsibility to be passed on to daughters.[40]
Another element is the support of right-wing political commentator
James Dobson. In 1991 and again in 2007, Dobson gave Anderson and
cofounder Cheryl Lightle the limelight on his *Focus on the Family* radio
show. Both times he praised Creative Memories for allowing women to
work at home, that is, especially in traditional roles as wives and mothers.[41] Yet another feature of the Creative Memories story is the use of testimonials placing emphasis on positive memories in building family unity.
Recalling Rhonda Anderson's scrapbooks, for example, the lawyer who
first helped in the establishment of the company, noted that

> every day he dealt with people who had given up on each other,
> their marriages, their children, their jobs and their lives in general.
> He was sure that if they'd preserved positive, cherished memories in
> the same loving way she had, they wouldn't be in his office.[42]

Creative Memories maintains that album making can hold society together, a coded message to women about their role as caregivers and nurturers. The work proceeds "page by page, out of your heart and onto the page." The work of so many women, given the title of consultants, forms "more than just a photo album company." As the publicity states: "We are about tradition, and we have been since the beginning. We are about legacies. Without this higher purpose, we would be just another album company."[43]

Yet Creative Memories also can be seen as providing alternate roles to women not given many opportunities for a public voice. Any cursory glance at these online scrapbooks reveals that these scrapbookers preserve the same culture that Todd Gernes found among nineteenth-century women: they become producers of local history, groups with considerable creativity that allow women to achieve their own identity without the forced hand of professional, structured history. They practice on the sidelines—yes, liminality again—but with specific goals, adaptive responses in recording the world as they see it, and efficiency, especially given the power of sharing with wide circles of people via the Internet.[44]

Genealogical Amnesia or Genealogical Complexity?

Why would this identity be so important? One reason is found in the genealogical amnesia mentioned at the beginning of this essay—the "compensation prize" mentioned by one of my informants. Laurel Thatcher Ulrich phrased it this way: women have a need to create "narratives lost in conventional political narratives, and writing—with a needle as well as a pen—[establishing] . . . identity beyond death."[45] Two stories told to me involve the permutations of such identity-narratives shaped by patterns of transmission dependent on specific social circumstances and suggestive of the complexity of gendered recordkeeping changing over time.

As with most family histories in the United States, both stories begin with migration, a focus on a person who is sometimes called the "crossing ancestor" (one who made the journey across an ocean to North America) who inspires by his or her passage "from the Old World to this one."[46] Most often this ancestor is a male because, according to the family historians and album makers, his records can be more easily found.

This tradition of male lineage illuminates legacy practices of ancient families selectively preserving patriarchal records and searching history through names of male family members.[47] In addition, Donald Harman Akenson notes a remaining patriarchal bias in what he calls the "kernel genealogical narrative." His example shows the names, dates of death, and ages at deaths of two people ("John Teskey" and "Anne, Beloved Wife").[48] The omission of the wife's last name is purposeful, according to Akenson. In contrast, all that is actually needed for any genealogical trail is that a woman gives birth to a child who lives. The fact that many genealogies begin with a male and sometimes even leave out his female partner reveals that genealogies can be seen as being "dictated by cultural desires rather than by biological reality."[49] In short, the practice, as Dhuoda described in the ninth century, of concentrating on the male line, continued.[50] Consider the fact that even a recent exhibit on women's needlework showing colonial US family lineage took the vernacular title, "Who's Your Daddy?"[51]

Yet I was lucky enough to hear one dramatic family history that evolved from a female "crossing ancestor." I begin with that one here, since it especially has to do with women as childbearers who also have the advantage of longer lives than men—another kernel narrative common to the lives of many women.

Marie Rosalie Préjean Pécot (1741–1813)

In this first family case, Carolyn Ivy Shimek (b. 1934) told me of tracing genealogy through records; her distant cousin, Mary Anne DeBoisblanc (b. 1925), a primitive artist, told of using genealogy to find subjects for many of her paintings.[52] Their shared ancestor is a woman named Marie Rosalie Préjean (later Pécot, 1741–1813) who, along with her family and many others, was expelled from Acadie (now Nova Scotia, Canada) by the British in the mid-1700s in an event remembered as

The Reunion of the Prejean Sisters by Mary Anne DeBoisblanc.
Photograph of acrylic painting on wood. Private collection.

Le Grand Dérangement. The teenager Marie Rosalie, her younger sister, four brothers, and their mother were put on one ship; two older sisters and their husbands were put on another ship. Some forty-five years later, the sisters as very old women were reunited, but not before a succession of moves in North America and the Caribbean.

All of these moves have been traced by Carolyn and then made publicly accessible by Mary Anne. They are not happy stories, but rather ones of persistence: besides the sadness of the expulsion from Acadie, there are tales of sicknesses, no chance for the education of children, harsh labor, revolutions, beheadings, dangerous ship voyages, horrible decisions handed down from governments in France and England often "destroying countless lives," and yet a community of kinship enduring through time.[53]

Before the late nineteenth century, the memories of Marie Rosalie's life were not inscribed within the family and only scantily inscribed by church and governmental authorities. Narratives, it is said, "simplify." The presence of a beginning, middle, end, or an "original state of equilibrium, a disruption, and a resolution," make the past both tenable and interest-ing.[54] But in genealogy this simplification can take decades, awaiting the time until the story is "needed" (thus attending to identity) and the time when records can be gathered (thus attending to evidence). For the broader Pecot family (whose name was Americanized in dropping the accent), a story from the years 1750 to 1815 has been told in increments over more than two centuries and told in different ways by men and women.

Carolyn first encountered the story of Marie Rosalie in the 1960s via a 1924 newspaper clipping and another small piece of paper discussing this clipping. According to both, around 1890, two granddaughters of Marie Rosalie (Hermina Bouillet Martel and Mathilda Perret) had been told by their mother (a daughter of Marie Rosalie) of the family's experiences of Le Grand Dérangement. They spoke in French, and Hermina's grandson, Gabriel Scully, translated their words to English and wrote them down. According to the published article, Hermina's son, J. Scully Martel, is the "heroic custodian" of the story. Why? Because he "went to great lengths to track down the story of the four exiled sisters." One of Marie Rosalie's sons, Charles Pecot, is also praised since he was "one of the French pio-neers who settled on the [Bayou] Teche."[55] The focus here, then, was on the two grown men, away from their female storytellers, but Carolyn was riveted by the account of the sisters' reunion and, as a genealogist, was interested in the two granddaughters who told the story.

Carolyn also recalled immediately another public male voice as found in "a little book." Written by a distant male cousin, Thomas Frère Kramer, this 2002 book repeats the importance of J. Scully Martel in making known the story of Marie Rosalie.[56] This pattern of the male voice finding the more public role could be seen as both an "appropriation of voice" and an example of the complexity of gender within family history. Robert Fisher, in tracing a similar account that was told within a family by women but brought to public hearing by local male historians, noted:

> Feminist scholars might read . . . a struggle of [women] to make
> their voices heard. . . . Historians of a contrary bent could argue
> that these members of the masculine elite recognized the value and
> ensured the survival of their feminine voices. Still others might

see it as proof that the bonds of family are stronger than those of gender, class or time.[57]

Disregarding the questions of voice and assignation of authority, the reunion of the four sisters remains the focus of the Pecot family story. The longevity of the sisters again enters the picture as one factor in how public memories are formed. None of the brothers of the family lived as long, according to Carolyn, and Marie Rosalie especially had "so many children. Her descendants are everywhere. So they are interested in her."

Mary Anne and Carolyn also linked their family history to a collective memory about Acadie and Acadian Louisiana, another reunion of those parted in Le Grand Dérangement. This is the statue of literary heroine Evangeline in St. Martinville, Louisiana. In one of her exhibition catalogs, Mary Anne wrote:

> Ever since childhood, Evangeline has had a mystical hold on me as an Acadian woman. . . . It was Evangeline's spirit that guided me to the Acadian Memorial. . . . It was here, I realized that Marie Rosalie's story belonged. Then my Pecot cousin [and here she is referring to Carolyn] told me Marie Rosalie was actually buried on February 11, 1813 at St. Martin de Tours [a nearby cemetery].[58]

Symbolically and in reality, Mary Anne made Evangeline a part of her own family. In other exhibition catalogs, a photograph of the statue and a drawing of Longfellow are always near her own Acadian family images.[59]

The 1847 epic poem "Evangeline" by Henry Wadsworth Longfellow itself has been memorized by countless schoolchildren, but is worth exploring in terms of the transmission of gendered memories and the formation of public memory in general. The poem follows a young Acadian woman in her search for her lost love, Gabriel. The two have been parted from one another, much as the sisters were, during the expulsion of the French from their homes. Longfellow based his story on a secondhand account told by a Massachusetts Episcopal priest. To learn the landscape of Louisiana, the poet relied upon his sister's telling of a journey to New Orleans and a panorama called "Three-Mile Painting," a moving screen that allowed viewers to sit in Boston and experience what a journey down

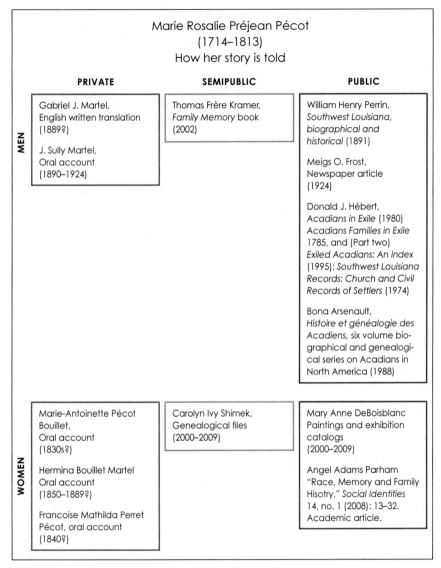

Figure 1: Marie Rosalie Préjean Pécot: How her story is told.

the Mississippi River would be like.[60] Longfellow also visited libraries and read T. C. Halliburton's *Historical and Statistical Account of Nova Scotia* (1829) and Guillaume Thomas François Raynal's account of the expulsion published in 1770.[61] It is notable that Longfellow did not rely upon genealogical records, though one scholar at least speculates on his use of the Massachusetts Historical Society.[62]

The Louisiana statue was sculpted during the making of the 1929 film *Evangeline* produced by the Edwin Carewe Company of Hollywood. The famous actress Dolores Del Rio, who played the role of Evangeline, paid for the monument and had it fashioned in her likeness. It became an immediate tourist attraction. The unveiling was attended by some fifteen thousand people, including a group of Acadians from Canada.[63]

Both the poem and the statue changed many lives, not only as markers of the past, but also in specific personal ways. The name *Evangeline*, for example, began to be chosen for girl children, and contests crowning selected teenagers as Evangeline and Gabriel became yearly events.

Before the poem's popularity, the name *Evangeline* was not an Acadian one. Rather, Longfellow chose it to represent both the angelic nature and the messenger role of an ideal and patient woman—a woman who carried and lived memory.[64] Evangeline—the exiled woman, the statue, the song, the poem itself, and its popularity—functions as a gendered history within a larger international history. Marie Rosalie functions also in much this same way on a smaller scale.

Miho Baccich (1859–1935)

Another crossing-ancestor account came from a family whose members center their history around the story of a Croatian ship captain named Miho Baccich (1859–1935). A great-grandson of Miho, Jonathan Jordan (b. 1953), introduced me to what he called "our family story." He spoke of the 1990 publication of a book by his cousin, Gus Rathe (b. 1921). The book tells the story of a handwritten family manuscript describing Miho's survival of a shipwreck in the late nineteenth century.[65] Three women in the family also began their interview about family history with mention of this book—with the published record of the male storyteller.

The family members, both male and female, then told of a teenaged Miho who left his home in Croatia in 1875 as a worker aboard his uncle's barque, the *Stefano*, bound for England to take coal to Hong Kong. Off the western coast of Australia, the ship ran aground and only Miho and another teenager survived. After near starvation, cannibalism of dead sailors,

Baccich Family Portrait. Eunice Baccich Collection,
Newcomb Archives, Tulane University.

and treks through the hot desert, the boys were saved by Aborigines who
fed them until they healed enough for a trek to a distant village. Here, the
survivors met the captain of a pearling ship who secured passage back
to Europe. At home, Miho and the other survivor dictated all they could
remember to a Jesuit scholar who recorded the experiences of the shipwreck, the long journey of survival, the flora and fauna of the land, the
rescue by Aborigines, and the assistance of colonial white Australians.
Two copies of the manuscript were made. One was given to Miho and one
remained with his parents, eventually passing to his sister "since she never
emigrated."

The society in which Miho lived influenced how the story was told,
of course. Miho's account in the manuscript begins with his recollection
of his mother's fear for him on the day of his departure. This beginning
demonstrates more than the dynamics of the family; it tells us about the
record of his memory and the milieu of recordkeeping among seafaring
families. Such families then, as now, understood the possibility of death at

sea. They also understood the need to keep records of goods and people, and the need to give thankfulness for survival. Jonathan's mother, Peggy Jordan (b. 1926), showed a page in Gus's book with a votive painting, circa 1877, still hanging in Our Lady of Mercy Church in Dubrovnik, commissioned by Miho's mother in gratitude for the survival of the boys[66]—evidence of these memory traditions.

Ordered chronologically, the Baccich archives dates from 1876, with the first letter Miho wrote to tell of his survival, to a 2008 annotation of the account by some descendants of the Aborigines who rescued him.

The family and others have spread these various texts literally and figuratively among various people and repositories across three continents and now also in a number of online pages. Some of the records still exist in their original form within the family; others are located in archives, museums, a church, and within other families. Each generation reshapes the "collection" of the memory but it is ordered in relation to the story of Miho—his shipwreck and survival, and then too his passage to New Orleans where he settled in the 1880s.

Gus's book indirectly describes how he found records via the first translation of the manuscript by his grandmother, Angelina Cietcovich Baccich. Family members today recall that Angelina (whose name, so like that of Evangeline, means angel and messenger) was "a scholar," a new role for women of her time. The grandchildren's and great-grandchildren's pride in this achievement, so many generations later, was noticeable. Angelina's translation of the Italian manuscript written by the Jesuit priest allowed her children and grandchildren to read the account. She wrote in a simple notebook, from which one daughter typed the account and another daughter, who was skilled at bookbinding, bound in

> dark green leather (a very stiff, substantial cover, just like a commercial book). On the front in the upper third is imprinted (embossed? into the leather) a shield with three seahorses, behind which are the wavy lines of the sea. Above that is the title, again embossed.[67]

Each of the seven children of Angelina and Miho was given a copy of the translation. The bound volume and the notebook were given to the oldest daughter. Translation, Bruno Latour reminds us, is not just about the shift from one language to another, but about "displacement, drift, invention, mediation, the creation of a link that did not exist before . . . [the modification of] two elements or agents."[68] Transmission too depends upon these other steps. Today, online, an Australian scholar has provided another translation of the manuscript and annotated it to discuss issues of authorship and translation, noting what Angelina added and what she left out from the original Italian. The Italian manuscript was itself a translation of the Croatian account into the language of the priest recorder, the language of commerce in that part of the Dalmatian coast.[69]

Meanwhile, family history was told as being lived through Miho's and Angelina's examples in other ways too. Peggy and her daughters cast present activities of the family, especially the making of family albums, alongside this larger account of Miho, which can then be told to future generations. Their albums are huge (three inches in depth) loose-leaf binders with photocopied pages, very like the albums popularized as family memory books by Marielen Christensen in Utah. Each binder was duplicated to be given by the women as gifts to family members.

The Baccich account is relevant to a gendered history in another way also. Miho had not only an educated wife to translate the story, but also six daughters and one son—a female-dominated family in which the youngest daughter, Anna, typed the translation from her mother's notebooks and gave them to the next generation. Much about family history depends upon these types of circumstances of transmission: who is taught to type (or use other technology), who is allowed to study bookbinding, and who lives surrounded by the circumstances that present opportunities and reasons for recordkeeping.

Miho himself represented his survival in Australia in another way that his descendants continue to articulate via women in the family. A name—that most familiar and living form of a genealogical legacy—was given to one of his daughters to convey the way Miho and Angelina wanted the story remembered. She was born on 27 October 1890, the fifteenth anniversary of his shipwreck. He initially chose the name "Australia," but his multilingual New Orleanian wife had different ideas. She suggested a Greek name—Euxenia—from *eu-xenos*, which translated literally as "high [regard for] the stranger"[70] and was chosen because "of the lifesaving care bestowed on their husband and father, the stranger, by the people of the distant land."[71] Today the name has been passed down through three generations of female descendants.

One of the great-granddaughters, Mary Lee (b. 1945), evokes naming practices in another way, easily available to her because she lives in the early twenty-first century:

> I changed my [last] name to Baccich when I entered the seminary, to invoke the strong spirit of Miho. After doing so, I have gone to Australia twice and am rebuilding in New Orleans, the [part of the] city here [that] he and his partners built, the Gentilly Terrace area. I believe changing my name evoked all his genetic material within me and influenced my life to include his own history. Meeting with the Aborigines fulfilled a dream he had of returning to Australia and meeting with them again.

She reverses in part the genealogical amnesia of women's names, the "patrilineal problem."[72] There were once very few other ways to re-enter into family trees the many married names of the female family members. On a mundane level, an album from 1915 tried to do so. It was *Bailey's Family Ancestral Album*, in which one could find maternal lines through "strategically placed cutaways," a kind of linking before the Internet, allowing jumps across the convention of taking a male surname.[73] But it was far from popular.

Family Stories, Personal Archives, Public Memory

Like other family accounts, the Marie Rosalie and the Miho stories will have future meanings, different layers of personal and public relevance, gendered or not. After all, record users of whatever sex choose what to study, and they write according to their particular view of the world.[74]

Such circumstances, however, will more and more be shaped by the very fact that personal archives, again a new term for archivists in the early twenty-first century, are becoming more plentiful and accessible, both in their addition to repositories and their presence online.[75] What makes private records "an archives" is both the use of the term by increasing numbers of people outside traditional repositories and academia and, within archival science, their function as public presentations.[76]

Family history records, then, are often seen as both public *and* private. This mixture too remains important to the study of gender and archives because of the historic alignment of so much about archives with public records and of so much about women with the private or personal realm. Consider that Tom Nesmith's interpretation of a record includes consideration of the "evolving" nature, the continuing "mediation of understanding about some phenomena which a given society deems to be in the public domain."[77] This domain itself changes over time, and thus what qualifies as a record also changes. What was his 1999 example? Women's records, which in the past, he noted, had often not been considered worthy of placement in archives at all.[78]

The lacunae of women's records within public archives and their overarching presence in personal archives tell then of the gendered traditions in archival recordkeeping. Women (along with others whose records were not transmitted to the public arena) had good reason to employ a number of steps to manage memories in private and to make sure those private memories found some way to the next generation, so they did not remain forever private, did not remain liminal. The growing awareness of "personal archives" reveals this evolution toward public transmission of family memory performed by women. Future study turns on the conceptual framework of those who were prototypical personal archivists long before the use of such a term was present in our literature.

NOTES

[1] I am indebted here to Robert C. Fisher and Eric Ketelaar who, as far as I can tell, were among the first to ask about the position of women as record and memory keepers in archival studies. Fisher, "'The Grandmother's Story': Oral Tradition, Family Memory, and a Mysterious Manuscript," *Archivaria* 57 (Spring 2004): 126–27; Ketelaar, "Sharing: Collected Memories in Communities of Records," *Archives and Manuscripts* 33, no. 1 (May 2005): 49.

[2] Pamela J. Drake, "Findings from the Fullerton Genealogy Study, A Master's Thesis Project" (master's thesis, California State University, Psychology Department, 2001), http://psych.fullerton.edu/genealogy/#RESULT, accessed 13 August 2012. Jean Cooper, "The Librarian and the Genealogist Should Be Friends" (presentation at the Virginia Library Association Annual Conference, Williamsburg, Virginia, 20 October 2005), http://www.vla.org/demo/Conference/05Conf/Presentations/IntrotoGenealogy.ppt, accessed 5 October 2008. Note that Cooper quotes statistics from ALA Library Fact Sheet 6, "Public Library Use," 2002, http://www.ala.org/Template.cfm?Section=libraryfactsheet&Template=/ContentManagement/ContentDisplay.cfm&ContentID=112163, accessed 7 April 2006. Women make up 77 percent, 62 percent, 71 percent, respectively, of current members from three genealogical societies studied extensively from 2006 to 2009 in Alabama and Louisiana in the ethnography mentioned below in endnote 6.

[3] "Find a Genealogist," Board for Certification of Genealogists, http://www.bcgcertification.org/ associates/index.php, accessed 13 August 2012.

[4] Ronald D. Lambert, "Looking for Genealogical Motivation," *Families* 34, no. 3 (August 1995): 158–59; Lambert, "Profile of the Membership of the Ontario Genealogical Society," *Families* 34, no. 2 (May 1995): 74–75. See also Roy Rosenzweig and David P. Thelen, *The Presence of the Past: Popular Uses of History in American Life* (New York: Columbia University Press, 1998), 23.

[5] Pierre Bourdieu, *Photography: A Middle Brow Art*, trans. Shaun Whiteside (Stanford, CA: Stanford University Press, 1990), 19; Claire Grey, "Theories of Relativity" in *Family Snaps: The Meanings of Domestic Photography*, ed. Patricia Holland and Jo Spence (London: Virago, 1991), 107; Deborah Chambers, "Family as Place: Family Photograph Albums and the Domestication of Public and Private Space," in *Picturing Place: Photography and the Geographical Imagination*, ed. Joan M. Schwartz and James Ryan (New York: Palgrave Macmillan, 2003), 97.

[6] Susan Tucker, "The Most Public of All History: Family History and Heritage Albums in the Transmission of Records/Genealogie en Familiealbums als

Dragers van Collectieve Herinnering" (PhD diss., University of Amsterdam, 2009).

[7] Manuals on family history begin with the private records, for example, one chapter among ten to twenty on public records. See, for example, various editions of *The Source: A Guidebook of American Genealogy* (Provo, UT: Ancestry Publishing, 2006). See also Penelope Papailias, *Genres of Recollection: Archival Poetics and Modern Greece* (New York: Palgrave MacMillan, 2005), 2.

[8] F. Wilbur Helmbold, *Tracing Your Ancestry: A Step-by-Step Guide to Researching Your Family History* (Birmingham, AL: Oxmoor House, 1976), 91. See also Sandra Hargreaves Luebking and Loretto Dennis Szucs, "The Foundations of Family History Research," in Szucs and Luebking, *The Source*, 3rd ed. (Provo, UT: Ancestry Publishing, 2006), 2–16; Bev Kirschner Braun, *Crafting Your Own Heritage Album* (Cincinnati: Betterway Books, 2000).

[9] The question was phrased as "In general, some of the publications on family history that I have seen begin with the statement that every family has its own historian, someone who keeps family records. Can you tell me what you think about this statement and also how this plays out in your own family?" If it did not become apparent who such a person was, they were then asked, "In general, is this person more likely to be a woman or a man?"

[10] Elisabeth van Houts, *Gender and Memory in Medieval Europe* (Toronto: University of Toronto Press, 1999), 66.

[11] Michael Innes, "Keeping It in the Family: Women and Aristocratic Memory, 700–1200," in *Medieval Memories: Men, Women and the Past, 700–1300*, ed. Elisabeth van Houts (Essex, UK.: Pearson Education, 2001), 17.

[12] Van Houts, *Gender and Memory*; Van Houts, ed., *Medieval Memories*; Patrick J. Geary, *Phantoms of Remembrance: Memory and Oblivion at the End of the First Millennium* (Princeton, NJ: Princeton University Press, 1994); Daniel R. Woolf, "A Feminine Past? Gender, Genre, and Historical Knowledge in England, 1500–1800," *American Historical Review* 102, no. 3 (June 1997), 645–79.

[13] "Domesticity," in *The Routledge Companion to Feminism and Postfeminism*, ed. Sarah Gamble (New York: Routledge, 2001), 218.

[14] Dale Spender, *Man-Made Language*, 2nd ed. (London: Routledge, 1985), 192.

[15] Todd Steven Gernes, "Recasting the Culture of Ephemera: Young Women's Literary Culture in Nineteenth Century America" (PhD diss., Brown University, 1992), 281, 280–353; Katherine Ott, Susan Tucker, and Patricia P. Buckler, "An Introduction to the History of Scrapbooks," in *The Scrapbook in American Life*, ed. Susan Tucker, Katherine Ott, and Patricia Buckler (Philadelphia: Temple

University Press, 2006), 3–27. Tamar Katriel and Thomas Farrell, "Scrapbooks as Cultural Texts: An American Art of Memory," *Text and Performance Quarterly* 11, no. 1 (January 1991): 7; Ellen Gruber Garvey, *The Adman in the Parlor: Magazines and the Gendering of Consumer Culture, 1880s to 1910s* (New York: Oxford University Press, 1996); Juliana Kuipers, "Scrapbooks: Intrinsic Value and Material Culture," *Journal of Archival Organization* 2, no. 3 (2004): 83–91.

[16] Corinne Earnest and Russell Earnest, *To the Latest Posterity: Pennsylvania–German Family Registers in the Fraktur Tradition* (University Park: Pennsylvania State University Press, 2004), 6–8; Gloria Seaman Allen, *Family Record: Genealogical Watercolors and Needlework* (Washington, DC: DAR Museum, 1989), 7. See also Free Library of Philadelphia, "Welcome to the Free Library of Philadelphia's Digital Collection of Fraktur," http://libwww.library.phila.gov/fraktur, accessed 13 August 2012.

[17] Earnest and Earnest, *To the Latest Posterity*, 17, 40, 30–31, 35, 40, 81, 99, 107–111, 114.

[18] Peter Benes, "Decorated New England Family Registers, 1770 to 1850," in *The Art of Family: Genealogical Artifacts in New England*, ed. D. Brenton Simons and Peter Benes (Boston: New England Historic Genealogical Society, 2002), 15.

[19] Sally Griffith, *Serving History in a Changing World: The Historical Society of Pennsylvania in the Twentieth Century* (Philadelphia: Historical Society of Pennsylvania, 2005), 21, 24. This effort, however, also muddied the waters when later leaders of the society considered genealogists as less appealing users. Women also were not given full membership until 1860.

[20] Griffith, *Serving History in a Changing World*, 24.

[21] William Carroll Hill, *A Century of Genealogical Progress, Being a History of the New England Historic Genealogical Society, 1845–1945* (Boston: New England Historic Genealogical Society, 1945).

[22] Hill, *A Century of Genealogical Progress*, 41, 42–43. In 1898, thirty-six women immediately were allowed to join this prestigious group.

[23] Richard Harvey Brown and Beth Davis-Brown, "The Making of Memory: The Politics of Archives, Libraries and Museums in the Construction of National Consciousness," *History of the Human Sciences* 11, no. 4 (November 1998): 21.

[24] Brown and Davis-Brown, "The Making of Memory," 19; Ian Robertson, "Emile Durkheim," in *Encyclopedia of Sociology* (Guilford, CT: Duskin Publishing Group, 1974), 92.

[25] Bonnie G. Smith, *The Gender of History: Men, Women, and Historical Practice* (Cambridge, MA: Harvard University Press, 1998), 165.

[26] Papailias, *Genres of Recollection*, 2.

[27] This thinking in accounts of early local history societies in the United States is documented in Griffith, *Serving History in a Changing World*, and Hill, *A Century of Genealogical Progress*. It may not be true for other countries outside the United States, a comparison I am now making in other work.

[28] James B. Allen and Jessie L. Embry, "Provoking the Brethren to Good Works: Susa Young Gates, the Relief Society, and Genealogy," *BYU Studies* 31 (1991): 115–38.

[29] Wallace Evan Davies, *Patriotism on Parade: The Story of Veterans' and Hereditary Organizations in America, 1783–1900* (Cambridge, MA: Harvard University Press, 1955), 58–63, 227–32; Francesca Constance Morgan, "'Home and Country': Women, Nation, and the Daughters of the American Revolution, 1890–1939" (PhD diss., Columbia University, 1998), 151–217.

[30] Morgan, "'Home and Country,'" 151–54, 170–75.

[31] Kory L. Meyerink, ed., *Printed Sources: A Guide to Published Genealogical Records* (Provo, UT: Ancestry Publishing, 1998), 474. See, for example, Daughters of the American Revolution, Delaware State Society, *Bible Records— Delaware* (Newark, DE: The Society, 1944–1967).

[32] Mary Ann Sheble, "Genealogical Libraries and Collections," in *Encyclopedia of Library History*, Garland Reference Library of Social Science, vol. 503, ed. Wayne A. Wiegand and Donald G. Davis Jr., (New York: Garland Publishing, 1994), 232.

[33] Shirley Langdon Weaver, *The National Genealogical Society: A Look at Its First One Hundred Years* (Washington, DC: National Genealogical Society, 2003), http://www.ngsgenealogy.org/history_of_ngs_4.0.pdf, accessed 1 December 2008; see especially the appendices.

[34] Morgan, "'Home and Country,'" 170–75.

[35] "NGS Board of Directors," National Genealogical Society, http://www.ngsgenealogy.org/aboard.cfm, accessed 13 June 2011; Jan Alpert, President of the National Genealogical Society, email to author, 21 May 2011.

[36] All names from the interviews, unless specifically noted, are pseudonyms.

[37] EK Success Reports, February 2007; see also Creative Memories website, My Creative Memory, "Scrapbooking Statistics," http://www.mycreativememory

.com/main.asp?page=%7B3B764E60-ACFE-4555-B447-4AE0BFBF7D69%7D, accessed 13 August 2012.

[38] "Keeping Memories Alive" website, "KMA History—We Invented Scrapbooking," Scrapbook.com, http://www.scrapbook.com/history.php, accessed 13 August 2012.

[39] Kelly Crow, "Scrapbook Industry Woos Male Crafters," *The Wall Street Journal*, 7 April 2007.

[40] Company History, "The Webway Opportunity," Antioch Company, http://www.antiochcompany.com/webwayopp.htm, accessed 10 July 2008.

[41] "Making Memories that Last," sound recording; "Making Memories that Last, Focus on the Family: Years Later," DVD.

[42] Katherine B. Ponder, "Company Spotlight: Creative Memories" (April 2007), Direct Selling News, http://www.directsellingnews.com/index.php/site/comments/company_spotlight_creative_memories, accessed 12 August 2008.

[43] Cheryl Lightle and Rhonda Anderson, *The Creative Memories Way* (Colorado Springs: WaterBrook Press, 2002), 4.

[44] Todd Steven Gernes, "Recasting the Culture of Ephemera: Young Women's Literary Culture in Nineteenth Century America" (PhD diss., Brown University, 1992), 281, 280–353.

[45] Laurel Thatcher Ulrich, "Creating Lineages," in Simons and Benes, *The Art of Family*, 11.

[46] John Seabrook, "A Reporter at Large: The Tree of Me," *New Yorker Magazine*, March 2001, 60.

[47] A Google search with the subject "crossing ancestor" in July 2009 turned up 166 links, with 150 devoted to a male ancestor; the other ten were not devoted to women but to topics not concerned with family history per se.

[48] Donald Harmon Akenson, *Some Family: The Mormons and How Humanity Keeps Track of Itself* (Montreal: McGill-Queen's University Press, 2007), 75, 80–81.

[49] Akenson, *Some Family*, 75.

[50] Francesca Morgan, "Lineage as Capital: Genealogy in Antebellum New England," *New England Quarterly* 83, no. 2 (June 2010): 263–69.

[51] Winterthur Museum, "Who's Your Daddy?," webcast exploring 2009 exhibition, http://www.winterthur.org/?p=804, accessed 13 August 2012.

[52] Because of the public nature of the work of Mary Anne DeBoisblanc and the Miho Baccich story, the names here are not pseudonyms.

[53] Donald J. Hébert, *Acadian Families in Exile, 1785* (Cecilia, LA: Hébert Publications, 1980), 347.

[54] Michael Schudson, "Dynamics of Distortion in Collective Memory," in *Memory Distortion: How Minds, Brains, and Societies Reconstruct the Past*, ed. Daniel L. Schacter and Joseph T. Coyle (Cambridge, MA: Harvard University Press, 1995), 355.

[55] Meigs O. Frost, "Strange Romance of 4 Sisters, Acadian Exiles, in Teche: 4 Parted in Youth are Joined at Life's Eve. Prejean Sisters Found Numerous Family In Bayou Teche," *New Orleans States*, 16 March 1924, 1–2. Note: The headline on page 2 of the continuation of this story from the title page 1 is "Strange Romance of Acadian Exiles: 4 Prejean Sisters, Parted in Youth, Reunited in Life's Sunset."

[56] Thomas Frère Kramer, *A Family Montage* (Lafayette, LA: Center for Louisiana Studies, 2002), 81.

[57] Robert C. Fisher, "'The Grandmother's Story': Oral Tradition, Family Memory, and a Mysterious Manuscript," *Archivaria* 57 (Spring 2004): 126–27.

[58] Bethany Ewald Bultman and Mary Anne DeBoisblanc, *A String of Pearls—The Lustrous Lives of Acadian Women*, exhibition catalog (St. Martinville, LA: Acadian Memorial Foundation, 2007), 1.

[59] Bultman and DeBoisblanc, *A String of Pearls*, 1–7. Exhibits were at the Acadian Memorial Foundation (2005, 2007); Louisiana State Old Courthouse Museum, Natchitoches, LA (2008); Newcomb Archives, Tulane University, New Orleans, LA (2009).

[60] Harry Hansen, *Longfellow's New England* (New York: Hastings House, 1972), 96–97.

[61] A. J. B. (John) Johnston, "Evangeline," in *France and the Americas: Culture, Politics, and History*, ed. Bill Marshall, Will Kaufman, and Cristina Johnston (Santa Barbara, CA: ABC-CLIO, 2005), 421–22; Barbara LeBlanc, "Evangeline as Identity Myth," *Canadian Folklore Canadien* 15, no. 2 (1993): 139–51.

[62] Barbara LeBlanc, "The Dynamic Relationship between Historic Site and Identity Construction: Grand-Pré and the Acadians" (PhD diss., Université Laval, 1994), 97.

[63] Ted Fitzgerald, "Evangeline Mourns in Louisiana," *Western Catholic Reporter*, 29 October 2003, http://www.wcr.ab.ca/columns/tedfitzgerald/2003/fitzgerald110303.shtml, accessed 23 February 2009; LeBlanc, "Dynamic Relationship," 109–13.

[64] LeBlanc, " Dynamic Relationship," 109.

[65] As in the previous example, because of the public nature of this family's story, the actual names have been used. Gustave Rathe, *The Wreck of the Barque* Stefano

Off the North West Cape of Australia in 1875 (Edinburgh, UK: Cannongate Press, 1992); Gustave Rathe, *The Wreck of the Barque* Stefano *Off the North West Cape of Australia in 1875* (Victoria Park, AUS: Hesperian Press, 1990).

[66] See Rathe, within a middle section of the book with other images (on unnumbered pages).

[67] Leslie Crowell Rathe, email to author, 16 April 2009. The bookbinder was Eunice Baccich.

[68] Bruno Latour, "On Technical Mediation—Philosophy, Sociology, Genealogy," *Common Knowledge* 3, no. 2 (Fall 1994): 32.

[69] Josko Petkovic, "The 1920 Translation of the *Stefano* Manuscript: Notes from the Editor," http://nass.murdoch.edu.au/docs/STEFANO_EDITING_TRANSLATION.pdf, accessed 13 August 2012; Josko Petkovic, "Who Is the Author of the 1876 *Stefano* Manuscript?," http://nass.murdoch.edu.au/docs/STEFANO_AUTHORSHIP.pdf, accessed 13 August 2012.

[70] Rathe, *The Wreck of the Barque* Stefano (Edinburgh ed.), 114.

[71] Rathe, *The Wreck of the Barque* Stefano (Edinburgh ed.), 114.

[72] Ulrich, "Creating Lineages," 11.

[73] Stefan Helmreich, "Kinship in Hypertext: Transubstantiating Fatherhood and Information Flow in Artificial Life," in *Relative Values: Reconfiguring Kinship Studies*, ed. Sarah Franklin and Susan McKinnon (Durham, NC: Duke University Press, 2001), 116–17.

[74] Hannah Arendt, "Truth and Politics," in Hannah Arendt, *Between Past and Future: Eight Exercises in Political Thought* (Hammondworth, UK.: Penguin Books, 1977), 238–39; Eric Ketelaar, "A Living Archive, Shared by Communities of Records: Truths, Memories and Histories in the Archive of the International Criminal Tribunal for the Former Yugoslavia," in *Communities and Their Archives: Creating and Sustaining Memory*, eds. Jeannette Bastian and Ben Alexander (London: Facet Publishing, 2010), 109–32; Elisabeth Kaplan, "We Are What We Collect, We Collect What We Are: Archives and the Construction of Identity," *American Archivist* 63 (Spring/Summer 2000): 126–51.

[75] Richard J. Cox, *Personal Archives and a New Archival Calling: Readings, Reflections and Ruminations* (Duluth, MN: Litwin Books, 2008), vii, 1.

[76] Geoffrey Yeo, "Concepts of Record (2): Prototypes and Boundary Objects," *American Archivist* 71, no.1 (2008): 118–43.

[77] Tom Nesmith, "Still Fuzzy, But More Accurate: Some Thoughts on the 'Ghosts' of Archival Theory," *Archivaria* 47 (Spring 1999): 147.

[78] Nesmith, "Still Fuzzy, But More Accurate," 144.

CHAPTER 9

From Annals to Heritage Centers: The Archives of Women's Religious Communities

FERNANDA PERRONE

TWENTY YEARS AGO, HISTORIAN MARY OATES, CSJ, STATED, "RELIGIOUS COMMUNITY ARCHIVES REPRESENT A FIRST-RATE SOURCE OF PRIMARY MATERIAL ON AMERICAN WOMEN. Their coverage is comprehensive in time span, in geographic and ethnic representation, and in types of work undertaken."[1] This statement has only become more apparent in the ensuing two decades. Women's religious communities and their archives still, however, remain somewhat mysterious. Compared to the more familiar archives of Catholic dioceses or major Protestant denominations, they are small, numerous, dispersed, diverse, and not easy to locate or access. Women's religious communities are associations of women bound by religious vows.[2] While the vast majority are Catholic, women's religious communities are found in the Episcopal and Orthodox Churches, and, in the past, in several Protestant denominations in the form of deaconess communities. Since the 1960s, those seeking to create a new monastic tradition have founded ecumenical communities that accept both men and women.[3] Others have embraced Buddhism, and monasteries from various Buddhist traditions have been established. The records of these new institutions will become the religious community archives of the future.[4]

This essay focuses on the archives of Catholic women's religious communities, although archives from other traditions are included if information was available. The scope of the study is limited to the United States, although it is virtually impossible to discuss women's religious communities without referring to their connections throughout the globe. The types of records in these archives reflect the gender roles imposed on women religious, who, unlike their male counterparts, did not have the option of ordination or, until the late twentieth century, of parish ministry. A *religious* refers to any member of a vowed community, either male or female. A *sister* is a member of an apostolic women's religious order whose members work outside the community—as teachers, nurses, social workers, parish workers, and in an increasing variety of occupations. *Nuns* are technically members of contemplative communities, whose chief mission is prayer.

The development of religious community archives as self-conscious entities began in the mid–1970s. In subsequent years, historians and women's studies scholars have used these archives to explore little-known aspects of women's experiences. This essay throws light on the unique resources of women's religious communities, analyzes some of the challenges community archives and their users face, and shows how they are adapting to changing times.

Literature Review

Relatively few studies exist on the archives of women's religious communities. The last major Society of American Archivists (SAA) publication on religious archives was longtime Lutheran Church archivist August Suelflow's 1980 contribution to the Basic Manuals series. Although Suelflow credited a religious community archivist as a consultant, he focused on the repositories of the major Protestant denominations, reflecting the religious archives universe up to the 1970s.[5] Subsequent years saw a great expansion in the number of religious archives and resulting scholarship. Several articles focused on the value of these archives for researchers. The idea that religious archives could provide raw materials for subjects other than religion was pioneered by David Haury in "The Research Potential of Religious Archives: The Mennonite Experience," in 1986. Haury identified women's history as one of seven broad areas of secular history documented at the Mennonite Library and Archives.[6] In articles aimed at the library community, Rosalie McQuaide, CSJP, and Mary Oates, CSJ, demonstrated how the archives of women's religious communities provide rich resources for studies of women's leadership and agency.[7] More recently, Malachy McCarthy of the Claretian Missionaries Archives showed how the archives of both male and female religious communities illuminate the hidden history of marginalized groups.[8] The archives of women's religious communities constitute a novel resource for medical research. In a 2004 *American Archivist* article, Gari-Anne Patzwald and Carol Marie Wildt, SSND, showed how the development of the School Sisters of Notre Dame's archives program facilitated the provision of data for the Nun Study, a longitudinal study of aging and cognitive function.[9]

Other studies have focused on the challenges of maintaining and using these archives. In 1992, Peter Wosh and Elizabeth Yakel reported on the results of a two-year National Historical Publications and Records Commission–funded project designed to improve religious archives in the metropolitan New York region. Their study, which included the archives of twelve women's religious communities, revealed the difficulty of providing systematic training and other meaningful support for these small, underfunded repositories.[10] This author's research on the records of closed Catholic women's colleges suggests that archivists of religious communities still struggle to find adequate training and support.[11] Users of religious community archives encounter a wide variety of professionalism and conditions of access. Furthermore, the merging and consolidating of many communities has created new challenges for archivists and researchers alike.[12]

Over the past twenty-five years, the amount of historical scholarship on women religious has exploded. Women religious have been viewed through the lenses of gender and power; ethnicity and Catholic identities; the development of the teaching, nursing, and social work professions;

race; postcolonial theory; feminism; leadership studies; and spirituality. Many of these studies are based on the archival resources of women's
religious communities.[13] Writing on women's archives has not, however,
devoted much space to religious communities. Andrea Hinding's pioneering *Women's History Sources* included some religious community archives,
but the descriptions tend to be brief, and many archives were apparently
closed to researchers.[14] The scholarship on women's archives has mainly
focused on repositories—usually university special collections or other
research libraries—that collect the papers of women and records of wom-
en's organizations.[15] Religious archives, on the other hand, are similar to
the archives of businesses or nonprofit organizations; they do not collect
as much as document themselves in the course of their daily existence.

History

Recordkeeping in religious archives dates back to the earliest days of
foundations. Catholic sisters follow canon law, which mandates the keeping of records by religious organizations.[16] In the past, the constitutions of
many Catholic women's religious communities required that each house
keep a diary of daily events, which were compiled at the end of each year
into annals or chronicles. As communities expanded and branch houses
were founded, these diaries served as a way to transmit information to the
community headquarters or mother house.[17] Episcopalian and Orthodox
women's communities did not place the same emphasis on recordkeeping, although some communities, like St. John Baptist in Mendham, New
Jersey, kept and continues to keep annals. Deaconess communities did
not keep house diaries, but they maintained records of governance and
administration of institutions, correspondence of individuals, photographs, and other materials.[18]

In 1965, *Perfectae Caritatis*, the document on religious life issued by
the Second Vatican Council, encouraged religious institutes to rediscover
their roots and return to the charism and spirit of their founders. This
document promoted an interest in archives and history among many

communities.[19] This trend was encouraged by the publication of the 1974
National Conference of Catholic Bishops' *Document on Ecclesiastical
Archives*, which urged dioceses, religious communities, and institutions
to inaugurate a nationwide effort to preserve and organize all existing
records and papers.[20] From 1976 to 1980, the Leadership Conference of
Women Religious (LCWR), the organization for superiors of women's
religious communities, received funding from the National Historical
Publications and Records Commission to launch a national archives project, which funded workshops for hundreds of community archivists. A
second federal grant, from the National Endowment for the Humanities,
funded a survey of the holdings of 569 congregations throughout the
United States. This survey, which included Orthodox and Episcopal
nuns and deaconess communities, resulted in the publication of *Women
Religious History Sources*, edited by Evangeline Thomas, CSJ, which
became the standard resource in the field.[21] Organized by state, this guide
included short descriptions and histories of each community; holdings
and extent information for each archives; and whether finding aids were
available. In some cases, access restrictions were noted. Thomas's criteria
for inclusion was any congregation/community of vowed religious that
had maintained a continuity over many years in manuscript and archival collections documenting its corporate and individual contributions to
church and American society.[22] According to these criteria, some newer
foundations were not included, nor were communities that did not maintain an archives *as such*, although they might hold old records.

The archives of religious communities flourished in the late 1970s and
1980s. Organizations such as the New York–area Archivists of Religious
Institutions and the New England Archivists of Religious Institutions were
founded. Religious community archivists, most of whom were themselves
community members, became active in regional professional associations
and in the SAA Religious Archives Section. In the late 1980s, a group of
archivists of Catholic religious communities began to meet informally to
discuss the possibility of forming a new organization. They sought a forum
to discuss common administrative and professional issues, noting the
foundation of another special interest group, the Association of Catholic

Diocesan Archives, in 1982. Community archivists pointed to the upsurge of scholarly interest in the history of women religious, illustrated by the foundation of the History of Women Religious Network in 1989. Another important concern was the declining membership and dwindling financial resources of religious communities and the implications of this trend for archives and archivists.[23]

The Ad Hoc Committee of Women Religious Archivists sought advice from archivists, historians, and community leaders. Among the issues to be resolved was the relationship of the new group to the SAA. While the committee members did not want to isolate the organization from mainstream archival debates and practices, they sought to serve congregation archivists who had little or no archival training, very small shops, little administrative support or understanding, little or no contact with professional archives organizations such as SAA, Mid-Atlantic Regional Archives Conference (MARAC), or Midwest Archives Conference (MAC), for the very reason that these organizations are "big," "national," groups that have "nothing for small people like me."[24] The committee sought support from the LCWR, which agreed to raise seed money for the new organization, requesting a contribution of $100 from each member community.[25] A decision was made to rename the committee the Archivists of Congregations of Women Religious (ACWR), so as not to appear to limit eligibility to members of religious communities. The committee debated admitting archivists of men's religious communities, who faced some of the same professional issues, but ultimately decided that while they did not want to exclude representatives of men's communities, the organization's focus would be on women's archives.[26] While ACWR was not restricted to Catholic communities, it is unclear if any archivists from Episcopalian or Orthodox communities have ever been members.

The desire to retain some connection with the SAA, partly driven by the very practical need to secure meeting space at the annual conference, led to the establishment of ACWR as an SAA roundtable, meeting for the first time in 1991. It soon became clear that many of ACWR's plans, such as writing a constitution and bylaws, fund-raising, and creating internships, were not appropriate activities for a roundtable meant to be an opportunity for archivists with similar interests to gather informally.[27] This anomalous situation resulted in an uneasy compromise that created two groups, the Women Religious Archives Roundtable (WRA) and ACWR, a separate, affiliated organization that was allowed space at SAA meetings on a first-come, first-served basis.[28] The roundtable continued to meet for several years, although some members questioned its purpose, and tensions continued with the SAA over the roundtable's relationship with ACWR.[29] The Women Religious Archives Roundtable was finally discontinued in 2001.[30] ACWR remains a thriving organization that holds triennial conferences, publishes a semi-annual newsletter, and provides networking and mentoring opportunities for archivists of women's religious communities.[31]

Scope

With over 250 members, the ACWR is a key resource for any study of the archives of women's religious communities. Many religious community archivists do not, however, participate in the organization. The complicated and evolving structures of Catholic women's religious communities make it difficult to count the number of community archives with accuracy. Some communities have multiple archives at various levels, while others have one centralized repository. ACWR is affiliated with the LCWR, which has 1,500 members, representing more than 80 percent of the 57,000 Catholic women religious in the United States.[32] The remaining sisters are represented by the traditionalist Council of Major Superiors of Women Religious (CMSWR). The CMSWR represents a few important communities like the Nashville-based Dominican Sisters of St. Cecilia, but most member communities appear to be too small and new to have amassed significant archival collections.[33]

Women's religious communities from other faith traditions are more easily counted. The Conference of Anglican Religious Orders in the Americas (CAROA) includes twenty-three religious communities that are part of the Worldwide Anglican Communion, of which sixteen are communities of women.[34] The first Anglican sisterhood, the short-lived Park Village Sisters, was founded in England in 1845 at the height of the Tractarian movement. Sisterhoods multiplied in the late nineteenth century, and several communities set up houses in the United States. Anglican (or Episcopalian as they were known in the United States) sisterhoods were modeled on Roman Catholic religious orders. Entrants took vows, lived in community, and were active in education, nursing, and social work, although they were independent of the church hierarchy.[35] Always small, the numbers of Episcopalian sisterhoods declined in the twentieth century. Those that remain maintain their own archives.

In the nineteenth century, American Protestant women served their churches in numerous ways—through fund-raising, social service, education, and missionary work.[36] The Protestant institutions most closely resembling women's religious communities were deaconess houses. The deaconess movement in the United States was inspired by the founding, in 1836, of the *Frauendiakonie* in Kaiserwerth, Germany, by Lutheran pastor Theodor Fliedner. Fliedner deliberately sought to restore the ancient order of deaconess from the early centuries of Christianity as a way to counteract the influence of Roman Catholic charitable foundations in his native Rhineland. At Kaiserwerth, Fliedner and his wife, Fredericke, set up a home and asylum for women just released from prison and began to train working-class and lower-middle-class single women for nursing and hospital administration. German immigrants to the United States brought the deaconess movement with them to provide social services for their ethnic communities. Deaconess communities were most widespread in the Lutheran and Methodist Churches, although they were also found in the Evangelical Synod (United Church of Christ) and Mennonite Church.[37] Women living in deaconess communities worked in hospitals, nursing homes, and other social service agencies. While they pledged to remain single, they were free to leave the order when they wished.[38] Deaconess communities declined in the mid-twentieth century, as other opportunities for leadership in the church opened for women.[39] In the early 1980s, Evangeline Thomas surveyed the records of several hospitals and homes where deaconesses lived communally, such as the Lutheran Deaconess

Motherhouse and School in Baltimore and the Eben-Ezer Lutheran Care Center in Colorado. Since then, those communities have closed and their records have been absorbed by denominational archives—the Evangelical Lutheran Church in America Archives in Chicago; the Archives of the United Methodist Church in Madison, New Jersey; the Evangelical Synod Archives in St. Louis; and the Mennonite Library and Archives in North Newton, Kansas.

Although women's monasticism in Eastern and Western Christianity had similar roots in the fourth-century Christian communities of Egypt and Asia Minor, women's monasteries in the East retained more characteristics of the early period than did their Western counterparts. The Eastern communities focused on prayer and asceticism, although they occasionally taught children or cared for the sick within their walls.[40] With the exception of Eastern-rite Catholic communities like the Ukrainian Sisters of Saint Basil the Great, Eastern women religious therefore did not fulfill the same educational and charitable functions within immigrant communities in the United States as did communities from Western Europe. The first Orthodox women's community in the country, Holy Assumption Monastery in Calistoga, California, was founded by a small group of nuns fleeing Russia and China in 1941.[41] Since 1970, Orthodox monasticism in the United States has experienced a unique renewal with over twenty monasteries being founded. Although many of these are small and financially insecure, they have active publishing and retreat programs, influencing many people both within and outside the Orthodox faith tradition.[42] There are about ten women's monasteries in the United States within the Orthodox Church of America (OCA). As well as the former Russian Orthodox and Greek Catholic Church, OCA encompasses the Romanian Orthodox Episcopate, the Albanian Orthodox Archdiocese, and the Bulgarian Orthodox Diocese.[43] In addition, monasteries affiliated with various other national Orthodox churches not part of the OCA have been established in the United States, such as St. Paisius Serbian Orthodox Monastery, founded in 1993.[44] Like Episcopalian sisterhoods, these communities maintain their own archives.

Method

In this brief essay, it is not possible to fully cover the wide range of different types of women's religious community archives in the United States. Rather than attempting a large-scale survey through, for example, distributing questionnaires, the author made personal visits to a sample of community archives from different religious traditions, which pursue a variety of ministries in diverse locations. This method enabled firsthand observation of the archives from the perspective of the user. Not counting the denominational archives that hold deaconesses' records, forty-four women's religious community archives were contacted (see table). Thirty-four of these were Catholic, including one community following the Eastern Rite. Five Episcopalian communities and three of the larger women's Orthodox monasteries were approached, in addition to two Roman Catholic men's communities for the sake of comparison. The author was able to arrange visits to twenty-seven Catholic women's communities, one Episcopalian community, and the two men's communities. Among the Catholic communities, those selected represented major traditions—Benedictines, Franciscans, Dominicans, Sisters of Charity, Sisters of Mercy, and Josephites—as well as communities with unique missions such as the Medical Mission Sisters and the Sisters of the Good Shepherd. Earlier visits to the archives of the Religious of the Sacred Heart, Ursuline Sisters of Louisville, the Sisters of Mercy of Baltimore, and the Congregation of the Holy Cross, although not strictly part of this study, inform it to some degree. Communities were also chosen that have historically ministered to diverse racial, national, and ethnic groups, such as the Religious Teachers Filippini, originally based in Italian-speaking parishes. Visits to two contemplative communities suggested how archivists can document women's spirituality. The religious communities visited are located throughout the country—from Boston, Massachusetts, to Portland, Oregon—but because of financial and time constraints, a disproportionate number are in the mid-Atlantic region. At each community archives, the author toured the facility, interviewed the staff, reviewed finding aids, and examined selected documents.

Types of Documents

The most basic type of record found in the archives of women's religious communities are records of membership.[45] These are found in religious communities of all faith traditions. Records of current membership, which are akin to personnel records, are usually held by the community administration and are not accessible to researchers. Some archivists maintain drop files on living members containing newspaper clippings, programs, awards, and other items that document the work of individual sisters. When a sister dies, her personnel file is transferred to the archives and merged with the drop file. As well as documentation of the various steps in the religious life—entrance, profession, and vows—these files may contain diaries, letters, transcripts, diplomas, and writings. Communities and individuals vary in the amount of material that they retain.[46] In some communities, health and employment information is not transferred to the archives. Membership records are also kept in handwritten ledgers. Since 1908, the Poor Clare Sisters of Chesterfield, New Jersey, a small contemplative community, have maintained an entrance book where they record information about each sister from her arrival until her death or departure. A separate register records what postulants, those desiring to enter the community, bring with them when they arrive, including clothing, money, and other possessions. This register ensures that if a postulant leaves, she can take whatever she brought with her.[47]

All religious communities hold records of administration and governance. These records vary in complexity, depending on the size and structure of the community. In most Catholic communities, the highest level of governance is known as the generalate, which, in an international community, may be located in Europe. The minutes of general chapters or meetings record the highest level of decision making within the community. All communities have constitutions, rules, and directories or manuals of practice that define the mission, structure, and customs of the group. Emendations to these basic documents are debated and decided at chapters. The second level of governance, usually known as the provincialate, can comprise the United States or a region within it. The records of the provincial leaders document policy making and administration at the local level. Small, independent communities like the New Jersey Poor Clares are governed by meetings of the abbess and sisters living in the monastery.

Another important type of record in community archives is records of formation. Formation is the process by which new members are educated and inculcated into the customs, practices, and spirituality of a particular community. In some communities, new members or novices are asked to write autobiographies, which are found in formation records, along with educational materials and evaluations by the formation director. Historically, some communities operated high schools, known as aspirancies, for girls considering entering religious life. More commonly, communities established mother house or sisters' colleges to provide higher education and religious training for young members. In 1960, there were ninety-three sisters' colleges in the United States.[48] Some of the sisters' colleges became colleges for lay students, but the majority closed, so their records can be found in community archives.

A final basic type of record is community annals. In the past, most religious communities required annals to be kept at any house where sisters lived. Some annals from the nineteenth century are detailed, candid, and rich with information. In 1859, the Sisters of the Holy Names traveled from Quebec to Oregon to establish a new mission. Their six-week journey—by train, steamer, and ocean steamship—is described in the community annals.[49] The early annals of the Holy Names Sisters were written in French; similarly, annals from European communities were initially written in the language of their country of origin. Not every community, however, kept detailed annals. The early ministry of the Sisters of Bon Secours, who, as nurses visited the homes of the sick, focused on patients' needs, not the keeping of annals.[50] The Sisters of the Good Shepherd were described as so totally preoccupied with their ministry that keeping annals was not a feasible priority, except in the form of the mandatory reports sent to the Generalate in France.[51] After the changes in religious life following the Second Vatican Council, 1962–1965, most communities ceased keeping annals. In the 1970s, with many sisters living independently and working in different places, keeping a house diary was no longer meaningful.[52]

In the twenty-first century, many community archivists have become the compilers or in some cases the writers of annals, which usually take the form of reports from individual sisters or small groups.

The next important category of records is those of ministry. Contemplative communities tend not to hold this type of record,[53] since their primary ministry is prayer, nor do some men's communities, whose members work as parish priests. Records of ministry can be divided into the records of active institutions, those of closed institutions, and those of projects that may overlap with membership records. Many colleges, schools, hospitals, and social service programs sponsored by women religious have their own archives. Community archivists collect publications like yearbooks, newsletters, and annual reports from these institutions. If the community owns the institution, its archives will hold high-level records such as incorporation documents and board minutes. Community archives often retain records of the foundation and early history of a sponsored or formerly sponsored institution, dating from a time when it was impossible to separate the records of the community from those of its works.

Over the past forty years, many religious communities have divested themselves of major institutional commitments, as sisters age and their focus shifts to new ministries. Community archives consequently hold the records of many closed colleges, private academies, hospitals, orphanages, and other institutions. These records vary greatly in quality, quantity, and completeness. Some contain virtually the entire administrative history of an institution, while others are more fragmentary. The records of a closed institution can overwhelm a small archives. Community archives are reluctant to take student records, patient records, and case files, except those from a very early period, because of legal concerns, although some archivists regularly provide transcripts for graduates of the community's closed colleges and schools.

The archives of women's religious communities contain many record formats common to all institutional archives. Most hold architectural and property records of buildings owned by the community, photographs, audiovisual records such as tapes of meetings, film footage of events, and oral histories of community members. Some archivists are beginning to receive electronic records, but most of these are retained in the community's administrative offices by the records creators. Some religious community archivists scan photographs, create electronic finding aids, and design databases to more efficiently answer reference questions pertaining to the lives and ministries of individual sisters. Several communities, such as the School Sisters of Notre Dame, have created centralized, online databases of all past and present members of the congregation, which can be searched on their websites.[54]

Finally, most community archivists are responsible for collections of artifacts. As well as being important sources of documentation and memory, artifacts can have spiritual significance. The director of archives of the Sisters of the Blessed Sacrament has helped identify relics of the community's founder, Katharine Drexel, who was canonized in 2000.[55] Objects like bells, religious habits, candles, rings, and rosary beads serve as physical evidence of the internal prayer life of community members.[56] Emblems of religious life are often displayed in community archives or heritage rooms. Among the artifacts displayed in the heritage room at the School Sisters of Notre Dame's Baltimore mother house are rule books and crowns of dried flowers encircling hair cut at reception ceremonies. Community archives also acquire artifacts documenting ministry such as textbooks, medical equipment, and crafts brought back from foreign missions. In 1999, the Sisters of Christian Charity in Wilmette, Illinois, left their historic mother house to move to a smaller building. Built in 1918, the grand and ornate mother house had accumulated items from former religious houses for years. Numerous objects were brought from the mother house to the new building and incorporated into an elaborate historical display curated by the community's archivist. As well as documenting the history of the community, the heritage room preserves the memory of the mother house and the works of the sisters who lived there.[57]

Documenting Women's Experiences

The archives of women's religious communities are rich resources on women's experiences. They document both the lives of the thousands of

women who entered religious communities and those of the millions of
women and girls who attended their schools and colleges, were patients
in their hospitals, or used the services they provided. Women religious
had the opportunity to assume leadership roles denied most women until
the late twentieth century. They served as school principals, presidents
and faculty members of colleges, and administrators of major social welfare institutions. This record of service is well documented in community
archives. The records do not, however, reveal only simple narratives of
achievement. Historian Margaret Susan Thompson wrote that the dominant paradigm in the history of women's religious orders is one of conflict.[58] Women religious negotiated a minefield of gender, class, race, and
ethnic tensions.

Women religious frequently clashed with the male clerical hierarchy. Numerous examples of these conflicts can be found in community records. In 1874, a group of Sisters of the Holy Names established a
mission in Baker City, Oregon. They soon experienced tension with the
mission's pastor, the Flemish priest Peter de Roo. The relationship dete-
riorated so much that, in 1884, de Roo sent letters to the Plenary Council
of Baltimore to "expose the many errors of our system of teaching and to
reform the many so-called abuses in our Community." Despite the inter-
vention of another priest who urged de Roo to stop "torturing" the sisters,
the congregational leadership in Montreal decided to close the school,
although de Roo himself was also asked to leave.[59] The Sisters of the Holy
Names did not return to eastern Oregon until the 1970s.

Margaret Susan Thompson and other historians have traced the complex relationship between race and class in nineteenth-century religious
communities.[60] The earliest communities that came to North America in
the eighteenth century replicated the class divisions of European convents, while wealthy women sometimes brought slaves with them as part
of their dowries.[61] One early community, the Oblate Sisters of Providence,
was founded in 1829 for free black women whose families had emigrated
to Baltimore from the Caribbean.[62] The Oblate Sisters would be the first
of four communities established expressly for African American women.
Their archives in Baltimore holds manumission certificates and certificates

of freedom for former slaves who joined the community and for children in its orphanage. In the nineteenth century, Caucasian communities like the Sisters of the Blessed Sacrament were founded to provide education for African American and Native American children. In the mid-twentieth century, sisters confronted issues of race in the segregated South, in urban neighborhoods, and in the Southwest; many became involved in the civil rights movement.[63]

The encounter of women's religious communities with ethnicity is as complex as the history of nineteenth-century immigration. Beginning in the 1850s, women religious arrived from Europe to minister to the growing number of Irish and German immigrants. Later in the century, women religious emigrated from Italy, Poland, the Ukraine, and other areas to serve in ethnic parishes defined by the language and culture of the local community. At the same time, working-class and lower-middle-class daughters of immigrants increasingly entered religious communities.[64] There were never enough sisters, however, to adequately staff ethnic

Archives assistants Sr. Felicia Avila, OSP, and Sr. Constance Fenwick, OSP,
discuss a photograph at the Oblate Sisters of Providence Archives.
Courtesy, Oblate Sisters of Providence Archives, Baltimore, Maryland.

parishes. In 1901 Wisconsin, encouraged by a Polish priest who needed
teachers for his parish school, forty-six Polish-speaking women left the
School Sisters of Saint Francis to form a new community. According to
one chronicler, "The Sisters who separated loved our Community, but
acted as they did on account of their language."[65] The new community,
the Sisters of St. Joseph of the Third Order of St. Francis, published a
somewhat different account of its founding.[66]

Despite the rich layers of history within their archives, some aspects
of the lives of women religious remain undocumented. Thompson notes
the difficulty of envisioning day-to-day life in the nineteenth-century
convent: "the substantive limitation of sisters' archives are, it seems to me,
largely a direct consequence of the terms under which religious life was
understood and lived—at least until the last quarter century . . . consider,
for example, the emphasis that congregations used to place on 'detach-
ment': selflessness, suppression of human emotion and relationships,
minimizing of contact with 'the world,' etc."[67] In the twentieth century,
during what one historian has called the Great Repression,[68] the archival record becomes even more opaque. In 1900 and 1901, the Vatican
officially recognized apostolic orders of sisters as real religious, an eleva-
tion in status that ironically made them more subject to the power of the
hierarchy. The changes in Canon Law of 1917 restricted the movement of
sisters outside the convent and standardized the regulations under which
communities operated.[69] The sisters' correspondence was limited, often
read by superiors, and sometimes destroyed. During this period, sisters
were not encouraged to save papers or memorabilia and were reluctant to
have their pictures taken, even though their predecessors had been photo-
graphed in the late nineteenth century.[70] The highly descriptive accounts
of all aspects of life, including conflict, that appeared in early annals were
replaced by routine listings of mundane events.[71]

Even in the most comprehensive community archives, the fundamental problem of how to document spirituality remains.[72] The underlying
charism of a community is revealed by documents such as the constitution, rule, custom book, breviaries, and liturgical scores. Some sisters
wrote religious poetry. The Sisters of the Blessed Sacrament Archives hold

3,200 writings by Katharine Drexel, including letters, retreat notes, and meditations. The Carmelite Sisters of Baltimore from 1790 on served as spiritual companions to figures like Thomas Price, one of the founders of Maryknoll, whose correspondence is in their archives. Although there are several exceptions, most sisters did not leave a written record of their inner life. For instance, one prioress of the Baltimore Carmelites left numerous letters but no personal spiritual writings except a few scattered notes.[73]

James O'Toole emphasizes the importance of retaining artifacts, not traditionally collected by archivists, to document religious life.[74] In recent years, religious community archivists have made an effort to document important events like profession ceremonies and jubilees—the celebrations of twenty-five, fifty, sixty, and seventy years in religious life—and collect programs from retreats and workshops conducted by sisters. Miriam Therese MacGillis, OP, is a leader in the eco-feminist and eco-spirituality movements. In 1980, MacGillis cofounded Genesis Farm in northwestern New Jersey on land donated to her community, the Dominican Sisters of Caldwell. Genesis Farm offers a variety of workshops and courses in ecology and the environment, as well as maintaining an organic community garden.[75] While Genesis Farm retains its own records, documentation of MacGillis's role can be found in her file at the Dominican Sisters archives.

Users of Religious Community Archives

A variety of patrons uses religious community archives. Although use depends on the size of the archives, types of materials held, and accessibility, some generalizations can be made. The primary users of community archives are internal; they are used by the leadership of the community for administrative purposes and by the members of the community, who work with the archivist to prepare displays and written materials for jubilee celebrations and funeral services. New members of the Franciscan Sisters of Joliet, Illinois, spend time with the archivist studying the history of the congregation during the prenovitiate and novitiate. Lay men and women who are preparing to be associates of the congregation also spend time with the archivist learning about the congregation in brief sessions, and novices spend a semester learning about the history of the community.[76] A second large group of users is genealogists seeking relatives who may have been sisters. Alumni groups preparing for reunions and members of parishes celebrating anniversaries want to know which sisters were in a particular school or parish at a given time. Academic researchers represent a growing cohort of users. Like the archives of many Protestant denominations, the Maryknoll Archives in New York hold rich documentation of women's missionary work throughout the globe. The Maryknoll Archives are used by missiologists, social historians, and scholars of colonialism. Film footage of the Los Baños concentration camp in the Philippines, where Maryknoll sisters were interned during the Second World War, was used in a History Channel documentary.[77] Communities like the Sisters of the Blessed Sacrament that ministered to African Americans and other racial and ethnic minorities are of particular interest to historians of diversity. Concurrently, Katharine Drexel's celebrity status has brought the archives new types of users, including elementary school students, artists seeking to verify Drexel's appearance, and boosters seeking to induct her into a local hall of fame.[78] All the community archivists surveyed reported that the vast majority of requests came via electronic mail or telephone call, rather than personal visit. The number of requests varied from two or three a year at one of the smaller archives to several hundred a year at the more prominent institutions.[79]

Access Issues

The archives of women's religious communities are private entities with no real obligation to admit researchers. Following the lead of other church bodies, however, religious communities have cautiously welcomed researchers into their archives.[80] Indeed, the mission of the ACWR includes collaborating actively and effectively with the Conference on the History of Women Religious and all historians who conduct research in the field of women's studies and church history.[81] Because of privacy concerns, however, access and restriction policies at the archives of women's religious communities are stricter than those at other repositories.

Access to almost all religious community archives is by appointment only. Like other small institutional archives, most community archives are one-person shops, where the reading room closes when the archivist is away. Most religious community archives restrict access to legitimate researchers. A typical access policy reads: "The Maryland Province Archives are open to all Sisters of Notre Dame de Namur and other authorized persons having a legitimate interest in the history of the Province, its apostolates or its members."[82] Some archives require researchers to submit applications in advance, stating the purpose of their research and signing a statement of responsibility for infringement of copyright, right-to-privacy, libel, slander, and other applicable statutes.[83] The application has to be approved by the archivist and in some cases by the community leadership. Some archivists prefer to do research for patrons, rather than encouraging them to visit the archives, although they are painfully aware of the need to balance access with privacy considerations.

Within religious community archives, a range of restriction policies is in force. Membership records are generally restricted, as are records of general and provincial chapters, and leadership correspondence. Some archivists place time restrictions on these records, but, most commonly, they allow access on a case-by-case basis. Archivists are concerned about protecting the privacy of living sisters, noting the difficulty of separating out sensitive materials from minute books or other file formats. They also want to maintain a positive image of the community for public relations purposes. A few communities ask researchers to send copies of manuscripts for approval prior to publication. As one archivist commented, "in religious communities, the life and the work of the members are intertwined, and community records are also the records of families."[84]

Particularly sensitive are the records of children in orphanages and other protective institutions. Although many community archives retain this type of record, the Sisters of the Good Shepherd archives holds a large quantity because of the community's mission. In the nineteenth century, the Good Shepherd sisters ran homes for orphans and preservates—at-risk children—and for sinners and penitents—delinquent women and girls. In the twentieth century, these institutions came under the umbrella of Catholic Charities, and after the Second World War, the sisters were increasingly employed as social workers in a deinstitutionalized environment.[85] The Sisters of the Good Shepherd New York Province Archives holds the records of all the community's former facilities in Manhattan and Brooklyn, so the archivist frequently receives requests for information from former residents or relatives. The notoriety caused by Peter Mullan's feature film *The Magdalene Sisters* (2002), which depicts young women forced to work as laundresses in a fictionalized Irish protective institution, and reports of abuses in Irish industrial schools have brought unwanted attention to the Good Shepherd archives.[86] In response to an influx of inquiries from former residents and supporters of their homes, journalists, and the curious, the archivist devised two forms asking for details about the inquirer, the subject of the inquiry, and the purpose of the inquiry, which are carefully tracked. She also facilitates requests from former residents trying to arrange reunions, being careful not to divulge the identities of classmates without their consent. Indeed, many residents were given assumed names to protect their privacy.[87]

In 2008, the Vatican launched two major investigations of American sisters. One investigation probed the quality of life of women religious institutes through questionnaires and site visits, while the other found serious doctrinal problems at the Leadership Conference of Women Religious and has called upon the organization to reform.[88] These long-running investigations have made religious communities understandably wary of research visits and studies.

Challenges

Balancing the desire to provide access with the need to protect privacy is only one of many challenges archivists of women's religious communities face. Their greatest need is for adequate financial support. More than twenty-five years ago, James O'Toole asked, "As the economic base of religious organizations shrinks with declining membership, will there not be increased competition for scarce funds, with the archives losing out to activities, such as social welfare programs for the benefit of the poor, that are deemed a more central part of those organizations' mission?"[89] In 2012, religious communities face competing demands as they struggle to maintain institutions and programs, while caring for their retired members. The number of women religious in the United States has declined by 68 percent since 1965; and, in 2009, nine in ten women who had made final vows were age sixty or older.[90] Since archivists are often older members of the community, there is much attrition among them and a constant need for training new recruits.[91] ACWR regularly advocates for the appointment of qualified archivists: "Who ever is chosen . . . should be a full-time worker, not encumbered with other jobs, should be relatively young and healthy, not retired."[92] In reality, it is unlikely that community leadership will move a sister from active ministry, where she brings income into the community, to the internal ministry of archives. Despite these challenges, many communities do support their archives. A recent trend is the employment of lay archivists by religious communities. The 2012 ACWR *Membership Directory* includes thirty-five lay archivists, including four men.

Some larger communities like the Sisters of Charity of Cincinnati and the Congregation of the Holy Cross in Indiana employ two or three professional archivists and a cadre of volunteers. The availability of volunteers drawn from the ranks of retired sisters is an advantage that religious community archives possess over other institutional repositories. The more typical community archivist is the proverbial lone arranger. These archivists supply information for community leadership, answer reference questions for everyone from elementary school children to university professors, appraise records from deceased sisters and closed institutions, process collections, and try to make their archives visible through exhibitions and presentations.

Challenging as the role of lone arranger may be, many small religious community archives struggle to maintain the most basic level of care for their old records. Of the thirteen religious communities that the author was unable to visit, two never responded to her messages, two were in transition and not able to receive visitors, and one archivist felt that her archives was too small to be included in the study (see table). The members of the tiny Episcopalian communities and even smaller Orthodox monasteries have little time and few resources to devote to archives. The Community of Saint Mary, the first surviving Episcopalian religious order for women founded in the United States, holds materials dating from 1865 onward in the archives of the Eastern Province in Greenwich, New York. Although these archives are maintained for internal use, researchers are given access to some materials.[93] The three Orthodox communities contacted were all founded in the last third of the twentieth century. Although they hold old records, none has had the opportunity to create an archives yet. One abbess summed up the problem: "I am sorry to tell you that we do not have an established archives here at the monastery. It would be a dream to establish one, but there always seems to be more work than people to do it."[94]

The restructuring of religious communities as they adapt to changing times, new forms of ministry, and an aging membership has created further challenges for community archivists. In 1925, Anna Dengel, an Austrian-born doctor, founded the Medical Mission Sisters to provide health care for Muslim women not permitted to see male doctors. Under her leadership, the sisters became the first Roman Catholic women's congregation to work as physicians, obstetricians, and surgeons, establishing hospitals in India, Africa, the Philippines, Jordan, Venezuela, and other locales.[95] Between 1957 and 1967, in response to decolonialization, the Medical Mission Sisters reorganized into six sectors: Asia, East Asia, Africa, Europe, Latin America, and North America.[96] Rather than decisions being made from a distance, the hospitals and other programs established in various countries in these sectors were now to be administered and staffed by communities of sisters of increasingly national origin. They were to be responsible for decisions and the subsequent implementation. Archival documentation from 1967 onward was to be maintained at sector level while records prior to 1967 remained where decisions were formerly made—in Philadelphia.[97]

Beginning in the 1960s, with the period of experimentation with governance and new types of ministry that followed Vatican II, record-keeping became more haphazard. Constantly evolving structures were challenging to document, while individual and small group projects did not yield the same organized sets of files as large institutions. In 1990, after trying various governance models, the Sisters of Notre Dame de Namur Maryland Province split into three provinces: the Maryland Province, the Chesapeake Province, and the Base Communities, which has a nonhier-archical structure.[98] Each province established its own archives, all in the Baltimore-Washington metropolitan area.

In the 1990s, many local religious congregations, provinces, and inde-pendent communities merged into larger regional bodies. Beginning in 2005, the Sisters of Mercy of the Americas consolidated from twenty-five local to six regional communities. While new archives were established in each region, the local community archives continued to maintain existing records. In 2008, the Congregation of Saint Joseph was founded by seven former independent Josephite communities in the Midwest.[99] Again, each local community retained its archives, while a new regional reposi-tory in Cleveland, the administrative headquarters, will collect materials generated from the time of the merger. Besides the inevitable disruption of moving archives and personnel, consolidation results in loss of local identity, increasing complexity of structure, and the need to standardize policies. The community must decide where to locate the merged archives and who will staff it. The new arrangement requires more travel, commu-nication, and education for archivists not familiar with local contexts.[100]

Creative Solutions

In the past five years, religious community archivists have found creative solutions to some of the challenges facing their archives, while congrega-tional leadership, historians, and the general public have increasingly rec-ognized the importance and value of these unique resources. One solution is for religious communities to combine forces to create a joint archives

center. The Religious of the Sacred Heart North American Province and
the Ursuline Sisters Central Province share such a facility in St. Louis,
Missouri. Building on this model, in 2008, the Claretians, a Chicago-
based men's community, established the Catholic Archive Collaborative
in a renovated downtown skyscraper. The Cenacle Sisters, a community
specializing in retreats, had merged into one province in 2000. Although
their provincial headquarters was in Chicago, their archives was in New
York. In 2009, the Cenacle Sisters moved their archives to the Claretians'
Chicago building. The arrangement allows community archives to pool
resources by sharing reading rooms, processing areas, photocopiers, scan-
ners, and storage space.[101] The shared facilities in St. Louis and Chicago
are located in major urban centers easily accessible to researchers.

Larger communities are creating centralized community heritage
and archives centers. The first of these was the Holy Names Heritage
Center, adjacent to the campus of Marylhurst University in Lake Oswego,
Oregon. The Holy Names Heritage Center was founded in 2007, following the merger of the North American provinces of the Sisters of the Holy
Names of Jesus and Mary. The Heritage Center is a purpose-built, sus-
tainable structure next to the new province headquarters. As well as the
archives and a library, the center offers educational programming, outreach to schools, and rental of the facility.[102] The Holy Names Heritage
Center has served as a model for other communities seeking to restructure their archives. In 2008, the leadership of the Institute of the Sisters
of Mercy of the Americas voted to set up a central heritage, archives, and
research center in Belmont, North Carolina, where a suitable building,
the library of the former Sacred Heart College, was available. At its centralized archives, the Mercy Heritage Center is absorbing the archives of
the former regional centers.[103] Heritage centers have also been created
by the Daughters of Charity in Emmitsburg, Maryland, and the Loretto
Community in Nerinx, Kentucky.

For several years, the ACWR leadership has been grappling with the
issue of what happens to archives when communities close. Initially, they
hoped to find one institution that could become a central repository for
the archives of communities that could no longer maintain their own

records.[104] After approaching several university libraries, they came to the conclusion that no one repository could fulfill this need: "Decisions [should] be made individually based on factors like size, reference use, how active a congregation is. . . ."[105] The Archives of the University of Notre Dame holds the records of a discontinued community, the Indianapolis Carmel, and the records of an active community, the American Province of the Poor Handmaids of Jesus Christ.[106] The Sisters of Our Lady of Christian Doctrine, a small New York community, donated its archives to Fordham University in 2006. The deed of gift safeguards access for members of the community and sets up a restriction policy for other users. The community archivist continues to maintain certain materials, answers reference questions, does in-house exhibitions, and serves as a liaison between Fordham and the community.[107]

In 2009, the growing commitment of religious community leaders to heritage was dramatically illustrated by the LCWR's sponsorship of the *Women and Spirit* exhibition. The opening of the exhibition in Cincinnati was the culmination of a multiyear project to amass archival documents, photographs, and artifacts from women's religious communities throughout the United States and to work with historians, archivists, and museum professionals to create a meaningful and accurate interpretation. For the next three years, the exhibition traveled the United States, with stops in Dallas; Washington, DC; Cleveland; New York; Dubuque; Iowa; Los Angeles; South Bend, Indiana; and Sacramento.[108] Seen by thousands of people, the *Women and Spirit* exhibit and accompanying educational materials successfully created awareness of the contribution of women religious to American history. In 2011, *Women and Spirit* received the Service to Catholic Studies Award from the American Catholic Historical Association. For the LCWR, the exhibition had an added subtext of encouraging religious vocations and countering negative publicity.

Women and Spirit and other exhibitions have rendered women's religious communities less mysterious. They clearly demonstrate the value of community archives for understanding women's historical experience. Increasingly, historians, students, fellow archivists, and the general public are discovering these archives. Community archivists struggle to serve new users, even as they face a shortage of resources and an aging membership. In 2012, the archives of women's religious communities are in a period of transition. As communities consolidate, restructure, and in some cases, disband, archives are being moved and reconfigured to reflect these changes. Regrettably, some of the more isolated community archives may be lost in this process. Increased attention to the heritage of religious communities, however, can only help ensure their future and that of their archives.

Location of Archives	Religion/Denomination	Notes
Elizabeth, NJ	RC Women/Benedictine	
Bensalem, PA	RC Women	
Mariottsville, MD	RC Women	
Towson, MD	RC Women	
Chicago, IL	RC Men	
Mendham, NJ	Episcopalian Women	
Albany, NY	RC Women/Setonian	As of 2012, these archives have merged with another province.
Caldwell, NJ	RC Women/Dominican	
Queens, NY	RC Women	
Silver Spring, MD	RC Women/Mercy	As of 2012, these archives have moved to the new Heritage Center.
Ossining, NY	RC Women/Missionary	
Philadelphia, PA	RC Women/Missionary	
Paterson, NJ	RC Women/Franciscan	
Baltimore, MD	RC Women/African American	
Union City, NJ	RC Men	As of 2012, these archives are moving to a new location.
Chesterfield, NJ	RC Women	
San Francisco, CA	RC Women	
Morristown, NJ	RC Women/Italian	
Milwaukee, WI	RC Women/Franciscan	
Baltimore, MD	RC Women	
Delhi, OH	RC Women/Setonian	
Convent Station, NJ	RC Women/Setonian	
Wilmette, IL	RC Women	
Oswego, OR	RC Women	
Chicago, IL	RC Women/Mercy	
Watchung, NJ	RC Women/Mercy	
Steventon, MD	RC Women	
Philadelphia, PA	Catholic Eastern Rite/ Ukrainian	
Joliet, IL	RC Women/Franciscan	
Brighton, MA	RC Women/Josephite diocesan	

NOTES

[1] Mary J. Oates, CSJ, "Religious Archives Undo Stereotypes about the Role of Sisters," *Catholic Library World* 63, no. 1 (1991): 47.

[2] Increasingly, women's religious communities also include nonvowed members.

[3] See for example, the New Monasticism Network: A Network of Ecclesial Communities Arising Out of Contextual Mission, 2012, http://new-monasticism-network.ning.com, accessed 22 July 2012.

[4] For more information on Buddhist nuns in the United States, see Sandy Boucher, *Turning the Wheel: American Women Creating the New Buddhism* (Boston: Beacon Press, 1993). For a description of a recent foundation, see "Buddhists Honor Fremont Nun Active in Starting Monastery," *The Oakland Tribune,* 7 March 2006, Newsbank Access World News (3576912), 5 August 2012, http://www.highbeam.com/doc/1P2-7036082.html.

[5] August R. Suelflow, *Religious Archives* (Chicago: Society of American Archivists), 1980. See also Peter J. Wosh and Elizabeth Yakel, "Smaller Archives and Professional Development: Some New York Stories," *American Archivist* 55, no. 3 (1992): 475, n. 1.

[6] David Haury, "The Research Potential of Religious Archives: The Mennonite Experience," *Midwestern Archivist* 1 (1986): 135–40.

[7] Rosalie McQuaide, CSJP, "A Well-Kept Secret: The Religious Archive as Reference Resource," *Reference Librarian* 13 (Winter 1986): 137–47 and Oates, "Religious Archives Undo Stereotypes," 47–57.

[8] Malachy R. McCarthy, "Navigating the Labyrinth: Understanding and Getting the Most from Catholic Archives," *Catholic Library World* 76, no. 2 (2005): 118–24.

[9] Gari-Anne Patzwald and Sister Carol Marie Wildt, "The Use of Convent Archival Records in Medical Research: The School Sisters of Notre Dame Archives and the Nun Study," *American Archivist* 67, no. 1 (2004): 86–106.

[10] Wosh and Yakel, "Smaller Archives and Professional Development," 474–82.

[11] Fernanda Perrone, "Vanished Worlds: Searching for the Records of Closed Catholic Women's Colleges," *Archival Issues* 30, no. 2 (2006): 119–49.

[12] Fernanda Perrone, "Whose History Is It? Doing Research in the Archives of Women's Religious Communities," *Catholic Library World* 80, no. 1 (2009): 27–31; and Rita Beaudoin, SUSC, "Merging the Archives of the Sisters of the Holy Union," *Catholic Library World* 72, no. 1 (2001): 24–27.

[13] See Carol Coburn, "An Overview of the History of Women Religious: A Twenty-Five Year Retrospective," *U.S. Catholic Historian* 22, no. 1 (2004): 1–26; and Margaret Susan Thompson, "Women, Feminism and the New Religious History: Catholic Sisters as a Case Study," in *Belief and Behavior: Essays in the New Religious History*, ed. Philip R. VanderMeer and Robert P. Swierenga (New Brunswick, NJ: Rutgers University Press, 1991): 136–61.

[14] Andrea Hinding, ed., *Women's History Sources: A Guide to Archives and Manuscript Collections in the United States*, 2 vols. (New York: R. R. Bowker, 1979).

[15] For example, see Kären M. Mason and Tanya Zanish-Belcher, "A Room of One's Own: Women's Archives in the Year 2000," *Archival Issues* 24, no. 1 (1999): 37–54; and Kären M. Mason and Tanya Zanish-Belcher, "Raising the Archival Consciousness: How Women's Archives Challenge Traditional Approaches to Collecting and Use, Or What's in a Name?," *Library Trends* 56, no. 2 (2007): 344–59.

[16] McQuaide, "A Well-Kept Secret," 138.

[17] Elizabeth Yakel shows how diaries were used by the Maryknoll Sisters of St. Dominic for recordkeeping, communication, and public relations. "Reading, Reporting, and Remembering: A Case Study of the Maryknoll Sisters' Diaries," *Archivaria* 57 (2004): 89–105.

[18] Dale Patterson, Archivist, General Commission of Archives and History, United Methodist Church of America, conversation with the author, Madison, NJ, 6 July 2009; and Archives of the Evangelical Lutheran Church in America, http://www.elca.org/Who-We-Are/History/ELCA-Archives.aspx, accessed 12 July 2012.

[19] James M. O'Toole, "What's Different about Religious Archives?," *Midwestern Archivist* 9, no. 2 (1984): 96.

[20] Peter J. Wosh, "Keeping the Faith: Bishops, Historians, and Catholic Diocesan Archivists, 1790–1980," *Midwestern Archivist* 9, no. 1 (1984): 15.

[21] M. Evangeline Thomas, CSJ, ed., *Women Religious History Sources: A Guide to Repositories in the United States* (New York and London: R. R. Bowker, 1983).

[22] Thomas, *Women Religious History Sources*, xiv.

[23] Rosalie McQuaide, CSJP, "Draft Proposal," Ad Hoc Committee of Women Religious Archivists, 12 December 1989, and "History/Formation of ACWR," "History" box, Archivists of Congregations of Women Religious Archives, Mount Saint Joseph, Delhi, OH (hereafter cited as ACWRA).

[24] Mary Serbacki, OSF, "Thoughts on ACWR," 19 October 1990, "History" box, ACWRA.

[25] Grace McDonald, FSPA, "History of the Relationship between the LCWR and the ACWR" (paper presented at the third triennial conference of the ACWR, Cleveland, OH, 30 September 2000). Used by permission of the ACWR.

[26] Janet Roesener, CSJ, Executive Director, LCWR to Rosalie McQuaide, 12 January 1990; and Minutes, Formational Meeting, 1 September 1990; and Minutes, Board Meeting, ACWR, 4–5 October 1996, "History" box, ACWRA.

[27] Elizabeth Yakel to Anne Diffendal, 16 June 1992, SAA 200/6/9/4, Box 2, Folder 19, UWM MSS 172, University of Wisconsin–Milwaukee Archives Department (hereafter cited as SAAA).

[28] Dolores Liptak, RSM to Anne R. Kenney, President, SAA, 13 November 1992, SAA 200/6/9/4, Box 2, Folder 19, SAAA.

[29] Minutes, ACWR Board Meeting, 4–6 October 1996, "History" box, ACWRA.

[30] Minutes, ACWR Board Meeting, 18–20 May 2001, "History" box, ACWRA.

[31] Archivists for Congregations of Women Religious, http://www.archivistsacwr. org/, accessed 19 July 2012.

[32] Leadership Conference of Women Religious, https://www.lcwr.org/index.htm, accessed 19 July 2012.

[33] Council of Major Superiors of Women Religious, http://www.cmswr.org/, accessed 14 July 2012. Some communities, like the Religious Teachers Filippini, are members of both organizations.

[34] Conference of Anglican Religious Orders in the Americas (CAROA), http:// www.caroa.net/, accessed 14 July 2012. One of these sixteen, the All Saints Sisters of the Poor, left the Episcopal Church and was received into the Catholic Church in September 2009, after the Episcopal General Convention declared homosexuals eligible for any ordained ministry within the church. See Mary Gail Hare and Matthew Hay Brown, "Episcopal nuns' exit widens rift," *Baltimore Sun*, 4 September 2009, American Anglican Council News Archive, http://www.americananglican.org/episcopal-nuns-exit-widens-rift, accessed 5 August 2012.

[35] On Anglican women's religious communities in the United Kingdom, see Susan Mumm, *Stolen Daughters, Virgin Mothers: Anglican Sisterhoods in Victorian Britain* (London: Leicester University Press, 1999); and Martha Vicinus, *Independent Women: Work and Community for Single Women 1850-1920* (London: Virago Press, 1985), 46–84.

[36] See Catherine A. Brekus, ed., *The Religious History of American Women* (Chapel Hill: University of North Carolina Press, 2007); and Susan Hill Lindley, *"You Have Stept Out of Your Place": A History of Women and Religion in America* (Louisville, KY: Westminster John Knox Press, 1996).

[37] See Mary Agnes Dougherty, *My Calling to Fulfill: Deaconesses in the United Methodist Tradition* (New York: Women's Division General Board of Global Ministries, The United Methodist Church, 1997); Carolyn De Swarte Gifford, ed., *The American Deaconess Movement in the Early Twentieth Century* (New York: Garland, 1987); L. DeAne Lagerquist, *From Our Mothers' Arms: A History of Women in the American Lutheran Church* (Minneapolis: Augsburg Publishing House, 1987), 66–70; and Ruth W. Rasche, "The Deaconess Sisters: Pioneer Professional Women," in *Hidden Histories in the United Church of Christ*, ed. Barbara Brown Zikmund (New York: United Church Press, 1984).

[38] Catherine M. Prelinger and Rosemary S. Keller, "The Function of Female Bonding: The Restored Dianconessate of the Nineteenth Century," in *Women in New Worlds*, vol. 2, ed. Rosemary Skinner Keller (Nashville, TN: Abingdon, 1982), 318–25.

[39] Lindley, *You Have Stept Out of Your Place*, 134.

[40] *Encyclopedia of Monasticism*, ed. William M. Johnston (Chicago: Fitzroy Dearborn, 2000), s.v. "Women's Monasteries: Eastern Christian." See also Brenda Meehan-Water, "From Contemplative Practice to Charitable Activity: Russian Women's Religious Communities and the Development of Charitable Work, 1861–1917," in *Lady Bountiful: Women, Philanthropy, and Power*, ed. Kathleen D. McCarthy (New Brunswick, NJ: Rutgers University Press, 1990), 142–56.

[41] Orthodox Church in America, "Holy Assumption Monastery," http://oca.org/parishes/oca-we-calham, accessed 15 July 2012.

[42] *Encyclopedia of Women and Religion in North America*, ed. Rosemary Skinner Keller and Rosemary Radford Ruether (Bloomington: Indiana University Press, 2006), s.v. "Women in Orthodox Christian Traditions."

[43] John Matusiak, "A History and Introduction of the Orthodox Church in America," 2012, Orthodox Church in America, http://oca.org/history-archives/oca-history-intro, accessed 15 July 2012.

[44] OrthodoxWiki, "List of American Monasteries," http://orthodoxwiki.org/List_of_American_monasteries, last modified 27 March 2012.

[45] Practically every type of document that can be found in the archives of religious communities is covered in Denis Sennett, SA, ed., *A Divine Legacy:*

Record Keeping for Religious Congregations/Orders (Graymoor, NY: Franciscan Friars of the Atonement, 1993).

[46] Historian Margaret Susan Thompson comments on the unevenness of demographic information found in community archives in "Women, Feminism, and the New Religious History," 138–39.

[47] Entrance Book and Ledger, Archives of the Poor Clare Sisters of New Jersey, Chesterfield, NJ.

[48] Marjorie Noterman Beane, *From Framework to Freedom: A History of the Sister Formation Conference* (Lanham, MD: University Press of America, 1994), 81–82.

[49] Chronicles, St. Mary's Academy, vol. 2, Portland, Oregon, 1859–1885, Archives of the Sisters of the Holy Names of Jesus and Mary, U.S.-Ontario Province, Holy Names Heritage Center, Lake Oswego, OR (hereafter cited as HNHC).

[50] Mary Herbert, Special Collections Archivist, Sisters of Bon Secours, USA, conversation with the author, Marriottsville, MD, 18 June 2009. Used by permission.

[51] Winifred Doyle, CSJ, Archivist, Sisters of the Good Shepherd, New York Province, conversation with the author, Astoria, NY, 26 October 2009. Used by permission.

[52] Yakel notes that by the late 1960s, many of the Maryknoll Sisters felt that diary-keeping was outdated. Yakel, "Reading, Reporting, and Remembering," 101.

[53] Historically, contemplative communities have done various types of work to support themselves, such as farming, sewing vestments, and baking altar breads, while more recently they have operated retreat houses and given spiritual direction, so their archives document these activities.

[54] For example, see School Sisters of Notre Dame North American Major Area Coordinating Center, "Search for a Sister," http://www.ssnd.org/search-for-a-sister, accessed 15 July 2012.

[55] Stephanie Morris, conversation with the author, Bensalem, PA, 23 November 2009. Used by permission.

[56] Elizabeth W. McGahan, "Inside the Hallowed Walls: Convent Life through Material History," *Material History Bulletin/Bulletin d'histoire de la culture materielle* 25 (Spring/Printemps 1987): 1–9.

[57] Anastasia Sanford, SCC, *SCC Archives Center Timeline and Heritage Room*, ca. 2008, Sisters of Christian Charity Western Province Archives Center, Wilmette, IL.

58 Thompson, "Women, Feminism, and the New Religious History," 142.

59 Chronicle, Baker City, Oregon, 1874–1884, HNHC.

60 Margaret Susan Thompson, "Sisterhood and Power: Class, Culture, and Ethnicity in the American Convent," *Colby Library Quarterly* (Fall 1989): 149–75; and Margaret Susan Thompson, "Philemon's Dilemma: Nuns and the Black Community in Nineteenth-Century America: Some Findings," *Records of the American Catholic Historical Society* 96 (1985): 3–8.

61 See Emily Clark, *Masterless Mistresses: The New Orleans Ursulines and the Development of a New World Society, 1727–1834* (Chapel Hill: University of North Carolina Press, 2007); and Barbara Misner, *Highly Respectable and Accomplished Ladies: Catholic Women Religious in America, 1790–1850* (New York: Garland, 1988).

62 See Diane Batts Morrow, *Persons of Color and Religious at the Same Time: The Oblate Sisters of Providence, 1828–1860* (Chapel Hill: University of North Carolina Press, 2002).

63 Amy Koehlinger, *The New Nuns: Racial Justice and Religious Reform in the 1960s* (Cambridge, MA: Harvard University Press, 2007); Suellen Hoy, *Good Hearts: Catholic Sisters in Chicago's Past* (Urbana: University of Illinois Press, 2006); and Roberto R. Treviño, "Facing Jim Crow: Catholic Sisters and the 'Mexican Problem' in Texas," *The Western Historical Quarterly* 34, no. 2 (2003).

64 Carol K. Coburn and Martha Smith, *Spirited Lives: How Nuns Shaped Catholic Culture and American Life, 1836–1920* (Chapel Hill: University of North Carolina Press, 1999), 70–71 and 140–41.

65 Account, 17 January 1931, "Polish separation file," Generalate/Founding Era Sources, Series 1-015A, Box 4, Archives, School Sisters of Saint Francis, Milwaukee.

66 Josephine Marie Peplinski, SSJ-TOSF, *A Fitting Response: The History of the Sisters of St. Joseph of the Third Order of St. Francis*, 2 vols. (South Bend, IN: Sisters of St. Joseph of the Third Order of St. Francis, 1982).

67 Margaret Susan Thompson, "Catholic Women's Religious Archives: A Historian's Perspective" (paper presented at the annual meeting of the Society of American Archivists, New York, September 1987), 5–6. Used by permission.

68 Mary Ewens, OP, "Removing the Veil: The Liberated American Nun," in *Women of Spirit: Female Leadership in the Jewish and Christian Traditions*, ed. Rosemary Ruether Radford and Eleanor McLaughlin (New York: Simon and Schuster, 1979): 272.

69 Coburn and Smith, *Spirited Lives*, 223–24.

[70] Patricia McKearney, Archivist, Dominican Sisters of Caldwell, conversation with the author, Caldwell, NJ, 15 December 2009. Used by permission.

[71] Sarah Cantor, Director of Archives, Holy Names Heritage Center, conversation with the author, Lake Oswego, OR, 4 November 2009. Used by permission.

[72] On this subject, see Robert Shuster, "Documenting the Spirit," *American Archivist* 45 (Spring 1982).

[73] Constance Fitzgerald, Archivist, Carmelite Sisters of Baltimore, conversation with the author, Towson, MD, 19 June 2009. Used by permission.

[74] James M. O'Toole, "Things of the Spirit: Documenting Religion in New England," *The American Archivist* 50 (Fall 1987): 513.

[75] Genesis Farm, "Mission and Vision," 2012, http://www.genesisfarm.org/about .taf, accessed 15 July 2012.

[76] Marian Voelker, OSF, Archivist, Sisters of Saint Francis of Mary Immaculate, conversation with the author, Joliet, IL, 19 August 2009. Used by permission.

[77] Ellen Pierce, Director of Archives, Maryknoll Mission Center, conversation with the author, Maryknoll, NY, 19 October 2009. Used by permission.

[78] Stephanie Morris, "Reference and Other Requests, January–November 16, 2009," Archives, Sisters of the Blessed Sacrament, Bensalem, PA (hereafter cited as SBSA). Used by permission.

[79] The director of archives of the Sisters of the Blessed Sacrament reported 364 requests in 2009. Morris, "Reference and Other Requests," SBSA.

[80] In 1997, the Pontifical Commission on the Pastoral Formation of Church Archives recommended that church archives be made available "without prejudice." See Archbishop Francesco Marchisano, "The Pastoral Function of Church Archives," 2 February 1997, The Holy See, http://www.vatican.va/roman_curia/ pontifical_commissions/pcchc/documents/rc_com_pcchc_19970202_archivi-ecclesiastici_en.html, accessed 22 July 2012.

[81] Archivists for Congregations of Women Religious, "Mission," http://www. archivistsacwr.org/Mission.htm, accessed 22 July 2012.

[82] "Policy for Use of the Archives of the Maryland Province/Sisters of Notre Dame de Namur," 22 August 2001. Archives, Maryland Province, Sisters of Notre Dame de Namur, Steventon, MD.

[83] Researcher Application, Sisters of Mercy Archives West Midwest Chicago Community, 2010, Archives, Sisters of Mercy Chicago Regional Community, Chicago.

[84] Sharon Knecht, Archivist, Oblate Sisters of Providence, conversation with the author, Baltimore, 16 June 2009. Used by permission.

[85] Margaret Regensburg, "The Good Shepherd Sisters of New York City and the Professionalization of Social Work, 1857–1962" (PhD diss., State University of New York at Stony Brook, 2007), 95–105.

[86] Elizabeth Butler Cullingford, "'Our Nuns Are *Not* a Nation': Politicizing the Convent in Irish Literature and Film," *Éire-Ireland* 41, no. 1 (2006): 9–12; and The Commission to Inquire into Child Abuse, 2009, http://www.childabusecommission.com/rpt, 21 accessed July 2012.

[87] Request for Information, Sisters of the Good Shepherd, New York Province, 2009. Archives, Good Shepherd Province Center, Astoria, NY; and Doyle, conversation with the author. Used by permission.

[88] Laurie Goodstein, "U.S. Nuns Facing Vatican Scrutiny," *New York Times*, 1 July 2009, http://www.nytimes.com/2009/07/02/us/02nuns.html, accessed 5 August 2012; and Laurie Goodstein, "Vatican Reprimands a Group of U.S. Nuns and Plans Changes," *New York Times*, 18 April 2012, http://www.nytimes.com/2012/04/19/us/vatican-reprimands-us-nuns-group.html?_r=0, accessed 5 August 2012.

[89] James M. O'Toole, "What's Different about Religious Archives?," *The Midwestern Archivist* 9, no. 2 (1984): 97.

[90] "Frequently Requested Church Statistics," Center for Applied Research in the Apostolate, Georgetown University "Services," http://cara.georgetown.edu/CARAServices/requestedchurchstats.html, accessed 5 August 2012; and Mary E. Bendyna, RSM, and Mary L. Gautier, *Recent Vocations to Religious Life: A Report for the National Religious Vocation Conference* (August 2009), http://www.nrvc.net/study_overview/, accessed 5 August 2012.

[91] Perrone, "Whose History Is It?," 28.

[92] Edna McKeever, presentation at LCWR regional meeting, ca. 2001, 2, "History" box, ACWRA.

[93] Sister Mary Jean, CSM, Archivist, Community of St. Mary, email message to the author, 14 September 2009; and Community of St. Mary Eastern Province, "Community History," http://www.stmaryseast.org/History.html, accessed 22 July 2012. Used by permission.

[94] Mother Christophora, Abbess, Orthodox Monastery of the Transfiguration, email message to the author, 11 December 2009. Used by permission.

[95] Angelyn Dries, OSF, "American Catholic 'Woman's Work for Woman,'" in *Gospel Bearers, Gender Barriers: Missionary Women in the Twentieth Century*, ed. Dana L. Robert (Maryknoll, NY: Orbis Books, 2002), 134–36.

[96] Marie-Jose Stoffers, MMS, *History of the Society of Catholic Medical Missionaries Pre-foundation to 1968* (London: Medical Mission Sisters, 1991), 106.

[97] Jane Gates, MMS, Archivist, Medical Mission Sisters North America, conversation with the author, Philadelphia, 7 December 2009. Used by permission.

[98] Mary Reilly, SNDdeN, *Courageous Women: Sisters of Notre Dame de Namur Chesapeake Province* (Baltimore: Sisters of Notre Dame de Namur Chesapeake Province, 2005), iv–vi.

[99] Congregation of Saint Joseph, "Our Founding Communities," http://www.csjoseph.org/our_founding_communities.aspx, accessed 22 July 2012.

[100] June Hansen, CSJ, "Merging, Moving, and Closing Archives" (panel session at the ACWR triennial conference, Milwaukee, 18 September 2009). Used by permission.

[101] Malachy McCarthy, "Merging, Moving, and Closing Archives" (panel session at the ACWR triennial conference, Milwaukee, 18 September 2009). Used by permission.

[102] Holy Names Heritage Center, http://www.holynamesheritagecenter.org, accessed 22 July 2012.

[103] "Fall Happenings at the Mercy Heritage Center, Belmont," Mercy International Association, 8 November 2011, http://www.mercyworld.org/news_centre/view_article.cfm?id=567.

[104] Minutes, ACWR Board Meeting, Brentwood, NY (6–8 October 1997), "History," box, ACWRA.

[105] Report on Repositories, ACWR Board Meeting, 16–19 May 2002, "History," box, ACWRA.

[106] Archives of the University of Notre Dame, "Search Our Collections," http://archives.nd.edu/search/index.htm, accessed 22 July 2012.

[107] Archives Agreement between the Sisters of Our Lady of Christian Doctrine and the Walsh Library Archives of Fordham University, 2006, Sisters of Our Lady of Christian Doctrine, Nyack, NY; and Virginia Johnson, RCD, "Merging, Moving, and Closing Archives" (panel session at the ACWR triennial conference, Milwaukee, 18 September 2009). Used by permission.

[108] Women and Spirit: Catholic Sisters in America, http://www.womenandspirit.org, accessed 22 July 2012.

CHAPTER 10

The Lesbian in the Archives: An Overview of the History, Themes, and Challenges

MARY A. CALDERA

IN 1973, THE LESBIAN HERSTORY ARCHIVES (LHA) WAS ESTABLISHED IN NEW YORK CITY. The LHA was a response by lesbian women to the perceived neglect and complicity by historians, libraries, archives, and publishers in perpetuating the invisibility of lesbians. Though still unique, it is no longer the only repository where one may find the lesbian in the archives. She lives in community archives and large research libraries. She lies buried under archaic or ambiguous terms and is highlighted with modern labels. The story of the lesbian in the archives parallels the lesbian experience from invisibility and isolation to community and to the mainstream. It is also a story in which the subject appears and disappears, comes in and out of focus, and changes shape. It is a story that starts with the question, "Where is she?"; asks, "Who is she?"; and ends with the question, "Who is she now?"

Researchers have long decried the difficulty in locating the lesbian in the archives. My own experience with this began in the early 1990s when, as a college student, I came across a copy of the LHA newsletter. I worked in a women's collection but failed to encounter the lesbian, much less the lesbian of color, in the archives. After reading about the LHA, I had a better sense of why that was. As I explored the topic further as a graduate student and followed the emerging literature, I was infused with righteous indignation at the failure of archives to document lesbians' lives. I was also excited about the emerging interest by libraries and archives in documenting lesbian, gay, bisexual, and transgender (LGBT) lives and history. I dreamed of working in an LGBT community archives or women's collection, where I could contribute to the documentation endeavor. Practical considerations necessitated my finding a position in the traditional archives where I have been employed for the last ten years. Fortunately, my institution embarked on an LGBT collecting initiative several years ago, allowing me to fulfill my early aspirations.

Through my work in both a women's collection and an LGBT collecting initiative, I have encountered many of the issues and challenges inherent in documenting lesbians' lives. I have encountered the absence of lesbians in the archives; heard of donors who did not want to be associated with particular collections; grappled with my desire to highlight potentially interesting collections without mislabeling them as *lesbian*; and faced the reality that lesbians of color are harder to document. I participated in ongoing discussions about definitions and description. In essence, this essay represents my own evolving understanding of what it means to find or place the lesbian in the archives.

This essay provides an overview of the history of the lesbian in the archives from the beginnings of the social justice movements of the 1960s and 1970s to the present. By necessity, this story is told with the lesbian sometimes embedded within the LGBT community, but where possible I specifically speak of lesbians. The essay also discusses three recurring themes and challenges of documenting lesbian women: privacy and confidentiality, paucity of the record, and definition and description.

Explanatory notes are needed on the use of the term *lesbian* and on the term's embeddedness within the umbrella term *LGBT*. *Lesbian* is a highly contested construct, the historical development of which is beyond the scope of this essay,[1] but which will be elaborated upon later. To begin the discussion, *lesbian* signifies women whose primary emotional/sexual attraction is to other women, no matter what her time period or what she may have been called or called herself. Though only one of many possible definitions for the term, it serves as a starting point for the discussion to follow. It was also the dominant definition for many activists in the decades when the lesbian archival project outlined in this essay began. In regard to the use of *gay* and *lesbian* or *LGBT* [2] herein rather than simply *lesbian*, particularly within the historical sections of the essay: in much of the literature on the topic of documenting lesbian, gay, bisexual, and transgender individuals and communities, they are discussed as a group rather than separately. I do my best to extricate the lesbian from this enmeshed history. Often it is impossible and, at times, unwise to do so because—as I hope will become evident—that is her context.

Historical Context

The story of lesbian and gay and women's archiving is deeply rooted in the social justice movements of the 1960s and 1970s. It was during those decades that women, lesbians and gays, and people of color found their collective voices, articulated their dissatisfaction, and formed movements for liberation from legal, cultural, and societal oppression. Given their multiple identities, lesbians' place in these identity-based movements posed some issues. Prior to the emergence of the women's movement, many activist lesbians found kinship with gay men important, and worked with them in the homophile movement, a precursor to the gay liberation movement. Some lesbians also had worked in the civil rights and antiwar movements. During the sixties and seventies, many activist-minded lesbian women, attracted by the ideals of feminism, joined the women's movement. While lesbians were participants in the women's movement, they were tolerated only as long as they remained invisible as lesbians. When large numbers became vocal in the movement as lesbians, they experienced a backlash from the more conservative and homophobic members of the women's movement. Lesbianism was seen as a threat to the movement because many heterosexual women feared being labeled lesbian.[3] Antifeminists effectively used the term *lesbian-baiting*, accusing all feminists of being lesbian man-haters. This alienated some lesbians, as they found themselves battling homophobia and heterosexism within the women's movement.

Not all lesbian activists focused their energy on the women's movement. Some chose to work in the gay liberation movement, or to work in both simultaneously. The gay movement was a natural fit for some lesbians, and many had already been involved in the homophile movement.[4] After the onset of the feminist critique, however, it became apparent to many lesbians that the only kinship they had with gay men was oppression as a sexual minority.[5] As some lesbians in the gay movement became more feminist, a rift between gay men and women emerged.[6] By fighting homophobia and heterosexism in the women's movement and sexism in the gay movement, lesbians began to form a separate sociopolitical identity. Tired of being subsumed in the generic (male) gay and women's movements, the concept of lesbian separatism emerged.

The intersectional[7] and generally subordinate position of lesbians (particularly lesbians of color)—which could include being a woman in a patriarchal society, a lesbian in a heterosexual society, and/or a person of color in a predominantly white society—made them particularly difficult to situate within the emerging movements, fields of study, and, eventually, cultural collections. This multiple positionality, some have suggested, continually threatens to relegate lesbians to a marginalized *other*. To use the field of women's studies as an example, Marilyn Frye criticized the field for being heterosexist,[8] and Barbara Smith saw it as white.[9] In their introduction to *The New Lesbian Studies*, Toni A. H. McNaron and Bonnie Zimmerman state the issue:

> In the early days of women's studies programs lesbian students and faculty were often encouraged to subsume our history, culture, and critical questions under the presumably more palatable rubric of "woman" or, on more liberal campuses, under that of "feminist." . . . Now, with the growth of gay studies and queer theory, lesbians once again find ourselves in danger of becoming invisible. In place of gendered terms, "lesbian" or "dyke," we are invited to place ourselves under the sign of "queer."[10]

In short, lesbians were keenly aware of their marginal status.

The social justice movements of the sixties and seventies left many legacies, including the claiming of collective identities, an empowering search for each group's history,[11] new fields of study,[12] and challenges to existing fields of study. Both women's and gay and lesbian studies (inside and outside of the academy) were direct outgrowths of the movements,[13] and in the beginning, history was a main focus.[14] The people's movements demanded a people's history, and social history helped pave the way for the new researchers.

The women's and gay movements, in particular, gave rise to an increased awareness of the absence of women, lesbians, and gays in the annals and citadels of history.[15] For gays and lesbians, once an identity as a minority was claimed, it became a political imperative to prove gays and lesbians always existed. According to Jeffrey Escoffier, "the search for authenticity underlay the impulse that led gay and lesbian scholars to track down the history of homosexuals."[16] As researchers began the task of "reclaiming the gay and lesbian past," they soon decried the lack of sources on women and racial and sexual minorities in libraries and archives. It quickly became apparent that traditional libraries and archives did not meet the needs of these new researchers.[17] Early researchers realized that if a true record were to be left for future generations, they themselves would have to collect it, write it, and, in some cases, publish it.

Responding to the Call

The library profession, and by extension the archival profession, experienced an onslaught of criticism by feminists in the 1970s and 1980s.[18] Feminists' main criticisms were sex discrimination in the profession, lack of positive materials by and about women, sexism in subject headings, and difficulty in accessing materials by and about women.[19] Like academic institutions, libraries and archives responded relatively quickly to the demands of women and women's studies scholars, possibly because the critics from within the library profession were in positions to enact the changes they sought.[20] Librarians demanded and collected more

women-positive materials, ensured sexist subject headings were eliminated, called for nonsexist subject headings, and wrote bibliographies that
helped researchers locate materials on women.[21] Some college and university libraries developed women's collections or increased the visibility of
already existing ones.[22] The enormous task of identifying manuscripts and
archives collections related to women across the country was undertaken
and the results published in 1979 as *Women's History Sources: A Guide to
Archives and Manuscript Collections in the United States.*[23]

The library and archival professions were much slower to respond to
the needs of lesbians and gays. There are several reasons for this, including the continued oppression of gays and lesbians in society itself and the
reluctance of academia to accept lesbian studies.[24] Additionally, sexuality
itself was not deemed an appropriate or even possible subject of study[25]
and documentation until relatively recently. Despite the fact that the
library profession can boast the first gay and lesbian professional organization, the American Library Association's Gay and Lesbian Task Force,[26]
it was not until the late 1980s and early 1990s that mainstream libraries
truly responded to the call for better documentation of lesbians and gays
in their collections. Before the 1980s, those who sought information on
lesbians and gays in libraries encountered several problems. Gay-positive
materials were often censored or completely absent from the library.
What was available, generally materials on medical and moral treatments,
portrayed gay men and lesbians as sick or morally depraved. Censorship
by librarians, archivists, administrators, or patrons further decreased the
likelihood that materials on gays and lesbians would be collected or made
easily accessible.[27]

A small number of librarians were strong critics of homophobic
collection policies. Janet Cooper and Israel Fisherman established the
Task Force on Gay Liberation, a section of the Social Responsibilities
Roundtable of the American Library Association, in 1970. Under the
leadership of Barbara Gittings, it was instrumental in many positive
developments within the library profession.[28] But again, support lagged
far behind that of women's issues. Even though the task force initiated
positive changes, researchers continued to experience many of the same

problems that earlier researchers identified. This was particularly true in archives.[29] As Steven Maynard put it, "Given the exclusion of lesbian and gay history from universities and academic journals, and the conscious and unconscious suppression of lesbian/gay materials in mainstream archives, the sources and locations of gay history have by necessity, emerged outside these institutions."[30]

Lesbian and Gay Community Archives

The lesbian and gay community archives movement needs to be considered in the context of the broader community archives movement. Additionally, it is helpful to provide some useful definitions of the term *community archives*. Andrew Flinn, in his discussion of the movement in England, states: "Community histories or community archives are the grassroots activities of documenting, recording and exploring community heritage in which community participation, control and ownership of the project is essential." On the nature of the archival sources themselves, Flinn indicates that

> the "archives" in community archives includes collections of material objects, paper and digital records, audio-visual material, and personal testimonies, all created or collected and held within the community. This definition might engender some debate as to whether these "created" or "artificial" collections are archives, but the movement has chosen, correctly I believe, to use the broadest most inclusive definitions possible.[31]

Private collections of gay and lesbian sources existed prior to the seventies. In fact, some of today's most substantial collections were started by individuals or organizations in the 1940s, 1950s, and 1960s. For example, the ONE International Gay and Lesbian Archives was begun by Jim Kepner as a private collection in 1943, and Barbara Grier's collection of gay-themed literature was started well before 1963.[32] However, the roots of community lesbian and gay libraries and archives developed directly out of and in conjunction with the lesbian and gay liberation movement and its precursor, the homophile movement. Even in cases where the collections preceded the 1970s, the movement led to increasing the visibility of existing private and semiprivate collections. Community archives and libraries were born of the activist impulse to remember, or reclaim, lesbian and gay history, and to show the world that lesbians and gays had always existed. Analyzing the mission statements of gay and lesbian libraries and archives, Bill Lukenbill states that they "reflect concerns for their history, heritage and the need to correct past neglect of their role in society. These mission statements clearly reflect the need for positive identification, self-imagery, and social and cultural recognition."[33]

The culture-producing endeavor gave birth to several repositories, including the Stonewall Library and Archives (1970–1971); the Atlantic Lesbian Feminist Alliance Archives (1972); the ONE International Gay and Lesbian Archives (opened to the public in 1979); and the June L. Mazer Collection (1981).[34] One of the earliest and exclusively lesbian archives still in existence is the Lesbian Herstory Archives (LHA), founded in 1973 and opened in the home of Joan Nestle and Deb Edel in 1974.[35] As stated in an early description, the archives

> began as an outgrowth of a Lesbian consciousness-raising group. . . . The founders were concerned about the failure of mainstream publishers, libraries, archives, and research institutions to value lesbian culture. It became obvious that the only way to insure the preservation of lesbian culture and history was to establish an independent archive, governed by Lesbians.[36]

Nestle described the need for and philosophy of the archives. She stated in 1990 that the

> strongest reason for creating the archives was to end the silence of patriarchal history about us—women who loved women. Furthermore, we wanted our story told by us, shared by and preserved by us. We were tired of being the medical, legal, and religious other.[37]

The founders of the LHA were deeply influenced by the women's and lesbian and gay movements. Their philosophy epitomizes Lukenbill's observation that positive identification and the claiming of history were central to gay and lesbian archives.

Not all gay activists approved of the grassroots community archives movement. By 1979, enough lesbian and gay community archives existed that an issue of the *Gay Insurgent* included a section titled, "Archives, Access, and Availability." Author Jim Monahan argued that the aim of collecting gay archives should be "to integrate the gay past into historical thinking, promoting the use of that information in the analysis of broad historical questions."[38] He opposed "separatist lesbian and gay institutions" because he believed the best places for gay and lesbian archival collections are academic institutions, where only qualified activists, academics, and students would have access to them, and where historians would have to take note of them.[39] Many of his arguments against separate community lesbian and gay archives were based on traditional archival principles such as archival organization, physical preservation, and security, and concerns about privacy and confidentiality. While his arguments were sound, they were also, in many respects, unrealistic. At the time, traditional archival institutions were not interested in documenting lesbians and gay men. Nestle, in the same journal issue, responded that it was for that very reason that the LHA existed. The traditional institutions had failed lesbians. She stated, "[we] cannot trust 'historical understandings' or 'academic institutions.'" Nestle insisted that "our concept of an archives must be different; we are different."[40]

Aside from emerging outside of established cultural institutions and generally being established and run by activist volunteers (some of which were professional librarians and archivists), lesbian and gay community archives, like other identity-based archives, differed from traditional repositories in several significant ways. They moved lesbians and gays from the margins to the center. They recognized "gay" and "lesbian" as encompassing lives instead of just sexual activities. Community archives democratized the archival process by insisting on inclusiveness to ensure documentation of the many, not just the prominent and famous. They saw self-definition as an imperative. They also saw community ownership of and participation in the documentation process as essential. This is evidenced by the level of outreach in which community archives traditionally engage, taking the archives into the community through slideshows, presentations, and representation at community events. They recognized the value of and need to document by any means necessary, including expanding the parameters of the archives. They encouraged the establishment of additional regional archives and self-archiving.[41] They were radical; they needed to be. According to Ann Cvetkovich,

> Lesbian and gay history demands a radical archive of emotion in order to document intimacy, sexuality, love, and activism, all areas of experience that are difficult to chronicle through the materials of a traditional archive. Moreover, gay and lesbian archives address the traumatic loss of history that has accompanied sexual life and the formation of sexual politics, and assert the role of memory and affect in compensating for institutional neglect.[42]

Community archives were special not only for what they held, but as spaces in and of themselves. In her description of her first visit to the LHA, Paula Bennet wrote: "The cramped New York City apartment was overflowing with women. . . . I figured we could come and run. But we stayed. We stayed because the archives is there and it is a warm and beautiful place."[43]

Lesbian and gay community archives were highly important to the lesbian and gay community; these community archives and libraries became lesbian and gay cultural institutions when there were no others.[44] Repositories were established throughout the country. The 1979 Lesbian Herstory Archives newsletter listed five other community-based, grassroots archives: the New Alexandria Lesbian Library, White Mare Archives, Tennessee Regional Archives, San Francisco Gay History Project, and the Washington DC Area Archives.[45] By 1985, less than ten years after the first community repositories were established, the Canadian Gay Archives listed forty gay archives in the United States and Canada.[46] Leading by example, these repositories not only preserved countless collections, they also challenged the way traditional archives selected, preserved, and made accessible materials documenting gay and lesbian (and later, bisexual, transgender, and queer) individuals and organizations. It would take more than a decade before traditional archives also began to document lesbian lives and history.

Mainstream Archival Repositories and the Response of the Archival Profession

Mainstream archival repositories eventually heeded the call for LGBT sources, albeit slowly. Women's collections acquired the papers of lesbians in the course of their collecting on women. However, this aspect of their collecting was not highlighted until recently. For example, in Andrea Hinding's 1979 *Women's History Sources: A Guide to Archives and Manuscript Collections in the United States*, only three of over eighteen thousand entries are indexed under lesbian and lesbianism. In Suzanne Hildenbrand's 1986 *Women's Collections: Libraries, Archives, and Consciousness*, the major women's repositories are represented, but none indicated that they specifically collected lesbian sources. Lesbians fared even worse in repositories that did not focus specifically on women.

In the 1980s, few mainstream archival repositories were collecting gay and lesbian materials. Brenda Marston cites as the reason she became an archivist the obstacles to studying lesbian lives, such as the lack of sources and discouragement from advisors, that still existed in the early eighties.[47] In 1986, Elizabeth Knowlton conducted a survey of forty gay and lesbian archives in the United States and Canada to assess the documentation of the gay movement. She also surveyed twelve traditional archives in the same geographic areas as the gay archives to ascertain what, if any, collecting they were doing and if they knew of the nearby gay archives. Except for one institution, all the traditional archives said they had no records documenting the gay movement, and more than half were unaware of the gay archives in their areas. Additionally, most claimed that the subject of gay records was not mentioned at all in their repositories.[48] Much would change in the next few years, including an increased awareness of LGBT issues within the archival profession and the beginnings of core LGBT collections within major research repositories.

The Kinsey Institute for Research in Sex, Gender, and Reproduction at Indiana University, founded in 1947, and the Minnesota Historical Society, which began collecting LGBT materials in the early 1970s,[49] may be the first mainstream repositories to document LGBT sexuality and lives; however, they were very much exceptions. It was not until 1988, when the New York City Public Library and the Cornell University Library received major LGBT collections, which led to new collecting programs, that traditional repositories began to make sexuality and LGBT history and experience collecting priorities.[50] The donations marked a shift in the tide for mainstream collecting. With few exceptions, the archival profession had remained silent on issues related to LGBT collecting. Little in the professional archival literature even alluded to LGBT archival issues. In the nineties that began to change, paralleling the growth and acceptance of lesbian and gay history and studies in colleges and universities. On discussing the rise of gay and lesbian history, George Chauncey Jr., Martin Bauml Duberman, and Martha Vicinus credit early pioneers outside of the academy, such as Jonathan Katz and the founders of the LHA, for the initial advances in the field. On the field's eventual inclusion in the academy, they credit gay and lesbian activists within the history profession as well as the ascendance of social history within the academy. Social history, with its focus on ordinary people, everyday life, and the private sphere; and women's history, with its focus on gender and sexuality, helped bring lesbian and gay history into the mainstream of the archival profession.[51]

Many gay and lesbian professional archivists were well aware of LGBT documentation issues and the work being done in community archives; some even volunteered at them. It was not until 1989, however, that professional archivists formed their own group to address LGBT issues within the archival profession. Members of the Society of American Archivists (SAA) formed the Lesbian and Gay Archives Roundtable (LAGAR) in 1989. For Stephen Novak, a founding member, three factors sparked the creation of LAGAR: the precarious state of community archives, which concerned professional lesbian and gay archivists; the 1985 formation of the International Association of Lesbian and Gay Archives and Libraries; and Elizabeth Knowlton's 1986 presentation at SAA on documenting the gay rights movement.[52] LAGAR's mission included making LGBT issues in archives and history more visible within SAA and educating archivists about the importance of identifying and preserving historical records documenting LGBT individuals.[53]

By the 1990s, the library profession was well on its way to addressing critiques of its treatment of LGBT documentation. The profession had seen an increase in women's and lesbian- and gay-positive publishing and collecting. Effective activism, especially of Barbara Gittings through the American Library Association's Lesbian and Gay Roundtable (the successor of the task force), ensured a robust professional dialogue among librarians. Publication of two landmark compilations, Cal Gough and Ellen Greenblatt's *Gay and Lesbian Library Service* (1990) and James Carmichael's *Daring to Find Our Names: The Search for Lesbigay Library History* (1998), further ensured that LGBT issues would receive attention by librarians. While both publications included chapters on archives, the archival professional literature remained relatively silent on the issues.[54]

Despite the lack of public dialogue among professional archivists as a group, several mainstream archival repositories had begun actively documenting the lesbian and gay movement, organizations, and (to a lesser extent) private lives. Collecting repositories, particularly research libraries and college and university libraries, turned a collecting eye to LGBT organizations and individuals. Many traditional repositories (including college and university libraries, public libraries, and historical societies) now list LGBT as an area of collecting focus.[55] Additionally, most of the major women's collections now actively and publicly document lesbians. According to LAGAR's 2003 list of repositories (which depends on self-reporting and is by no means exhaustive), there were fifty mainstream repositories with significant LGBT collections, compared to thirty-six just five years before.[56] The SAA annual meeting often includes sessions covering LGBT issues.[57] Further, LGBT archives, libraries, and special collections have been the subject of an international conference and smaller symposia.[58]

While traditional archives began to collect and to contend with the challenges LGBT documentation presents, community archives continued to collect and make LGBT documentation accessible. New lesbian and gay archives (including virtual ones) continue to be created, despite the fact that some older community archives grapple with tensions arising from the number of sources being created and donated, increased researcher interest, and limited resources. Two recent examples of new repositories include the Madeline Davis GLBT Archives of Western New York (2001)[59] and the Pacific Northwest Lesbian Archives (2006).[60] The continued establishment of community archives, generally regional in scope, suggests that traditional repositories are still not adequately documenting LGBT life and culture and that the archival record is still not representative of the diversity of LGBT communities. But it also might reflect the fact that documentation efforts in mainstream repositories, often national in scope, do not replace the localism and community-building aspects that are such an integral part of community archives.

Meeting in the Middle?

The influence of LGBT community archives on mainstream archives, and vice-versa, is evidenced in two trends affecting both: the trend toward more professionalism[61] in community archives and the trend toward more inclusiveness in traditional archives. Each type of repository (community and traditional) serves a purpose and has its particular strengths and weaknesses. Traditional archives often have more resources and paid staff who are trained and knowledgeable about archival principles and techniques. Traditional archives offer more accessibility by disseminating information about their holdings to a wider audience and providing longer hours of operation. However, they have been perceived by some as exclusionary and elitist. Community archives allow a community of people to actively gather and preserve a record of themselves, and, by the

very act of archiving, define themselves and their experiences. They are
deeply connected to (if not embedded in) their communities and trusted
by them. They are usually staffed by volunteer members of the communities they document and, as such, are at the forefront of documenting the
people, events, and issues relevant to those communities. Because community repositories lack the restraints of archival tradition, they can be
creative in what they acquire and how they describe those acquisitions,
resulting in incredibly rich and varied collections. Some see community
archives' holdings, however, as vulnerable and relatively inaccessible to
the larger scholarly community.[62]

Resources of some community repositories were strained by the
quantity of materials donated, in conjunction with increased demands
for access to them. Such community archives recognized the benefits of
becoming affiliated with an established repository with more resources,
seeking and finding homes or close collaborations with receptive traditional archives.[63] The benefits are mutual as the traditional archives
receive an established collection and the energy and connections of
members. Further, several community archives have, themselves, become
established repositories, complete with grant funding and professionally trained archivists.[64] The Internet allows community archives to share
information about their projects and holdings with the broader research
community.

There is ample evidence that the archival profession is heeding the
call for a more inclusive archival record,[65] and archivists are examining
issues of diversity from various angles.[66] The changes traditional archives
have undergone over the last thirty years are not, of course, attributable
solely to the community archives movement. The development of social
history, women's studies, LGBT studies, and the recognition of the value
of diversity and inclusiveness in the information professions have all
worked to effect change in the nature of archives. As such, the impact
community and traditional archives have had on each other and on the
historical record may have been inevitable. As early as 1981, Fredric C.
Miller recognized that the new social history that emerged in the previous decades would or should change traditional archives; he stated that

"archival practices and principles are not immutable" and "it is now time to reevaluate the conventional wisdom of our profession, discarding what has become outmoded, reordering priorities, and retaining what is useful."[67] LGBT community archives, women's archives,[68] and other identity-based archives projects, demanded just that of the profession, and perhaps forever changed the traditional archives.

Themes and Challenges of Situating the Lesbian in the Archives

In the thirty or so years of archival discourse on LGBT documentation—including professional literature, listserv postings, and presentations at conferences—a few recurring themes and challenges emerge, and all are related to naming: privacy and confidentiality, paucity of the record, and definition and description. While this essay does not discuss privacy and confidentiality issues in detail, it is important to note their recurrence as issues. Suffice it to say that, by their very nature, personal papers of lesbians can contain intimate details of their own and others' lives. Given the ambiguous state of societal acceptance, stigma, violence, and challenges to civil rights are still very much a part of LGBT people's lives. As such, outing[69] and labeling (or mislabeling) are still powerful arguments against categorizations (for example, subject headings) when ambiguity is involved or third parties are concerned. Even when there is no question about the appropriateness of the applied descriptors, third-party privacy and confidentiality in intimately personal papers and legal and medical records pose ethical dilemmas for those attempting to ensure that LGBT life is documented in the historical record.

When grappling with concerns about privacy and confidentiality, however, it is necessary for us to examine our assumptions and motives. In her thoughtful article, "The Archivist's Balancing Act: Helping Researchers While Protecting Individual Privacy," Judith Schwarz provides examples of censorship disguised as concern for privacy. She suggests that

> [t]he impulse to suppress material or at least to restrict its use for
> a time seems to spring from desires to protect both the reputations
> of individuals and families and the welfare of the institution. . . .
> As long as lesbians and gay men are seen as a threat to the estab-
> lished order, and lesbianism stays a slanderous accusation long
> after a woman's death, we will continue to face angry protectors of a
> deceased relative's or colleague's reputation.[70]

Open discussion with donors and among members of the archival community is critical to addressing privacy and confidentiality issues. Increased
transparency in our collecting, arrangement and description, and access
policies will help archivists develop best practice guidelines. Such guidelines might help us answer questions such as, "What is an appropriate
number of years to restrict material?"; "When should we make items
available online?"; "Should we archive legal or medical records?"; and
"Who should decide?"

A second recurring challenge is evident in the extent of the representation of lesbian women in archives today. Without hard data, we must
make inferences about the equity or adequateness of the archival record
on lesbians, but it is not hard to conclude that there is a paucity of the
record. It is clearly no longer true to say that there are not enough archival
sources to support the study of contemporary lesbian lives. One would
be hard-pressed to locate a research library that does not have some primary source materials on lesbians. But the questions remain: is that adequate? Is it representative? It is likely that a sample of source materials
on lesbians would overrepresent white, middle-class, educated, activist
women from cities and underrepresent lesbians who are poor or disenfranchised, come from rural communities, are religious or conservative,
or are women of color.

As repositories have become more inclusive in their collecting scopes,
they have attempted to ensure representation of diverse communities
within their collections. Many major LGBT organizations, despite their
relative youth, are represented in archives—lesbian organizations, or
individual lesbians, perhaps less so. Repositories that focus specifically
on women or LGBT women have understandably done a better job of

documenting individual lesbian women's lives. Even they, however, have had less success documenting women of color, despite much effort.[71] (A notable exception might be the LHA, which, from its beginning, made a concerted effort to document lesbians outside of the white, middle-class demographic.) Lesbians and gay archivists of color have tapped their own communities in efforts to fill the documentation gap. For example, Yolanda Retter began the Lesbian Legacy Collection at the International Lesbian and Gay Archives (now the ONE Institute), and Steven Fullwood began the Black Gay and Lesbian Archives at the Schomburg Center for Research in Black Culture. Efforts such as these are essential to ensuring a broad representation of lesbian diversity.

Despite the increase in documentation efforts, researchers and critics within the profession continue to point out the difficulties they encounter in finding evidence of sexuality, particularly LGBT sexuality, in the archives— so much so that a small body of literature has emerged on reading the silences around sexuality in archives.[72] In addition to collecting more, a few traditional archives have reviewed their holdings in an attempt to assess whether collections contained evidence of women's same-sex erotic relations.[73] Such projects are invaluable in uncovering potentially useful collections, but also indicate the amount of effort required to locate the lesbian in the archive. Perhaps this is more related to past silences and suppressions. It is a fact that most people in the past did not document their sexual lives, particularly their homosexual ones, to the extent that some do today. The issue today, however, may be not so much what is and is not in the archives but defining the subject herself. In "The Problems in Writing the History of Sexuality: Sources, Theory and Interpretation," Estelle B. Freedman and John D'Emilio conclude, "the main problem is not a lack of sources but rather a need to define more clearly the subject matter."[74]

The greatest challenge to documenting lesbian women is definition and description. The label *lesbian* is a problem for archives. Our main problem is that we do not know what a lesbian is, or was, or will be. As Martha Vicinus states, "Put bluntly, we lack any general agreement about what constitutes a lesbian."[75] Historically, there have been several terms used to describe women who engage in same-sex sexual behavior or have same-sex orientations: the terms *tribads, sapphists, romantic friends, inverts, homosexuals, dykes, lesbians, bisexuals, transsexuals, gays,* and *queers* are just a few. More recently, homosexuality became understood as something that a person *is* (identity) as opposed to a set of behaviors he or she engages in. The scholarship is far from definitive; and even the "experts"—scholars in women's, gender, and sexuality studies—disagree on what the subject *lesbian* really is.[76] This question has occupied scholars since they took up the subject, and the answer is relevant not only to how we describe the materials that may document lesbians, but also to how we define our collecting.

As archivists, it is helpful to review the ways historians have understood lesbian homosexuality since the seventies. The definition put forth at the beginning of this essay—women whose primary emotional/sexual attraction is to other women, no matter what her time period or what she may have been called or called herself—would have rung true to the early activists/archivists who initiated the LGBT archival project in the 1970s, with their orientations firmly rooted in the identity politics of the time. Early documentation efforts focused on the reclamation of a lost (or suppressed) gay and lesbian past. This, of course, assumed a gay and lesbian past, however, and was later challenged by those who questioned the legitimacy of imposing the present-day category *homosexual* or *lesbian* on individuals who lived in a time when those categories did not exist.[77]

At the core of the debate are the competing essentialism and social constructivism theories of gender and sexuality. In short, the essentialist view holds that homosexuality is inherent and, therefore, transhistorical, while the social constructivist view holds that sexuality and sexual expression (even gender) are culturally constructed and therefore vary through time and space.[78] A parallel debate, particularly in lesbian historiography, is the question of genital sex, whether it is a necessary factor in defining the lesbian: the "did they or didn't they?" question.[79] Queer theory and other postmodernist approaches to the study of gender and sexuality, such as deconstructivism and literary theory, have further destabilized and questioned the category *lesbian*, challenging as they do the very foundations of historical knowledge and the sources by which it is attained.

Given the continuing debates, it seems almost impossible to come to a nonproblematic understanding of the lesbian in the archives.

One of our primary functions as archivists is description, and how we describe anything is based on our understanding of it. How, then, are we to describe the seemingly indefinable lesbian? Archivists have to do what the scholars do: read the texts and contexts, sift through evidence, and ultimately, decide for themselves what to call it (whatever "it" is), how to categorize it, how to describe it. John D. Wrathall, put it thus:

> The work of archivists is not any more value neutral than other historical endeavors. . . . To illuminate rather than obscure such problems, archivists need to understand the epistemological problems in the fields of research. This analysis implies that good archival work requires substantial historical analysis and interpretation.[80]

Archivists, particularly those of us who work on documenting gender and sexuality, have to analyze and interpret, because the alternative is to not name, to not categorize, to continue the silence, and to perpetuate the invisibility. This is particularly difficult for LGBT materials created prior to the gay rights movement, when language around same-sex sexuality is absent, coded, or unrecognizable. Additionally, we must, as Elisabeth Kaplan suggests, acknowledge that our work is "critical in shaping history," and admit, "we are major players in the business of identity construction and identity politics."[81] Doing so can help us remain critical of our own biases.

While it was the demand for documentation of lesbians and gays that began the archival project, I have come to believe that *lesbian* is, in fact, too narrow a term for the concept of female same-sex sexual behavior and/or orientation. We need to expand the documentation project beyond (but still include) lesbians to document female same-sex sexuality, a term favored by Leila Rupp, because it "gets beyond the use of terms such as 'queer,' 'gay,' 'lesbian,' or 'homosexuality.'"[82] Only then can we effectively respond to the evolving scholarship and needs of researchers. Approaching the topic from the perspective of same-sex sexuality rather than LGBT allows us not only to expand the scope of our collecting, it also helps us to avoid the pitfalls of ahistoricism.

Two primary concerns regarding description are the mislabeling of individuals or collections as LGBT and the lack and (later) inadequacy of subject headings for LGBT subjects. Concerns about mislabeling or applying historical descriptors ahistorically are valid. Faced with describing the early twentieth-century letters of two nonfamilial women in an obviously devoted and passionate relationship, the archivist might choose not to highlight that aspect of the collection. The time period and the fact that the women did not themselves use the term *lesbian* to describe their relationship would naturally pose problems with the use of the term in the description. While heeding the warnings against projecting current concepts and understandings onto materials created in a different era,[83] it is also necessary to ensure that we describe our collections in ways that make their research potential evident. Finding aids, like other texts, do and should use contemporary lenses (understandings) to situate and describe materials and the context in which they were created. As such, it is appropriate to judiciously highlight the collections' potential value for gender and sexuality research.

While a finding aid describes a specific collection, one of the main purposes of a subject heading is to allow for the collation under one heading of many different sources. Critics point out the limits of subject headings, especially Library of Congress subject headings, as descriptors for the LGBT experience.[84] The main issue here, of course, is the ever-evolving terminology and the slow response of the information profession to such changes. Additionally, in many collections, the sexuality of the creator or subject is not explicitly stated or documented in the materials, so the assignment of an LGBT subject heading is questionable. Individual repositories have found alternative ways to address the issue. My institution developed a local subject heading, *LGBTQ resource*, to bring out the potential of some collections for gender and sexuality research, where a lesbian, gay, bisexual, or transgender subject heading may not be appropriate.[85] Another uses *female friendships* as a descriptor for some of its collections.[86] These approaches are necessary, though less than satisfactory, responses to the problem. Another, and for our purposes probably better, way to collate collections is with subject guides. Subject guides allow the archivist to pull together for the researcher same-sex sexuality collections that otherwise may be inaccessible through keywords (such as *lesbian*, *gay*, or *homosexual*) or increasingly specific subject headings.

However we choose to describe and make accessible the materials that document the lesbian or female same-sex sexuality (by whatever definition is imposed), our descriptions need to be as diverse and contextually nuanced as the concepts themselves. Further, we need to accept that our descriptions cannot be static, but need to be dynamic and evolving. In short, our descriptions need to evolve with the scholarship.

Looking Forward

Not until the 1960s and 1970s, when activists, archivists, librarians, public historians, and individual collectors within the lesbian and gay community undertook documentation projects, did libraries and archives began to address the problem of lesbians' invisibility in the public record. Encouraged by the lesbian and gay-liberation movements, these pioneers' efforts, though sometimes unconventional, led to the creation and preservation of countless collections. Though traditional archives responded slowly to the demand for source materials by researchers in the nascent fields of women's and gay and lesbian studies, over the last thirty years, documenting the lesbian has gained academic legitimacy. These advances can be attributed to many factors including the activist archivists (professionally trained and not) and the establishment of community archives; the rise of social, women's, and LGBT history; the successes of the LGBT civil rights movement toward destigmatizing homosexuality; and the library and archives professions' move toward increased diversity and inclusiveness.

That many traditional repositories now recognize the value of documenting LGBT lives, culture, and history is encouraging. Community archives continue to save the stories of their communities from fading back into silence. An LGBT individual or organization can now potentially choose from among several appropriate repositories based on location, collecting focus, or repository type. Thus, more source materials have been made available to a broader audience.

While the lesbian is no longer absent from the archives, we are far from reaching the proposed goal of establishing what Brenda Marston calls "a full, complex representative lesbian, gay, bisexual, transgendered archival record."[87] The recurring challenges, particularly the issue of definition, suggest a need to expand the scope of the lesbian archival project. While we may never be able to come to an unproblematic understanding of what constitutes a lesbian and, by extension, how to document her, the last thirty years of progress demonstrate that we need not stop trying.

NOTES

The author wishes to thank the reviewers whose comments and suggestions proved helpful in the writing of this essay. Portions of this essay are based in large part on a presentation I gave titled, "From Grassroots to Ivory Towers: The Search for the Lesbian in the Archive" (paper presented at the annual meeting of the Society of American Archivists, 14–21 August 2005).

[1] For an overview, the reader is referred to George Chauncey Jr., Martin Bauml Duberman, and Martha Vicinus, introduction, *Hidden from History: Reclaiming the Gay and Lesbian Past* (New York: NAL Books, 1989), 1–13. See also Lillian Faderman, "Surpassing the Love of Men Revisited," *Harvard Gay and Lesbian Review* 6, no. 2 (1999): 26–29; and Leila Rupp, "'Imagine My Surprise': Women's Relationships in Historical Perspective," *Frontiers: A Journal of Women's Studies* 5, no. 3 (1980): 61–70.

[2] From the 1960s to the 1980s, it was common to use *gay* and *lesbian* when discussing the gay and lesbian community. As the gay and lesbian rights movement become more inclusive, *bisexual* and *transsexual*, or *transgender*, were included as well. Current usage is even more inclusive and acknowledges the diversity within the community and includes *lesbian, gay, bisexual, transgender,* and sometimes *queer* and *intersex* or *LGBTQI*.

[3] Marilyn Murphy, "Sisterhood Is Painful or What's All the Fuss about the Lesbian Issue," *University of Michigan Papers in Women's Studies* 2, no. 4 (1978): 55–64; Marilyn Frye, "Willful Virgin or Do You Have to Be a Lesbian to Be a Feminist?," *Willful Virgin: Essays in Feminism 1976–1992* (Freedom, CA: Crossing Press, 1992), 124–37.

[4] John D'Emilio, *Sexual Politics, Sexual Communities: The Making of the Homosexual Minority in the United States, 1940–1970* (Chicago: University of Chicago Press, 1983).

[5] Julia Penelope (Stanley) and Susan J. Wolfe, "Sexist Slang and the Gay Community: Are You One Too?" *Michigan Occasional Papers in Women's Studies* 14 (1979): 1–19.

[6] Penelope and Wolfe, "Sexist Slang and the Gay Community," 1–19.

[7] Intersectionality was originally posited by African American feminists and dispelled the dominant notion of a unified feminist sisterhood. Intersectionality recognizes the influence of multiple intersecting factors—notably race, gender, class, sexuality, and nationality—in people's lives and interactions. See Michele Tracy Berger and Kathleen Guidoz, eds., *The Intersectional Approach: Transforming the Academy through Race, Class, and Gender* (Chapel Hill: University of North Carolina Press, 2009).

[8] Marilyn Frye, "A Lesbian Perspective on Women's Studies," in *Lesbian Studies Present and Future*, ed. Margaret Cruikshank (Old Westbury, NY: Feminist Press, 1982), 194–98.

[9] Barbara Smith, "Building Black Women's Studies," *The Politics of Women's Studies: Testimony from 30 Founding Mothers*, ed. Florence Howe (New York: Feminist Press, 2000), 194–203.

[10] Toni A. H. McNaron and Bonnie Zimmerman, introduction, *The New Lesbian Studies* (New York: Feminist Press, 1996), xv.

[11] Margaret Cruikshank, *The Gay and Lesbian Liberation Movement* (New York: Routledge, 1992); and Barbara Haber, "The New Feminism: Implications for Librarians," *RQ* 20, no. 1 (1980): 76–78.

[12] Maria Mies, "Women's Studies: Science, Violence, and Responsibility," *Women's Studies International Forum* 13, no. 5 (1990): 433–41; Will Roscoe, "History's Future: Reflections on Lesbian and Gay History in the Community," in *Gay and Lesbian Studies*, ed. Henry L. Minton (New York: Haworth, 1991), 161–79.

[13] Mies, "Women's Studies"; and Roscoe, "History's Future."

[14] Cruikshank, *Gay and Lesbian Liberation Movement*; and Haber, "New Feminism."

[15] John D'Emilio, "Not a Simple Matter: Gay History and Gay Historians," *Journal of American History* 76, no. 2 (1989): 435–42; and Salvatore J. Licata, "The Homosexual Movement in the United States: A Traditionally Overlooked Area in American History," *Journal of Homosexuality* 6, nos. 1–2 (1980–81): 161–89.

[16] Jeffrey Escoffier, "Generations and Paradigms: Mainstreams in Lesbian and Gay Studies," in *Gay and Lesbian Studies*, ed. Henry L. Minton (New York: Harrington Park Press, 1992), 7–26.

[17] Many writers have outlined the problems with doing research on gays and lesbians, including: Steven Maynard, "'The Burning Willful Evidence': Lesbian/ Gay History and Archival Research," *Archivaria* 33 (Winter 1991–92): 195–201; D'Emilio, "Not a Simple Matter"; Estelle Freedman, "Resources for Lesbian History," in *Lesbian Studies*; Marvin J. Taylor, "Queer Things from Old Closets: Libraries—Gay and Lesbian Studies—Queer Theory," *Rare Books and Librarianship* 8, no. 1 (1993): 19–34; Martin Duberman, "'Writhing Bedfellows' in Antebellum South Carolina: Historical Interpretation and the Politics of Evidence," in *Hidden from History: Reclaiming the Gay and Lesbian Past*, ed. Martin Duberman, Martha Vicinus, and George Chauncey Jr. (New York: New American Library), 153–68.

[18] Some of this discussion is based on critiques of libraries and library practices, but as archives are often part of libraries and have increasingly used the models and tools of librarianship, particularly in description, I believe they apply to archives as well.

[19] Patricia Glass Shumann and Kathleen Weibel, "The Women Arisen," *American Libraries* 10, no. 6 (1979): 322–26; Margaret Rogers, "'Are We On Equal Terms Yet?' Subject Headings Concerning Women in LCSH, 1975–1991," *Library Resources and Technical Services* 37, no. 2 (1993): 181–96.

[20] Susan E. Searing, "A Quiet Revolution," *Women's Review of Books* 6, no. 5 (1989): 19; Haber, "The New Feminism," 76–78.

[21] Janet Freedman, "Work that Is Real: Perspectives on Feminist Librarianship," *Alternative Library Literature* (1990–91): 24–25.

[22] The history of women's collections precedes the modern feminist critiques by several decades. For information on the history of women's collections, see Martha S. Bell, "Special Women's Collections in United States Libraries," *College and Research Libraries* 20, no. 3 (1959): 235–42; Suzanne Hildenbrand, ed., *Women's Collections: Libraries, Archives, Consciousness* (New York: Haworth, 1986); and Anke Voss-Hubbard, "'No Documents—No History': Mary Ritter Beard and the Early History of Women's Archives," *American Archivist* 58 (Winter 1995): 16–30.

[23] Andrea Hinding, ed., *Women's History Sources: A Guide to Archives and Manuscript Collections in the United States*, 2 vols. (New York: R. R. Bowker, 1979).

[24] For a good review of the literature on service to gays and lesbians from a library perspective, see Steven L. Joyce, "Lesbian, Gay, and Bisexual Library Service: A Review of the Literature," *Public Libraries* 39, no. 5 (2000): 270–79.

[25] David M. Halperin, "Is There a History of Sexuality?," in *Lesbian and Gay Studies Reader*, ed. Henry Abelove, Michèle Aina Barale, and David M. Halperin (New York: Routledge, 1993), 416–31.

[26] The American Library Association Gay and Lesbian Task Force (now GLBT Roundtable) was established in 1970.

[27] For an overview of the issues, see Cal Gough and Ellen Greenblatt, eds., *Gay and Lesbian Library Service* (Jefferson, NC: McFarland, 1990); and "Services to Gay and Lesbian Patrons: Examining the Myths," *Library Journal* 117, no. 1 (1992): 59–63. See also Glen Creason, "Anatomy of a Hate Crime," *Communicator* 23, nos. 9–12 (1990): 19–20.

[28] For the history of the Lesbian and Gay Task Force on Gay Liberation, now the Gay, Lesbian, Bisexual, Transgender Round Table, see Barbara Gittings, "Gays in Libraryland: The Gay and Lesbian Task Force of the American Library Association: The First Sixteen Years," *WLW Journal* 14, no. 3 (1991): 7–13; and James V. Carmichael Jr., "Homosexuality and United States Libraries: Land of the Free, But Not Home to the Gay," *Proceedings 64th IFLA General Conference* (1998).

[29] Alisa Klinger, "Resources for Lesbian Ethnographic Research in the Lavender Archives," *Journal of Homosexuality* 34, nos. 3–4 (1998): 206–7.

[30] Maynard, "The Burning Willful Evidence," 196.

[31] Andrew Flinn, "Community Histories, Community Archives: Some Opportunities and Challenges," *Journal of the Society of Archivists* 28, no. 2 (2007): 153.

[32] Paul D. Cain, "Barbara Grier," *Leading the Parade* (Lanham, MD: Scarecrow Press, 2002), 145–53.

[33] Bill Lukenbill, "Modern Gay and Lesbian Libraries and Archives in North America: A Study in Community Identity and Affirmation," *Library Management* 23, nos. 1–2 (2002): 96.

[34] Ellen Embardo, "Directories of Special Collections on Social Movements Evolving from the Vietnam Era," *Reference Services Review* 18, no. 2 (1990): 59–95.

[35] Polly Thistlewaite, "The Lesbian Herstory Archives," in *Gay and Lesbian Library Service*, 61–64.

[36] Lesbian Herstory Archives, "Background on the Lesbian Herstory Archives," undated.

[37] Joan Nestle, "The Will to Remember: The Lesbian Herstory Archives of New York," *Feminist Review* 34 (Spring 1990): 87.

[38] Jim Monahan, "Considerations in the Organization of Gay Archives," *Gay Insurgent,* nos. 4–5 (1979): 8.

[39] Monahan, "Considerations in the Organization of Gay Archives," 8.

[40] Joan Nestle, "Radical Archiving: A Lesbian Feminist Perspective," *Gay Insurgent,* nos. 4–5 (1979): 10.

[41] For example, the *Lesbian Herstory Archives News* 8 (1984) includes a section on "Preserving Your Own Records," 12.

[42] Ann Cvetkovich, "In the Archives of Lesbian Feelings: Documentary and Popular Culture," *Camera Obscura 49* 17, no. 1 (2002): 110.

[43] Quoted in the *Lesbian Herstory Archives News* 5 (1979), 2.

[44] The importance of LGBT community archives and libraries is evidenced by the number of times community libraries and archives and history projects are covered in the gay press. For just a few examples, see Cal Gough, Michel Dee, and Stephen Kline, *Gays and Lesbians, Libraries and Archives: A Checklist of Publications, 1970–1989* (Minneapolis: GLTF Clearinghouse, 1989). According to Ann Cvetkovich, the Lesbian Herstory Archives was even featured, though mildly disguised, as the Center for Lesbian Information and Technology (CLIT), in a lesbian film by Cheryl Dunye, *The Watermelon Woman.* See Ann Cvetkovich, "In the Archives of Lesbian Feelings: Documentary and Popular Culture," *Camera Obscura 49* 17, no. 1 (2002): 107–47.

[45] *Lesbian Herstory Archives News* 5 (1979), 5.

[46] Elizabeth Knowlton, "Documenting the Gay Rights Movement," *Provenance* 5, no. 1 (1987): 19.

[47] Brenda J. Marston, "Archivists, Activists, and Scholars: Creating a Queer History," in *Daring to Find Our Names: The Search for Lesbigay Library History,* ed. James V. Carmichael Jr. (Westport, CT: Greenwood Press, 1998), 137.

[48] Knowlton, "Documenting the Gay Rights Movement," 19–21.

[49] Minnesota Historical Society Collections, "The Gay, Lesbian, Bisexual and Transgender Collection," http://www.mnhs.org/collections/museum/glbt/glbt .htm, accessed 5 July 2010.

[50] Brenda Marston, "History, Projects, Libraries, and Archives," *Encyclopedia of Lesbian, Gay, Bisexual, and Transgender History in America*, vol. 2, ed. Marc Stein (Detroit: Charles Scribner's Sons, 2004), 43–48. The New York Public Library received the International Gay and Lesbian Information Center Archives and the Cornell University Library received the Mariposa Educational Research Foundation. It is interesting to note that the cores of many mainstream collections originated in just this way.

[51] Chauncey, Duberman, and Vicinus, introduction, *Hidden from History*, 2.

[52] Stephen E. Novak, "Outreach and Inreach: The SAA Lesbian and Gay Archives Roundtable, 1988–2004" (paper presented at the annual meeting of the Society of American Archivists, Boston, Massachusetts, 2–8 August 2004).

[53] Novak, "Outreach and Inreach."

[54] There are certainly exceptions; several archivists have worked to fill this information gap in the professional literature, including Elizabeth Knowlton and Brenda Marston. Most of what has been written, however, has been written by nonarchivists.

[55] For example, Sophia Smith Collection (Smith College), Manuscripts and Archives (Yale University), the Labadie Collection (University of Michigan), Northeastern University Libraries Archives and Special Collections, just to name a few.

[56] Lesbian and Gay Archives Roundtable, Society of American Archivists, "Repositories with LGBT Materials in the U.S. and Canada," published as an appendix in *Encyclopedia of Lesbian, Gay, Bisexual and Transgendered History in America*, 307–19.

[57] Novak, "Outreach and Inreach."

[58] For example, the Lesbian, Gay, Bisexual, Transgender, Archives, Libraries, Museums, and Special Collections Conference was held Minneapolis in 2006 and in New York City in 2008, with another scheduled in 2011. Smaller symposia include "Sex in the Stacks: A Zwickler Memorial Symposium on Sexuality and the Archives," held at Cornell University in 2002, and the "Out of the Closet and Into the Vaults" symposium held at the University of California, Los Angeles.

[59] Madeline Davis, "The Madeline Davis LGBT Archives of Western New York," http://www.madelinedavisglbtarchives.org/index.html, accessed 5 June 2010.

[60] "Frequently Asked Questions About PNLA," http://www.pnwlesbianarchives
.org/faq/, accessed 5 July 2010).

[61] By professionalism, I mean conformance to established archival principles and
techniques, not to devalue the standards by which the community archives
were run. In fact, several founders and volunteers at community archives are
trained librarians and archivists.

[62] Novak, "Outreach and Inreach."

[63] Two recent examples include the Jean Tretter Collection and the Pacific
Northwest Lesbian Archives. Tretter donated his collection to the University
of Minnesota Libraries; see Lisa Vecoli, "From the Chair," *Tretter Letter* 1,
no. 1 (2006). Lisa Cohen's Pacific Northwest Lesbian Archives now operates from within the Washington State Historical Society (WSHS) in
Tacoma, Washington. See Cohen, "Great Big Wonderful News!," http://www
.pnwlesbianarchives.org, accessed 17 October 2009.

[64] See, for example, the ONE Institute and the LGBT Historical Society in San
Francisco.

[65] There has been a significant increase in the number of articles in the archival
literature pertaining to diversity, particularly in the last ten years. *RBM* 8, no. 2
(2007), edited by Penny Welbourne and Kathleen Burns, is entirely devoted to
highlighting diverse collections and projects. Additionally, archivists are beginning to critically examine diversity in archives.

[66] For just one example, Elisabeth Kaplan, "We Are What We Collect, We Collect
What We Are: Archives and the Construction of Identity," *American Archivist*
63, no. 1 (2000): 126–51.

[67] Fredric M. Miller, "Social History and Archival Practice," *American Archivist*
44, no. 2 (1981): 124.

[68] Kären M. Mason and Tanya Zanish-Belcher, "Raising the Archival
Consciousness: How Women's Archives Challenge Traditional Approaches to
Collecting and Use, Or, What's in a Name?" *Library Trends* 56, no. 2 (2007):
344–59.

[69] *Outing* refers to publicly disclosing that someone is LGBT.

[70] Judith Schwarz, "The Archivist's Balancing Act: Helping Researchers while
Protecting Individual Privacy," *Journal of American History* 79, no. 1 (1992):
185.

[71] People of color are often included as subjects in discussions of underrepresented groups in the archives. A recent example is a program at the
GLBT Historical Society on hurdles to documenting LGBT people of color:

"Collecting the Spectrum: Diversity Challenges in Queer Archives," *History Happens: Newsletter of the GLBT Historical Society* (June 2009), http://archive.constantcontact.com/fs029/1101960178690/archive/1102594119311.html, accessed 11 September 2010.

[72] Several writers have suggested alternate ways of reading the silences around sexuality in archives. See Bronwyn Dalley, "Creeping in Sideways: Reading Sexuality in the Archives," *PHANZA: E-Journal,* http://www.phanza.org.nz/journal/sex-archive-bronD.htm; and John D. Wrathall, "Provenance as Text: Reading the Silences in Manuscript Collections," *Journal of American History* 79, no. 1 (1992): 165–78. Writings on reading the postcolonial archives are especially intriguing in this respect. See, for example, Anjali Arondekar, "Without a Trace: Sexuality and the Colonial Archives," *Journal of the History of Sexuality* 14, nos. 1–2 (2005): 10–27.

[73] For example, archivists in Manuscripts and Archives, Yale University Library, undertook a project to uncover women's collections within their holdings that may be of use for research in gender and sexuality. See Christine Weideman and Mary Caldera, "Uncovering the Hidden: Finding GLBTQ Resources in Archives and Libraries" (paper presented at the annual meeting of the Society of American Archivists, Washington, DC, 30 July–6 August 2006).

[74] Estelle B. Freedman and John D'Emilio, "The Problems in Writing the History of Sexuality: Sources, Theory and Interpretation," *Journal of Sex Research* 27, no. 4 (1990): 481–95.

[75] Martha Vicinus, "They Wonder to Which Sex I Belong," in *Lesbian Subjects: A Feminist Studies Reader,* ed. Martha Vicinus (Bloomington: Indiana University Press, 1990), 234.

[76] See Judith Schwarz, "Researching Lesbian History," *Sinister Wisdom* 5 (Winter 1978): 55–59; Frances Doughty, "Lesbian Biography, Biography of Lesbian," *Frontiers* 4, no. 3 (1979): 76–79; Adrienne Rich, "Compulsory Heterosexuality and Lesbian Experience," *Signs: Journal of Women in Culture and Society* 5, no. 4 (1980): 631–60; Lisa Duggan, "The Theory Wars, or, Who's Afraid of Judith Butler?," *Journal of Women's History* 10, no. 1 (1998): 9–18.

[77] Chauncey, Duberman, and Vicinus, introduction, *Hidden from History.*

[78] Freedman and D'Emilio, "Problems Encountered."

[79] Rich, "Compulsary Heterosexuality."

[80] John D. Wrathall, "Provenance as Text: Reading the Silences around Sexuality in Manuscript Collections," *Journal of American History* 79 (1992): 178.

[81] Kaplan, "We Are What We Collect," 147.

[82] Leila J. Rupp, "Toward a Global History of Same-Sex Sexuality," *Journal of the History of Sexuality* 10 (2001): 287.

[83] Rupp, "Imagine My Surprise," 61–70.

[84] A recent example of this is a post by Jenna Freedman, "Queering LCSH," on the need for a subject heading for "Queer," *Lower East Side Librarian*, 3 February 2009, http://jenna.openflows.com/whatshouldbelcshforqueer, accessed 16 October 2009). The 2006 and 2008 Lesbian, Gay, Bisexual, Transgender, Archives, Libraries, Museums, and Archives conferences each included presentations on subject headings. As additional terminology is introduced to the discourse on same-sex sexuality, continued critiques are likely. For earlier critiques of subject headings in the library literature, see Berman Sanford, *Prejudices and Antipathies: A Tract on the LC Subject Headings Concerning People* (Jefferson, NC: McFarland, 1993); Gough and Greenblatt, *Gay and Lesbian Library Service* and "Services to Gay and Lesbian Patrons"; Joan Marshall, "LC Labeling: An Indictment," in *Revolting Librarians*, ed. Celeste West, Elizabeth Katz et al. (San Francisco: Booklegger, 1972), 45–49; Rogers, "Are We On Equal Terms Yet?, 181–96. Berman continued to keep a watchful eye on Library of Congress subject headings and, as late as 2007, recommended new headings. See "Memoranda to Interested Colleagues dated November 16, 2007," posted on Sanford Berman's website, www.sanfordberman.org/headings/headings111607.pdf, accessed 16 October 2009).

[85] Yale University Library began using *LGBTQ resource* as a local subject heading in 2007. The author was a member of the committee that recommended the establishment of the local subject heading.

[86] The Schlesinger Library as per Susan Von Salis, "When Subject Headings Aren't Enough" (paper presented at the annual meeting of the Society of American Archivists, 1994).

[87] Marston, "Archivists, Activists, and Scholars," 142.

CHAPTER 11

"A Culture of Concealment": Revealing the Records of Human Reproduction

TANYA ZANISH-BELCHER

HUMAN REPRODUCTION IS A MESSY AND COMPLICATED ISSUE, AND SO TOO IS THE WORK OF DOCUMENTING AND PROVIDING ACCESS TO PRIMARY SOURCES ABOUT IT. The concept of human reproduction encompasses many biological and cultural functions in society, including pregnancy, birth experiences, birth control, fertility and infertility, abortion, adoption, menstruation, menopause, reproductive technologies, political movements such as the pro-choice and pro-life movements, sexuality, and gendered identities. While collecting and preserving documentation on human reproduction may be difficult, it is essential that archives fully document such an integral part of human existence. Societal taboos regarding sexuality and cultural discomfort surrounding the topic may inhibit the creation of documents in the first place and subsequently make it difficult to acquire, describe, and even locate collections associated with the act of procreation and human biology. While human reproduction does affect the entire population, it has historically been seen as a women's issue and part of women's history, and accorded less significance as a result. Certainly, the development of second-wave feminism and the modern women's movement furthered the importance of collecting women's materials, which in many cases included materials on human reproduction and sexuality. Today, records on the subject exist in a variety of formats and repositories and are wide ranging in source and scope. Many are also governed by complex legal restrictions, privacy considerations, or other confidentiality concerns, which raise significant issues for archivists and researchers. The biggest challenge in documenting human reproduction however, remains in the fact that the topics represent "unspeakable" and hidden aspects of our lives, in what has been called "a culture of concealment."[1]

This essay reviews the scholarship in the field of human reproduction and the primary sources scholars have used, and then explores the challenges of locating sources. It is unclear whether there are simply too few primary sources, or too many with inadequate description. The essay also examines how archivists acquire and administer these records, how they assist researchers in locating relevant sources, and other preservation and access issues. The collecting and preserving of these papers and records is important work, not only for the history of women, but also for the history of humankind.

Scholarship on Human Reproduction

There has been considerable scholarship in monographic form about the human experience of reproduction in the latter half of the twentieth century, primarily about the experience of women.[2] Judith Leavitt's *Brought to Bed: Childbearing in America, 1750 to 1950* (1986) and *Women and Health in America: Historical Readings of the Issues* (1984) illustrate some of the broad themes involved. There have also been a number of cultural histories focusing on the development, history, and role of birth control; Linda Gordon's *Woman's Body, Woman's Right: A Social History of Birth Control in America* (1976) is one of the earliest. Also notable are Andrea Tone's *Devices and Desires: A History of Contraceptives in America* (2001) and *Controlling Reproduction: An American History* (1997), as well as Simone M. Caron's *Who Chooses? American Reproductive History since 1830* (2008). Published primary sources such as Laurel Thatcher Ulrich's classic, *A Midwife's Tale: The Life of Martha Ballard, Based on Her Diary, 1785–1812* have offered explorations of the early and distinct American female role in childbirth. Independent scholar Autumn Stanley devoted an entire chapter to women and their creative contributions to reproductive technologies in *Mothers and Daughters of Invention: Notes for a Revised History of Technology* (1993). Women developed numerous inventions specifically designed for the female physiology, such as alternative birth techniques, contraceptive douching, sponge tampons, menstrual cups, diaphragms, and other antifertility devices.[3] There have also been several recent cultural studies relating to menstruation, menopause, and the history of the feminine hygiene industry. Significant works include Elissa Stein and Susan Kim's *Flow: The Cultural Story of Menstruation* (2009); Lara Freidenfeld's *The Modern Period: Menstruation in Twentieth-Century America* (2009); Judith A. Houck's *Hot and Bothered: Women, Medicine, and Menopause in Modern America* (2008); Gabriella Burger's *Menopause and Culture* (1999); and Karen Houppert's *The Curse: Confronting the Last Unmentionable Taboo: Menstruation* (1999).

Historical articles focusing on the various biological and historical issues for women include Carroll Smith-Rosenberg's scholarship on the biological experiences of women in the nineteenth century beginning with 1973's "Female Animal: Medical and Biological Views of Women and Her Role in Nineteenth Century America" and "Puberty to Menopause: The Cycle of Femininity in Nineteenth Century America" published in the *Journal of American History* and *Feminist Studies*, respectively.[4] The *Journal of Women's History* has included research such as Johanna Schoen's "Between Choice and Coercion: Women and the Politics of Sterilization in North Carolina, 1929–1975" (2001) and "'All this that has happened to me shouldn't happen to nobody else': Loretta Ross and the Women of Color Reproductive Freedom Movement of the 1980s" (2010), as well as book and literature reviews.[5] *Feminist Review, Feminist Studies, Journal of the History of Sexuality*, the *National Women's Studies Association Journal*, and the *Women's History Review* all publish related scholarship. Primary sources used by these scholars include public records, private manuscripts, oral histories, and self-generated research data. Mary Hawkesworth recently analyzed the thematic content of *Signs: Journal of Women in Culture and Society* over a five-year period (2005–2010) and determined that 10 percent of the articles (twenty) were dedicated to topics related to sexualities and reproductive and genetic technologies.[6] A 2011 issue of the same journal was dedicated to "Gender and Medical Tourism" and included articles on abortion rights and international access to reproductive technologies. A cursory review of the sources used in these articles indicates a reliance on author-generated data in the form of surveys, oral history interviews, and public records. Anthropology, ethnology, and folklore journals and research collections document related topics such as contraception and midwifery. Specialized groups and organizations such as the Society for Menstrual Cycle Research and the Alliance for the Study of Adoption and Culture have organized symposia or conferences as part of their scholarly disciplines. The alliance hosted a 2012 conference to examine "not only adoption in its many historical and cultural variations but also parallel institutions such as foster care, orphanages, and technologically-assisted reproduction." Historians specializing in women and gender history have published consistently on this topic, especially since the advent of women's studies in the 1970s and 1980s. Many have focused on deeply imbedded biological beliefs based in the medical profession and the impact of these beliefs on social gender constructs.

In contrast to this rich record of academic scholarship, the archival community has produced little professional discussion or scholarship on the topic.[7] *The Selected Papers of Margaret Sanger* (2002) and *Emma Goldman: A Documentary History of the American Years* (2003)—both books documenting birth control activists—represent documentary editions of papers residing at various university and other repositories. The archival literature on collection development has touched on the often-politicized cultural topics of abortion and sexuality.[8] Timothy J. Gilfoyle's "Prostitutes in the Archives: Problems and Possibilities in Documenting the History of Sexuality" raises questions about working with the archival record when researching such a controversial subject. R. Jackson Armstrong-Ingram, in "The Givenness of Kin: Legal and Ethical Issues in Accessing Adoption Records," discusses the conflict between current

practice for records access and archival principles. Certainly, some articles on women's archives and collections, though limited in number, occasionally mention reproductive issues in the broader context of collecting.[9]
There are also examples of articles dealing with broader archival issues that
could be applied to records of this type, such as Barbara L. Craig, "Hospital
Records and Record-Keeping, c. 1850–c. 1950, Part 1: The Development
of Records in Hospitals"; Sara Hodsen's "In Secret Kept, In Silence
Sealed: Privacy in the Papers of Authors and Celebrities"; and Karen M.
Lamoree's "Documenting the Difficult or Collecting the Controversial."[10]
Unfortunately, there has been little published research dealing specifically
with any archival efforts to document human reproduction.

A 2005 Society of American Archivists session, "Controlling
Reproduction: Documenting the Post–World War II Revolution," focused
for the first time on the wide-ranging issues confronting archivists interested in collecting in this area. Kathryn Jacob's "Our Bodies, Ourselves,
Our Documents: The Challenges of Documenting the Struggle to Control
Women's Reproductive Lives" focused on the issues of acquiring and
accessing any materials related to human reproduction and the potential public relations quagmire. Jacob also presented a framework for
a documentation strategy for her institution, the Schlesinger Library.
Jennie Guilbard Diaz's paper, "Dr. Strangelove, or How I Learned to Stop
Worrying and Love the Pill," described Food and Drug Administration
(FDA) documentation of the Pill as it wound its way through bureau-
cratic review for final approval. Deborah Armentrout from the National
Archives (NARA) described the initial appraisal of the Pill's application as
a permanent record in "Enovid's Journey: From Approval to Appraisal of
the Pill." The session's final presentation (and earlier version of this essay),
"Biological Necessity: Reproductive Issues in U.S. Archival Collections,"
focused on the status of reproductive records in the United States and
examined the issues facing both researchers and archivists. Other than
this one SAA session, there has been little analysis or assessment of overall American recordkeeping practices in this area.

The Challenge for Researchers: Locating Sources on Human Reproduction

How do researchers locate and use records that possess such complex prov-enance and accessibility issues? They must first overcome several barriers. These include the functional and structural challenges of provenance-organized archives, the inherent difficulties in locating collections that document such private matters, and the increasing "fragmentation of context" in the digital environment.[11] In many cases, women's collec-tions (along with those of other ethnic and marginalized groups) have been obscured in repositories largely dedicated to economic and political elites, predominantly white males. While the concept of human repro-duction certainly concerns both men and women, the fact remains that human reproduction has historically been considered a women's issue, and thus women's collections will more likely include source materials on the subject. Archivists responsible for these collections have struggled to make them more accessible through improved description.[12] In addi-tion, marginalized groups have responded to the neglect of mainstream repositories by creating their own repositories "to retain control over their own documentation, over its presentation and interpretation, and over the very terms of access," as Rand Jimerson notes.[13] The proliferation of women's archives can certainly be considered evidence of this, although these repositories may not necessarily focus their collecting in this area.[14] Both mainstream and women-focused repositories have collected records and papers documenting human reproduction, sometimes purposefully, sometimes purely coincidentally.

Human reproduction has never been considered a topic for polite soci-ety; to a large degree, people are uncomfortable speaking about it except in the abstract. Thoughts and opinions on contraception, childbirth, infertility, menstruation, and menopause—while they may be shared in private—are not often recorded or written down. Therefore, such docu-mentation does not routinely make its way into mainstream repositories. Nineteenth-century documentation is certainly rare, primarily found in

diaries and letters.[15] Twentieth-century records reflect the impact of feminism, the increasing politicization of reproduction, and the impact of
reproductive and hygiene technologies, with evidence found in corporate
and organizational records, personal papers, and public records. The issue
is to assess and survey a wide variety of electronic and traditional collections, created by an overwhelming variety of creators and deposited in a
dizzying array of repositories, and still find relevant materials. In addition,
these collections are sometimes governed by conflicting ethical and legal
policies that can affect access. These can range from privacy issues for personal papers, patient confidentiality for medical records, and restrictions
on corporate records in regard to potential patent infringement.[16]

Researchers increasingly rely on the Internet and web resources, in
addition to bibliographic databases and union catalogs such as OCLC
and ArchivesUSA. It is unclear how successfully researchers are able to
navigate these complicated paths to sources. Doris Malkmus found in
her survey of history faculty that they located "online primary sources
in informal and unsystematic ways—equally often through e-mail, professional publications, online browsing, and word of mouth."[17] It would
seem that while online access through web and catalogs, and metasearch
engines including OCLC and Primo, may certainly have improved access
to selected women's collections, their successful retrieval still depends on
the quality of the description provided for each collection.

When simple searches were conducted in the Archival Materials category (1.5 million MARC records) in OCLC, the following catalog records
were returned. These searches were limited to Library of Congress subject
headings and keywords:

Abortion	1,057 records
Birth control	850 records
Childbirth	402 records
Fertility and human fertility	Little or none, due to association of term *fertility* with farming and agriculture
Infertility	42 records
Human reproduction (sexuality)	14 records
Human sexuality	299 records
Menopause	34 records
Menstruation	44 records
Pregnancy	377 records
Reproductive health	128 records
Reproductive technologies	13 records
Right to life movement	690 records

Conducting basic searches in Proquest's Archive Finder, which searches contributed finding aids, produced similar results:[18]

Abortion	285 finding aids
Fertility	23 finding aids
Menopause	5 finding aids
Pregnancy	46 finding aids
Right to life	333 finding aids
Sexuality	13 finding aids

ArchiveGrid, currently in beta testing by OCLC, potentially holds promise in this area by providing searches of WorldCat's 1.5 million MARC records, EAD finding aids, pdfs, html pages, and other Word documents.[19] Some of its numbers were much higher than those found in WorldCat or ArchiveFinder, but also included a wide variety of additional published materials and reports:[20]

Abortion	2,647 records
Contraception	281 records
Human fertility	238 records
Menopause	113 records
Menstruation	145 records
Pregnancy	1,156 records
Pro-life	3,005 records
Sexuality	1,555 records

Several observations can be made about these very general results. The political and cultural battles over the issue of abortion have produced a rich documentary record, and archivists have reaped the benefits. By contrast, it is striking to note how few results are returned for pregnancy and childbirth, and the more taboo subjects of menopause and menstruation. It would appear that these female experiences are extremely underdocumented in archival collections. There are a number of reasons that may result in such a lack of documentation. Individuals may simply not be recording or sharing this private information; or, if they do create or record it, it is perhaps subsequently destroyed.[21] Archivists may simply not be collecting it. It may be hiding in larger collections or in diaries or oral histories that lack indexing or description. Is it squeamishness about describing such topics in finding aids? Or is it that archivists cannot possibly describe collections at such a granular level? The latter seems more likely, when one considers the likelihood of a donor even recording such personal experiences. Even with the advent of digitizing and keyword searching, it is unlikely that enough specific keywords will exist to be found in every potential case.[22]

How archivists can provide descriptions that allow users to seamlessly find archival collections, let alone locate those materials documenting human reproduction, has long been problematic. One need only examine the history of archival descriptive standards development over the last thirty years to comprehend the underlying issues. Initially, complex archival descriptions for collections were forced to fit, uncomfortably, into library cataloging systems, whether a card catalog or MARC record.

Library of Congress subject headings, the primary pointers leading to archives collections, also had serious limitations. This had, and continues to have, serious implications for postfeminist women's collections; as librarian Sue Searing notes, "Modern subjects . . . must be squeezed into pre-existing outlines of knowledge that no longer fit the shape of current scholarly output."[23] These limitations led to the development of MARC-AMC (MAchine Readable Cataloging: Archival and Manuscripts Control Format) and the descriptive standard *Archives, Personal Papers, and Manuscripts* (APPM). Finding aids were simply left out of the initial cataloging discussion as they were too limited to share broadly, only being available in-house. Even with the eventual development of Encoded Archival Description (EAD) for finding aids and *Describing Archives: A Content Standard* (DACS, which replaced APPM), the difficulties in capturing archival complexity or volume still remain. The process of writing descriptions is subjective. As Wendy M. Duff and Verne Harris observe, "What we choose to stress and what we choose to ignore is always an unavoidable subjective, and the value judgments that archivists make affect in turn how our researchers find, perceive, and use records." These choices can certainly have a detrimental impact on locating collections that may have that one valuable reference to a childbirth experience; the reference may be lost because there is an incorrect subject heading, or it may have disappeared in the miasma of a generalized folder title. "More Product, Less Process" has certainly reinvigorated processing and access efforts for many, but archivists need to remember there may be a price to pay. Even with the promise of growing access through digitization, keywords, tagging, and "metadata as the interface," archivists still struggle with collection backlogs and an inability to completely and fully describe collections under their care.[24] One still finds archival finding aids existing in siloed databases or websites, albeit online, but the challenge is now to share this information in the aggregate. One can hope that as description or metadata and the linked data structures that provide them become more robust, archivists will be able to share more detailed and accurate information about what is in their collections. This could provide new outlets for collections documenting human reproduction. The web alone gives some access based on the individual repository and collection names, limited though this is.

One benefit of the web is that, from its very beginning, it has provided links to archival repositories as well as specialized subject guides that were previously unavailable. These include several national listings of women's collections, organized by state, and lists of primary sources and guides focusing on abortion, birth control, motherhood, and sexuality.[25] Many repositories also provide subject-based guides online for their own collections. Rutgers University's Special Collections provides a thorough subject-based guide to its manuscripts, including entries for abortion, adoption, birth control, childbirth, eugenic sterilization, genetics, midwives, obstetrics, pregnant women, sterilization, and teenage pregnancy. Other repositories such as the Minnesota Historical Society, the State Historical Society of Wisconsin, and Smith College have produced subject guides describing their collections related to reproductive rights and pro-choice and anti-abortion movements.[26] One potential solution for the future may be a guide for reproductive collections along the lines of the Mapping the World of Women's Information Services database, a project of the Aletta Institute for Women's History, which provides contact information for repositories focusing on women. As of 2012, there was no straightforward and broad-based intellectual access to these materials at the national level.[27]

A Range of Collections

A brief review of some collections demonstrates the difficulties researchers might face in locating sources on human reproduction. The majority of these collections were found using simple keyword searches relating to human reproduction and archives in Google, or relying on online guides to women's collections. For most of history, reproduction (and sexuality) has been considered part of private life that individuals have been reticent to discuss, let alone record in any way. Nonetheless, some documentation of these experiences can be found in personal papers and diaries. Family papers at the University of Texas contain nineteenth-century descriptions of contraceptive methods and abortifacients.[28] In addition to the voluminous and important collections of Margaret Sanger and Emma Goldman, there are also small collections of personal papers found at the Andover-Harvard Theological Library and Duke University. The papers of Ethel P. Storey are archived at the University of Washington. Her oral history, captured in the 1980s, explores depression-era issues relating to abortion, childbearing, and motherhood. The American Heritage Center contains the papers of Paul Popenoe, who worked with the Human Betterment Foundation as part of the eugenics movement. The Library of Congress holds the papers of Supreme Court Justice Harry Blackmun, who wrote the majority opinion for *Roe v. Wade*. Blackmun's papers also include related cases such as *Doe v. Bolton* and *Webster v. Reproductive Health Services*.[29] All letters regarding the subject of abortion to which Blackmun responded were retained, and a 10 percent sampling of the unanswered correspondence was also kept, as part of the Correspondence series.

Social and political movements, particularly those related to family activism, health, law, and policy, have spawned organizations that in turn have generated records. Many of these are preserved in archival repositories such as the Social Welfare History Archives at the University of Minnesota. These collections can be excellent sources of information on sexual practices and attitudes, as well as on the movements themselves. Examples include the Association for Voluntary Sterilization at the Social Welfare History Archives and the papers of Marian Stephenson Olden, a proponent of compulsory sterilization, located at Rutgers University. Under the twentieth-century construct of "reproductive rights," there are collections such as the records of American Citizens Concerned for Life, Inc., held at the Gerald R. Ford Presidential Library; Planned Parenthood, whose national records are housed at the Sophia Smith Collection at Smith College; the American Civil Liberties Union collection at Princeton University; and the Human Betterment Foundation at the California Institute of Technology. Other related collections include the La Leche League International records housed by DePaul University and the documents of the Midwives' Alliance of North America, also located at Smith. The number of smaller, localized or regional collections is simply astounding, including the records of the Campaign for Choice at the Nevada Women's Archives, the Philadelphia Reproductive Rights Organization at Temple University, and the Planned Parenthood of Pittsburgh at the University of Pittsburgh. Planned Parenthood of Mid-Michigan and the Right to Life of Michigan collections are located at the Bentley Library at the University of Michigan, and the papers of Nell Goodrich DeGolyer, the founder of the Dallas chapter of Planned Parenthood, are located at Southern Methodist University. Major human sexuality collections are also housed at Cornell University, the Kinsey Institute at Indiana University, and Duke University.

A wide range of local, state, and federal governmental agencies contain relevant records, including the Center for Reproductive Law and Policy, the US Food and Drug Administration, the National Institutes of Health, and the National Library of Medicine. The Alabama Department of Archives and History contains state records of interest including the records of the Department of Public Health and the Lieutenant Governor's Administrative files on infant mortality and abortion legislation, as well as the files of the Alabama Medical Services Administration program, which oversees abortion services and birth control in the state. One would expect to find similar collections in other state archives. The National Archives holds numerous records documenting reproductive health, including legal and legislative records, and a variety of films, photographs, and text documenting fertility and family planning. Medical archives are located at a large number of universities and medical schools, such as Harvard and Duke Universities. Finally, there are also ethnographic and folk collections that may shed light on experiences related to human reproduction, such as midwifery.[30]

Not surprisingly, a large number of collections documenting the business of reproduction reside in corporate and legal archives. The "Big Four" in feminine hygiene—Johnson & Johnson, Kimberly-Clark, Procter and Gamble, and Playtex—possess a wealth of cultural information on a wide variety of products through the years, including menstrual products, pregnancy testing, Viagra, and other reproductive technologies. The

Kimberly-Clark Corporate Archives includes advertisements, published works, memoranda, marketing reports, photographs, films and videos, product and packaging samples, contracts, patents, and other materials that document the creation, production, marketing, and distribution of Kotex from 1919 to the present.[31] However, the Kimberly-Clark collection is private, and access is restricted to the company's employees. Outside researchers may request access to and information from the collection, but it is granted on a case-by-case basis. In most cases, at least some information is supplied to the researcher. As in most business-related collections, some records have legitimate additional restrictions for legal, privacy, or competitiveness reasons.[32] A number of consumer advertising collections also exist in academic repositories, such as Duke University's Ad*Access Project, which includes over seven thousand advertisements printed in US and Canadian newspapers and magazines between 1911 and 1955. Of special note are advertisements for feminine hygiene products from the 1920s through the 1950s.[33] These secondary sources can provide valuable information and cultural context based on what was being communicated to potential customers.

Consumer use of birth control, fertility, and other reproductive technologies also needs to be collected and documented. Legal records held by law libraries and academic repositories are valuable sources of information and reflect the contentious legal issues raised by contraceptive and reproductive technologies. For example, two major legal collections document the trauma and legal wrangling related to the Dalkon Shield alone. The Dalkon Shield, a contraceptive intrauterine device (IUD), was manufactured and sold by the A.H. Robins Company at a time when women and their physicians were looking for a safe and simple alternative to the birth control pill. It later proved to produce harmful side effects to those who used it, resulting in litigation. The Harvard Law School Library acquired a voluminous collection of papers from the Dalkon Shield litigation, a tort case involving nearly four hundred thousand claims. The papers were donated in 2005 by the Ohio law firm Brown and Szaller, whose managing attorney, James Szaller, had been involved in the suit since 1975. The Dalkon papers include trial transcripts, medical information on the shield's effects, documents relating to company bankruptcy proceedings, and depositions and testimony from expert witnesses. A related collection, held by the University of Virginia, documents the Dalkon Shield Trust, which was created to distribute financial awards to claimants in this lawsuit.[34] According to the finding aid, the collection consists of 170,000 items extending some 327.5 linear feet and traces the history of the shield, from purchase of the device in 1970 through tort litigation and bankruptcy settlement in 1988. The collection also documents the establishment and ten-year history of the trust, which paid out almost $3 billion to over 218,000 claimants. Archival records documenting this topic will only continue to grow as technology plays an even larger role in human efforts to manage reproduction. This brief yet overwhelming review demonstrates the sheer range, variety, and volume of archives, records, and repositories documenting human reproduction, and the challenge it presents for researchers and historians.

Challenges from the Archivist's Perspective

While the challenges may appear daunting for the researcher and scholar, in many cases they are even greater for the archivist who determines what is to be collected and saved. A repository develops a collecting policy based on its institutional mission, and the archivist implements this policy by the solicitation, selection, and appraisal of relevant collections. These acts, circumscribed by space, time, and value of the records, determine what is seen of the past. As Eva Moseley, curator of manuscripts at the Schlesinger Library, observed in 1992, "Selection or appraisal is not only intellectually but also emotionally demanding. With no other function does an archivist's responsibility weigh so heavily."[35] As archivists, we face the ultimate balancing act of coordinating acquisition, appraisal, and access with staffing and space. A number of repositories that specialize in collecting women's history sources, such as the Schlesinger Library, the Sophia Smith Collection, and the Sallie Bingham Center at Duke University, already possess materials documenting reproduction because it has been such an integral part of women's lives. Other mainstream repositories can reassess their holdings to locate related materials or decide whether they wish to proactively collect on this topic. However, it is difficult to put out one more call for proactive collecting in this time of limited resources; perhaps it makes more sense to simply ask for awareness. A first priority in addressing the gap in primary sources related to human reproduction is for archivists to document and survey what has already been collected. Simply knowing what is in the collections—and ensuring good descriptive records for both traditional and digitized materials, finding aids, and subject guides—should be the first priority of any archivist. Archivists should investigate whether the collections include anything documenting human reproduction and, if so, consider focusing digitizing efforts on those collections. As well, archivists should assist those repositories without professional staffing to describe or share their resources with a wider audience. Information about the relevant collections should be submitted to the appropriate guides or lists, such as the biennially published US National Library of Medicine's *Directory of History of Medicine Collections*, or its newly established pilot project, History of Medicine Finding Aids Consortium.[36]

For other repositories wishing to actively collect, the challenge is more of a collection development issue based on the mission of the archives. A variety of collecting and documentation strategies may offer options for more fully documenting human reproduction, although it is debatable as to which repositories even possess the resources for these kinds of projects. Larry Hackman and Joan Warnow-Blewett describe a documentation strategy as "the case for broad, ongoing analysis of the adequacy of archival documentation and for coordinated action to improve the identification, retention, and treatment of records of enduring value."[37] The use of documentation strategies has received decidedly mixed reviews in the archival community. As previously noted, Kathryn Jacob of the Schlesinger Library provided a framework for her library's "documentation strategy" in 2005.[38] She conceded from the outset the difficulty in selecting precise criteria, but the Schlesinger's general focus is on reproductive choice, infertility, global population, female control of reproductive life, science and medicine, law and legislation, outreach and providing services, political activism, and funding and fund-raising. New areas include lesbian families, stem cell research, and cloning. She admitted that these broad categories could result in hundreds of collections.[39] Admittedly, the size and collecting scope of the Schlesinger make it a special case. Each archivist will need to make localized decisions regarding acquisition strategies, determining what works best for any given repository. But beyond the collecting efforts of individual repositories, what might be done nationally? A documentation strategy could provide an answer with an intellectual construct, developed by a national board or a national organization, similar to the American Institute of Physics, to drive collecting and consolidate resources in support of this work. The issues really relate, however, to the likelihood of any repository or organized group having the resources to explore these possibilities. The primary responsibility of many archivists remains localized: working one-on-one with individual donors and organizations for the deposit of their papers and records.

Archival collections with personal or potentially sensitive information can greatly complicate all archival functions "from appraisal and donor relations through description and reference."[40] Any archivist is keenly aware of the delicate give-and-take of working with donors, and issues of privacy may also influence whether this information is ever considered for donation in the first place. Oral history may provide some options for archivists interested in documenting rarely captured experiences. Working one-on-one is different, however, from documenting organizations involved in such sensitive topics. In this politically charged era, collection development for organizations working in these areas can be especially difficult. As Kathryn Jacob notes, when writing to conservative groups on behalf of the Schlesinger Library for the History of Women, "perhaps nothing I could write could dispel the preconceived notion of an ivy-covered bastion of East Coast liberalism and feminism."[41] This can work in both directions on the ideological spectrum. Conservative donors might fear that what they perceive as a left-leaning archives will downplay or even discard their records. To an archivist, it may seem obvious that any archives would want to document all aspects of an issue, but this may have to be elucidated clearly to potential donors, particularly in an area as sensitive and controversial as abortion. How does Jacob combat this perception? She contacts all potential donors, without regard to ideologies, emphasizing the educational component. She urges organizations to save records, even if they do not donate to the Schlesinger. She subscribes to newsletters, publications, and zines that in many cases are rare and unique. Karen M. Lamoree argues that the "key to success lies in a strategy for documenting an issue rather than a side, group, or individual."[42] It is important for the archivist to remain as professional and objective as is humanly possible and to recognize the politics of each individual situation. Any archives documenting the pro-choice and pro-life movements must also be aware of the potential for attracting unwanted negative attention. When the Iowa Women's Archives of the University of Iowa planned an open house to celebrate its acquisition of the records of a feminist health clinic (and abortion provider), a well-known anti-abortion activist visited the archives and its exterior hallway exhibit in advance. The event was not disrupted, due to, as the curator assumed, the archives' out-of-the-way location.[43] The safety and security of an archives could be compromised by the acquisition of a collection that touches a sensitive ideological nerve in the community at large. Some potential donors may question whether an archives, particularly one associated with an academic community, is genuinely willing to document all sides of an issue, including unpopular views. Archivists must work hard to dispel this notion, while at the same time, recognizing how their own inherent biases may drive their collecting.[44] A majority of institutions, one would hope, will have already created basic access policies for their collections, based on the profession's Code of Ethics.[45] Archivists must review requirements on a regular basis and incorporate changes into archives policy. They must also continually and proactively reevaluate potential legal and ethical issues, such as privacy, and know whom to contact in case of a problem.

What precisely are the definitions of *privacy* and *confidentiality*? According to Menzi Behrnd-Klodt, "these rights . . . primarily protect feelings and sensibilities and protect persons from undesirable and undesired publicity of matters that they want to keep private."[46] The need for this protection can certainly be applied to any documentation relating to the private life of an individual and, in some cases, third parties. Complicating these matters is the idea that "Privacy concepts have changed over time and differ from place to place."[47] Archivists must act with great care and sensitivity, balancing the information needs of researchers with other individuals' right to privacy. As just one example, the state of Iowa at one time provided Iowa State University with orphaned babies (prior to their adoption) to be housed in home economics cottages to teach students about parenting skills. The university archives now possesses records documenting this program and scrapbooks on individual babies; it created, in consultation with University Legal Services, a specialized policy governing access.[48] The creation and enforcement of detailed policies ensure the equitable treatment of researchers while also protecting privacy, and, at the same time, can encourage and reassure potential donors to save and donate unique and revealing materials. For women's collections, this is particularly important. Donors who are brave enough to write personal thoughts about childbirth or sexuality may still not be brave enough to open their papers to the public immediately. Giving donors an assurance of privacy for the long term can make them much more comfortable about sharing details of their private lives that—if disclosed immediately—could potentially be embarrassing.[49] Faculty researchers, who may conduct interviews on any number of reproduction-related topics, will in many cases be unable to provide access due to individual confidentiality agreements or their institutional review boards.[50] Medical records, or medical collections in mainstream, specialized, or data-based archives may also contain sensitive information that donors do not wish to have revealed.[51]

Corporations, maintaining records that are related to human reproduction vis-à-vis fertility technology development or the design of menstrual commercial merchandise, can also be impacted by these issues. In many cases, corporations may close their records to the public because these records provide internal information that could be used to advantage by competing entities. From the perspective of corporate archivists, their mission is to focus on the preservation of official records for internal purposes, as opposed to public access. Kimberly-Clark has outsourced the processing of its records to an external archival service company and does not allow public access to its records. Any scholar researching the records of a company's products and their impact on the female experience of menstruation may therefore find their access somewhat limited.[52]

An even more demanding challenge faced by archivists is the long-term preservation of records in their physical format. Artifacts and ephemera ranging from contraception kits to pamphlets, zines, and digital objects are a special challenge for any archivist due to their nonpermanent status and fragility. These formats can also include three-dimensional objects such as forceps and ultrasound equipment, sanitary napkins, and printed materials such as distributed pamphlets, posters, and advertising broadsides.[53] Large medical artifact collections housed at the American College of Obstetricians and Gynecologists, Virginia Commonwealth University, and Yale's Collection of Obstetrical Instruments contain objects dating back to the sixteenth century. Case Western Reserve

Percy Skuy History of Contraception Museum,
Dittrick Medical History Center, Case Western Reserve University.

University's Dittrick Museum houses the Percy Skuy Collection on the History of Contraception, which contains birth control apparatuses, such as intracervical devices (sponge, seaweed, and pebbles), modern devices (IUDs and cervical caps), and the odd (including animal dung, herbs, pessaries, condoms, pills, potions and plants, and rhythm method kits). The conservation, display, and storage challenges for these artifacts are obvious.[54] There are also a number of unique menstrual artifact collections, in both museums and private hands. The Museum of Menstruation, collected by a private individual interested in the topic, contains over four thousand items. These range from a 1914 Sears and Roebuck menstrual apron to advertisements, booklets, films, and sample belts and pads. No longer available to the public as of 1998, one can only hope the collection will be donated to an appropriate repository.[55] One mentioned as a potential recipient is the Powerhouse Museum in Sydney, Australia, which has focused its collecting efforts in this area. A recent exhibit, *The Rags: Paraphernalia of Menstruation*, utilized its collection and noted in its introduction, "Menstruation is a matter for private lives, not public exhibition, so few museums collect artifacts associated with this defining occurrence in women's lives."[56] History Factory archivist Sarah Souther, responsible for the archives collections of Kotex, observes that product and packaging samples are potential preservation challenges because they were often composites that included paper, plastic, rubber, and adhesives. The Kotex artifact collection also includes samples of sanitary napkins, sanitary pads, tampons, and various types of belts. Souther states, "Other than some minor discoloring or embrittlement of older cardboard product boxes and some rubber components of the belts, most samples seem to be surviving in good condition."[57] Unfortunately for the archivist, the majority of these objects have not been perceived as being historically valuable, but ephemeral and transitory.[58] Many women will recognize the Kotex pamphlet they were given in grade school, but very few will have saved them.

All archivists, including those documenting human reproduction, face unique preservation and access challenges in handling digital, electronic, and web-based collections and records. While sensitive subject matter does not alter the inherent nature of electronic records, it simply adds that additional layer of complexity to their management, ownership, and access.[59] Broad-based data collections as well as digital humanities research projects illustrate the continual challenges related to the long-term preservation of electronic records.[60] The growing likelihood that reproductive information will exist as electronic data will only add to these curatorial challenges with continued concerns over privacy.

The most significant challenge, however, may come from individuals, groups, and corporations participating in social media. Personal and public discussions have shifted away from traditional communication such as paper newsletters to an online presence in websites, individual personalized blogs, and social media; while this documentation may have previously only existed in analog form, it now only exists in the online environment. This presents both appraisal and preservation challenges for the archivist. These sites fall primarily into three topical categories: personal, political, and corporate. Numerous individual personal blogs and Facebook pages focus on adoption, fatherhood, infertility, parenthood, pregnancy, childbirth, and, in rarer cases, menopause.[61] Reflecting wider social politics, numerous personal and political blogs focus on the pro-choice and pro-life movements, and reproductive rights in general. However, there are also more neutral voices educating women about their health, their bodies, and the choices they must make. A number of groups and sites, including Bloodsisters and the Museum of Menovulatory Lifetime, are also celebrating the positive elements of the menstrual cycle with events such as blood-ins and other elements of menstrual activism.[62] However, the majority appear to focus on the menstrual experience as an "illness or hygiene problem" to be solved by the feminine products produced by mainstream corporate entities, such as Johnson and Johnson or Procter and Gamble. In response, many activist groups and sites offer alternative options.[63] In 2000, the Student Environmental Action Coalition (SEAC), an online activist group, began focusing on the issue of dioxins in tampons and the sustainability issue raised with the discarding of tampons and pads in its program Tampaction.[64] According to the SEAC blog, this eco-feminist movement seeks to educate the public on "the unhealthy consequences of tampons on menstruators' bodies and how corporate control and male corporate control has affected menstruators." The group provides links to alternatives such as organic tampons, Diva cups, pads, and sea sponges, and sponsors an electronic newsletter. The fight over the female consumer and where and why she spends her purchase dollars is nothing new; in the past, the primary documentation for menstruation has always been corporate-created ephemera.[65] What remains unclear is whether any repository is collecting these materials, or arranging for the appropriate permissions for any of it to be saved permanently. The prospect seems unlikely, as these blogs are not part of an official web-based repository's collection (where it might be crawled and preserved by a website preservation service such as Archive-It), and any physical records generated, such as brochures and zines, are transitory.[66] Given current trends, the loss of these virtual communities will continue to escalate as online communities and content continue to grow and then fade away.[67] Social media technologies such as Facebook, Twitter, and wikis pose similar preservation problems for the archivist.[68] While the archival community as a whole faces these issues, again, the subject matter and sensitivities involved with human reproduction raise the urgency for preservation to an even higher level.

Responsibility for the Future

The records documenting human reproduction present many challenges, ranging from cultural biases that restrict their creation to collecting, processing, preserving, and providing access. They pose distinct difficulties for researchers as well as archivists. However, archivists must remember to proactively collect these materials with sensitivity. The archivist should be knowledgeable about the potential legal and social implications of collecting these kinds of records. Policies governing the collecting, access, and use of such records should already be established. Preservation of both the physical and electronic records should also be a priority, ensuring long-term access for future scholars. We have barely begun to scratch the surface of documenting a core part of the human experience that is, in many ways, still hidden. Archivists for all collections, but for women's collections in particular, must work together to ensure these records—regardless of format—are preserved and made accessible to researchers and the general public. Archivists need to understand the many complexities and sensitivities involved with collecting these kinds of records and also to take responsibility for making them available to as wide an audience as possible.

NOTES

[1] Term used in Karen Houppert, *The Curse: Confronting the Last Unmentionable Taboo: Menstruation* (New York: Farrar, Straus and Giroux, 2000).

[2] Historian Joan W. Scott discusses related issues and the history of women in her essay, "Feminism's History," *Journal of Women's History* 16, no. 2 (2004): 10–29. She notes there has been "far more success in introducing women into the picture than in reconceiving it in terms of gender" (11). See also Anne Firor Scott, "Unfinished Business," *Journal of Women's History* 8, no. 2 (1996): 111–20.

[3] Stanley's collection is housed at Iowa State University and includes a reusable menstrual pad invented, marketed, and sold by a woman—an example, according to Stanley, of women proactively caring for their own physiology. Stanley's collection also includes biographical information about the women who developed numerous sanitary products, specifically for Johnson & Johnson and Kimberly-Clark.

[4] About Victorian women, Carroll Smith-Rosenberg and Charles Rosenberg state, "All women were prisoners of the cyclical aspects of their bodies, of the great reproductive cycle bounded by puberty and menopause, and by the shorter but recurrent cycles of childbearing and menstruation," in "The Female Animal: Medical and Biological Views of Women and her Role in 19th Century America," *Journal of American History* 60, no. 2 (1973): 336. Also see Carroll Smith-Rosenberg, "The New Woman and the New History," *Feminist Studies* 3, nos. 1–2 (1975): 185–98.

[5] Schoen later published *Choice and Coercion: Birth Control, Sterilization, and Abortion in Public Health and Welfare* (Chapel Hill: University of North Carolina Press, 2005).

[6] Mary Hawkesworth, "Signs 2005–2010: Reflections on the Nature and Global Reach of Interdisciplinary Feminist Knowledge Production," *Signs: Journal of Women in Culture and Society* 36, no. 3 (2011): 512. There is certainly more writing done on sexuality and archives, an example being John D. Wrathall's "Provenance as Text: Reading the Silences around Sexuality in Manuscript Collections," *Journal of American History* (June 1992): 165–78.

[7] Based on a review of *American Archivist, Archival Issues: Journal of the Midwest Archives Conference, Provenance, Journal of Archival Organization, Archivaria,* and published secondary works.

[8] Brief references to collecting in these areas are made in Linda Henry, "Collecting Policies of Special-Subject Repositories," *American Archivist* 43 (Winter 1980): 57–63; H. Thomas Hickerson, "Ten Challenges for the Archival Profession," *American Archivist* 64 (Spring/Summer 2011): 6–16; and Christine Weideman, "A New Field Map for Field Work: Impact of Collections Analysis on the Bentley Historical Library," *American Archivist* 54, no. 1 (1991): 54–60.

[9] Andrea Hinding, ed., *Women's History Sources: A Guide to Archives and Manuscript Collections in the United States,* 2 vols. (New York: R. R. Bowker, 1979). This survey, the first of its kind to specifically survey US women's collections, does include references to relevant collections.

[10] Barbara L. Craig, "Hospital Records and Record-Keeping, c. 1850–c. 1950, Part 1: The Development of Records in Hospitals," *Archivaria* 29 (Winter 1989–1990): 57–87; Sara Hodsen, "In Secret Kept, In Silence Sealed: Privacy in the Papers of Authors and Celebrities," *American Archivist* 67, no. 2 (2004): 194–211; and Karen M. Lamoree, "Documenting the Difficult or Collecting the Controversial," *Archival Issues: Journal of the Midwest Archives Conference* 20, no. 2 (1995): 149–53.

[11] Noted in Anne J. Gilliland's 1995 article, "Health Sciences Documentation and Networked Hypermedia: An Integrative Approach," *Archivaria* 41 (1995): 41–56. Jennifer Shaffner discusses these issues in "The Metadata *Is* the Interface: Better Description for Better Discovery of Archives and Special Collections, Synthesized from User Studies" (Columbus: OCLC Research, 2009).

[12] A 1994 SAA session, "Research Strategies: When Subject Headings Aren't Enough," included "Lost in the Archives: Uncovering Hidden Sources on the History of Women" by Kären M. Mason, the curator of the Iowa Women's Archives (University of Iowa). While the focus may have been subject headings, many of the observations could also be applied to any sort of archival description.

[13] Randall C. Jimerson, "Embracing the Power of Archives," *American Archivist* 69 (Spring–Summer 2006): 31. There are also distinct skill sets involved in the development of "archival intelligence" in attempting to locate and use these records referred to as a "basic conceptual knowledge and the development of a general framework of archival management, representation and descriptive practices" as articulated by Elizabeth Yakel and Deborah A. Torres, "AI: Archival Intelligence and User Expertise," *American Archivist* 66 (Spring–Summer 2003): 54.

[14] Kären Mason and Tanya Zanish-Belcher, "A Room of One's Own: Women's Archives in the Year 2000," *Archival Issues: Journal of the Midwest Archives Conference* 24, no. 1 (1999): 37–54. While this article specifically focused on US archives, there are also international archives, such as Aletta, that have records documenting reproduction.

[15] An interesting discussion of birth control, childbirth, and abortion (based on primary sources) on the nineteenth-century frontier is offered in Sandra L. Myres, *Westering Women and the Frontier Experience, 1800–1915* (Albuquerque: University of New Mexico Press, 1986), 154–56. The author comments in the footnote: "Careful study of a number of collections of women's papers has led me to conclude that references to marital intimacy, contraception, and other delicate matters related to sex were carefully expurgated from the materials before they were placed in libraries, archives, and other depositories. This was probably done not by the original writers but by children or grandchildren horrified to think their parents ever 'talked about things like that.' . . . The existence of some rather explicit material on sexual matters and the tantalizing omissions from letter collections, missing pages, or inked or cut out paragraphs of diaries when the proceeding or succeeding materials suggest that intimate topics might have been discussed leads one to suspect latter-day censorship." See also *Inscribing the Daily: Critical Essays on Women's Diaries*, ed. Suzanne L. Bunkers and Cynthia A. Huff (Amherst: University of Massachusetts Press, 1996).

[16] Erik Moore, "Hiding Information or Providing Access to Archives (HIPAA): Protected Health Information in University Archives" (presentation at the Midwest Archives Conference, Columbus, Ohio, 4 May 2007). See also Menzi L. Behrnd-Klodt, *Navigating Legal Issues in Archives* (Chicago: Society of American Archivists, 2008); Menzi L. Behrnd-Klodt and Peter J. Wosh, eds., *Privacy and Confidentiality Perspectives: Archivists and Archival Records* (Chicago: Society of American Archivists, 2005); and Heather MacNeil, *Without Consent: The Ethics of Disclosing Personal Information in Public Archives* (Chicago: Society of American Archivists and Scarecrow Press, 1992).

[17] Doris Malkmus, "'Old Stuff' for New Teaching Methods: Outreach to History Faculty Teaching with Primary Sources," *portal: Libraries and the Academy* 10, no. 4 (2010): 424. Helen R. Tibbo noted in her ACRL conference presentation paper, "How Historians Locate Primary Resource Materials: Educating and Serving the Next Generation of Scholars" (Charlottesville, VA, 2003), that only "48 percent of historians frequently or always tell their students to search the OCLC or RLIN union databases" and "Only 35 percent of the professors frequently suggested to their students in classes that they search the web to discover the location of relevant primary sources." See also Wendy M. Duff and Catherine A. Johnson, "Accidentally Found on Purpose: Information Seeking Behavior of Historians in Archives," *Library Quarterly* 72 (October 2002): 472–96; Kathleen Feeney, "Retrieval of Archival Finding Aids Using World Wide Web Search Engines," *American Archivist* 62 (Fall 1999): 206–28; Shaffner, "The Metadata *Is* the Interface"; and Elizabeth Yakel, "Listening to Users," *Archival Issues: Journal of the Midwest Archives Conference* 26, no. 2 (2002): 111–27.

[18] It should be noted, of course, that although this is a profit-based subscription service, any repository can submit finding aids.

[19] Jennifer Shaffner, OCLC, email, 6 September 2012. ArchiveGrid, "About ArchiveGrid," http://beta.worldcat.org/archivegrid/about/, accessed 26 October 2012. In addition to harvesting OCLC records, repositories may also submit finding aids.

[20] Searches conducted 23 August 2012.

[21] Based on the author's personal experience in collecting an oral history interview specifically focusing on women in agriculture. The interviewee, whom I knew fairly well, shared that she had gotten pregnant out of wedlock and had to marry. One wonders, without that personal relationship and comfort level, would that information have even been shared? And mixed in an interview focusing on another issue, would it have been identified or indexed in any way for researchers to find?

[22] It is intriguing to consider the juxtaposition in the cultural changes for women's sharing through the years when considering the cases described by Sandra Myres in note 15 with the modern ease of "publishing" personal information in blogging and zines. Virginia Corvid's "Building Community through Self-expression: Zines as Archival Materials," published in this volume, illustrates women proactively creating primary source materials, in many cases to share private information about such things as abortion or sexuality. Zines and other self-published works have played a significant role in the feminist movement. The first publication of the now famous *Our Bodies, Ourselves* was a self-designed and published booklet by the Boston Women's Health Book Collective. See also

Andreas Kitzmann, "That Different Place: Documenting the Self within Online Environments," *Biography* 26, no. 1 (2003): 48–65; and Catherine O'Sullivan, "Diaries, On-line Diaries, and the Future Loss to Archives; or, Blogs and the Blogging Bloggers Who Blog Them," *American Archivist* 68 (Spring/Summer 2005): 53–73.

[23] Susan E. Searing, "How Libraries Cope with Interdisciplinarity: The Case of Women's Studies," *Issues in Integrative Studies* 10 (1992): 8. Kären Mason also discussed this issue in regard to women's collections in her 1994 Society of American Archivists presentation mentioned in note 12.

[24] Shaffner, "The Metadata *Is* the Interface."

[25] Archives for Research on Women and Gender at the University of Texas at San Antonio Libraries, "Special Collections," http://lib.utsa.edu/SpecialCollections/WomenGender/links.html, accessed 6 July 2011; American Women's History: A Research Guide, Middle Tennessee State University, "Birth Control and Abortion," http://frank.mtsu.edu/~kmiddlet/history/women/wh-birthcontrol.html, and "Sexualtiy," http://frank.mtsu.edu/~kmiddlet/history/women/wh-sexuality.html, accessed 6 July 2011. And, of course, library catalogs and metasearch engines still provide access to secondary materials, such as advice manuals, textbooks, and women's magazines.

[26] Minnesota Historical Society Library, "History Topics: Abortion Rights, Pro-Life Movements," http://www.mnhs.org/library/tips/history_topics/96choicelife.html, accessed 21 June 2011; Rutgers University Libraries, "Women's History Sources: A Guide," http://www.libraries.rutgers.edu/rul/libs/scua/womens_fa/womensubjects.shtml, accessed 21 June 2011; Smith College Libraries, Sophia Smith Collection, "Reproductive Rights and Women's Health," http://www.smith.edu/library/libs/ssc/subjbc.html, accessed 22 June 2011.

[27] Aletta Institute for Women's History, "Mapping the World of Women's Information Services," http://www.aletta.nu/aletta/eng/projects/mapping-the-world, accessed 16 November 2011.

[28] The Neblett and Newcomb Collections and the Clow Papers were all used in Sandra L. Myres's *Westering Women and the Frontier Experience, 1800–1915.* Letters and diaries both contain relevant discussions concerning the management and prevention of pregnancy.

[29] Roe v. Wade, 410 US 113 (1973); Doe v. Bolton, 410 US 179 (1973); Webster v. Reproductive Health Services, 492 US 490 (1989). Justice Warren Burger's papers are at the University of William and Mary and are closed until 2026.

[30] Examples include the Archive of American Folk Medicine (UCLA); the National Anthropological Archives (Smithsonian); and the Archives of Appalachia (East

Tennessee State University). The particular subject matter of human reproduction, or in many cases, "female concerns," can also introduce challenges for researchers working with original texts, as demonstrated in Pamela Innes, "Ethical Problems in Archival Research: Beyond Accessibility," *Journal of Language Communications* (2009), doi: 10.1016/j.langcom.2009.11.006.

[31] A number of works examine corporate impact on the various areas of human reproduction technologies, such as Elizabeth Arveda Kissling, *Capitalizing on the Curse: The Business of Menstruation* (Boulder, CO: Lynne Rienner, 2006); and Thomas Heinrich and Bob Batchelor, eds., *Kotex, Kleenex, Huggies: Kimberly-Clark and the Consumer Revolution in American Business* (Columbus: Ohio State University Press, 2004). Recent studies have focused on the various aspects of reproductive technologies, including class and race issues in accessing these technologies, such as Lorraine Hudson Culley and Nicky Van Rooij, eds., *Marginalized Reproduction: Ethnicity, Infertility and Reproductive Technologies* (London: Earthscan, 2009).

[32] As NARA senior records analyst Deborah Holland Armentrout noted in her appraisal of Enovid (the Pill), she had to also consider confidentiality and trade secrets during the appraisal process, "Controlling Human Reproduction: The Challenges of Documenting the Post–World War II Revolution," Society of American Archivists Annual Meeting presentation, 2005.

[33] Duke University, http://library.duke.edu/digitalcollections/adaccess/, accessed 30 July 2012. This collection is organized by product, company, date, publication, subject, and medium. The advertising techniques (using many of the images from Duke's collection) utilized for menstrual products are described in detail in Elissa Stein and Susan Kim, *Flow: The Cultural Story of Menstruation* (New York: St. Martin's, 2009).

[34] A collection description also appears in Worldcat; Harvard's does not, although it may not yet be processed.

[35] Eva Moseley, "Collecting the Taboo/Past for the Future" (paper presented at the Society of American Archivists Annual Meeting, 1992). She also notes, "Of course, most people don't record much about the most intense and intimate matters."

[36] The directory is available online, http://wwwcf.nlm.nih.gov/hmddirectory/index.cfm. The consortium currently indexes over three thousand finding aids from twenty institutions and is also available online, US National Library of Medicine, "History of Medicine Finding Aid Consortium," http://www.nlm.nih.gov/hmd/consortium/index.html, accessed 7 December 2011.

[37] Doris Malkmus provides a cogent and concise review of the history of documentation strategy, "Documentation Strategy: Mastodon or Retro-Success?" *American Archivist* 71 (Fall/Winter 2008): 384–409.

[38] Which is which? Terry Abraham assesses the difference in "Collection Policy or Documentation Strategy: Theory and Practice," *American Archivist* 54 (Winter 1991): 44–52.

[39] Kathryn Jacob, "Controlling Human Reproduction: Documenting the Post–World War II Revolution," (paper presented at the Society of American Archivists Annual Meeting, 2005), 3.

[40] Moseley, "Collecting the Taboo," 3.

[41] Jacob, "Controlling Human Reproduction," 4–5.

[42] Lamoree, "Documenting the Difficult," 149. See also Brian Keough, "Documenting Diversity: Developing Special Collections of Underdocumented Groups," *Library Collections, Acquisitions and Technical Services* 26 (2002): 241–51.

[43] Kären Mason, curator, Iowa Women's Archives, University of Iowa, email to author, 6 November 2012.

[44] See Elisabeth Kaplan, "We Are What We Collect, We Collect What We Are: Archives and the Construction of Identity," *American Archivist* 63 (Spring/ Summer 2000): 126–51.

[45] *Society of American Archivists Code of Ethics*, www2.archivists.org/saa-core-values-statement-and-code-of-ethics, accessed 13 December 2011.

[46] Menzi Behrnd-Klodt, *Navigating Legal Issues in Archives* (Chicago: Society of American Archivists, 2008), 107.

[47] Behrnd-Klodt, *Navigating Legal Issues in Archives*, 106.

[48] See also Tim Pyatt, "Balancing Issues of Privacy and Confidentiality in College and University Archives," in *College and University Archives: Readings in Theory and Practice*, ed. Christopher J. Prom and Ellen D. Swain (Chicago: Society of American Archivists, 2008), 211–26.

[49] Judith Schwarz, "The Archivist's Balancing Act: Helping Researchers While Protecting Individual Privacy," *Journal of American History* 29 (June 1992): 179; reprinted in Behrnd-Klodt and Wosh, eds., *Privacy and Confidentiality Perspectives*. While most of Schwarz's commentary related to LGBT issues, certainly it can be applied to any aspect of sexual and reproductive privacy.

[50] As an example, Dr. Christa Craven (College of Wooster) has retained tape recordings and transcriptions from interviews with homebirth mothers, but

these are unavailable as the participants were promised confidentiality. She destroyed interviews she conducted with midwives due to legal issues in the state of Virginia; however, the results of her research have been published in *Pushing for Midwives: Homebirth Mothers and the Reproductive Rights Movement* (Philadelphia: Temple University Press, 2010). Craven, email exchange with author, 2 August 2012. Interviews conducted under the rubric of research will certainly have additional restrictions through university Institutional Research Boards (IRBs).

[51] The Health Insurance Portability and Accountability Act of 1996 (HIPAA) has had a special impact on archives. The Privacy Rule protects all "individually identifiable health information" held or transmitted by a covered entity (primarily health care providers), in any form or media, whether electronic, paper, or oral. The Privacy Rule calls this information "protected health information (PHI)." Martin L. Levitt, "Ethical Issues in Constructing a Eugenics Web Site," in Behrnd-Klodt and Wosh, eds., *Privacy and Confidentiality Perspectives*, 122.

[52] Paul C. Lasewicz, "Riding Out the Apocalypse: The Obsolescence of Traditional Archivy in the Face of Modern Corporate Dynamics," *Archival Issues: Journal of the Midwest Archives Conference* 22, no. 1 (1997): 61–76.

[53] Ken Arnold and Thomas Söderqvist observe, when examining forceps in the Wellcome Collection (London), "And finally, for those with a concern for power relations, the asymmetry of those forceps might symbolize how, throughout history, instruments have enabled professional practitioners (most often men) at one end to control patients (in this case always women) at the other." In Ken Arnold and Thomas Söderqvist, "Medical Instruments in Museums: Immediate Impressions and Historical Meaning," *FOCUS-ISIS* 102, no. 4 (2011): 727–28.

[54] Case Western Reserve University, Dittrick Medical History Center, *Virtue, Vice, and Contraband: A History of Contraception*, "The Percy Skuy Collection," http://www.case.edu/affil/skuyhistcontraception/index.html, accessed 21 March 2012.

[55] The Museum of Menstruation and Women's Health is now only available online, http://www.mum.org, accessed 6 July 2011.

[56] Powerhouse Museum *The Rags: Paraphernalia of Menstruation*, curated by Megan Hicks, curator of Health and Medicine, http://www.powerhousemuseum.com/rags/, accessed 15 November 2011.

[57] Sarah Souther, archivist, email exchange with author, 25 March 2004. Analyzing corporate archives and access to records documenting aspects of human reproduction certainly is a possible research project for the future; Jenny Kane, email exchange with author, 19 April 2005. Access to artifacts (as well as audio, film,

multimedia, and videotape) in archival collections can also be problematic for researchers.

[58] While employed at the Alabama Department of Archives and History (ADAH), the author was able to obtain a copy of an anti-abortion flyer that targeted Dr. David Gunn, an Alabama doctor providing abortion (who was murdered in Pensacola in 1993). It was added to ADAH's collections and is available as SPR408. This pro-life flier measures eleven by fourteen inches, and is on bright yellow paper. Included is a photograph of Dr. Gunn, Dr. Gunn's professional and home addresses, a copy of his daily itinerary, and suggestions on what to do (such as prayer and direct contact with Dr. Gunn).

[59] Susan Legène, "Flatirons and the Folds of History: On Archives, Cultural Heritage and Colonial Legacies," in *Traveling Heritages: New Perspectives on Collecting, Preserving and Sharing Women's History*, ed. Saskia Wieringa (Amsterdam: Aksant Academic Publishers, 2008), 47.

[60] See also Bruce Ambacher, *Thirty Years of Electronic Records* (New York: Scarecrow Press, 2003); Philip C. Bantin, *Understanding Data and Information Systems for Recordkeeping* (New York: Neal-Schuman Publishers, 2008); Christopher (Cal) Lee, ed., *I, DIGITAL: Personal Collections in the Digital Era* (Chicago: Society of American Archivists, 2011); and William Saffady, *Managing Electronic Records*, 4th ed. (New York: ARMA International and Neal-Schuman Publishers, 2009).

[61] See the following examples: *Childfree Me: Choosing to be Childless when the World Wants Me to Breed*, http://childfreeme.blogspot.com; *Childless by Marriage*, http://childlessbymarriage.blogspot.com/; *Adoptions Together Birth Parent Blog*, http://www.birthparentblog.com; Sandy Robertson, *Infertility-Fertility Over 40*, http://infertility-fertility.blogspot.com; *Tales from My Dusty Ovaries*, http://mydustyovaries.blogspot.com; *Human Reproduction*, http://humanreproduction.blogspot.com; *Radical Midwife*, http://radicalmidwife.blogspot.com; *Ob/Gyn Kenobi*, http://obgynkenobi.blogspot.com; *Un-Expecting*, http://myabortionblog.tumblr.com; *The Abortioneers* http://abortioneers.blogspot.com; ProLifeBlogs.com, http://www.prolifeblogs.com; *Reproductive Rights Prof Blog*, http://lawprofessors.typepad.com/reproductive_rights; Menopause Goddess Blog, http://www.menopausegoddessblog.com/ Menopause and Wellness, http://www.shmirshky.com/menopause-blog/ category/menopause-blog, all accessed 1 October 2012.

[62] Bloodsisters.org; Museum of Menovulatory Lifetime, http://www.moltx.org, accessed 5 November 2012.

[63] See, for example, Bloodsisters.org; Cloth Menstrual Pad Database, "Patterns and Guides," http://clothpads.wikidot.com/patterns; GladRags. http://gladrags.com/; Lunapads, http://lunapads.com/; *Menstrualcupinfo's Blog* http://

menstrualcupinfo.wordpress.com/; Society for Menstrual Cycle Research (which sponsors the Blood, Body and Brand Conference), http://menstruation-research.org/; *Cycling*, http://menstruationresearch.org/blog/; This Is Personal, http://www.coalitiontoprotectwomenshealth.org/; and S.P.O.T. The Tampon Health Site at http://www.spotsite.org/, all accessed 30 July 2012.

[64] SEAC Tampaction Campaign, http://tampaction.wordpress.com/about/, accessed 21 March 2012.

[65] See Stein and Kim, *Flow: Cultural Story of Menstruation*.

[66] Archive-It is available as a subscription service for archives and libraries, http://www.archive-it.org/. For many of the technical and collection development issues relating to the preservation of web-based materials and blogs, see Amy Benson and Kathryn Allamong Jacob, "No Documents, No History: Traditional Genres, New Formats," in *Make Your Own History: Documenting Feminist and Queer Activism in the 21st Century*, ed. Lyz Bly and Kelly Wooten (Los Angeles: Litwin Books, 2012), 123–40.

[67] Link rot and website loss are a continual problems and also indicate the need for preservation. For additional information, see Gunther Eysenbach and Mathieu Trudel, "Going, Going, Still There: Using the WebCite Service to Permanently Archive Cited Web Pages," *Journal of Medical Internet Research* 7, no. 5 (2005): e60; Daniel Gomes and Mário J. Silva, "Modeling Information Persistence on the Web," *International Conference on Web Engineering* (2006); and Hany M. SalahEldeen and Michael L. Nelson, "Losing My Revolution: How Many Resources Shared on Social Media Have Been Lost?," http://arxiv.org/abs/1209.3026, 13 September 2012, 1–12. Also see Benson and Jacob, "No Documents, No History." One example of a lost e-zine is *The Whirling Cervix*, posted by activist Carol Church, which is no longer available online.

[68] And, of course, the same issues in regard to confidentiality, ethics, and privacy may still apply to these materials as well.

Documenting Women's Experiences

CHAPTER 12

Raising the Archival Consciousness: How Women's Archives Challenge Traditional Approaches to Collecting and Use, Or, What's in a Name?

KÄREN M. MASON AND TANYA ZANISH-BELCHER

ABSTRACT

This article examines archival collecting, taking as case studies two women's archives. Drawing on their experiences building the collections of the Archives of Women in Science and Engineering (Iowa State University) and the Iowa Women's Archives (University of Iowa), the authors explore how such efforts challenge traditional approaches to collecting. Proactive collecting, such as oral history projects focused on Latinas or women scientists, helps fill gaps in the historical record by encouraging people who have not traditionally been donors to participate in building and using diverse archival collections.

IN 2000, WE COAUTHORED "A ROOM OF ONE'S OWN: WOMEN'S ARCHIVES IN THE YEAR 2000," AN ARTICLE FOCUSED ON THE GROWING NUMBER OF WOMEN'S ARCHIVES IN THE UNITED STATES AND THE IMPETUS FOR THEIR CREATION.[1] We argued that women's archives were founded on the premise that women's lives and activities were not being adequately documented in traditional repositories and that women's archives turned collection development on its head in the 1970s by insisting that the papers of women be preserved and made accessible to researchers. These early archives, like the incipient field of women's history, focused on the contributions made by women to American society and history, high-lighting prominent women with public roles. Like the field of women's history itself, however, women's archives have evolved over the past several decades, gradually broadening their collecting scope to include previously underdocumented groups. Women's archives continue to seek out the papers of groups and subjects whose histories are not being preserved to document a broad range of women and to build a diverse set of collections. Women's collections archivists work proactively to capture the parts of society so often left out of the mainstream and in so doing give a voice to the disempowered. As a result, women's archives have altered the landscape of archival collecting, improving the overall documentation of culture and society in the United States. This article considers the methods and techniques women's archives utilize to document underrepresented groups and the uses that are made of the collections thus acquired.

Literature Review

Since the early 1970s, there have been occasional articles on the subject of women's archives in the library and archival literature, but analyses of the cultural context and impact of women's collections have not kept pace with the establishment of women's archives. For the most part, publications on the subject have been concerned with compiling and disseminating information about women's history resources in archives. It is important, however, to view the articles specifically about women's archives in the context of a larger scholarly literature on the nature of historical documentation of women. Archivists do not work in a vacuum; they interact with scholars and other researchers and respond to and encourage new areas of research.

When Martha Bell's article on women's collections appeared in *College and Research Libraries* in 1959, it focused primarily on collections of published materials, reflecting how few women's archives existed at the time. By 1973, the women's movement had sufficient influence on the fields of archives and history that *American Archivist* devoted an entire issue to the role of women in the archival profession and to the necessity of rethinking archival collecting and description to include women. Articles by archivist Eva Moseley and historian Joanna Schneider Zangrando considered the impact of feminism on history and archives.[2] Moseley's article reflected the uncertainty that surrounded this new field of women's history. She argued that women should be included in history and that archivists have a responsibility to preserve women's papers, but if all archivists did a good job of documenting women there might be no need for separate women's archives in the future.[3] Three women's studies journals founded in the 1970s—*Feminist Studies, Signs,* and *Frontiers*—helped solidify the scholarly claims of the field. Each included articles in the field of women's history, and *Signs* had a section entitled "Archives," which printed documents along with introductions by archivists or historians. The Archives section underscored the existence of varied, interesting archival sources for women's history. The 1970s also witnessed the publication of a number of guides to women's collections within mainstream repositories, as well as the mammoth *Women's History Sources*, a compendium of brief descriptions of manuscript collections held by repositories across the country.[4] The 1970s were, thus, a time of making the case for women's history by demonstrating that there were indeed enough historical resources to support this field of study.

By 1980, the field of women's history was maturing and changing, increasingly influenced by social history. No longer were historians interested solely in "great" women—those active and prominent in the public sphere. Writing history "from the bottom up," social historians brought to the foreground groups that had previously been ignored or forgotten by historians. The underlying philosophy of social history likewise influenced the perspective and functioning of women's history and women's archives. Eva Moseley explained the changes in women's history to her archival audience and suggested to mainstream archivists how one goes about collecting women's papers. Furthermore, she noted the lack of sources created by groups such as working-class women, but was not yet ready to embrace the concept of an activist archival profession in which archivists would create documentation through means such as oral history to fill gaps in the historical record.[5] To her (and to many other archivists), the notion of the *activist archivist* was still a somewhat radical idea. The implication was that *historians* should conduct oral history interviews, not *archivists*.

In fact, women historians did undertake oral history projects when they were unable to find adequate sources in archives. Most famously, Darlene Clark Hine's *The Black Women in the Middle West Project* enlisted volunteers to scout their local communities for sources and to capture their community's history through oral history interviews. Moseley's own institution—the Schlesinger Library—likewise undertook an oral history project to record interviews with African American women.[6]

Publications such as *Feminist Collections*, launched in 1980, disseminated information about print and nonprint resources, while archivists and historians compiled printed guides to sources on particular topics or geographical areas.[7] By 1986, the field had developed sufficiently to warrant an issue of *Special Collections* focused on women's collections. While celebrating the emergence of these new women's collections, editor Suzanne Hildenbrand expressed an increasing concern among curators of women's collections about the lack of diversity in their holdings. Hildenbrand also warned:

> The success of women's collections today should not obscure the limited and fragile nature of that success. There are numerous women for whom there are no adequate research collections and whose past and present suffer accordingly. These include the Hispanic women of the US, Francophone women of Canada, Native American women of both nations, the poor and others.[8]

She worried that the link between feminism and women's collections could be a liability, threatening marginal collections if support for feminism waned. Women's historians likewise questioned the focus on white women and in fact on studying women apart from men. By the end of the 1980s, the field could support a new journal devoted specifically to women's history, *The Journal of Women's History*, which began publication in 1989, as well as the journal *Gender and History* (also begun in 1989), which signaled the rise of gender studies alongside women's history.

The archival literature of the 1990s looked to the past but also to the future. Anke Voss-Hubbard explored the emergence of the first women's archives in the 1930s and 1940s, while a 1995 conference hosted by the Schlesinger Library addressed the growing impact of the technological revolution on archives. A selection of papers presented at the conference was published as *Women, Information, and the Future: Collecting and Sharing Resources Worldwide*.[9] This broadened the discussion of women's information sources to include global initiatives and resources outside archival repositories and suggested the possibilities for closer connections among repositories through the web. The explosive growth of women's archives in the 1990s revealed a more activist bent among archivists. The literature also reflects a deepened understanding of the need for more diverse collections and the ways to bring that about. Responding to changes within the field of women's history, archivists intensified their efforts to gather the history of underrepresented groups. Kathryn Neal and Kären Mason reflected on the challenges of building archival collections that represented women of diverse backgrounds.[10]

Who Is Missing from the Historical Record?

The past four decades have seen an ever-expanding definition of who is to be included in history. However, constantly changing research interests expose deficiencies in our collections, reminding us that we must be ever vigilant about who is represented in our collections and who is not.

As Eva Moseley argued nearly thirty years ago, race and ethnicity are only part of the equation.[11] It is easier to acquire the papers of educated women of color, than poor, less formally educated women of any race or ethnicity. Educated people not only create more written records but are more comfortable with libraries and with institutions of higher learning and thus more open to donating their papers to an archival repository. Not long ago when scholars spoke of a lack of diversity in our collections they were referring mostly to the lack of sources on African American women. Other groups, however, did not spring so readily to mind: Iowa has many rural women, but their records are not abundant in archives. Domestic or service workers are common in society, but their records are sparse. As research interests have shifted toward new areas such as rural history, Latino studies, and disability studies, we have correspondingly broadened the scope of our collecting to include these and other groups formerly hidden from history. We now recognize that groups underrepresented in society tend to be underrepresented in archives, but that other factors also influence the shaping of the archival record.

Finally, how we define *underrepresented* groups depends upon the context. Well-educated women scientists who are not stars in their field may be as underrepresented in mainstream archives as Latina migrant workers, African American community activists, or white domestic workers, because their stories have not been valued and thus have not been solicited by archival institutions.

As special subject repositories, women's archives are able to craft our own collection development policies. Unlike state archives and other institutional repositories, we are unhampered by mandates that dictate what must be accepted. Instead, we have a great deal of latitude in our collecting, which enables us to document people and issues that often fall through the cracks of other repositories. But we are not immune from biases that can skew the archival record. Archivists tend to document what they know, and archival collections often reflect the interests and identities of their curators. This is not necessarily a bad thing.

Marie Bankhead Owen, the second director of the Alabama Department of Archives and History, was a formidable force in the state of Alabama, for a number of reasons. Not only was she the widow of the first director, Thomas M. Owen, she was also the sister of Alabama senator John H. Bankhead and Speaker of the House William B. Bankhead. Robert Jakeman describes the connections that enabled her to secure WPA funding for the construction of an archives building and how her connections helped in her collecting. During her tenure, the department accumulated a wide range of manuscript materials relating to women. Although the primary subjects were upper-class white women, at that time even their records were rarely included in archival collections. Bankhead Owen likely understood from her own experience that women play significant roles in society and that their papers are worth preserving. As a result of Bankhead Owen's efforts and the force of her personality, the department acquired rich collections that researchers still appreciate today.[12]

At a time when the history of women was not yet appreciated, it is unlikely that a male department head would have collected women's papers. By contrast, women's archives today may have a feminist bias and may fail to document groups that do not share these values or who actively oppose these values, such as right-wing organizations or right-to-life groups. Archivists must therefore be conscious of and open about their biases, carefully evaluating the decisions they make about collection development.

To avoid the omissions of the past, archivists of women's collections must conceive of women's papers broadly and be proactive in their collection development. Nonetheless, defining a collecting scope presents both challenges and opportunities for women's archives. All individuals have multifaceted identities;[6] as a result, their papers and records may fall within the scope of any number of archival repositories—based on geography, education, residence, sexuality, religion, occupation, or avocation.[13] The Iowa Women's Archives (IWA) has a geographic collecting scope; it seeks papers of women identified with the state of Iowa. The collection development policy of the Archives of Women in Science and Engineering (WISE) focuses on a woman's professional identity, regardless of where she lives or works. This means that collections donated to these repositories could easily go elsewhere. For example, a lesbian engineer born in Iowa who earned degrees at two out-of-state institutions and was employed by a third might choose to donate her papers to any one of the universities where she was educated or employed or to the Lesbian Herstory Archives rather than to either the IWA or the WISE Archives.

Cognizant of the overlapping nature of subject collections, we encourage collaboration with other archives to ensure that collections make their way into appropriate repositories. Oral history is one method of enhancing the historical record for underdocumented groups. It is especially critical for groups that do not create written records. Interviews can also provide valuable information and added perspectives concerning those whose papers are in archives.[14]

The Iowa Women's Archives has undertaken the Mujeres Latinas Project to preserve the history of Latinas in Iowa. Among the women interviewed are migrant workers who traveled to Iowa and other states from Mexico or Texas on a seasonal basis, following the crops from place to place in cars or pick-up trucks. These women were, for the most part, unable to create or keep personal papers because of the circumstances of their lives. Many had no more than a grade school education. Those who had the ability to write were unlikely to have the time or inclination to do so after long days working in the fields and preparing meals. The twentieth-century historical record of migrant work in Iowa is mostly limited to occasional newspaper articles about migrant workers and reports of social agencies such as the Migrant Action Program in Mason City, written from the perspective of observers. In general, there is little documentation of individual lives and experiences from their own point of view, apart from the occasional memoir. Oral history gives these women an opportunity to relate their experiences in their own words and voices. Oral recordings have the added value of conveying emotion and character in a way that papers cannot. For the researcher, listening to a recording and hearing the manner of speaking—accents, intonation, pauses, laughter, crying—creates a more intimate connection with the speaker and can contribute to a better understanding of her experience.

The Camille and Henry Dreyfus–funded oral history project of the Archives of Women in Science and Engineering seeks to document women at the other end of the class and educational spectrum: women in chemistry. Approximately fifty-five interviews have been conducted with women chemists from various fields and backgrounds. While these women may have paper collections, they have not necessarily seen their experiences as historically significant and for the most part have not donated their papers to an archival repository. In the past, the women scientists whose lives were well documented were the exceptions—those who achieved great prominence as a result of their work, such as Marie Curie.[15] The vast majority of women scientists who do research and teach are not stars, but their experience is as valuable to historians as that of the exceptional scientists. They may lay the groundwork, conduct research, or teach the next generation. For example, Nellie Naylor, an assistant professor at Iowa State University for nearly fifty years, taught basic chemistry courses. Her teaching inspired student Darleane C. Hoffman to change her major from art to chemistry; Hoffman eventually won the National Medal of Science in 1997. As Hoffman noted in a 1998 interview, "[Naylor] was not a mentor in the sense that we usually talk about because I don't think she even knew who I was. . . . It was the way she taught it."[16] Both women's lives are important: without Nellie Naylor, Darleane Hoffman might not have become a chemist. Without Hoffman's oral history, we would not know this story, because it does not appear in either Hoffman's or Naylor's personal papers in the WISE Archives.

Not only do oral histories document the past, the process of gathering them helps convince women about the significance of their role in history. Recording an oral history is an interactive experience, a collaboration between the archivist and the narrator (the person being interviewed). Archivists select interviewees, do background research, write questions, and conduct the interviews. They may steer an interview toward important subjects or events about which they wish to learn more. But more often than not, the narrator will take an interview in a different direction, providing rich but unexpected information. Participating in an oral history project helps the women interviewed see the value of their life stories and can also raise the consciousness of any community about the value of its history. For the narrator, oral history is an intensely personal experience; it offers women the opportunity to speak in their own voices and reflect upon their lives. The act of telling one's life story often creates a bond between narrator and interviewer. In some cases, this leads to the donation of papers, when they exist. In other cases, the oral histories complement existing collections at other repositories. Or they may be the only evidence of a particular life story, as is the case with some of the migrant workers interviewed. Providing a copy of the interview to these individuals is a way that archives can give back to the community and the individual. The trust that often develops between interviewer and participant can foster good will within the community toward the archives and its parent institution.

In framing our oral history projects, we attempt to be inclusive. Thus, the IWA promotes its Mujeres Latinas Project as a project to preserve community and family history, so that we can include some interviews with men, even while the focus remains on women. Likewise, the WISE Archives has at times interviewed spouses, family members, colleagues, and mentors to provide additional context on the work and lives of women scientists. Oral histories can also provide differing perspectives, especially when interviewing several people about the same event. However, it is not simply an individual's participation in a historical event that is of interest. Rather, his or her experience can provide significant insights about society and culture. Oral histories are especially helpful in providing a holistic view of women's lives and their multiple roles and responsibilities. The interviews often include discussions of family and home life, as well as career. It is difficult if not impossible to understand a woman's career without the context of her home and family, and vice versa. Conversely, women's experiences and perspectives shed light on the institutions of which they are a part, providing insight and perhaps a gendered perspective absent from other sources.

Outreach

Because women's archives seek to document groups that have been invisible to history, we must use a variety of methods to reach potential donors. Traditionally, archivists have identified individuals or organizations whose papers they wished to acquire and contacted them to solicit their papers. Such solicitations might include a letter introducing the repository and its goals to the potential donor and suggesting a meeting to discuss the repository's interest in her papers. A tour of the archives or a meeting in the donor's home or place of work might ensue. This approach assumes, first, that there is an identifiable group of individuals whose papers one wants to acquire (in essence, a list of people that one should document) and, second, that these people are prominent in some way (they are community leaders, elected officials, power brokers, scholars, celebrities). They hold some status that brings them to public attention and thus makes them candidates for this imagined list of potential or desired donors. Such an approach has limited applications to social history. If we are to document history fully, we must be interested in the broad spectrum of society—not only leaders, but also people who are not known outside their families or communities. We want to document how "ordinary" people lived their lives and how their everyday actions affected and were affected by the world around them. Like other archivists interested in preserving social history, women's archives have developed a variety of techniques to broaden the scope of our collections beyond those with a public role. These techniques include publicizing our activities and goals in print and broadcast media, hosting events in the archives, giving presentations in a variety of venues, attending community celebrations, creating tabletop displays, and distributing printed materials such as bookmarks and brochures.

At the Iowa Women's Archives, early efforts to solicit collections by writing letters to potential donors met with mixed results. The jargon we unconsciously used in our letters and the fact that most women had little or no knowledge of archives meant that few responded to these solicitations unless they were already aware of the Iowa Women's Archives. Such an approach works best for those who are well educated, understand the purpose of archives, and recognize their own place in history. Therefore, this approach has been more effective for the WISE Archives, because the women contacted are highly educated and may already know about the archives through their involvement in professional organizations. It is not an effective means of reaching the poor, working people who have less formal education, and those who for one reason or another are outside the mainstream of society—in short, the people who make up the majority of society.

Over the years, the Iowa Women's Archives and the WISE Archives have adapted their methods of soliciting collections, attempting to make appeals more inclusive and less intimidating. For the Mujeres Latinas Project, the IWA designed colorful brochures depicting women in everyday settings—sitting around a kitchen table, standing on a front porch, leaning against a car, riding a bike. The text was kept to a minimum and was consciously jargon-free, geared to people unfamiliar with archives. We also created bookmarks with the tag line, "Every woman has a story—tell us yours" superimposed over photographs of Iowa Latinas from the 1920s and 1960s. The only text besides the tag line was contact information and the URL of the Mujeres Latinas website printed on the back of the bookmark. We have likewise printed bookmarks reiterating our interest in African American women's papers. These bookmarks contain a photograph, a simple statement about the importance of preserving African American women's history, a list of types of materials collected, and contact information. Bookmarks are especially practical because they can be inexpensively produced and easily modified for a particular group, they find their way into unexpected places, and they are accessible to a broad audience.[17]

Our goal is to widely broadcast our interest so that others can help identify potential donors and interview subjects. Presentations at public libraries, community centers, historical societies, conferences, and meetings of women's organizations have been effective. The value of these is reaching a large audience that can spread the word to friends, family, acquaintances, and colleagues. Word of mouth is in fact our best tool for acquiring collections: it is much more effective for a woman to hear from a family member or colleague that we might be interested in her letters or photo albums than for us to contact her out of the blue. In these days of never-ending phone and mail solicitations and spam, people are suspicious of solicitations from unknown sources and are likely to ignore or dismiss them out of hand.

Special events can also be an effective method of publicizing an archives and its work. The WISE Archives has sponsored lectures by women scientists, class tours, open houses, and national exhibits from the Beckman Center for the History of Chemistry and the Society of Women in Engineering. Both the IWA and the WISE Archives have hosted receptions for organizations to get people in the door, illustrate what an archives is, and demonstrate the archives' interest in preserving their history. In 2001, the IWA hosted an open house for the University of Iowa's Latino-Native American Cultural Center, which was celebrating its thirtieth anniversary. This event helped the IWA lay the groundwork for the Mujeres Latinas Project and make contact with potential donors. It also showed people what the archives collects and what it does with the materials it acquires, and it let people know about our interest in gathering and preserving Latina history in Iowa. Traveling exhibits are also a good way to publicize and promote women's archives. Inexpensive tabletop displays have been a great boon to the IWA because they can be taken to talks, conferences, and events, and can be modified to appeal to particular audiences. The WISE Archives produced a traveling exhibit on women nutritionists that was displayed as part of a collaborative arrangement at community colleges throughout the state of Iowa.

Working with organizations to publicize what we wish to collect has also been of great value. The WISE Archives has placed items in the newsletters of women scientists' organizations and sent email messages to members. A good example is the archives' collaboration with Iota Sigma Pi, the nationwide women's chemistry honorary group. Working closely with the Iota Sigma Pi historian, the WISE curator made presentations at the group's centennial event and to local chapters. In turn, the chapters provided WISE with the names of potential interviewees for the Women in Chemistry Oral History Project. These groups are inclined to be receptive because they are already organized to support each other as women in the profession and therefore value and appreciate the idea of a women's archives. This feeling of deep connection to the archives can inspire a woman to donate her own papers and then share her positive experience with friends and family.

In 1995, Fann Harding, a senior administrator at the National Institutes of Health (NIH), donated her papers to the WISE Archives.[9] Harding was the founding president in 1970 of the NIH Organization for Women (now known as SHER: Self Help for Equal Rights) and was a founding member of both the Association for Women in Science (organized in 1971) and the Federation of Organizations for Professional Women (established in 1972). In the early 1970s, Harding filed the first sex discrimination complaint against NIH, winning her case in 1974.[18] After a 2005 reunion of the founding members of SHER, several additional collections were sent to the WISE Archives by NIH scientists. In 2006, Fann Harding hosted a reception in Washington, DC, so that the WISE curator could meet with these women scientists and with the incoming director of the Association of Women in Science. Women engineers and scientists often have nationwide networks of colleagues and friends, who may connect with a women's archives such as the WISE Archives and encourage each other to donate their papers, as did participants in the World War II Curtiss-Wright Engineering Cadettes Program. Such existing networks provide connections for women's archives and can directly contribute to their success, resulting in the donation of personal papers, organizational records, or financial contributions, often years after the initial contact.

The collection development methods discussed above are not unique to women's archives; they have been used in a variety of settings by archivists who wish to reach out to groups that are underrepresented in archives. However, women's archives have a particular stake in developing or refining innovative techniques so that they may rectify the omission of women from the historical record in the past and avoid making the mistake of preserving a historical record skewed by the absence of particular groups in the future. Targeted collecting initiatives, oral history projects, and outreach strategies that encourage a broad spectrum of women to donate their papers and records to archives have resulted in collections that have value to groups well outside traditional researchers.

Researchers and Use: Who Are Our Users?

Women's archives serve a wide range of clients and users. Because many women's archives are located on university or college campuses, students and scholars are often the largest clientele. Women's archives also have the opportunity to promote use of their collections through class orientations, tours, and connections with faculty members, with the result that students may be given class assignments or other projects in the archives. The WISE Archives has hosted national exhibits about women in chemistry and engineering that have brought alumnae groups, student organizations, and even potential future students into the reading room.

But online finding aids and websites are attracting a much broader range of researchers, as ever-widening access to the Internet has made archival collections more accessible to the ordinary person than ever imagined. Digital content not only dissolves the walls of the archives, it also expands the very concept of use. People who in the past would never have set foot in a university library or an archives are discovering collections relevant to their interests by simply typing keywords into a Google search engine. Genealogists searching for an ancestor, women looking for a recipe their mother baked, and people trying to reconnect with old friends or extended family members have been delighted to find all of these things through our websites. They contact the archives by email or phone to request photocopies or scans; some ultimately visit the archives. The result is more use by casual researchers, as well as journalists, writers, and other professionals. Online access democratizes the process of locating archival sources; the materials in women's archives are now available to all, not just to a select group of informed scholars. But online finding aids also make women's archives more transparent to traditional researchers, such as historians and other scholars, including those who might previously have dismissed women's archives as irrelevant to their field of study. This undercuts the argument that women's archives marginalize the history of women. Online access has also increased at the macro level, thanks to dedicated individuals and organizations that gather information about women's collections nationwide and worldwide, such as the

Mapping the World project of the International Information Centre and Archives for the Women's Movement in the Netherlands, the Society of American Archivists Women's Collections Roundtable Directory, and the University of Texas–San Antonio's Guide to Women's Collections. These have proved to be rich and valuable resources for users.

Yet, women's archives reach even farther beyond traditional researchers and scholars to a broader public of users. They connect with activists and community groups within and outside the local community. The open houses held by the Iowa Women's Archives for community groups are not intended simply to encourage collection development; by educating the public about the archives, these events encourage public use of the archives. Likewise, open houses and exhibits featuring a group's records can validate the history and memory of that group. When alumnae of two programs no longer in existence at the University of Iowa—Dental Hygiene and the Department of Physical Education for Women— attended receptions in the IWA during their reunions, the knowledge that their records were being preserved was particularly meaningful to them. Founding members of a women's health collective started in 1973 gathered at the IWA during the clinic's thirtieth anniversary. In all three cases, the archives not only preserved the history of the groups, but also provided a physical space in which women could recall their shared history. More recently, community activists have used the archives to learn about local history, examining IWA collections on second-wave feminism to create a timeline of local GLBT history for Pride Week.

Intent on creating archives that are inclusive in their holdings, women's archives strive to be welcoming to diverse users. To accomplish this, they actively encourage various educational activities as part of their mission, both within and beyond the walls of the archives. Hosting a county-wide reading event, speaking to an American Association of University Women chapter about the impact of Iowa women in science, and talking about Latina history to a group of third and fourth graders involved in a mentoring project in a neighboring town are collaborative efforts that bring the archives closer to the public. By working with such diverse groups, we create partnerships and foster connections as well as fulfill our educational mission. One result of this outward-looking educational impetus is evident in the rapidly increasing use of our collections by K–12 students. The willingness of archivists to host educational sessions for K–12 students opens up the archives and brings into the reading room groups not normally part of our regular clientele. Online access to topical lists and finding aids has facilitated K–12 use of our collections through remote reference, especially by junior and senior high students working on History Day projects. Other K–12 users include high school interns working on summer research projects with professors at Iowa State University who have utilized the papers of previous interns in the WISE Archives as models and inspiration. The WISE Archives' holistic approach to collection development—documenting family and personal life as well as career—has been important in demonstrating the discrimination women scientists have faced, the patchwork nature of their careers, particularly if they were married, and what they have achieved despite these barriers. Thus, WISE archives show high school and college students these role models of successful women scientists and engineers but also provide cautionary tales about the obstacles that women faced and may continue to face in pursuing nontraditional careers.

College students visiting the archives to learn about primary sources may experience a more personal connection to history. When an introductory Latino studies class visited the Iowa Women Archives, students read oral history excerpts and newspaper clippings about migrant workers in Iowa in the 1960s. They also examined photographs of the boxcar houses in which early twentieth-century Mexican workers lived with their families. Both Latina and non-Latina students were deeply affected by the experience. They were exposed to a history that had been omitted from textbooks and the history they learned in school.

Conclusion

Women's archives are both physical and symbolic spaces where women's experiences are valued and preserved. The fact that our repositories

include "women" in the name is important and has deep symbolic meaning for donors and users alike. The existence of women's archives can be
an impetus to people outside an institution to create and collect historical
documentation with the knowledge that it will be preserved and made
available to a broad audience. The connection women feel to women's
archives has led them to undertake oral history projects of their own
and donate the completed tapes and transcripts. Two examples are the
Iowa Women Artists Oral History Project and the Oral Histories of
Iowa Women Police, which were donated to the Iowa Women's Archives.
Similar projects are underway for the WISE Archives. Dedication to the
mission of each archives along with a commitment to ensure that women's
experiences are not forgotten has spurred individuals to document groups
that are not included in the historical record. For these people, the fact
that there are archives dedicated to women is critical.

Archivists of women's collections understand that a lack of knowledge of one's history has implications for any group's identity.[19] Recalling
the long-standing omission of women from the historical record, these
archivists now actively seek to document groups that have been denied
their history. As archivist Mark Greene states, "Our work [as archivists] is
about providing the building blocks and tools for assembling and interpreting the past—history and/or memory."[20] Women's collections archivists preserve the history of women and help women create, re-create, and
own their memories.

NOTES

This article was originally published in *Library Trends* 56 (2007), 344–59.

[1] Kären M. Mason and Tanya Zanish-Belcher, "A Room of One's Own: Women's Archives in the Year 2000" *Archival Issues* 24 (1999), 37–54.

[2] Martha S. Bell, "Special Women's Collections in United States Libraries," *College and Research Libraries* 20 (1959), 235–42; Eva Moseley, "Women in Archives: Documenting the History of Women in America," *American Archivist* 36 (1973), 215–22; Joanna Schneider Zangrando, "Women in Archives: An Historian's View on the Liberation of Clio," *American Archivist* 36 (1973), 203–14.

[3] Over the years, the concerns of women's collections archivists have often been conflated with issues pertaining to the status of female archivists. Thus, the Society of American Archivists (SAA) suggested in the late 1990s that the Women's Collections Roundtable and the Women Archivists Roundtable be combined, although the former was specifically geared to archivists who worked with women's collections while the latter was a roundtable devoted to issues concerning the status of women in archives.

[4] Andrea Hinding, ed., *Women's History Sources: A Guide to Archives and Manuscript Collections in the United States* (New York: R. R. Bowker Company, 1979). When the project began it was assumed that it would be a modest effort. The tens of thousands of collections by or about women included in the guide—merely the tip of the iceberg—effectively silenced the argument that there were not enough sources to support the study of women's history.

[5] Eva Moseley, "Sources for the New Women's History," *American Archivist* 43 (1980), 180–90.

[6] Darlene Clark Hine, *The Black Women in the Middle West Project: A Comprehensive Resource Guide* (Indianapolis: Indiana Historical Bureau, 1986); Ruth Edmonds Hill, *The Black Women Oral History Project: From the Arthur and Elizabeth Schlesinger Library on the History of Women in America, Radcliffe College* (Westport, CT: Meckler, 1991). Sometimes such sources existed but were hidden in collections, undescribed in card catalogs or finding aids. The Schlesinger Library surveyed its holdings in order to uncover sources on African American women hidden within larger collections. Susan J. Von Salis, *Revealing Documents: A Guide to African American Manuscript Sources in the Schlesinger Library and the Radcliffe College Archives* (Boston: G. K. Hall, 1993).

[7] Published guides were standard practice for disseminating information about archival sources until the mid-1990s. See for example University of North Carolina at Chapel Hill Faculty Working Group in Southern Studies, *Southern Research Report #3* (Chapel Hill: University of North Carolina, 1991). By the late 1990s, however, such printed guides were outmoded, as archivists increasingly placed collection descriptions, finding aids, and subject guides on their websites or in collaborative online databases. The SAA Women's Collections Roundtable created a directory of women's collections archivists with descriptions of the collections they administered in the 1990s, updating it several times; it was available online until recently.

[8] Suzanne Hildenbrand, ed., *Women's Collections: Libraries, Archives & Consciousness* (New York: The Haworth Press, 1986), 6–7.

[9] Anke Voss-Hubbard, "'No Documents—No History': Mary Ritter Beard and the Early History of Women's Archives," *American Archivist* 58 (Winter 1995), 16–30; Eva Steiner Moseley, ed., *Women, Information, and the Future: Collecting and Sharing Resources Worldwide* (Fort Atkinson, WI: Highsmith Press, 1995); Laura E. Micham, "A Repository of One's Own: An Examination of Activism within the General Field of Archives as Exemplified by Women's Studies Archivy," (unpublished thesis, University of North Carolina at Chapel Hill, 1997).

[10] Kathryn M. Neal, "Cultivating Diversity: The Donor Connection," *Collection Management* 27 (2002), 33–42; Kären M. Mason, "Fostering Diversity in Archival Collections: The Iowa Women's Archives," *Collection Management*, 27 (2002), 23–31.

[11] Eva S. Moseley, "Sources for the 'New Women's History,'" *American Archivist* 43 (1980), 180–190.

[12] Robert J. Jakeman, "Marie Bankhead Owen and the Alabama Department of Archives and History, 1920–1955," *Provenance* 21 (2003), 36–65.

[13] For a discussion of the complex issues related to identity-based collecting, see Elisabeth Kaplan, "We Are What We Collect, We Collect What We Are: Archives and the Construction of Identity," *American Archivist* 63 (2000), 126–51.

[14] Ellen D. Swain, "Oral History in the Archives: Its Documentary Role in the Twenty-first Century," *American Archivist* 66 (2003), 139–58.

[15] Marie Curie's papers are located in France at the Salle des Manuscripts of the Bibliothèque Nationale as well as the archive of the Institut Curie.

[16] Oral history interview with Darleane C. Hoffman, 1998, Women in Chemistry Oral History Project Interviews, Archives of Women in Science and Engineering, Iowa State University.

[17] The IWA received a call from a woman in Muscatine, Iowa, who had found a brochure in a pew at her church. She became a key contact for that area. She agreed to an oral history interview and suggested the names of several other Latinas who were also interviewed for the project. A woman in northwest Iowa called the archives offering to participate in the project after finding a Mujeres Latinas bookmark in a book lent to her by a friend.

[18] Fann Harding Papers, Archives of Women in Science and Engineering, Iowa State University.

[19] For discussion of this issue, see Joel Wurl, "Ethnicity as Provenance: In Search of Values and Principles for Documenting the Immigrant Experience," *Archival Issues* 29 (2005), 65–76, and Jeannette Allis Bastian, "A Question of Custody: The Colonial Archives of the United States Virgin Islands," *American Archivist* 64 (2001), 96–114.

[20] Mark A. Greene, "The Messy Business of Remembering: History, Memory, and Archives," *Archival Issues* 28 (2003/2004), 95–103.

CHAPTER 13

Documenting African American Women in the Archives of Historically Black Colleges and Universities

TARONDA SPENCER

As a community of institutions, Historically Black Colleges and Universities[1] (HBCUs) today are collecting materials that documents every aspect of the African American experience in the United States. HBCUs were established after the American Civil War with a mission to educate African Americans. The secondary mission has been to nurture and conserve the distinct character of the African American community. In pursuit of these missions, HBCUs have collected a unique body of primary source materials that chronicles not only the more than 150 years of black educational history, but also much of the social, economic, and cultural history of the communities they served. They have become the primary repositories of this experience. Stored in the archives and libraries of HBCUs are sources critical to the study of the history of education and of African Americans, and to an understanding of the larger society.

HBCUs have also been pioneers in documenting African American women's history. Their libraries and archives house significant collections and continue to be a primary resource for documentary evidence on African American women. Decades before the 1970s when women's history became a primary focus of scholarship and teaching, HBCUs were collecting the papers of African American women and their organizations. The diversity of the institutional records and special collections related to women provides scholars with invaluable sources related to women in the sciences, medicine, religion, and the arts; social and political movements; community development; black feminist thought; and the history of African American women in the United States and around the world.

Building an Archival Tradition at Historically Black Colleges and Universities

Historically Black Colleges and Universities are institutions of higher education, most established in the latter half of the nineteenth century to provide educational opportunities for newly freed slaves. By the opening of the twentieth century, through a combination of public and private efforts, a network of more than two thousand schools for African Americans had been established in the South, in the Midwest, and in Pennsylvania. Among them were nearly two hundred institutions founded as or that would become colleges and universities. HBCUs helped to transform an illiterate, enslaved people into a literate and free population, exercising their rights for full and equal citizenship. They would become the center of black intellectual, social, political, and cultural activity; and their administrators, faculty, and alumni would help shape public opinion about African Americans, including the idea that African Americans possess a significant history that preceded and extended beyond slavery. Today, HBCUs comprise 105 institutions, both private and public; single-sex and coeducational; two-year and four-year liberal arts, land-grant, and community colleges and universities; research universities and professional schools. Although HBCUs only account for 3 percent of colleges and universities in the United States, they graduate nearly 20 percent of African Americans who earn undergraduate degrees. More than 50 percent of

African American public school teachers, doctors, lawyers, entrepreneurs, scientists, and other professionals graduated from an HBCU.[2]

At their founding, HBCUs served a student body at the very bottom of the educational process. Few offered college courses within the first few years of opening. However, as literacy rates for African Americans rose, HBCUs evolved academically from preparatory schools, high schools, and normal schools into colleges and universities. By the late 1920s, most black colleges and universities had disbanded their high school departments and were offering collegiate courses in the liberal arts and sciences, as well as programs in law, medicine, and theological study. Institutions like Atlanta, Howard, and Fisk Universities became leading centers for black higher education with an expanded curriculum and a large, highly trained group of black faculty. Scholars such as W. E. B. DuBois, Alain Locke, and Charles S. Johnson, who were barred from teaching at white universities, used their training and intellect to cultivate new studies in social work, anthropology, agriculture, and African and African American history.[3] HBCUs were seedbeds for research, teaching, and publishing African American history and the study of social issues in the United States. Atlanta, Tuskegee, and Hampton Universities were in the forefront of these initiatives with annual conferences to study African American urban and rural life.[4] Similar work was also being done at Howard and Fisk in the areas of history, religion, and race relations. The development of archives and special collections at HBCUs dovetailed with these new developments in academic research and teaching. Institutional collections were augmented by the acquisition of special collections through gifts and purchases from private collectors who had systematically built collections of books, manuscripts, artifacts, and other materials by and about African Americans. Collections such as the Jesse E. Moorland and Arthur Spingarn Collections at Howard University, the Henry Slaughter and Countee Cullen/Harold Jackman Memorial Collections at Atlanta University, the George Foster Peabody Collection at Hampton University, Fisk University's International and Southern Young Men's Christian Association Graduate School Collections, the William Dorsey Collection at Cheyney University, and the Heartman Collection on Negro Life and

Culture at Texas Southern University provided the foundation for important HBCU special collections and archives. Jessie Carney Smith, university librarian and the William and Camille Cosby Professor at Fisk University, writes, "the depth that these collections achieved was directly attributable to the foresight of early librarians, sometimes faculty members, who were endowed with the determination, dedication, and interest necessary to preserve Black history and culture in records."[5]

The majority of HBCUs did not have collections as extensive as those at Howard, Fisk, Atlanta, or the other larger schools. This was due in large measure to the fact that the majority of HBCUs were undergraduate institutions. Faculty had heavy teaching loads and there was little support for scholarly research and writing, therefore they overlooked the importance of preserving their institutional records or developing special collections. Dorothy Porter, curator of the Moorland Foundation at Howard University, in a 1942 article in the *Journal of Negro Education* encouraged HBCU administrators and librarians to care for their institutional records, writing, "it is of special importance that Negro college and university administrators give some thought to and take definite steps towards the task of preserving their institutional records. University historians and educators would have drawn a far truer picture of the development of our educational institutions had our first generation of administrators possessed the foresight to collect and keep the various college memoranda with which they came in contact."[6]

By the mid-1960s, however, more schools were building collections and organizing their institutional records, particularly those colleges and universities preparing for centennial anniversaries and the publication of institutional histories. This new archival work at HBCUs also coincided with the social activism of the 1960s, which pushed schools to deepen their collections to reflect a broader view of the African American experience. In the 1970s, most major colleges and universities in the United States, both majority institutions and HBCUs, had begun to rework areas of their curricula incorporating meaningful courses in African American history and literature or establishing black studies programs. According to Robert L. Allen, one-time professor of black studies at San José State in California, by 1971, "nearly 500 schools had full-scale Black studies programs."[7]

In a study of black academic libraries published in 1977, Jessie Carney Smith noted that of the eighty-nine HBCUs surveyed for the study, thirty-five reported programs of black and African studies.[8] During these years, there was also a substantial increase in the number of scholars contributing to the historiography of the African American experience. New studies were done on the black working class, the black family, black nationalism, community development, and related topics that had previously received little or no attention in the mainstream of academic inquiry. Yet, missing from all of this new activity was a meaningful inclusion of scholarship on African American women.

Efforts to Document African American Women in History and Archives

Archival collections acquired by HBCUs were most often records related to African American men, as men were the primary focus of most historical research and scholarship. In contrast, the lives of African American women were placed on the periphery of history, if present at all. Authors Martha Pallante and Kathleen Thompson contend that, "any discussion of African and African American women is difficult given the documentary record and performance of 19th and early 20th century historians. Being Black and female places this cohort outside the mainstream of the historical record and academic discussion, their race and gender virtually guarantee that Black women show up in the record only when there has been a problem or when an individual has fallen outside of the norm."[9] Of the women who were included in history books and other texts, historian Patricia Morton writes, "Black women were never invisible in American historiography. On the contrary, they have been 'disfigured' and turned into highly visible racist-sexist stereotypes. The ubiquitous mammy, the devilish Jezebel, and the castrating matriarch all make their appearance in post–Civil War scholarship."[10]

The task of transforming the image of African American women was largely undertaken by African American women themselves. Among the first to address the issue were African American clubwomen, particularly those in organizations whose memberships included teachers and librarians. Women's clubs, societies, and associations promoted awareness and encouraged African American women's groups to write their own histories. In the years after World War II and into the 1970s, clubwomen were joined by African American women scholars, mostly historians, who would help to move African American women to the center of the historical narrative.

The African American women's club movement began in the 1890s in response to the dismal living conditions and unmet social, educational, and cultural needs affecting large sections of African Americans in the rural South and in the urban centers of the northern United States. African American women organized clubs, associations, missionary and literary societies, sewing circles, and other groups to address community conditions. They worked together to organize schools and health clinics, launched campaigns for improved sanitation in their neighborhoods, organized kindergartens and child care programs for the children of working women, and offered classes in reading, hygiene, home care, and citizenship.[11]

In cities, clubs were active in the settlement house movement. They established working-girl homes that provided employment information and job training to mostly southern women migrating north. By the end of the century, the women in these organizations began to turn their attention to national issues and concerns. Using the leadership skills honed in their local and state organizations, clubwomen joined to form a national organization that would give a powerful and unified voice to their work for social change and racial uplift and to advance the interests of African American women. These independent groups of local and state clubs, societies, and associations came together to form the National Association of Colored Women (NACW).

Founded in 1896, NACW was the outcome of the merger of the National Federation of Afro-American Women and the National League of Colored Women. The NACW served as an umbrella organization, bringing together local clubs at the base, which were supported by state and regional federations, which were, in turn, supported by a national body. At the top, NACW operations were managed by an executive committee and departments that worked to address specific issues such as rural conditions, education, antilynching, temperance, and suffrage.[12] NACW provided local leaders with a national platform from which they could address the systematic exclusion of African Americans from federal protections, programs, and services as well as the crippling effects of second-class citizenship, economic disparities, and political disenfranchisement. NACW also became an instrument to refute negative perceptions of black women. African people had been characterized as inferior as part of the rationale for slavery, and demeaning the moral character of black women was deeply intertwined into this concept of inferiority. Even after emancipation, black women continued to be the target of malicious attacks on their moral character.

Many historians agree that one of the reasons for the coalition that led to the formation of NACW was the circulation of a letter by southern journalist James W. Jacks, president of the Missouri Press Association, written to Florence Balgarnie, a British reformer. The letter slandered Ida B. Wells Barnett[13] and her antilynching activities in England specifically and the morality of black women generally. Historian Lillian Serece Williams asserts that, although attacks against the character of African American women were not new, with the founding of NACW, there was now an organization comprised of a "large body of articulate, college-educated women to refute the charges."[14]

One of the methods used by NACW to counter the negative stereotypes was to showcase the accomplishments and contributions of black women. Historian Jacqueline Rouse writes that "local clubs and regional federations developed and staffed libraries and reading rooms with volumes on historic figures and events from African and African American pasts."[15] Mary Church Terrell, president of NACW from 1896 to 1901, published a pamphlet titled "The Progress of Colored Women" and wrote numerous articles and gave speeches about the successes of African

American women and their rise from difficult circumstances to become leaders in their professions and communities. She believed that publicizing African American women's contributions would be transformative, inspiring African Americans throughout the country to develop pride in their people and become exemplary citizens.[16]

Clubwomen also authored histories of the club movement and biographical sketches of individual women. Fannie Barrier Williams's "Club Movement among Negro Women" and Margaret Murray Washington's "Club Work among Negro Women" were published in *Progress of the Race: or the Remarkable Advancement of the Afro American Race*.[17] Gertrude Bustill Mossell's *The Work of the Afro American Woman* was published in 1908. Elizabeth Lindsay Davis published two histories, *The Story of the Illinois Federation of Colored Women's Clubs, 1900–1922* and *Lifting As They Climb: An Historical Record of the National Association of Colored Women*. In 1926, Hallie Q. Brown, NACW president from 1920 to 1924, published *Homespun Heroines*, a collection of sixty biographies of important African American women. In 1933, Sadie Iola Daniel published *Women Builders*, a collection of biographical sketches on seven important clubwomen: Maggie Lena Walker, Janie Porter Barrett, Nannie Helen Burroughs, Lucy Craft Laney, Mary McLeod Bethune, Jane Edna Hunter, and Charlotte Hawkins Brown.[18]

In an article recounting the history of *National Association Notes*, the official publication of the NACW, Dulcie Straughan writes that a recurring theme in the publication was the "Black woman as role model." She states, "By publishing success stories about Black women, readers could take pride in their accomplishments and have hope for the future."[19] During the administration of Mary McLeod Bethune from 1924 to 1928, NACW purchased a national headquarters building in Washington, DC. In 1927, Bethune wrote, "for thirty years, the National Association has been shifting its headquarters every four years. Its archives have been the suitcases or trunks of its officers. Its records have been scattered to the four winds of heaven."[20] Now they would have an official archives where the achievements of NACW and its members could be preserved and studied.

Bethune's historical consciousness was also a major component of the work of the National Council of Negro Women (NCNW), the organization founded by Bethune in 1935. The National Council began as a federation of fourteen African American women's organizations. It was conceived as a "national organization of national organizations" that brought into coalition the larger national African American women's religious, political, and professional organizations and academic sororities to address issues critical to the progress of the African American community.[21] Within the NCNW, Bethune established an archives committee with Dorothy Porter as the chair. The committee also included Sue Bailey Thurman and Juanita Mitchell, as well as Mary Church Terrell and Elizabeth Carter Brooks, who were, like Bethune, past presidents of the National Association of Colored Women. Through the archives committee and its subsequent National Archives and Museum Department, the National Council began collecting materials with an aim to document "women of many vocations and walks of life including teachers, physicians, artists, housewives, authors, and domestic employees."[22]

In 1940, Sue Bailey Thurman founded and became editor of the *Aframerican Women's Journal,* the official publication of the National Council. Thurman used the *Journal* to promote historical awareness and to solicit historical materials. She also published articles in the *Chicago Defender* and *Pittsburgh Courier* urging women to "retrieve material from their attics and trunks and send it to the archives." [23] In 1944, Thurman became chair of the archives committee. Her efforts to collect materials through the 1940s, 1950s, and 1960s would eventually become the core of the National Black Women's Archives, located in the National Park Service Mary McLeod Bethune Council Home in Washington, DC.[24] In November 1979, the Mary McLeod Bethune Memorial Museum and National Archives for Black Women's History was formally dedicated, becoming the first archival repository exclusively devoted to collecting primary source materials about African American women.

Many of the women who were involved in the African American women's club movement were also affiliated with HBCUs. In addition to serving as president of NACW and founder and president of the NCNW,

Bethune was also the founder and president of the Daytona Normal and Industrial Institute for Girls and its successor school, Bethune-Cookman College. Margaret Murray Washington and Jennie Booth Moton were wives of the first and second presidents of the Tuskegee Institute, Booker T. Washington and Robert Russa Moton, respectively. Margaret Washington, president of NACW from 1914 to 1918, was lady principal at Tuskegee and founder of the Tuskegee Women's Club. Jennie Booth Moton, NACW president from 1937 to 1941, was director of women's industries at the school and president of the Tuskegee Women's Club.

A charter member of the Atlanta Branch of NACW, Lugenia Burns Hope was founder of the Neighborhood Union, a social welfare agency in Atlanta, and wife of John Hope, president of Atlanta University. Marion Birnie Wilkinson, a founder of the South Carolina Federation of Colored Women's Clubs, was the wife of Robert S. Wilkinson, president of South Carolina State College. Mary Jackson McCrorey, who served as an executive committee member of NACW and corresponding secretary of the International Council of Women of the Darker Races, was the wife of Henry L. McCrorey, president of Biddle University (now Johnson C. Smith University). Hallie Quinn Brown, president of the NACW, was a member of the faculty and a fund-raiser for Wilberforce University.

The personal papers of these women were among the earliest collections in the libraries and archives at these HBCUs. In 1936, Louie Davis Shivery, a master's student at Atlanta University, completed her thesis— "History of Organized Social Work among Atlanta Negroes"— under the direction of W. E. B. DuBois, using the records of the Neighborhood Union.[25] In a 1959 survey, "Special Women's Collections in United States Libraries" in *College and Research Libraries*, Martha S. Bell included the Hallie Q. Brown Collection at Central State University and the Women's Collection at Bennett College for Women on a list of special collections of materials by and about women and their activities.[26]

At Howard University in the late 1950s, Dorothy Porter began to collect the papers of African American women with the acquisition of the Mary Church Terrell papers. In a 1995 interview with Avril Madison, Porter remembered how she acquired the Terrell papers left behind by the

Library of Congress. She said "they didn't look in the basement and the closets. I got for Howard about six manuscript boxes of papers that [were] just trash they thought. It's a valuable collection." Porter worked to bring the papers of Angelina Weld Grimké to Howard in the early 1960s.[27] By the early 1970s, there were more than fifty collections by and about African American women and organizations at Howard University. Moorland-Spingarn Research Center encouraged the use of the records and papers with the publication of the *List of References to Women* in 1975. The *List* was updated in 1988 and published as the *Guide to Resources on Women in the Manuscript Division of the Moorland Spingarn Research Center.*

Of collecting women's resources at Fisk, archivist Ann Allen Shockley wrote, "the civil rights movement inspired the women's movement and caused an awakening to the importance of documenting both women's and Black history. In 1970, under my curatorship, the Special Collections began actively to solicit papers of Black women. There were already a few collections, Pauline E. Hopkins and Constance Fisher . . . augmenting the women's collections are the papers of Dorothy L. Brown, Ophelia Settle Egypt, Grace James, Naomi Long Madgett and Eileen Southern and the research papers and tapes used by historian Gerda Lerner in the writing of *Black Women in White America.*"[28]

Taking advantage of newly acquired collections—as well as those that lay unexamined in the libraries and archives of HBCUs and other repositories—scholars, including a group of young African American women historians, began to focus their teaching, research, and writing on African American women, demonstrating that black women's history is a rich, albeit neglected, area within African American and women's studies. In 1978, Sharon Harley and Rosalyn Terborg-Penn published the first volume of historical essays on African American women, *The Afro-American Woman: Struggles and Images.* The anthology of original essays examined black women's experiences from a historical and bio-graphical perspective. In a review of the book, historian Francille Rusan Wilson commended the authors, noting that they had "illustrated how Black women's history might be recovered from primary sources using traditional methods of historical analysis." She further wrote, "it is worth noting that five of the seven authors (of the book) received their under-graduate or graduate degrees in history from Howard University and that their research on Black women drew upon Howard's half-century of leadership in Black historical studies."[29] The book's foreword was written by Moorland-Spingarn's curator and mentor to these young historians, Dorothy Porter.

This new focus on African American women encouraged scholars from a variety of academic disciplines to research and to publish ground-breaking work about African American women. The 1980s and 1990s saw a proliferation of scholarly monographs on topics relating to African American women, including work on black women in slavery, religion, civil rights, and education; the black women's club movement; and the roles and work of African American women in the black community, the nation, and around the world. More articles related to African American women began to appear in refereed journals and periodicals. To encourage new scholarship, support the growing number of historians who were teaching and researching black women's history, and professionalize the new discipline of black women's studies, Rosalyn Terborg-Penn, Eleanor Smith, and Elizabeth Parker founded the Association of Black Women's Historians in 1979.[30]

New courses and programs in black women's studies were growing in colleges and universities across the country. In 1977, Alice Walker introduced the first course on black women writers at Wellesley College in Massachusetts; this was followed soon after by courses at San José State University, the University of Maryland, and the University of Massachusetts at Amherst.[31] In 1981, Beverly Guy-Sheftall established the Women's Research and Resource Center at Spelman College, the first of its kind at an HBCU. Spelman was also the first HBCU to offer a comparative women's studies major and minor and the first with an endowed professorship named in honor of a black female intellectual—Anna Julia Cooper. In 1983, Guy-Sheftall cofounded, with Patricia Bell Scott, the periodical *SAGE: A Scholarly Journal on Black Women.* Issued from 1984 to 1995, *SAGE* was a critical resource for black women's studies. It was the first explicitly black feminist publication devoted exclusively to the experiences of women of African descent. Author Paula Giddings described the journal as "the only place where, every time you pick it up, there's a concentrated emphasis on . . . the scholarship on Black Women."[32]

New scholarship brought with it a demand for new resources. Scholars needing original materials were anxious to identify potential sources for their research. Historian Bettye Collier-Thomas observed that while the research and writing of women's history resulted in archives and libraries being inundated by requests for primary and secondary sources, there was a lack of identifiable, readily accessible resources. This raised a growing concern among researchers who were anxious about the preservation and identification of materials.[33] Historian Deborah Gray White, in her essay "Mining the Forgotten: Manuscript Sources for Black Women's History," agreed with Collier-Thomas's assessment, writing that the discovery of new or newly opened archival collections and documents was paramount if African American women's history was to come out of the shadows.

White asserted that the roles of race and gender in the lives of African American women shaped the ways in which documentary evidence of African American women was created and preserved. A strong oral tradition in the black community, combined with the reluctance of black women to donate their papers to mainstream manuscript repositories due to concerns over perceptions and a somewhat adversarial relationship, resulted in a scarcity of documentation. White further asserts that "our ability to understand the complex ways in which race and gender have shaped Black women's lives depends on intensive work in primary sources."[34]

Hearing the concerns of historians and other researchers, the larger HBCU libraries and archives responded by expanding their collecting focus and increasing accessibility to existing sources. To bridge the larger gap between the smaller repositories and researchers, archivists and librarians who were experienced in managing rare book and manuscript collections moved quickly to assist HBCUs where the libraries had insufficiently trained staff and inadequate funding. Workshops and conferences were convened, and there was an outpouring of publications, all providing guidelines and practical advice to the growing number of librarians who suddenly needed to build or expand collections and better manage their repositories.

E. J. Josey, librarian and prolific author of more than a dozen books on black librarians and librarianship, included chapters on the development of archives in two of his works, *Ethnic Collections* and *The Black Librarian in America Revisited*.[35] In *Ethnic Libraries*, Stanton Biddle and Verdia Jenkins contributed a chapter on developing ethnic archives, outlining basic factors necessary in establishing and developing an archival repository. In an article entitled "Librarians, Archivists and Writers: A Personal Perspective" in *The Black Librarian Revisited*, Ann Allen Shockley provided a retrospective view of the development of libraries and archives as well as insights into the future of both professions, noting particularly the role of automation in cataloging and access.

Shockley had been at the forefront of the movement to assist college and university libraries with the administration of their collections. In 1970, she published *A Handbook for the Administration of Special Negro Collections*. The handbook was designed as a guide to librarians who were suddenly "curators or librarians in charge of Black collections."[36] Using the collection at Fisk as the example, Shockley guided the reader through administrative policies and procedures, proper budgeting, as well as acquisition policies and procedures for securing both book and manuscript collections.

HBCU archives were the focus of the first national conference of the Black Caucus of the American Library Association, *Culture Keeping: The Plight of Archives in Black Colleges and Universities,* in 1992. One session, comprised of HBCU library directors and archivists, presented an overview of the importance of archives at HBCUs. The presenters stressed the need for resources and programs to enhance the development of the archival programs, particularly the necessity for trained staff and adequate facilities. One panelist, archivist Karen Jefferson, observed that while administrators are quick to point to successes achieved by librarians and archivists, this recognition was a "double edge sword." She stated, "These collections and the research scholarship they support are often noted by our college administrators as outstanding features that Black schools have to offer. Yet these accolades on the values of the Black college archives rarely result in the corresponding support that is necessary to meet the needs of archival programs."[37]

These discussions would also spark projects to locate, identify, and describe collections of African American materials. In 1967, the Race Relations Information Center began the first national initiative to provide bibliographic information about African American primary and secondary sources. In 1970, the center published the *Directory of Afro-American Resources,* edited by Walter Schatz. The guide provided an extensive list of two thousand organizations and institutions with holdings of five thousand collections of primary and secondary materials on African Americans. It was the first national guide to contain references to HBCU holdings.[38] Another reference guide that included HBCU collections was *Women's History Sources: A Guide to Archives and Manuscript Collections in the United States,* edited by Andrea Hinding.[39] *Women's History Sources,* published in 1979, is still the most comprehensive guide to women's collections in public and private repositories nationwide. It contains entries on many collections that had not been previously described in national or local guides and lists references to collections in twelve HBCU archives.

There were also projects specifically targeting HBCUs to help improve access to materials. In 1971, North Carolina Central University initiated a project funded by the Office of Education to identify and describe African American materials in North Carolina, South Carolina, Virginia, Georgia, Tennessee, and Alabama. In 1980, the National Endowment for the Humanities (NEH) and the United Negro College Fund (UNCF) sponsored a conference of archivists, librarians, and administrators from UNCF's member institutions to discuss the importance of archives to their institutions. The conference was followed by a workshop to teach basic archival skills. In 1993, the Margaret Walker Alexander Research Center at Jackson State University and the Mississippi Department of Archives and History conducted a two-year statewide survey of African American records in private hands. In the same year, the North Carolina Historical Advisory Board of the National Publications and Records Commission, the North Carolina Division of Archives and History, and North Carolina

Central University formed the North Carolina African American Advisory Group to survey African American sources in North Carolina.

Perhaps the most extensive project to work with HBCU archives was the Cooperative HBCU Archival Survey Project (CHASP) at Wayne State University in Detroit. In 1995, the African American Educational Archives Initiative at Wayne State, in partnership with North Carolina Central University, received funding from NEH to conduct a comprehensive survey of the archives at HBCUs. CHASP conducted on-site surveys of archival holdings at eighty-one institutions in twenty-one states and the District of Columbia. The administration of the project was transferred from Wayne State to the Women's Research and Resource Center at Spelman College in Atlanta, where it was completed in 2000. As a result of the survey, a total of 1,473 collections were identified. Of that number, nearly two hundred individual collections related to African American women were found, confirming that the libraries and archives of HBCUs are invaluable resources for documenting African American women.[40]

African American Women's Collections in HBCU Archives and Special Collections

Bibliographic surveys such as CHASP revealed the presence of an extraordinary body of primary source materials related to African American women throughout the HBCU community. The diversity of the institutional records and special collections in these repositories records how black women have empowered themselves and others, and highlights their roles and work in family life, education, religion, medicine and law; as artists, writers, and musicians; and as social workers, political activists, and community builders.

Predominant among the collections at HBCUs are the administrative records of the institution. Usually, this body of materials is the most substantial housed in the repository and is the most tangible evidence of the school's founding and development. The records relate to governing boards, presidents and administrators, academic departments, faculty and staff, students and alumni. These collections include items such as reports, catalogs, publications, photographs, audiovisual materials, scrapbooks, and other records that detail the experiences of African American women students, faculty, staff, and administrators who were an integral part of the life of most institutions.

Among the institutional collections—and alongside the papers of notable HBCU presidents such as Booker T. Washington, Mordecai Johnson, John Hope, and Charles S. Johnson—are the records of African American women founders and presidents of HBCUs. These collections chronicle the efforts, some pioneering, of African American women in shaping the educational process at all academic levels. Evelyn Elizabeth Wright is one such example. While many have heard of Mary McLeod Bethune and Lucy Laney, the Wright Collection alerts us to others of equal importance. Wright is generally not included in most academic histories as the founder of Voorhees College in South Carolina. The institutional records of Voorhees and Wright's papers provide a rare glimpse of the struggles and triumph of a black female educator to establish a school. While her first two attempts at opening a school were thwarted by arson, Wright succeeded in opening the Denmark Industrial School, a high school in Denmark, South Carolina, in 1897. With the help of Jessie Dorsey, Booker T. Washington, northern philanthropists, and local churches, Wright was able to sustain the school, which survives today as a four-year liberal arts college.[41]

Like Wright, there are many other extraordinary examples African American women who have led black colleges and universities. Many of these women were the first to serve as presidents of the schools. Having moved up the ranks, they were chosen because of their academic achievements in teaching and scholarship, administrative acumen, and service.[42] One of the earliest women to assume leadership of an institution was Artemisia Bowden at St. Philip's College in Texas. Bowden served as chief administrator of the school for fifty-two years, guiding its development from a parochial school to a two-year college from 1902 to 1950. The records of Bowden's administration are in St. Philip's College archives. In the archives of Huston-Tillotson University (Texas) are the records of

Mary E. Branch, president of Tillotson College from 1930 to 1944. Branch was the first African American woman college president in Texas and the second African American woman to lead a senior-level college.

One of the first black women to assume the presidency of a coeducational university was Niara Sudarkasa who served as the first woman president of Lincoln University in Pennsylvania from 1986 to 1998. The records of her presidency are in the university's archives. The archives of Southern University, Baton Rouge (Louisiana), is the repository for the records of Dolores R. Spikes, who served as the first female head of a university system in the United States and of a Louisiana public university from 1988 to 1996. The archives at Johnson C. Smith University (North Carolina) house the papers of Dorothy Cowser Yancy, who served as the twelfth president of the university, and the first woman to so serve, from 1994 to 2008. Clinton Junior College (South Carolina) is the repository for the records of presidents Sallie V. Moreland, who served from 1946 to 1994, and Cynthia McCullough Russell, who served from 1996 to 2002. The archives at Philander Smith College (Arkansas) house the records of Trudie Kibbe Reed, the eleventh president of the college and the first woman to so serve, from 1998 to 2004. Paine College (Georgia) houses the records of Shirley A. R. Lewis, who served as the thirteenth president of the college, and the first woman to so serve, from 1994 to 2007.

Archival Records of Historically Black Women's Colleges

Unique among HBCU collections are the records of black women's institutions. Since most women were educated in coeducational settings, the records of these schools provide scholars with essential information on how the schools pursued their roles as educational institutions for the exclusive education of black women and girls. The Board of Freedmen of the Presbyterian Church, USA, established the first schools for African American women and girls in the South. Scotia Seminary was established in Concord, North Carolina, in 1867, and Barber Memorial Seminary was founded in 1869 in Anniston, Alabama. In 1930, the two schools merged forming Barber-Scotia Junior College for Women in Concord. In 1954, the school became a coeducational college. Mary Allen Seminary was established in 1886 in Crockett, Texas. Mary Holmes College was founded as a secondary school in 1892 in Jackson, Mississippi. The American Missionary Association opened Tillotson Collegiate and Normal Institute in Austin, Texas, in 1877. In 1952, Tillotson College merged with Samuel Huston College becoming Huston-Tillotson College.

Bennett College for Women in Greensboro, North Carolina, was founded in 1873 as a coeducational school. It was reorganized as a women's college in 1926 by the Women's Home Missionary Society of the Methodist Episcopal Church. Spelman College was established in 1881 in Atlanta, Georgia, by Sophia Packard and Harriet Giles, missionaries commissioned by the Woman's American Baptist Home Mission Society. Hartshorn Memorial College was founded in 1883 in Richmond, Virginia, by the American Baptist Home Mission Society. Chartered as a college, it was the first of the black women's institutions to award baccalaureate degrees. Hartshorn merged with Virginia Union University in 1932.

In 1867, the Mather School was founded by Rachel Crane Mather in Beaufort, South Carolina. In 1882, the Woman's American Baptist Home Mission Society assumed support of the school, operating it as a normal school for black girls. In 1904, Mary McLeod Bethune established the Daytona Literary and Industrial School for Training Negro Girls in Daytona Beach, Florida. Primarily a vocational school, the educational program focused on basic literacy skills and industrial training. In 1923, this school merged with Cookman Institute of Jacksonville, Florida. This partnership would eventually become Bethune-Cookman University.

The records of Barber and Scotia Seminaries are in the archives of Barber-Scotia College. The records of Hartshorn Memorial College are in the archives of Virginia Union University. The records of Tillotson College are at Huston-Tillotson College, and the Mather Institute archives are at Benedict College (South Carolina). Among the records at Bethune-Cookman are the Mary McLeod Bethune Papers, which document Bethune's efforts to start and sustain the Daytona Literary and

Industrial School for Training Negro Girls and her years as president of Bethune-Cookman.

The institutional records of Spelman College and Bennett College for Women document more than one hundred years of continuous education of African American women and girls. The materials, which are unavailable elsewhere, offer researchers a unique opportunity to evaluate the impact of attending a single-sex educational institution on African American women and girls over an extended period of time. Both collections provide an opportunity for significant comparisons between colleges for white women and girls and Bennett and Spelman in the areas of curriculum development, student enrollment, mission of the college, early childhood education, student activism, leadership development, and family and career choices of alumnae.

Records of the African American women who led these institutions can also be found among the institutional records. At Bennett are the papers of Willa Player, the first woman president of Bennett, who served from 1956 to 1966. The papers chronicle Player's career as a professor, vice president, and president of Bennett. In addition to the Player Collection, the archives also hold the presidential records of Gloria Randle Scott, who served from 1987 to 2001; Johnnetta B. Cole, who served from 2001 to 2005; and Julianne Malveaux, who served from 2007 to 2012. The Spelman archives contains records documenting the tenures of Johnnetta B. Cole, Spelman's seventh president and the first African American woman to so serve, and Audrey Forbes Manley, the eighth president and Spelman's first alumna president.

In HBCU archives and libraries are also important special collections related to African American women. These collections differ greatly in size and scope. Some collections are comprised of a few items; others, hundreds of boxes. They document the lives African American women who were internationally and nationally prominent as well as women who were known only in their local communities. Collection policies and resources at the research universities and larger colleges with broad educational missions have allowed these institutions to build collections that are national (sometimes international) in focus. Smaller schools, on the other hand, have tended to concentrate their efforts on collecting the papers of faculty, staff, alumnae, and local community leaders and groups. In all, HBCUs have assembled outstanding collections which ensure that the contributions of black women to the nation and the world are preserved.

Foremost among HBCU libraries and archival repositories is the Moorland-Spingarn Research Center at Howard University. The research center houses one of the most comprehensive collections for the study of African Americans and the African Diaspora. Among its 600 collections are more than 150 collections of personal papers and organizational records documenting African American women across a broad spectrum of fields and activities. Included among the collections are personal papers of African American women such as educator and author Anna Julia Cooper. The collection contains materials relating to Cooper's tenure as president of Frelinghuysen University from 1930 to 1941. The Moorland-Spingarn Research Center also houses the papers of Lucy Diggs Slowe, first dean of women at Howard from 1922 to 1937 and president of the National Association of College Women and Deans and Advisors of Women in Colored Schools; Eva B. Dykes, professor of history and leader in the Seventh Day Adventist Church; Carlotta Stewart Lai (as part of the Stewart-Flippin Family Papers), pioneer in the public education system in Hawaii; artist Lois Mailou Jones; and Ophelia Settle Egypt, sociologist, educator, and author.

There is also a small collection of materials regarding the controversy arising out of the denial of the use of Constitution Hall to Marian Anderson by the Daughters of the American Revolution; the papers of Georgia Douglass Johnson, musician, author, and playwright; and the papers of Gregoria Fraser Goins, which detail Goins's work in the National Association of Negro Musicians, the Washington Music Teachers Association, and the Gregorian Studio of Music, which she operated. That collection also includes the papers of Goins's sister, Marinda Fraser Lougen, one of the first black female physicians in the United States and the first woman physician in the Dominican Republic. The papers of medical professional Lena Edwards, an obstetrician-gynecologist, are also located at Moorland. Those materials document Edwards's activities as a physician, a community activist, and a volunteer with migrant workers at St. Joseph's Mission and Our Lady of Guadeloupe Maternity Clinic for migrant women in Hereford, Texas.

Also among the repository's collections are the papers of suffragist Mary Ann Shadd Cary; correspondence from Shirley Graham DuBois in the papers of Kwame Nkrumah, Ghana's first president after independence; the papers of activist Eslanda Goode Robeson; and the papers of Mary Frances Berry, historian and civil rights activist. Along with personal papers, Moorland-Spingarn is also the repository for the records of a number of major African American women's organizations. The center serves as the archives for Alpha Kappa Alpha, the first African American intercollegiate Greek-letter sorority. There are also records related to chapters of the Order of the Eastern Star, including the papers of Georgiana Thomas, one of the founders of the earliest chapter of the Prince Hall affiliate of the Order of the Eastern Star in Washington, DC, in 1874.

Prominent among the collections at the Atlanta University Center Robert W. Woodruff Library's Archival Research Center are the records of the Neighborhood Union. Established in 1908 by Lugenia Burns Hope, the union addressed the social, economic, and educational problems in the African American community surrounding the university. Personal papers of Lugenia Hope are also located in the John and Lugenia Burns Hope Papers. Present in the library's collection are the records of the Association of Southern Women for the Prevention of Lynching, an interracial women's organization based in Atlanta and an outgrowth of the Women's Committee of the Commission on Interracial Cooperation; the Chautauqua Circle, one of the oldest clubs for black women in Atlanta; and The Moles, an African American women's social organization. The collection also contains the personal papers of Eva Alberta Jessye, writer, singer, and civil rights activist, and a small collection from composer and collector Maud Cuney Hare. The library also holds the papers of Florence "Frankie" Adams, educator, author, and social worker, and Pauline A. Young. The Young Papers document her life as an educator and a civil rights and community activist, and they include a small amount of biographical information about her aunt, writer Alice Dunbar Nelson.

Similar in scope to the records at the Woodruff Library are the collections at Fisk University archives. Fisk University archives serves as the repository for a number of important collections documenting the lives and work of African American women in the arts. Among the most notable are the papers of Pauline E. Hopkins, the nineteenth- and twentieth-century novelist, editor, and musician; the diary of Ellen Shepherd, pianist and arranger for and an original member of the Jubilee Singers; a collection of letters from America Robinson, also an original Jubilee singer and a member of Fisk's first graduating class; and the of papers of Henrietta Crawley Myers, member and later director of the Jubilee Singers. Writer and book publisher Naomi Long Madgett's papers are in the Fisk collection, as well as those of Eileen Jackson Southern, musicologist and author of the seminal work *The Music of Black Americans* (1971). The archives also contains a small collection of letters and other materials from Mary McLeod Bethune; Olympian Alice Coachman Davis; sociologist Ophelia Settle Egypt; and Emma Bragg, registrar and director of admissions at Meharry Medical College. The papers of Juliette Derricotte, dean of women at Fisk, are in the Thomas Elsa Jones Papers. The materials in these papers document Derricotte's tenure at Fisk as dean of women from 1929 to 1931.

The library and archives at Tuskegee University are internationally known for their rare collections of primary and secondary sources of African American materials. Included among the archives and manuscripts collections at Tuskegee are the papers of African American women who were an integral part of the life of the university and the local community. Among the collections are the papers of Margaret Murray Washington, documenting her work as a teacher and lady principal at Tuskegee and as president of the National Association of Colored Women's Club, the Southern Federation of Colored Women's Clubs, the International Council of Women of the Darker Races, and of the Tuskegee Women's Club, whose records are also in the archives. The Tuskegee Women's Club was established in 1895 by the female faculty and the wives of male faculty members at Tuskegee. The club provided educational and social services to the rural communities. The papers of Edith Washington Shehee, daughter-in-law of Booker T. Washington and owner of the Washington Candies Company; Sadie Peterson Delaney, chief librarian and bibliotherapist at the Veterans Hospital in Tuskegee; and Jessie Parkhurst Guzman, director of Tuskegee's Department of Research and Records from 1944 to 1965, are also housed in the Tuskegee archives.

The Spelman College archives serves a dual mission at the college: first, to collect the permanently valuable records of the college and the personal papers and records of alumnae, faculty, and staff; and second, to collect the papers of contemporary African American feminist scholars, activists, and writers in support of the college's Women's Research and Resource Center's mission to be a major repository for scholarship on black feminism and feminist thought. These roles are reflected in the holdings of the archives, which, in combination, form a rich resource for the study of African American women.

Among the earliest collections in the archives are the letters of Spelman graduates Nora Gordon and Emma Delaney, nineteenth-century missionaries to schools in the Congo and Liberia in West Africa. In addition to these collections, there are papers of Spelman graduates Audrey Forbes Manley, pediatrician, public health professional, former acting surgeon general of the United States, and president of Spelman College; Eleanor Ison Franklin, associate dean of the College of Medicine and professor of physiology at Howard University; June Dobbs Butts, a therapist and family counselor and one of the first African American sexologists; and Josephine Harreld Love, a concert pianist, teacher, writer, and museum curator. The latter collection documents Love's career as a concert pianist and as cofounder and director of Your Heritage House, a fine arts museum for children in Detroit, Michigan.

The Audre Lorde Papers comprise one of the most significant collections among the holdings in the Spelman archives. The papers are the most comprehensive documentation of Lorde's life and work as a black lesbian feminist writer and activist. Other noteworthy collections include the papers of Toni Cade Bambara, writer, filmmaker, and community organizer; Selma H. Burke, pioneering African American female sculptor and educator, best known for her relief portrait of Franklin Delano Roosevelt used on the American dime; and Marion V. Cuthbert, leader in the Young Women's Christian Association (YWCA). The personal papers of Johnnetta B. Cole, which document her career as an educator and anthropologist, and her tenure as president of Bennett College for Women and as the current director of the Smithsonian's Museum of African Art, are also housed in the Spelman archives.

A rare collection of African American organization records can be found in the archives at Xavier University of Louisiana. The collection is composed of charters, minutes, and other documents that chronicle the history of New Orleans black benevolent associations. Contained in the collection are items related to associations organized by African American women, such as the Ladies of Catholic Benevolent Association of the Sacred Heart of Mary, 1875; Benevolent Daughters of Louisiana, 1936; Daughters of Zion Benevolent Association, 1936; Les Dames et Demoiselles de Bon Secours Societe D'Assistance Mutuelle, 1936; and Les Dames et Demoiselles Sinceres.

The archives at the University of Arkansas, Pine Bluff, has also focused its collecting on the records of local women's organizations. Among the collections are the records of the Arkansas Association of Colored Women; the Arkansas Association of Girls; and the Arkansas Association of Women, Young Adults and Youth Clubs, Inc., an affiliate of the National Association of Colored Women's Clubs, Inc. Also included are the files of the Arkansas State Girls Association and Young Adults; the National Association of Colored Girls Clubs; the National Association of Colored Women's Clubs, Inc.; and the Southwest Region of the National Association of Colored Women's Clubs, Inc.

Some HBCUs have built collections around the work of a single individual. Texas Southern University is the repository for the papers of United States congresswoman Barbara Jordan. The collection comprises more than four hundred linear feet of materials dating from 1950 to 1996. The materials document Jordan's career as the first African American woman to serve in the Texas state senate (1967), the first African American US representative from Texas (1972 to 1979), and the first African American to deliver a keynote speech at the Democratic National Convention (1976). The papers also provide detail about Jordan's law practice in Houston (1961 to 1966), her teaching experience at Tuskegee Institute (1960), and her professorship at the Lyndon B. Johnson School of Public Affairs at the University of Texas (1979 to 1995).

The institutional home of the Margaret Walker Alexander National Research Center is Jackson State University in Mississippi. The center is the successor of the Institute for the Study of the History, Life and Culture of Black People founded in 1968. The research center's principal collection is the papers of author, poet, and educator Margaret Walker Alexander. Alexander is best known for her epic poem *For My People* (1942), her novel *Jubilee* (1966), and the biography *Richard Wright: Daemonic Genius* (1987). The collection consists of 110 linear feet of materials dating from 1929 to 1998 and includes correspondence, 130 personal journals, and creative works by Alexander and others.

The archives of Talladega College (Alabama) is the repository for the papers of Hilda Davis, dean of women at Talladega College from 1937 to 1952. The collection consists of personal and professional correspondence, records, and speeches that document Davis's service as president of both the Association of Deans of Women and Advisers to Girls in Negro Schools and the National Association of College Women, as well as her work in other organizations. A portion of the Ragland Family Collection at the Talladega archives is made up of the papers of Mary Venus Ragland, Addie Ragland, and Gertrude Ragland, including class record books, class rolls, lesson plans for courses in business, remnants of a 1875 memory book kept by Addie Ragland while a student at Talladega College, yearbooks, and programs. Also included in the archives are the papers of Mattie Rivers Trammell. This collection consists almost entirely of programs and minutes of the Alabama Federation of Colored Women's Clubs, the Association of Colored Women's Clubs, and the City Federation of Colored Women's Clubs of Anniston, Alabama.

The Virginia State University Archives is especially strong in the documentation of African American women faculty members and community leaders. Significant among the collections are the papers of Virginia school teachers Amanda DeHart and Mabel Harris; community activist Helen Estes Baker; business owner Alice Atwell Jackson; and Virginia State faculty members M. E. V. Hunter (founder of the School of Home Economics), Altona Johns and Anna Laura Lindsay (of the Music Department), and Amaza Lee Meredith (of the Art Department). The Meredith Collection is especially noteworthy: comprised of nearly five thousand items, the papers document Meredith's teaching career as well as her business dealings with the Azurest North Syndicate, a real estate business firm in Sag Harbor, New York. The papers include correspondence and business records, blueprints, line drawings, sketches reflecting Meredith's interest in architecture, as well as scrapbooks and ephemera.

North Carolina Central University houses the William Tucker Collection of Black Authors and Illustrators, which includes eleven separate collections consisting of notes, working drafts, sketches, typescripts, galleys, correspondence, and autographed books. African American women represented include Dorothy Robinson, Beth Wilson, Eloise Greenfield, Alexis DeVeaux, Sharon Bell Mathis, Charlemae Hill Rollins, and Beth Pierre Wilson. The papers of African American librarians are also present in the archives; the Black Librarians Collection consists of the papers of fourteen African American librarians including African American women librarians Lille Day Carter, Rossie B. Caldwell, Vivian D. Hewitt, Mollie Huston Lee, Bernice Middleton, Annette Phinazee, Charlemae H. Rollins, and Mary Spaulding.

The collection at Meharry Medical College (Tennessee) includes documentation of the college's nursing school and African American nurses. A significant collection is that of Evelyn Tomes, chair and professor of the Division of Nursing. The Tomes Papers document the history of African American nursing and nursing schools. The Black Nurses History Collection also includes the records of nurses Hulda Lyttle Frazier, Rosa Mimms, and Iris R. Shannon.

The Impact of HBCU Archival Collections on Scholarship

In spite of the fact that African American women's collections in HBCUs have not been known in the broader academic and research communities, there are scholars and researchers who have made good use of these resources. Historian Gerda Lerner was among the first scholars to make use of African American women's collections at HBCUs. In *Black Women in White America: A Documentary History*, she cites records from the Neighborhood Union Collection and Association of Southern Women to Prevent Lynching at Atlanta University; the Ophelia Settle Egypt interviews in the Charles S. Johnson Papers at Fisk University; and a letter from Mary McLeod Bethune in the Rosenwald Fund Papers, also at Fisk University. From the Moorland-Spingarn Collection, Lerner used documents from the Grimké Family Collection and letters from the Works Progress Administration records; and from Tuskegee, the Margaret Murray Washington Papers. In documenting the political struggles of black women for gender equality, Dorothy Sterling used the Mary Ann Shadd Cary papers and the diaries of Charlotte Forten Grimké and Laura Hamilton Murray in the Francis Grimké and Freeman Murray Collections at Howard; she published *We Are Your Sisters—Black Women in the 19th Century* in 1984. Paula Giddings also used the Mary Ann Shadd Cary Papers and other collections at Moorland-Spingarn to write *When and Where I Enter: The Impact of Black Women on Race and Sex in America* (1984).[43]

In an article on biographical references about women, librarian Susan Searing wrote, "the 1990s saw the fullest flowering of biographical references published on African American women. One author, librarian Jessie Carney Smith, was responsible for much of the best material in the area."[44] Searing's review refers to the three-volume reference work, *Notable Black American Women*, edited by Smith. Published in 1992, 1996, and 2003, the volumes contain 1,100 biographies of African American women. Smith and her contributors took advantage of the sources from HBCU archival collections when compiling information on the women profiled in the volumes. In the introduction to the first volume, Smith writes that one of the goals of the publications was to help future researchers by "including reference notes and as far as possible, the identification of local or archival material."[45] Examples of the HBCU collections used to write biographies include the Constance Hill Marteena Papers at Bennett College; the records of the Carrie Steele Home for the biography of its founder, Carrie Steele, at the Atlanta University Center Woodruff Library; the Yvonne Walker Papers at Wilberforce University; and the Verda Freeman Welcome Papers at Morgan State University.

Recent scholars as well as emerging scholars are also using the sources in HBCU archives in their teaching and publications. Professor Joyce Hanson used the Bethune Papers at Bethune-Cookman University to write *Mary McLeod Bethune and Black Women's Political Activism* (2003). In her comparative study of white and black women in the South Carolina women's club movement, author Joan Marie Johnson cited the records of the South Carolina Federation of Colored Women Clubs and other black women's organizational records found in the archives at South Carolina State University; she published *Southern Ladies, New Women: Race, Region, and Clubwomen in South Carolina, 1890–1930* in 2005. Authors Yolanda L. Watson and Sheila T. Gregory made extensive use of the Spelman College archives and collections at the Atlanta University Center Woodruff Library in doing research for their publication, *Daring to Educate: The Legacy of the Early Spelman College Presidents.*[46]

Emerging scholars are using sources in HBCU archives for theses and dissertations. Such works include Cassandra Evans-Herring's 2003 dissertation on Mary E. Branch, president of Tillotson College. Bennett College for Women is the subject of a 2004 dissertation written by Nadine Lockwood at the State University of New York at Buffalo. Alexis Gumbs used the Audre Lorde Papers at Spelman to complete her dissertation "We Can Learn to Mother Ourselves: The Queer Survival of Black Feminism, 1968–1996."[47] GraceLynis Dubinson focused her master's thesis on the development of Azurest North, an African American summer community developed in the 1950s in Sag Harbor, New York. The Amaza Lee Meredith Collection at Virginia State University provided much of the documentation for this work.[48] Such use of HBCU archival collections by veteran and emerging scholars will ensure the preservation and the continued use of these invaluable resources.

Overcoming Obstacles: A Commitment to Future Growth

HBCUs are committed to the ongoing preservation of the history of African Americans. Their libraries and archival repositories will continue to grow, assuring users that they are in the forefront of the documentation of African American women. Scholarly disinterest in the history of African American women, inadequate funding for the professional development of archives by many HBCUs, and the underreporting of these collections in reference works and bibliographic aids have been major obstacles to achieving the level of access and preservation sought by scholars and researchers. For scholarship on African American women to continue to evolve, archivists and historians must work together to identify and preserve the primary source materials. HBCUs must also work collaboratively with each other and with other cultural institutions and funders so they can continue to strengthen their programs and increase their collections. Archivists and historians working in tandem can open new areas of scholarship by filling in the gaps in African American women's history.

HBCUs have a long and dedicated history of collecting, preserving, and making accessible documentation of African American history and culture in general, and African American women's history in particular. HBCU archives have an unending commitment to this mission and will continue to play a vital role in this documentation in the future. Author Alice Walker wrote that "people are known by the records they keep. . . . If it isn't in the records, it will be said it didn't happen. That is what history is: a keeping of records."[49] Historically Black Colleges and Universities have served as the keepers of records throughout much of their history and will continue to chronicle the past through "a keeping of records."

NOTES

[1] In Title III of the Higher Education Act of 1965, Congress officially defined institutions whose principal mission was the education of African Americans and were established and accredited before 1964 as HBCUs.

[2] United Negro College Fund, http://www.uncf.org/members/aboutHBCU.asp, accessed 11 January 2012.

[3] Richard I. McKinney, "Mordecai Johnson: An Early Pillar of African American Higher Education," *Journal of Blacks in Higher Education* 27 (2000): 99.

[4] Cynthia Neverdon-Morton, *Afro American Women of the South and the Advancement of the Race* (Knoxville: University of Tennessee Press, 1989), 7.

[5] Jessie Carney Smith, *Black Academic Libraries and Research Collections: An Historical Survey* (Westport, CT: Greenwood Press, 1977), 157.

[6] Dorothy B. Porter, "The Preservation of University Documents with Special Reference to Negro Colleges and Universities," *Journal of Negro Education* 11 (1942): 527.

[7] Robert L. Allen, "Politics of the Attack on Black Studies," *Black Scholar: Journal of Black Studies and Research* 6, no. 1 (1974): 2.

[8] Smith, *Black Academic Libraries and Research Collections*, 169.

[9] Martha I. Pallante and Kathleen Thompson, *Encyclopedia of African American History, 1619–1895: From the Colonial Period to the Age of Frederick Douglass*, ed. Paul Finkelman, Oxford African American Studies Center, http://www .oxfordaasc.com/article/opr/t0004/e0607, accessed 21 February 2012.

[10] Darlene Clark Hine, "Disfigured Images: The Historical Assault on Afro-American Women," quoted in Patricia Morton, review of *Contributions in Afro-American and African Studies, Journal of Southern History* 59, no. 4 (1993): 795.

[11] Jacqueline A. Rouse, "The Legacy of Community Organizing: Lugenia Burns Hope and the Neighborhood Union," *Journal of Negro History* 69, nos. 3–4 (1984): 114.

[12] Neverdon-Morton, *Afro American Women of the South*, 193.

[13] Ida B. Wells-Barnett (1862–1931), journalist, antilynching crusader, suffragist and clubwoman, was an outspoken social activist. In 1889, she became editor of and partner in the *Free Speech and Headlight,* a black Memphis newspaper. After the lynching of three friends in Memphis, Wells-Barnett used her editorials to crusade against lynching. She was an outspoken advocate for anti-lynching laws, authoring statements and publications critical of southern mob

violence. Wells-Barnett was a founding member of the National Association of Colored Women (NACW) and the National Association for the Advancement of Colored People (NAACP); "Ida B. Wells-Barnett," http://www.gale.cengage .com/free_resources/bhm/bio/wells_i.htm, accessed 6 December 2011.

[14] Lillian Serece Williams, *Records of the National Association of Colored Women's Clubs, 1892–1992* (Bethesda, MD: University Publications of America, 1994), vii.

[15] Jacqueline A. Rouse, "Out of the Shadow of Tuskegee: Margaret Murray Washington, Social Activism, and Race Vindication," *Journal of Negro History* 81, nos. 1–4 (1996): 39.

[16] Deborah F. Atwater, *African American Women's Rhetoric: The Search for Dignity, Personhood and Honor* (Lanham, MD: Lexington Books, 2009), 59.

[17] Fannie Barrier Williams, "Club Movement among Negro Women," in *Progress of a Race: or, the Remarkable Advancement of the Afro American Race*, eds. Henry F. Kletzing and William Henry Crogman (Atlanta: J. L. Nichols, 1903); Margaret Murray Washington, "Club Work among Negro Women," in *Progress of a Race: or the Remarkable Advancement of the Afro American Race*, eds. J. L. Nichols and William Henry Crogman (Naperville, IL: J. L. Nichols, 1920).

[18] Sadie Iola Daniel, *Women Builders* (Washington, DC: Associated Press, 1931); Elizabeth L. Davis, *Lifting as They Climb* (Chicago: National Association of Colored Women, 1933); Hallie Q. Brown, *Homespun Heroines and Women of Distinction* (Xenia, OH: Aldine Publishing Company, 1926).

[19] Dulcie Straughan, "'Lifting as We Climb': The Role of the *National Association Notes* in Furthering the Issues Agenda of the National Association of Colored Women, 1897–1920," *Media History Monographs* 8, no. 2 (2006): 10–15.

[20] Charles H. Wesley, *The History of the National Association of Colored Women's Clubs: A Legacy of Service* (Washington, DC: Association, 1984), 98.

[21] Minutes, National Council of Negro Women, 5 December 1935. NCWN Records, Series 2, Box 1, Folder 1, National Archives for Black Women's History, Washington, DC.

[22] Bettye Collier-Thomas, "Towards Black Feminism: The Creation of the Bethune Museum-Archives," in *Women's Collections: Libraries, Archives and Consciousness,* ed. Susan Hildenbrand (New York: Haworth Press, 1986), 58.

[23] Linda J. Henry, "Promoting Historical Consciousness: The Early Archives Committee of the National Council of Negro Women," *Signs* 7, no. 1 (1981): 254.

[24] Barbara Gamarekian, "Historian Fills Gaps in Black Women's Legacies," *Houston Chronicle*, 10 March 1985, http:// search.proquest.com/docview/295043406?, accessed 25 July 2011.

[25] Louie Davis Shivery, "The History of Organized Work among Atlanta Negroes, 1890–1935" (master's thesis, Atlanta University, 1936).

[26] Martha S. Bell, "Special Women's Collections in United States Libraries, *College and Research Libraries* (1959): 236.

[27] Avril Johnson Madison and Dorothy Porter Wesley, "Dorothy Burnett Porter Wesley: Enterprising Steward of Black Culture," *Public Historian* 17, no. 1 (1995): 29–30.

[28] Ann Allen Shockely, "Special Collections, Fisk University Library," in Thomas Battle and Ann Allen Shockley, "Research Notes: Resources for Scholars: Four Collections of Afro-Americana: Part 2 University Library Collections," *Library Quarterly* 58, no. 2 (1988): 160.

[29] Francille Rusan Wilson, "'This Past Was Waiting for Me When I Came': The Contextualization of Black Women's History," *Feminist Studies* 22, no. 2 (1996): 347. The five Howard-educated authors were Evelyn Brooks Higginbotham, MA, 1974; Rosalyn Terborg-Penn, PhD, 1978; Sharon Harley, PhD, 1981; Gerald Gill, MA, 1974, PhD, 1980; Cynthia Neverdon-Morton, PhD, 1977.

[30] Association of Black Women Historians, "History," http://www.abwh.org/index.php?, accessed 1 February 2012.

[31] Beverly Guy-Sheftall, "Black Women's Studies: The Interface of Women's Studies and Black Studies," in *African American Studies Reader*, ed. Nathaniel Norment Jr. (Durham, NC: Carolina Academic Press, 2001), 138.

[32] Quoted in Anne Johnson, "Beverly Guy-Sheftall, 1946–," *Contemporary Black Biography, 1997*, Encyclopedia.com, http://www.encyclopedia.com, accessed 11 February 2012.

[33] Bettye Collier Thomas, Foreword in *The Progress of Afro American Women: A Selected Bibliography and Resource Guide*, ed. Janet L. Sims (Westport, CT: Greenwood Press, 1980), ix.

[34] Deborah Gray White, "Mining the Forgotten: Manuscript Sources for Black Women's History," *Journal of American History* 74, no. 1 (1987): 237.

[35] E. J. Josey and Marva L. DeLoach, *Ethnic Collections in Libraries* (New York: Neal-Schuman, 1983); E. J. Josey, *The Black Librarian in America Revisited* (Metuchen, NJ: Scarecrow Press, 1994).

[36] Ann Allen Shockley, *A Handbook for the Administration of Special Negro Collections* (Washington, DC: US Department of Health, Education and Welfare, 1970), i.

[37] "The Plight of Archives in Black Colleges and Universities: Legacies Good and Bad," in *Culture Keepers: Enlightening and Empowering Our Communities: Proceedings of the First National Conference of African American Librarians*, ed. Stanton Biddle (Newark, NJ: Black Caucus of the American Library Association, 1993):105.

[38] Walter Schatz, ed., *Directory of Afro-American Resources* (New York: R. R. Bowker, 1970).

[39] Andrea Hinding, ed., *Women's History Sources: A Guide to Archives and Manuscripts Collections in the United States*, 2 vols. (New York: R. R. Bowker, 1979).

[40] More than seven hundred collection descriptions by CHASP were added to the *National Union Catalog of Manuscript Collections* (NUCMC). The completed records are available on the Library of Congress NUCMC website, http://lcweb.loc.gov/coll/nucmc.

[41] J. Kenneth Morris, *Elizabeth Evelyn Wright, 1872–1906, Founder of Voorhees College* (Sewanee, TN: University Press, 1983).

[42] Gerri Bates, "These Hallowed Halls: African American Women College and University Presidents," *Journal of Negro Education* 76, no. 3 (2007): 384.

[43] Gerda Lerner, ed., *Black Women in White America; A Documentary History* (New York: Pantheon Books, 1972); Dorothy Sterling, ed., *We Are Your Sisters: Black Women in the Nineteenth Century* (New York: W. W. Norton, 1984); Paula Giddings, *When and Where I Enter: The Impact of Black Women on Race and Sex in America* (New York: William Morrow, 1984).

[44] Susan E. Searing, "Biographical Reference Works for and about Women, from the Advent of the Women's Liberation Movement to the Present: An Exploratory Analysis," *Library Trends* 56, no. 2 (2007): 483.

[45] Jessie Carney Smith, *Notable Black American Women* (Detroit: Gale Research, 1992), xxxv.

[46] Joyce A. Hanson, *Mary McLeod Bethune and Black Women's Political Activism* (Columbia: University of Missouri Press, 2003); Joan Marie Johnson, *Southern Ladies, New Women: Race, Region and Clubwomen in South Carolina, 1890–1930* (Gainesville: University of Florida Press, 2005); Yolanda L. Watson and Sheila T. Gregory, *Daring to Educate: The Legacy of the Early Spelman College Presidents* (Sterling, VA: Stylus Publishing, 2005).

[47] Cassandra Evans-Herring, "An Intersectional Analysis of the Life Experiences of Mary Elizabeth Branch, the First Female Senior College President" (PhD diss., Georgia State University, 2003); Nadine Lockwood, "Bennett College for Women, 1926–1966" (PhD diss., State University of New York at Buffalo, 2004); Alexis Gumbs, "We Can Learn to Mother Ourselves: The Queer Survival of Black Feminism, 1968–1996" (PhD diss., Duke University, 2010); GraceLynis Dubinson, "Slowly, Surely, One Plat, One Binder at a Time: Choking Out Jim Crow and the Development of the Azurest Syndicate Incorporated" (master's thesis, Georgia State University, 2012) Georgia State University Digital Archive, http://digitalarchive.gsu.edu/history_theses/53.

[48] Amaza Lee Meredith Papers, 1912, 1930–1930, Accession #1982-20, Special Collections Dept., Johnson Memorial Library, Virginia State University, Petersburg, VA.

[49] Emory Libraries, Robert W. Woodruff Library, "A Keeping of Records: The Art and Life of Alive Walker," http://web.library.emory.edu/libraries/schatten-gallery/previous-exhibits/alice-walker, accessed 5 July 2011.

CHAPTER 14

Collecting, Describing, and Promoting Women's History at the Library of Congress

JANICE E. RUTH

THE LIBRARY OF CONGRESS, THE NATIONAL LIBRARY OF THE UNITED STATES AND THE COUNTRY'S OLDEST FEDERAL CULTURAL INSTITUTION, HAS BEEN COLLECTING BOOKS, MANUSCRIPTS, AND OTHER MATERIALS RELATING TO WOMEN SINCE SHORTLY AFTER ITS FOUNDING IN 1800. This was long before historian Mary Ritter Beard called for the creation of a World Center for Women's Archives in the 1930s and many decades prior to the founding of special women's history repositories at the country's leading women's colleges. Over the last two centuries, the Library of Congress has quietly, and in some cases unintentionally, assembled a remarkably broad and deep collection of resources for the study of women, especially women in the United States.

In the last fifteen years, Library of Congress staff have engaged in a concerted effort to uncover, describe, and promote the institution's women's history holdings through a variety of means: improved catalog records and finding aids; a repository-wide guide in both print and online versions; a two-day symposium; an ongoing staff-patron discussion group; publications ranging from knowledge cards to calendars to a *Women Who Dare* book series; digitization projects; a web capture initiative; and a collaborative endeavor with the photo-sharing site Flickr. This essay offers a brief overview of the library's collections, particularly its manuscript holdings relating to American women's history, followed by a detailed description of the staff's efforts to make those collections better known and more accessible. Researchers should gain from this essay an understanding of the library's resources and learn how to identify and access them. Archivists, on the other hand, may take away from the project descriptions and lessons learned some possible ideas for promoting their own holdings, employing technology to enhance access, and finding new ways of communicating with potential audiences.

Collecting Women's History at the Library of Congress

The holdings of the Library of Congress currently number nearly 151 million items, including many millions specifically devoted to the topic of women.[1] Located in the library's general and rare book collections are hundreds of thousands of monographs, almanacs, and encyclopedias; the country's most comprehensive collection of doctoral dissertations; published collections of women's letters and diaries; etiquette books, prescriptive literature, and sex manuals; autobiographies, genealogies, and scrapbooks; cookbooks and domestic journals; trade catalogs, hobby books, and school primers; and congressional, technical, and statistical reports on every topic imaginable. The library's Serial and Government Publications Division holds one of the world's largest collections of current and retrospective newspapers, periodicals, and government publications. Its Law Library contains the largest body of federal, state, and international legal sources in the world, and its special collections divisions are home to a diverse body of manuscripts, prints and photographs, maps, music, sound recordings, motion pictures, and broadsides replete with information about women.

Like many repositories, the library has acquired these collections over the last two centuries through purchases and gifts. In addition, it has enjoyed the unique advantage of receiving government transfers and copyright deposits to build its holdings. When Congress purchased

Thomas Jefferson's library in 1815 to replace the congressional library burned by the British during the War of 1812, it acquired for the new Library of Congress poems by Phillis Wheatley; a history of the American Revolution by Mercy Otis Warren; novels by Eliza Haywood, Mary Manley, and Anne Germaine; and *The Woman's Lawyer*, a 1632 British compilation of statutes and cases concerning women.[2] In the two hundred years since, the library has continued to use both appropriated and gift funds to buy women's history materials not available through other means, but the number of these purchases pales in comparison to the number of its holdings acquired by transfer, deposit, and gift.

A government transfer accounted for one of the library's first women's manuscript collections when the Smithsonian Institution sent to the library in 1866 the papers of Dolley Madison, seventeen years after the first lady's death. Transfers from the State Department and other entities followed, as did legislation requiring the mandatory deposit of government publications and copyrighted materials, especially Americana. Since 1870, as part of the copyright registration process, individuals and companies have submitted for deposit a wide variety of books, magazines, sound recordings, motion pictures, play scripts, maps, prints, posters, photographs, sheet music, and other materials. Many, but not all, of these items have found their way into the library's permanent collections.

The library has supplemented these copyright deposits, transfers, and purchases with countless gifts of personal papers, organizational records, photo archives, and other special collections. Most of the library's manuscript materials have been acquired through gifts, especially after the establishment of a separate Manuscript Division in 1897. Although most of the library's collections are universal in scope—embracing Thomas Jefferson's own view that there is "no subject to which a member of Congress may not have occasion to refer"—the collections in the Manuscript Division are generally limited in focus to American history and culture. They tend to reflect events, people, and organizations of national significance, although aspects of state and local history are documented in the state files of national groups and in the letters and diaries of women and men who lived in, traveled to, or otherwise represented communities across the country. Like other repositories that collect nationally, the Manuscript Division often must decline materials that focus on local topics or regionally prominent women. Although partly a question of priorities and budget resources, this policy also reflects the belief that locally focused collections will be of greatest interest to those who live nearby. A local or regional repository often holds complementary materials, and its staff has gained a specialized knowledge of an area's history and place in national events.

Estimated at more than 63 million items contained in approximately 11,500 collections, the library's manuscript collections account for nearly one-half of the institution's collection of 151 million items. These manuscripts differ from the holdings of the National Archives and Records Administration, which is required by law to maintain the official records of the United States government. Instead, most of the library's manuscript collections comprise the *personal* papers of individuals and families, along with a number of organizational records. They range in size from a single letter or diary to the more than 3.5 million records of a single organization—the National Association for the Advancement of Colored People (NAACP). A 1979 publication identified 506 collections in the Manuscript Division relating to women's history, but a more comprehensive listing compiled internally in 1985, which included references to women's papers in the collections of male family members, placed the figure at more than 1,400 collections.[3] This number has increased significantly, of course, in the twenty-five years since the 1985 survey, with a conservative estimate placing today's total in excess of two thousand collections.

The Manuscript Division's earliest chiefs actively solicited the collections of notable women who were involved in the suffrage and abolition campaigns. They also sought the papers of first ladies, of women who achieved various "firsts" in history, and of women who were pioneers in fields formerly restricted to men. To this day, those collections sustain heavy research use and continue to influence current collecting policies. Represented are prominent women from many walks of life and nearly every time period in our nation's history. Most of the women represented were white and from middle- and upper-middle-class families, although some important examples of documentation of African American women may be found. There are fewer sources written by Native Americans or by women of Asian, Hispanic, or other origin. Efforts are being made, however, to rectify these omissions.[4]

Included are the papers of suffragists and reformers Susan B. Anthony, Elizabeth Cady Stanton, Lucy Stone, Alice Stone Blackwell, Clara Barton, Anna E. Dickinson, Carrie Chapman Catt, Maud Wood Park, Mary Church Terrell, Margaret Sanger, Anna Kelton Wiley, Belle Case La Follette, Cornelia Pinchot, and Madeleine McDowell Breckinridge. Supreme Court justices Sandra Day O'Connor and Ruth Bader Ginsburg have donated their papers, as did the families of congresswomen Ruth Hanna McCormick, Clare Boothe Luce, and Patsy Mink. Also represented are diplomats, judges, and government officials Florence Jaffray Harriman, Florence E. Allen, Shirley Hufstedler, Patricia Harris, Pamela Harriman, and Alice Rivlin; writers and poets Shirley Jackson, Muriel Rukeyser, and Edna St. Vincent Millay; anthropologist Margaret Mead and scientists Vera Rubin, Lynn Margulis, and Frances Kelsey; actresses Minnie Maddern Fiske, Margaret Webster, Lillian Gish, and Jessica Tandy; and journalists Ruby Black, Janet Flanner, Ethel Payne, Bess Furman, Mary McGrory, Katharine Graham, and Nancy Dickerson.

The Manuscript Division also serves as the archival repository for a number of civil rights and reform organizations such as the National Association for the Advancement of Colored People, National American Woman Suffrage Association, National Woman's Party, League of Women Voters, National Consumers League, National Women's Trade Union League, National Council of Jewish Women, ERAmerica, National Coalition on Older Women's Issues, and the Center for a Woman's Own Name.

Other materials, which were not always consciously sought, are letters and diaries documenting women's everyday existence and revealing women's hopes, disappointments, and accomplishments. Although unsolicited, these items were also preserved, but as part of multigenerational family papers or as unnoticed groupings buried in the papers of a more famous husband, father, or brother. The papers of these unknown female relatives reflect the daily activities, concerns, and observations of

American women from the colonial period through the twentieth century. Used together with the papers of male family members, they provide important information on American family life, the relationships between men and women, and the impact of wars, politics, and other national and international events on individuals and families. Uncovering and describing these manuscript materials and other women's history holdings throughout the library has been a major institutional activity in the last fifteen years.

The Role of Catalog Records and Finding Aids

The search for women's history resources in the Manuscript Division has been aided by the fact that every collection held by the division (even if unprocessed) is represented by a full or preliminary MARC record in the Library of Congress Online Catalog. Available remotely via the Internet, these catalog records are useful for locating the most likely sources on a topic and for gaining an overview of the division's holdings. A search for Manuscript Division collections may be done in conjunction with an integrated search of the library's books and other formats, or it may be limited to Manuscript Division records only or to records that describe archival manuscript/mixed format collections in various divisions.[5] Familiarity with the *Library of Congress Subject Headings* (*LCSH*) is essential. Although long criticized by feminists and others for being slow to respond to societal changes, *LCSH* has become more effective in the last thirty years in cataloging women's topics, although identifying the precise authorized headings and subheadings remains difficult. For example, a search of the catalog for the keyword phrase *battered women* uncovers about 170 books, films, government reports, and other sources. If, however, the three authorized headings—*Abused women, Abused wives, Wife abuse*—are used, the search yields more than 2,300 records (with some overlap). Every new edition of *LCSH* includes an increasing number of terms relevant to women's studies. For example, the twenty-third edition of *LCSH* (2000) listed twenty-four pages of terms under the heading

Women, as well as additional pages containing other applicable headings, such as *Girls, Goddesses, Lesbians, Mistresses, Nuns, Queens,* and *Sisters.* The thirty-second edition of *LCSH* (2010) now contains thirty-two pages for the heading *Women.* The heading *Women* can also be followed by some of the more than three thousand authorized free-floating subdivisions, which can be geographical, topical, chronological, or by form.[6] In addition to searching by name and subject, the Library of Congress Online Catalog also permits various types of keyword searches, which are especially useful for locating words and phrases in the summary scope and content notes of manuscript records.

When searching the catalog, manuscript researchers should keep in mind that they will likely need to consult collections not because of any interest per se in the creator of those materials, but because the creator may have had an association with the person, events, or activities that are the real focus of their research. This is especially true when searching for women, whose presence in a collection may not have been captured by a cataloger years ago. Researchers often need to search not only for a woman's name but also for the names of her male family members, friends, colleagues, organizations, and anyone else with whom she may have corresponded. The catalog record, however, cannot describe the entire scope and diversity of the creator's experiences, nor can it identify every subject represented in a given collection. It distills in a few paragraphs the information contained in a multipage finding aid, which is routinely created by division archivists in the course of processing all but the smallest of collections. More than two thousand finding aids are available for use in the Manuscript Reading Room, of which the division has encoded and put online nearly 1,700 in EAD format.[7] Searching the online finding aids allows researchers to uncover more quickly than before the names of people, places, groups, and subjects that do not appear in the abbreviated catalog records. Yet, even with such enhancements, finding guides are still only aids to research. They cannot substitute for a detailed examination of the actual papers.

American Women Resource Guide

Although individual divisions promoted their women's history holdings through catalog records, finding aids, and the occasional press release or article in a library publication, there had never been an attempt to conduct an institution-wide survey or publish a comprehensive guide. The Manuscript and Music Divisions had contributed entries over the years to the *National Union Catalog of Manuscript Collections* and to the 1979 Andrea Hinding publication *Women's History Sources: A Guide to Archives and Manuscript Repositories in the United States*, but it was not until 1997 that the library began seriously planning the publication of the 456-page resource guide, *American Women: A Library of Congress*

Cover, *American Women: A Library of Congress Guide for the Study of Women's History and Culture in the United State.* (Washington, DC: Library of Congress, 2001). Design by Adrianne Onderdonk Dudden.

Guide for the Study of Women's History and Culture in the United States.
To offset some of the considerable printing and distribution costs, the
library's Publishing Office collaborated with a copublisher in this project;
the book was published in December 2001 with the University Press of
New England (UPNE). This collaboration was financially critical to the
book's publication.

At times, it seemed unlikely that the guide would ever reach the publication stage, but a strong commitment from the Publishing Office and
the determination of the five-person editorial team corralled the work
of eighteen catalogers, reference specialists, and editors over a four-year
period following the first all-group planning meeting in August 1997.
The task was daunting, and almost immediately hard choices had to
be made regarding the scope of the undertaking to ensure its feasibil-
ity. An especially painful early decision was to limit the guide to sources
for the study of women in the United States, eliminating coverage of the
library's strong international materials.[8] It also became quickly apparent
that although the guide would be the most comprehensive ever undertaken, the result could not be exhaustive. The institution's holdings were
simply too massive, and duplicating the library's online catalog would be
of questionable benefit. Much discussion focused on whether to weave
information about the collections into a single narrative history (comparable to the library's chronologically organized *African American Mosaic*
resource guide) or to arrange the book in chapters that coincided with
the library's organizational structure of special-format and subject-based
reading rooms (similar to *Many Nations*, the library's Indian and Native
Alaskan resource guide).

The result was a compromise, a blended approach. Twelve chapters
written by Library of Congress subject specialists are organized by major
reading rooms and cover the general collections, newspapers and periodicals, legal materials, rare books, manuscripts, prints and photographs,
maps, music, recorded sound, moving images, American folklife, and
foreign-language collections. Interspersed between the chapters are five
topical essays designed to demonstrate how to conduct interdisciplinary research across the library's twenty-one reading rooms. Essay topics

include the woman suffrage parade of 1913; the campaign to ratify the Equal Rights Amendment; woman as symbol; women's westward movement to California; and a biographical essay on the life and work of Marian MacDowell, founder of the MacDowell Colony for creative artists. More essays had initially been planned, and their loss was regretted, but as with any large-scale project, a willingness to be flexible and make sacrifices along the way protected the effort already invested and ensured a more timely and successful completion.

Participating in the discussion of the book's organization and the choice of essays was an academic advisory committee, which was hired by the Publishing Office to help the editorial team review the historical accuracy of the content and to provide insights into the type of information that would be desired by faculty and students working in the field. Twentieth-century historian Susan Ware, who had years of experience researching at the library, headed the advisory committee, which included five other women's studies scholars from around the country.[9] Although there was some precedent for a scholars' publications committee, most advisory boards at the library had been used in connection with exhibitions. Assembling such a committee for the resource guide provided the institution with valuable early feedback, an outside perspective, and exposure for the book within academic circles.

Each chapter author was allocated a page length based on his or her division's presumed collection strengths, and all agreed to follow a uniform organizational structure that included an introductory overview, information on how to find relevant collections, and highlights of the division's most important holdings related to women. The middle instructional section, titled "Using the Collections," occasionally delves into the division's collecting policies; explains how the materials are arranged and described; suggests appropriate research methodologies; and identifies the major catalogs, finding aids, and other tools essential for uncovering and interpreting a particular division's collections. Although regrettably this information is too often ignored by many researchers, it underscores the reality that while certain collections are well represented in the library's online catalogs and finding aids, others are not, for reasons as varied as the collections involved. In some cases, staffing shortages at the time of receipt led to minimal-level descriptions. In other cases, significant conservation problems, excessive access restrictions, or perceived lack of research interest curtailed descriptive efforts. In addition, several special-format divisions still rely on local card catalogs and other in-house finding aids and indexes. Explaining these access tools to researchers is critical at a time when most patrons believe that they can find all the information online.

The largest section of each chapter describes selected major holdings of that division. These selections are grouped by topic, format, date, or other criteria meaningful to the division, and considerable effort was expended to make these short descriptions as engaging and informative as possible. In addition, knowing that not all collections could be described, authors chose to highlight resources that could serve as representative examples of collection types with strong women's history possibilities. This approach—grouping representative holdings by type or major topic—allowed for a broad and varied overview without the presumption of comprehensiveness. Careful selection and captioning of the more than three hundred illustrations in the book allowed for additional collections and themes to be introduced.

The Publishing Office hired an experienced contractor to create the book's thirty-two-page index, but the editorial team and chapter authors contributed to the process and helped in drawing out the interconnections among divisions. As one of the authors noted, conducting research at the library invariably involves more than one reading room. Using a research study of Margaret Sanger as an example, she explained that numerous books on Sanger are found in the library's General Collections. The Manuscript Division houses Sanger's personal papers, and a pamphlet collection she gave to the library in 1931 is located in the Rare Book and Special Collections Division. Many photographs of her can be found in the Prints and Photographs Division; her voice may be heard on radio broadcasts held in the Recorded Sound Section of the Motion Picture, Broadcasting and Recorded Sound Division; and the Law Library provides information on the laws that Sanger challenged.[10] The book's index is essential for alerting researchers to these dispersed interdisciplinary materials.

Some of this dispersion is the result of materials being transferred by the receiving division to other custodial units with special playback equipment or storage conditions more appropriate for specific formats and media. Cross-representation also reflects related materials being acquired from different sources at different times. Individual collection guides can alert researchers to transferred materials, but integrated catalog systems, cross-divisional subject guides, and knowledgeable reference staff are necessary to help patrons identify relevant resources throughout a big institution or an even larger research universe.

From Print to Online Publication

As soon as the print publication of *American Women* had been sent off to press, the editorial team began discussing the idea of creating an online version that could reach additional audiences and offer enhanced functionality. The head of the Publishing Office supported the idea of an online publication, although he requested that the team wait until the book had been on sale for at least a year before launching the online site. Experience had shown him that although online versions cut into some potential print sales, they also generate interest in a book from audiences whose needs are not fully met by online publications. Now, ten years later, a reverse approach might be more likely. Given the direction of the library's publishing program, it is conceivable that the resource guide would be developed online in installments, with a potential print run, or print on demand function, becoming available when a critical stage is reached.

In discussing how best to digitize the guide, the goal was for it to become something more than a PDF version. The three members of the editorial team who championed the online version hoped that it could develop into a larger framework for describing and providing access to current and future analog and digital holdings in the area of American women's history. They enlisted the help of other library colleagues who were excited about promoting and making more accessible the library's women's history holdings by creating an American Women website within the library's pioneering American Memory program. The guide became the centerpiece of this larger American Women website, which its designers hoped would become the first stop for researchers interested in American women's history at the Library of Congress. As a gateway site, American Women built on the research guide by providing additional information on preparing for a research visit to the Library of Congress; tips on searching for women's history resources in the library's catalogs; guidance on finding materials relating to women within the library's American Memory collections; and helpful orientations to women's history sources in the library's online exhibitions and web broadcasts of lectures, readings, and symposia.[11]

The project team worked with the library's web designers and programming experts to preserve the resource guide's original organization and text, but supplemented the latter with significantly more illustrations and links to online catalog records, finding aids, and digital items throughout the library's web pages. Additionally, the online version provides both full-text searching and hyperlinks between sections, which improve the reader's ability to identify related materials across the library's complicated, multiformat organizational structure. It also theoretically allows authors to update and expand their chapters when new collections are acquired, processed, or digitized.[12]

In redesigning the print publication for online use, the team reformatted the text to make it more web friendly. Sections were subdivided. Information and links to others sections were added so that each web page could "stand on its own," since readers might land there as a result of search queries and not because they advanced to the next page sequentially, as when reading a book. Subheadings were added, longer paragraphs were divided, and text was reformatted to allow for easier skimming of pages and to accommodate expanding content. Bullets, numbered lists, italics, boldface, and other formatting conventions helped to break up dense narrative passages and draw attention to specific information. Catalog record links launch search strings (via the Z39.50 information retrieval

protocol) that retrieve formatted displays of the Library of Congress catalog records, which are likely to be updated more frequently than the text
in the research guide. Since catalog records sometimes contain their own
links, it is possible to move from a summary description in the women's
history research guide, to a potentially more detailed catalog record, and
ultimately via a link in the catalog record to an in-depth collection finding
aid or perhaps a digital surrogate of an item.[13]

All of this reformatting and creation of additional pages was a significant investment in staff time, but the effort has paid off. Aside from
the concrete development of an award-winning and well-reviewed website, the project further deepened the good relationships that had begun
to emerge during work on the well-received original resource guide.[14]
As expressed in the book's acknowledgments, the contributors reflected
"almost all corners of the institution and its holdings," and during the
four-plus years it took to complete the guide, "divisional walls [became]
windows."[15] This process continued during the development of the website, to the benefit of both staff and researchers.

Celebrating and Promoting with a Symposium

To celebrate the completion of the *American Women* print guide and the
forthcoming launch of the companion web resource, staff organized a free,
two-day symposium at the library on 19–20 June 2003 titled "Resourceful
Women: Researching and Interpreting American Women's History."[16]
Involving more than thirty speakers, the "Resourceful Women" symposium highlighted current research in the field of American women's history, showcased the library's multiformat collections, and explored how
various types of researchers are uncovering and presenting the story of
American women's experiences to different audiences. The symposium's
keynote session, focusing on "Women and the Law," included Supreme
Court justices Ruth Bader Ginsburg and Sandra Day O'Connor (both of
whose papers are held in the library's Manuscript Division), University
of Iowa historian Linda K. Kerber, and law professors Patricia J. Williams

of Columbia University Law School, and Wendy Webster Williams of
Georgetown University Law Center. National Public Radio special cor-
respondent Susan Stamberg gave the opening address on the second day.
Harvard University historian and Schlesinger library director Nancy F.
Cott delivered the closing plenary, and Susan Ware, who chaired the academic advisory board for the *American Women* guide, provided continuity with the earlier project by chairing the first session. Participants in the
other four panels, which were devoted to women's biographical research,
women's private lives, women and labor, and women's involvement in
social and political reform, reflected the diversity of the library's patrons
and collections. They included a librarian, actress, archaeologist, documentary editor, children's book author, historians, filmmakers, museum
specialists, and journalists.

The intention of the symposium, which drew more than three hundred people from across the country, was not to replicate the narrowly

Meeting before the "Resourceful Women" symposium keynote session on 19 June 2003,
were, from left, Librarian of Congress James H. Billington, Marjorie Billington, Supreme
Court justices Ruth Bader Ginsburg and Sandra Day O'Connor, and John O'Connor.
Photo by Charlynn Spencer Pyne, LC.

focused sessions that characterize scholarly conferences in the field, but instead to assemble speakers whose life experiences or research activities would help highlight the library's resources and services (both traditional and electronic) and share with a widely diverse audience creative ways to uncover and exploit the potential of archival and library materials. The goal was to bring together a mix of people working independently, within the academy, and in public history settings, who through the use of different mediums, are "doing" women's history. The conference focused on the interplay of sources, methodologies, and interpretation. The panelists described interesting sources and the strategies used to find them; discussed new ways of interpreting familiar sources; considered the effects of the electronic revolution on women's history research; offered ideas about how librarians and archivists can best assist researchers in preserving, accessing, and using resources; and suggested how the nation's library can sustain and promote cutting-edge research in the field. A related film series, arranged by one of the conference organizers and staff from the library's Motion Picture and Television Reading Room, ran throughout the month of June 2003 to celebrate the richness of the library's film holdings and to highlight the work of several symposium speakers.

Now, nearly ten years later, the library is still reaping the benefits of that two-day symposium. It helped to foster relations with two prominent donors (Justices O'Connor and Ginsburg); created contact with two potential new donors who were in attendance; raised the institution's profile with leading scholars who participated and who shared favorable accounts of the event with others; furthered communication among library staff with an interest in women's history; and, through the subsequent web release of the videotaped presentations, continues to expose new audiences to the library's programs and resources. The program's success, however, required a significant amount of work, careful planning, and luck. Summarizing the logistics involved might benefit other archivists interested in using symposia to promote their holdings.

Staff first broached the idea of a symposium with library administrators in November 2000, and they were encouraged to pull together a more detailed proposal, list of potential speakers, and budget, which were submitted in April 2001, following an email appeal and in-person brainstorming session with all staff who worked on the *American Women* resource guide. Partial funding was secured that summer from the chief of the Manuscript Division, and staff successfully applied for additional funds from a grants program that is intermittently available to support special staff projects.[17] With money in hand, planning began in earnest in fall 2002. The organizers focused first on lining up speakers with the highest name recognition, correctly assuming that their participation would garner commitments from others. Once a speaker accepted, she was mailed a contract, a copy of the printed *American Women* guide, a release form permitting the library to videotape and distribute her presentation online, and a carefully prepared list of questions, which was distributed to all speakers to provide guidance on the content of their remarks. These questions helped to reinforce the idea that the speaker should cover not just the subject of her work, but also the research process and sources that shaped it. One of the smartest decisions was to offer speakers an all-inclusive honorarium, which allowed them the flexibility to make their own travel arrangements and permitted staff to focus on being conference organizers and not travel agents. Also enhancing the success of the program was the degree to which the organizers budgeted both time and money for two receptions, which allowed more interaction among the participants—both speakers and attendees.

Preparing webcasts of the symposium allowed the event to reach larger audiences; preserved a permanent record of the proceedings, including its video and audio components; and eliminated the expense of subsequently publishing conference papers.[18] Yet this activity did not come without a cost in staff time. Anxious to get the taped versions of the speakers' remarks on the web sooner than the library's dedicated technical unit could schedule, two of the conference organizers arranged to have the video files digitized and then learned how to code the necessary RAM, RP, and SMI files themselves to enable the tape of the presentations to display in sync with the speakers' PowerPoint slides and video clips. This work was outside their normal scope of duties, but it was justified on grounds that it exposed them to new technical skills, established contact with library units with whom they would later do business, and allowed the organizers to roll out the presentations more quickly in two installments, each of which offered a new opportunity to publicize via listserv and press announcements the library's collections and services in women's history.

Women's History Discussion Group

Hoping to build on the success and scholarly exchange that characterized the "Resourceful Women" symposium, three of the conference organizers established the Library of Congress Women's History Discussion Group in July 2004 to promote the institution's collections and bring together staff and patrons for lunch-time meetings twice a month to discuss current research in the field and share information about sources and access tools. Among the thirty-plus people attending the first session on July 29 were visiting college professors, graduate students, independent researchers, and a diverse group of library staff, including catalogers, reference librarians, acquisitions specialists, editors, curriculum developers, and technology specialists. Subsequent meetings included announcements about new acquisitions and upcoming events, short presentations from group members about their research, and staff presentations about relevant collections, access tools, and new subscription databases. The group has pooled its knowledge to provide personalized research advice for many visiting scholars and has helped to educate staff about women's history resources at the Library of Congress and elsewhere.

For the first three years, the group met twice a month, but as the three organizers assumed more work assignments and managerial responsibilities, they scaled back the frequency of the meetings in July 2007 to monthly. By July 2012, when the group concluded its eighth year in existence, it had held approximately 124 meetings with more than 1,600 participants, including many regular attendees. Announcements and meeting summaries are emailed to an active list of more than 285 recipients, of whom two-thirds are outside the institution. This ensures that those who cannot attend the on-site meetings can learn of the resources and research trends discussed and can network digitally with other group members via the organizers. Even when staff members outnumber researchers at the meetings, both groups have benefited. Staff in particular have found it a good way to keep abreast of what their widely dispersed colleagues are doing and to elicit feedback from researchers about new library initiatives.

Women Who Dare Book Series

While the discussion group aimed to address the needs of the research community, other initiatives have reached out to the library's general audience and in particular to students and younger readers. Educational outreach tools appear on the library's website, and individual divisions have made various ad hoc efforts to support remote research for students' History Day projects. In addition, the library's Publishing Office has partnered with outside publishers to promote the library's collections through historical encyclopedias, calendars, knowledge cards, and general-interest books.[19] For many years, some of the library's women's history holdings gained exposure in this way, particularly through the popular Women Who Dare calendars, which the library copublished with Pomegranate Communications. In the 1990s, however, calendar sales began to fall off, and in late 2003 Pomegranate approached the library about doing a series of small-format books on this theme. The Publishing Office, which had begun to question the amount of work spent on ephemeral publications thrown away each December to make way for the new year's version, jumped at the idea of preparing two sets of Women Who Dare books. The concept was to condense for a general audience a complex topic or an individual's life into sixty-four small-format pages with space for forty-five or so illustrations and captions. After a year of preliminary planning, six topics and corresponding authors were selected, including books on women of the suffrage movement, women of the Civil War, women of the civil rights movement, and biographies of Helen Keller, Amelia Earhart, and Eleanor Roosevelt. Although the first three topics were well represented in the library's collections and information could certainly be found to support the biographies, division specialists had lobbied unsuccessfully for the biographies to focus on women whose papers were held in the institution. Pomegranate, however, controlled the final choice.

Authors had about six months to write their text and locate and reproduce illustrations. Book production took another six to seven months, and the first set of books arrived in February 2006 in time for Women's History Month. Based on the projected success of the first six books, Pomegranate commissioned another four, which focused on women explorers, women of change (reformers), Margaret Mead (whose papers are held by the library), and Marian Anderson (whose papers are not). An online review of the series observed that "in a 21st century preoccupied with visuals, the Women Who Dare series is an exceptionally useful way to help make history come alive for children and adults alike."[20] Although not initially as broadly disseminated as we hoped, at the end of 2010, Pomegranate exercised its rights under the book contract to produce and distribute electronic copies of the ten Women Who Dare books in collaboration with the company Zinio. The ebooks, which are exact snapshots of the physical books with several enhancements, can be read on desktops, notebooks, and iPads, and will eventually be available for the iPhone and iPod.

Remember the Ladies: Integrating Women's History into Other Library-wide Programs

Another recent publishing project, which in this case had its roots in the *American Women* resource guide, was a history of the MacDowell Colony written by one of the library's music specialists. Robin Rausch first became interested in the life of Marian MacDowell and the artists' colony she created in Peterborough, New Hampshire, when researching an essay on the topic for the *American Women* resource guide. Rausch leveraged the research she had done into a successful proposal to the library's Interpretive Programs Office for a major exhibition at the library on the MacDowell Colony. This, is turn, led to an invitation by the colony's directors to write a centennial history of the colony and MacDowell's role as founder. This steady, incremental approach allowed Rausch to promote the library's collections to various audiences through print and online resource guides, an exhibition, and an external publication and related book talks.[21]

Other staff also built on work initially begun during the preparation of the resource guide. For example, in at least two cases, items that had initially been considered for selected digitization as part of the online "American Women" portal grew into separate and significantly larger American Memory presentations several years later. In 2005, in celebration of the eighty-fifth anniversary of women's right to vote in the United States, the library's Manuscript Division released online "Women of Protest: Photographs from the Records of the National Woman's Party." Representing the militant wing of the suffrage movement, the National Woman's Party (NWP) used tableaus, parades, demonstrations, and picketing—as well as its members' arrests, imprisonment, and hunger strikes—to spur public discussion, garner publicity for the suffrage cause, and successfully lobby for women's voting rights. Initially, staff had planned to digitize only a handful of NWP photographs as part of the "American Women" portal, but institutional support grew for a larger-scale digital project that resulted in nearly 450 digitized images and a variety of contextual essays and time lines created by Barbara Bair and Janice E. Ruth, two Manuscript Division historical specialists.[22]

Similarly, Rare Book and Special Collections Division specialist Rosemary Fry Plakas initially recommended scanning for the "American Women" portal a few pages from one of the scrapbooks created between 1897 and 1911 by New York suffragists Elizabeth Smith Miller and her daughter Anne Fitzhugh Miller. Steady and persistent lobbying by Plakas, however, eventually resulted in all seven scrapbooks being digitized in their entirety as an American Memory site.[23] In 2010, Plakas worked with a library videographer to create a "Journeys and Crossings" online video presentation about the Miller scrapbooks, in a continued effort to bring to the attention of different audiences the research value of these sources. *American Women* coeditor Sheridan Harvey has also used the "Journeys and Crossings" technology to describe some of the library's holdings relating to women defense workers during World War II.[24] Harvey's fourteen-minute video, *Rosie the Riveter: Real Women Workers*, was among the hundreds of webcasts uploaded by the library to YouTube; as of August 2012, it had been viewed 74,137 times on that site.

Web Archiving and Flickr

Two other library-wide technology initiatives, which on first glance would appear to have little connection to women's history, have both been used effectively by women's history advocates to add to or promote the library's collections. In 2006, as part of a joint Library Services–Office of Strategic Initiatives web harvesting pilot project, the Manuscript Division identified and captured the websites of thirty organizations whose records it holds or with whom it has an existing relationship. The division's project director made certain that among the sites included were those of the MacDowell Colony, Society of Woman Geographers, National Consumers' League, National Council of Jewish Women, and League of Women Voters (LWV). The last included not only the website of the national office of the LWV, whose paper records are held in the division, but also the websites of several hundred state and local LWV offices, whose records are held elsewhere, allowing the Manuscript Division an opportunity to document the work being done by the local branches without committing staff and space to preserving their paper records. This pilot project, which was resumed in January 2010 as an ongoing activity, allowed the Manuscript Division an opportunity through the permissions process to reconnect with some donors with whom it had not been in contact for a few years. It also provided both the division and its donors the opportunity to document better the organizations' activities in the twenty-first century.[25]

Following on the heels of the web archiving project was the launch in January 2008 of two of the library's historical photograph collections on Flickr, the popular photo-sharing website and Web 2.0 innovator.[26] With the library's involvement, Flickr created a new space on its site called "The

Commons," where institutions can share their images and invite user comment and identification. The library's Prints and Photographs Division began by mounting more than 3,100 photographs drawn from two collections: all of the color photographs from the depression and World War II eras contained in the Farm Security Administration/Office of War Information Collection, and a portion of news photographs from the 1910s from the George Grantham Bain Collection. Many of these images are of women, including photographs of them at work during World War II or engaged in newsworthy events (such as suffrage activities) during the 1910s. Additional images were added at the rate of fifty per week, so that by August 2012, the library's Flickr site contained more than sixteen thousand images. Flickr statistics indicated that the photographs were viewed more than five million times during the first month they were available, and they now average about eight hundred thousand views a month.

In keeping with the social networking aspects of Flickr, people viewing the photographs have provided comments about the content of the images, added tags that allow them to retrieve pictures by words that are meaningful to them, and requested permission to include individual pictures in Flickr "groups" that focus on particular subject areas, including, for example, a "Women at Work" group. As noted by Barbara Orbach Natanson, head of the Prints and Photographs Reading Room, Flickr contributors have provided links to related textual documentation elsewhere on the web, offered biographical information about women depicted, and engaged in discussions ranging from woman suffrage in various countries to the presence of African American women in the World War II work force. In early February 2009, Natanson encouraged members of the Women's History Discussion Group to choose images from the library's Flickr site for a special selection to be compiled in honor of International Women's Day on March 8. She and her colleagues then used this special presentation as an opportunity to share information about the discussion group and to refer viewers to information on the Library of Congress website about the institution's women's history resources.[27]

Lessons Learned

Despite the overriding success of the various women's history projects that were undertaken in the last fifteen years, there were trade-offs along the way. Projects had to be scaled back to fit budgets and time constraints. In two instances—the *American Women* print guide and the Women Who Dare series—securing copublishers was critical to the projects' advancing, even though it meant less internal control over the final products and disappointment among some staff with the publishers' distribution methods. For example, despite favorable reviews, the Women Who Dare books did not enjoy a level of sales initially envisioned, partly because many major bookstores would not carry Pomegranate's products once the publisher adopted a no-return policy for remainders. For this reason, the publisher's new ebook partnership with Zinio was an especially welcome development.

Archival repositories looking for copublishers should be alert to such concerns and assess whether they can independently sell sufficient copies onsite and online. Collaborating with another nearby repository to produce a regional women's history guide might be more cost effective than undertaking a single institutional guide. Such multirepository works might also be more appealing to university presses in the region or, if done as online ventures, might attract sponsorship from local woman-owned companies. Another factor to consider is that because of the short deadlines that many copublishers demand, a subject specialist who already has a full slate of other duties may not be able to assume sole responsibility for authoring a book. In some cases, coauthoring may be an option so that the workload is split in half. In other cases, the specialist may be able to contribute her or his expertise by providing research guidance or by reviewing the draft text that a nonstaff member writes.

Collaboration is not without its problems, however. For example, the academic advisory committee assembled for the *American Women* guide was, on the whole, extremely helpful, and archivists should definitely consider using such committees, while keeping expectations realistic. Even if financially compensated, the time and effort that committee members

give to a project varies considerably, and in some cases, the main benefit
derived from the involvement of well-known and over-extended scholars is having their names and imprimaturs attached to the endeavor. In
other cases, the advisors will read every word, offer amazingly detailed
comments and corrections, help navigate sensitive or controversial issues,
offer encouragement, and assist in promoting the book once it is published. This was certainly true of Susan Ware—who wrote an important
historiographical survey for the guide—and some of the other advisors
who served on the *American Women* committee. In other instances, the
collaboration underscored the very different expectations that archivists
and academic researchers have concerning the levels of description and
access that repositories can provide.

Being receptive to new technologies and taking advantage of new
programs within the library, such as web archiving, webcasts, and the
Flickr collaboration, provided several staff with the opportunity to promote their divisions' women's history collections and reach new patrons,
while at the same time expanding personal skills and offering support
for an institutional initiative. Yet, at other times, the staff may have been
too eager to embrace a technology that may not have been the best fit
in the long run. For example, in lobbying to create an online version of
American Women, team members sought to transform a print publication into a dynamic framework that could be easily revised, expanded,
and integrated with the library's digital collections. In 2002 and 2003, the
best way to achieve that functionality was to position the project so that
it could benefit from the high-profile, strong searching capabilities and
future scanning resources of the American Memory program, not to mention the expertise and enthusiasm of an experienced American Memory
staff. Although there were important advantages in placing "American
Women" within the American Memory program, the site is something of
an anomaly, and its placement within American Memory has been con-
fusing for some staff and researchers. Unlike most American Memory
presentations, "American Women" is not a collection of digital items. It
is a gateway designed as a first stop for Library of Congress researchers
working in the field of American women's history. The team also likely

overestimated the degree to which staff would be able to keep the pages current, a situation partly exacerbated by increased security limits on the number of staff who can access various library servers. Also, as an early implementation of an XML DTD, the online resource guide poses some challenges to current staff attempting to migrate the older American Memory websites to new design templates.

Another example of technology falling a tad short of its promise was the product that resulted when the "Resourceful Women" symposium organizers encoded the webcasts themselves to quicken the presentations' online release. By tackling this work, the organizers may have inadvertently saddled these webcasts with the designation of somehow being "different" than those created by the library unit normally responsible for this type of work. The concern now is to make sure that the "Resourceful Women" web assets are not forgotten by the library's technical staff, so that despite their origin, they will be maintained and migrated to the same servers and search systems as other library webcasts. Remembering forgotten assets, however, should not pose too large an obstacle to a group of staff who in recent years has been systematically uncovering, describing, and celebrating the institution's sometimes hidden women's history collections.

Identifying, describing, and bringing these hidden materials to the attention of researchers and the general public had long been a goal of the library's staff, but in the last two decades, a happy combination of factors led to a series of accomplishments that had heretofore been unrealized: a multidivisional resource guide in both print and online versions, a scholarly symposium that attracted nearly three hundred people to the library, a monthly discussion group that has entered its ninth year of existence, numerous books and digital initiatives, and pilot projects in web archiving and crowdsourcing of photographic descriptions.

That so much has been accomplished in a relatively short span of time is due in part to at least three developments: the incredible synergy of a core group of staff members who have successfully moved from one project to the next, leveraging the work and contacts they created during the preceding projects; the support of library managers and resource

allocators who have provided funding or located external partners willing
to shoulder some of the expense; and the emergence of websites, webcasts, digital scanning, encoded finding aids, ebooks, social networking,
and other technologies that have provided new means and opportunities for accessing the library's collections and disseminating information
about the institution's resources and programs.

NOTES

[1] Library of Congress, "General Information," http://www.loc.gov/about/
generalinfo.html, accessed 17 August 2012.

[2] Rosemary Fry Plakas and Jacqueline Coleburn, "Rare Book and Special
Collections Division," in *American Women: A Library of Congress
Guide for the Study of Women's History and Culture in the United
States* (Washington, DC: Library of Congress, 2001), 101. Also avail-
able online, Library of Congress, "American Women," http://memory.loc
.gov/ammem/awhhtml/awrbc4/index.html, accessed 17 August 2012.

[3] Andrea Hinding, ed., *Women's History Sources: A Guide to Archives and
Manuscript Collections in the United States*, 2 vols. (New York: R. R. Bowker,
1979), 123–57; Marianne L. Roos, "Women's History Sources in the Library
of Congress Manuscript Division" (unpublished typescript, 276 pages, January
1985).

[4] The summary in this paragraph and in the subsequent three paragraphs is taken
from the author's chapter in *American Women*, 122–75. Also available online,
Library of Congress, "American Women," http://memory.loc.gov/ammem/
awhhtml/awmss5/index.html, accessed 17 August 2012.

[5] Library of Congress Online Catalog is available at http://catalog.loc.gov/.
Searches may be limited to Manuscript Division records only by selecting the
Add Limits option on any of the three types of searches—Browse, Advanced
Search, and Keyword Search, with the latter two being more appropriate for
searches of manuscript collections. To search just Manuscript Division col-
lections, choose "Manuscript" (not "Manuscript Reference Collection") from
the drop-down menu under Location in the Library. To search for Manuscript
Division collections along with archival collections in other custodial divisions, including the American Folklife Center and the Music Division, choose
Archival Manuscript/Mixed Formats under Type of Material.

[6] Sheridan Harvey, "The General Collections," in *American Women*, 5. See also Harvey, "Using the Library of Congress," in *American Women*, xxxii–xxxiv. Similar text is available online at Library of Congress, "American Women," http://memory.loc.gov/ammem/awhhtml/awsearchcat.htmlandhttp://memory .loc.gov/ammem/awhhtml/awgc1/lc_subject.html, accessed 17 August 2012. Library of Congress subject headings may also be searched online at "Library of Congress Authorities," http://authorities.loc.gov/, accessed 17 August 2012.

[7] For a listing of "Manuscript Division Finding Aids Online," see Library of Congress Manuscript Reading Room, http://www.loc.gov/rr/mss/f-aids/mssfa .html, accessed 26 June 2013. To search across all Library of Congress finding aids, go to the "Search Finding Aids" page at http://findingaids.loc.gov/, accessed 17 August 2012.

[8] Although the Manuscript Division's collections principally focus on the United States, information on foreign women may be found in the papers of Americans who served as diplomats or missionaries abroad or who visited foreign countries on personal travel or as journalists or members of the military. In addition, as authors Peggy K. Pearlstein and Barbara A. Tanenbaum noted in "Area Studies Collections," *American Women*, 341, "From its very beginnings, the Library of Congress has collected works in foreign languages. Today the Library's book collections number more than eighteen million volumes. Half of these are works written in languages other than English, representing about 450 different languages and 35 scripts. In many instances, the Library is considered to be the best repository outside the country of origin for Western-language books, periodicals, and other materials about a particular culture. Its non-roman-script-language collections are generally the largest and most extensive in the world outside of the countries where those languages are spoken. Foreign-language items published in the United States form yet another substantial segment of the Library's collections."

[9] In addition to Susan Ware, the advisory committee included Eileen Boris, University of California, Santa Barbara; Joanne M. Braxton, College of William and Mary; Carol F. Karlsen, University of Michigan; Alice Kessler-Harris, Columbia University; and Vicki L. Ruiz, Arizona State University.

[10] Robin Rausch, "American Women: Guide to Women's History Resources Published," *Library of Congress Information Bulletin* 61, no. 1 (2002), Library of Congress, http://www.loc.gov/loc/lcib/0201/herstory.html, accessed 17 August 2012.

[11] Library of Congress American Memory, "American Women: A Gateway to Library of Congress Resources for the Study of Women's History and Culture in the United States," http://memory.loc.gov/ammem/awhhtml/index.html.

[12] See author's unattributed essay, "About the Guide," describing changes to the print publication for online use, Library of Congress, "American Women," http://memory.loc.gov/ammem/awhhtml/awhabout.html, accessed 17 August 2012.

[13] "About the Guide."

[14] The print version of *American Women* won the 2003 Barbara "Penny" Kanner Award from the Western Association of Women's Historians for "distinguished achievement in the area of scholarly bibliographic and historiographic guides to research focused on women and/or gender history." A review in the publication *Feminist Collections* stated, "Any women's studies researcher embarking on a trip to the Library of Congress would find this book indispensable." As for the online version, from 2001 to 2006, the web browser Yahoo! chose only three women's history websites in the country as "Yahoo! Picks," and "American Women" (selected in July 2003) was one of them. "American Women" also made the list maintained by besthistorysites.net. See also the positive review of the "American Women" site by American history professor Anne Sarah Rubin, *Women and Social Movements in the United States, 1600–2000*, http://womhist .alexanderstreet.com/reviewrubin.htm, accessed 17 August 2012.

[15] Sara Day and Evelyn Sinclair, acknowledgments, in *American Women* (Washington, DC: Library of Congress, 2001), xv. Also available online, Library of Congress, "American Women," http://memory.loc.gov/ammem/awhhtml/ awhack/awack.html, accessed 17 August 2012.

[16] Library of Congress "Resourceful Women: Researching and Interpreting American Women's History," symposium, 19–20 June 2003, http://www.loc .gov/rr/women/, accessed 17 August 2012.

[17] Funding for the symposium and film series was made possible by grants from the Library of Congress Manuscript Division Benjamin Fund and the James H. Billington Endowment, funded by the generous support of Library of Congress Madison Council members Abraham and Julienne Krasnoff.

[18] Webcasts of the "Resourceful Women" symposium may be found online, Library of Congress, "American Women," http://www.loc.gov/rr/women/ awprogram.html, accessed 17 August 2012.

[19] See especially the "Teachers" page on the Library of Congress website, http:// www.loc.gov/teachers/, and the "General Publishing Program" description and highlights, http://www.loc.gov/publish/general/, accessed 17 August 2012.

[20] See "Daring and Caring," a four-star review of the Women Who Dare series, posted on 6 April 2006, on *INFODAD.com Family Focused Reviews*,

http://transcentury.blogspot.com/2006/04/daring-and-caring.html, accessed 17 August 2012.

[21] Robin Rausch, "The House that Marian Built: The MacDowell Colony of Peterborough, New Hampshire," in *American Women*, 270–77, Library of Congress, "American Women," http://memory.loc.gov/ammem/awhhtml/aw08e/aw08e.html, accessed 17 August 2012. See also Rausch, "The MacDowells and Their Legacy," in *A Place for the Arts: The MacDowell Colony, 1907–2007*, ed. Carter Wiseman (Peterborough, NH: MacDowell Colony, 2006), 50–135; "The MacDowell Colony Is Subject of New Book to Be Discussed on Oct. 30," Library of Congress press release, 22 October 2007, "News of the Library of Congress," http://www.loc.gov/today/pr/2007/07-210.html, accessed 17 August 2012; and the online exhibition *A Century of Creativity: The MacDowell Colony, 1907–2007*, http://www.loc.gov/exhibits/macdowell/, accessed 17 August 2012.

[22] "Women of Protest: Photographs from the Records of the National Woman's Party," http://memory.loc.gov/ammem/collections/suffrage/nwp/, accessed 17 August 2012.

[23] "Miller NAWSA Suffrage Scrapbooks, 1897–1911," http://memory.loc.gov/ammem/collections/suffrage/millerscrapbooks/, accessed 17 August 2012.

[24] Rosemary Fry Plakas, *Catch the Suffragists' Spirit: The Millers' Suffrage Scrapbooks*, Library of Congress Journeys and Crossings webcast recorded 22 February 2010, http://www.loc.gov/today/cyberlc/feature_wdesc.php?rec=4839, accessed 17 August 2012; and Sheridan Harvey, *Rosie the Riveter: Real Women Workers in World War II*, Library of Congress Journeys and Crossings webcast recorded 14 May 2003, http://www.loc.gov/rr/program/journey/rosie.html, accessed 17 August 2012.

[25] See the "Manuscript Division Archive of Organizational Web Sites" collected initially as part of the Selecting and Managing Content Captured from the Web (SMCCW) pilot project, Library of Congress Web Archives Minerva, at http://lcweb2.loc.gov/diglib/lcwa/html/orgs/orgs-overview.html, accessed 17 August 2012. Bibliographic records describing these archived websites appear in the Library of Congress Online Catalog and links to these related resources are included in the EAD finding aids to the paper records. For more information on the project, see Abbie Grotke and Janice E. Ruth, "Selecting and Managing Content Captured from the Web: Expanding Curatorial Expertise and Skills in Building Library of Congress Web Archives," *DigCCurr2007: An International Symposium in Digital Curation* (Chapel Hill: University of North Carolina, April 2007, http://www.ils.unc.edu/digccurr2007/papers/grotkeRuth_paper_9-3.pdf, accessed 17 August 2012.

[26] To view the Library of Congress Flickr photographic images and contributions, start at http://www.flickr.com/photos/library_of_congress/. For information on the pilot project, see the Prints and Photographs Division website, http://www.loc.gov/rr/print/flickr_pilot.html, accessed 17 August 2012.

[27] Flickr, "Women Striving Forward, 1910s–1940s," http://www.flickr.com/photos/library_of_congress/sets/72157614805050380/, accessed 17 August 2012.

CHAPTER 15

Regional Collections— Documenting the Feminist Experience

DANELLE MOON

MANY HISTORIANS HAVE USED THE METAPHOR OF "WAVES" TO DESCRIBE THE COMPLEX HISTORY OF WOMEN'S RIGHTS AND FEMINIST ACTIVISM. The "first wave" refers to the activism that began with the Seneca Falls Convention in 1848 and ended in 1920, when women finally were granted federal voting rights under the Nineteenth Amendment. The "second wave" generation includes women who were activists in the post–World War II years and younger women who came of age in the social movements of the 1950s and 1960s. The creation of the Presidential Commission on the Status of Women (PCSW) under President John F. Kennedy in 1961, the formation of the National Organization for Women (NOW) in 1966, and the emergence of the "Women's Liberation Movement" created a new revolution of feminism. Third- and fourth-wave movements have followed since, making clear the continuum of social movements and women's activism over time.[1]

Archivists have worked hard over the years to build collections that document and preserve the histories of US women's social movements. The work of the Library of Congress, the National Archives, and women's archives have clearly shaped twenty-first-century collecting practices focused on women's organizations, resulting in core collections that document national and regional organizations and their leaders. The growth of regional historical studies on the second-wave movement highlights the need to continue documenting the diversity of women's participation in US social movements. Regional repositories like San José State University Special Collections and Archives and other college and university libraries are uniquely and geographically positioned to document local women's organizational records, which can then be utilized by scholars to document the diversity of the feminist experience.

The Wave as a Feminist Metaphor

By 1968, feminists used the term "first wave" to recognize the contributions of their foremothers, yet in doing so they lumped together multiple decades of activism dating back to 1848. Feminist scholars writing about the second-wave movement tended to describe the first wave around the singular issue of suffrage. The postsuffrage movement that followed has been depicted as slow moving, while the second-wave movement has been described as transformative and revolutionary.[2] Third- and fourth-wave activists offer a more diverse—albeit a more diffused—movement, which is more attentive to race, class, sexuality, culture, and national identity than that of their foremothers.[3]

In *No Permanent Waves: Recasting Histories of U.S. Feminism*, historian Nancy Hewitt contends that the previous script of feminism as a revolution, as articulated by Sara Evans and Ruth Rosen, has disappeared. *No Permanent Waves* provides an interesting collection of articles that undo the rhetoric of feminist waves. Recent historiography trends appear to be focused on coalitions and the multiplicity of women and social movements. These studies represent an ideological shift that reaches beyond the wave metaphor, brings together new ideas of common challenges and assumptions about feminist priorities, and demonstrates the diversity of feminism over time. Many scholars have challenged the old circumscribed histories that define feminism based on traditional chronologies (or waves), reform agendas, and social ideologies. The use of the wave metaphor limits historical analysis and understanding. As Hewitt points out, feminist activism across time is messy and is not bound by chronological ideology, and this series explores and exposes the diversity of actors and their roles in forming diverse coalitions and resulting contestations between groups over reform agendas. Indeed, these studies make clear the relevancy of gender justice and the continuum of feminist mobilization on different fronts. Studies of this kind provide an intellectual framework for archival collection strategies to document the diversity of feminist and nonfeminist activism.[4]

Hewitt acknowledges that it may be impossible to completely eliminate the wave metaphor, and instead she prefers thinking about the variation of feminist surges in terms of "radio waves." As she suggests in her introduction, the metaphor of radio waves will advance our thinking about movements as having "different lengths and frequencies; movements that grow louder or fade out; that reach vast audiences across oceans or only a few listeners in a local area; movements that are marked by static interruption or frequent changes of channels; and movements that are temporarily drowned out by another frequency but then suddenly come in loud and clear. Rather than being members of the first, second, or third wave, we can be the National Public Radio of feminism." The beauty of radio waves, she writes, allows "signals to coexist, overlap, and intersect," and thereby produce histories that reflect the diversity of the American experience.[5]

No Permanent Waves presents a rich array of feminist research that can advance our collecting strategies in building feminist movement collections. This body of scholarship covers the spectrum of feminist waves, and includes articles that look at third- and fourth-wave identity politics, divergent cultural agendas, and hip-hop feminism. These treatments of the twenty-first-century movements push the historical narrative forward and provide some interesting case studies that can inform twenty-first-century collection development priorities. Whether we rely on the wave metaphor or think of social movements as radio frequencies, archivists need to be familiar with the historiography and theoretical changes as we build out collection strategies focused on the diverse experiences of women across time.

Moreover, the diffusive and fleeting nature of third- and fourth-wave feminism presents real documentation challenges, while the narrative of second-wave feminism—as explored in *Feminist Coalitions: Historical Perspectives on Second-Wave Feminism*—illustrates the range of feminist coalitions and activism during the second-wave movement that reaches beyond the standard histories that focus on the Equal Rights Amendment (ERA) and the role of NOW. *Feminist Coalitions* includes articles that look at the peace movement, abortion and health rights, the antirape movement, and welfare rights. Editor and historian Stephanie Gilmore reminds us that coalitions by nature are imperfect and frequently formed for a short period of time to address specific issues, and that they did not always achieve their original goals. In another publication, Gilmore studied three different NOW chapters and shows how women organized outside and within NOW to address specific regional problems, such as race discrimination, rape, and domestic violence. Gilmore's study highlights the importance of regional collections in expanding the historical narrative, and, as archivists, we play an important role in fostering new feminist history by building collections that are more inclusive of the diverse activism that has spanned three centuries.[6]

Early Women's Archives in the United States

The second-wave effort to document the rich and varied experiences of women in the late twentieth century was grounded in the work of historian and activist Mary Ritter Beard. As Anke Voss-Hubbard describes in "No Document—No History: Mary Ritter Beard and the Early History of Women's Archives," Beard played a significant role in the establishment of the Sophia Smith Collection at Smith College, and, with the support of Margaret Storrs Grierson, the founding archivist, in the establishment of the first US women's history collection in 1942. In 1943, Radcliffe College established the Woman's Rights Collection that began with the deposit of suffragist Maud Wood Park's papers; this collection later became the cornerstone of the Schlesinger Library. Beard offered important advice to

Radcliffe College president Wilbur K. Jordan on growing the women's collection in addition to providing personal financial support to the college. Beard brought in significant women's papers including those of Leonora Reilly and Inez Irwin, and she donated the World Center for Women's Archives as well. Beard's vision gave birth to new collecting initiatives that focused on documenting the first wave of feminism. Without this foundation, our understanding of the birth of feminism in the nineteenth century through the postsuffrage struggle would be all but lost.[7]

The effort to document the first-wave generation resulted in core collections at the Library of Congress and women's archives; slowly, colleges and universities recognized the value of women's history and provided the foundation for documenting the second-wave movement. The growth of women-centered archives and collections devoted to women's history since the 1960s to the present is remarkable. As Kären Mason and Tanya Zanish-Belcher summarize in "A Room of One's Own: Women's Archives in the Year 2000," the growth rate of independent women's collections and endowed programs blossomed as a result of diverse groups of feminist activists, scholars, oral historians, archivists, and librarians to preserve the history of feminism and the second-wave movement. This social activism to document and preserve second-wave history has resulted in significant holdings across the United States that support historical study. The growth of women's history and women's studies can be attributed to the spirit of activism that defined the second-wave movement. As historian Gerda Lerner demonstrates in her study "U.S. Women's History: Past, Present, and Future," the volume of scholarship for the past forty years is equally remarkable. This productivity is directly connected to the collecting practices that began with Smith and Radcliffe and that continues today nationwide. As Lerner reminds us, new conceptual models to study women's history and the new histories that document women of color, laboring women, class, race, and religion underscore the importance of women's collections, while illustrating the symbiotic relationship between scholars and archivists in building new disciplines and new rooms to discover the varied past of women's experiences. Recent scholarship focused on feminist coalitions moreover provides an intellectual framework for twenty-first-century collecting strategies.[8]

Oral History Strategies

As the second-wave movement took root in the early 1960s, a renewed interest to document second-wave activists inspired a new generation of archivists committed to documenting feminism.[9] Moreover, oral history documentation became a common method used by activists, scholars, and community members to build disciplines in women's history and women's studies.

The growth of women's history and women's studies programs coincided with the revolution of the second-wave movement, resulting in designated programs and new areas of academic study. The 1977 *Frontiers: A Journal of Women Studies* is a good representation of the feminist revolution and the role of oral history as a documentation strategy. The editors of *Frontiers* devoted a special issue to women's oral history. Historian Sherna Gluck openly challenged traditional historiography with her groundbreaking article, "What's so Special about Women? Women's Oral History." This pioneering effort to document women's experiences through oral history represents a cross-pollination between scholars and feminist activists. Western women scholars developed their own interviewing manual, and they gained experience interviewing diverse groups of women. As Gluck reflected in 1983, oral history became an important method for documenting the rich experiences of women and helped build the rationale for women's collections.[10] A flurry of oral history projects focused on the first wave of feminism filled important gaps in documenting women's experience. In *Women's Oral History*, the editors describe these early projects as collaborative, community based, and well funded.[11]

One of the notable early feminist oral history projects, funded by the Rockefeller Foundation, enabled the Regional Oral History Office (ROHO) of the Bancroft Library at the University of California, Berkeley, and the Feminist History Research Project of Los Angeles to record twelve firsthand accounts of the early leaders of the suffrage movement. Amelia Fry and Sherna Gluck conducted the interviews; ROHO has recently digitized the interview transcripts of Alice Paul, Sarah Bard Field, Jeannette Rankin, Burnita Shelton Matthews, Rebecca Hourwich Reyher, Helen Valeska Bary, and Mabel Vernon. In the early 1980s, the Center for Oral History and the Women's Studies Program at the University of Connecticut, supported by the Connecticut Humanities Council, launched a similar project, resulting in the recording of twenty-one women detailing political activism from 1915 to 1945. In 1983, Nancy D. Mann compiled a directory of women's oral history projects and collections, demonstrating the vitality of feminist activism.[12]

These early projects provided a foundation for understanding the historical context of the first-wave generation, while providing good models and interview strategies for second-wave projects. One of the challenges of doing oral history is the timing; interviews typically take place late in life, when memories have faded. The work of Fry and Gluck underscores the need to capture personal memories before the onset of advanced age and the deterioration of memory. Fry interviewed Alice Paul when she was age eighty-five and later reflected that Paul had a remarkable memory of her lobbying activities and had a running record of every congressman, including his past and present actions on the ERA; yet she had trouble recalling her early suffrage activities in England and in the United States, and she was very guarded when asked to describe the feminist conflicts. Moreover, she was very conscious of her own historical significance and aware that Fry was also interviewing Sarah Bard Field and Mabel Vernon. The issue of selective memory and addressing controversy is also a common problem when interviewing politicians and well-known leaders. Paul never wrote her autobiography, and her oral history provides significant details about her public life that would otherwise be lost.[13]

SJSU Collection Strategies and Oral History

San José State University Special Collections and Archives (SJSU) embarked on a major collecting initiative to document the regional experiences of women in politics and social movements in the South Bay region, which includes the city of San José in Santa Clara County, located south of San Francisco. SJSU's base of collecting political papers began in 1995 when Congressman Don Edwards donated his congressional papers and formed the SJSU Legislators' Archive. Since that time, this archive has grown significantly and includes the records of Congressman Norman Mineta and California state senator Alfred Alquist; the mayoral records of Janet Gray Hayes, Susan Hammer, and Ron Gonzales; as well as the papers of Rod Diridon and Dianne McKenna, who both served on the Santa Clara County Board of Supervisors.

These collections provided a foundation for an initiative to collect grassroots social organizations and to document women's experiences in politics through oral history. Since 2005, SJSU has acquired the records of several local women's organizations, including those of the local chapters of the Young Women's Christian Association (YWCA), NOW, the League of Women Voters (LWV), and the San José Woman's Club (SJWC). It has acquired community history records that include the Chinese American Women's Club (CAWC) records; the personal papers of Florene L. Poydue, founder of Parents Helping Parents; visual and print collections that document the experiences of South Bay lesbians and the LGBTQ community; and the SJSU Women's Studies Department records. More recently, SJSU acquired the International Museum of Women's records, which document the organization from its early formation as the Women's Heritage Museum to its development as an international digital archives devoted to documenting the lives of women worldwide. These collections provide significant primary source materials in the form of letters, diaries, journals, scrapbooks, news clippings, minute records, outreach materials, photographs, and oral histories. Collectively, the focus on political papers and social movements provides a diverse group of materials that documents identity politics and shows how different groups have aligned, separated, split off completely, and in some cases disbanded. The disbanding of the local chapter of NOW in 2005 underscores the importance of capturing the experiences of the members through oral history.[14]

Significant scholarship on the history of politics in the region reinforced the need to build on the strengths of the Legislators' Archive. Historian Glenna Matthews in *Silicon Valley, Women, and the California Dream: Gender, Class, and Opportunity in the Twentieth Century* and political scientist Janet Flammang in *Women's Political Voice: How Women Are Transforming the Practice and Study of Politics* document the rich history of this region and the role of women in the public sector as politicians, activists, and workers. Both scholars focus entire chapters on the building of the "Feminist Capital" in the South Bay region, and they both use oral history as a method to gather firsthand accounts. Flammang interviewed several female office holders, but she never deposited her research with a local institution. Matthews, an alumna of SJSU, donated her collection of thirty-seven oral interviews to SJSU in 2005. Her book documents the social and economic history of the region, with a specific focus on women workers; she interviewed both male and female politicians, activists, and laboring women to help fill in the historical and documentation gaps. Her analysis brings to light the extreme differences between classes and gender employment. She shows how poor and immigrant women have shouldered the work production from the agricultural heyday to semiconductor chip–making industries in the Silicon Valley, while highlighting the political advancement of middle-class women and ethnic minority women from the 1960s to 1990s. These oral histories provide primary sources that document the diverse experiences of individuals living in this region, from the very poor to the very rich.

Matthews's seminal work in the region provided the foundation for a new department initiative to document the specific experiences of the women who were pioneers in politics and as social activists. The South Bay Second Wave Feminist Oral History Project (South Bay Project), funded by SJSU, was conducted from 2006 to 2009 and has resulted in thirteen oral histories that captured the voices of some of the feminist politicians and organizational leaders in San José and Santa Clara County. The initial project was developed to fill in some of the collecting gaps and to give voice to the key feminist leaders in politics during the heyday of the "Feminist Capital."[15] This history is tied to the new demands by women for political and economic opportunity during the second-wave movement. Betty Freidan, through her bestselling book *The Feminine Mystique*, helped galvanize a new generation of feminist activists; this, combined with the growth of the female labor market sector and New Left politics demanding equality, created a perfect storm for political change across the United States. Second-wave feminists, like their foremothers, represented a cross-section of women who belonged to a variety of organizations and developed different strategies, techniques, and goals. Understanding the historical context and diversity of the movement is a necessary component to building a solid oral history project and is needed to develop diverse collecting practices.[16]

Feminist Capital in Santa Clara County

Janet Gray Hayes became nationally recognized as the first woman to be elected mayor of a large city. Gray Hayes won her bids for mayor in 1974 and 1978, which helped propel Santa Clara County to recognition as the Feminist Capital of the nation. The use of the term "Feminist Capital," as noted by Flammang, was meant for local consumption, but was also picked up in the international and national press corps. The combined success of female candidates across the United States led a number of national magazines to run stories on the role of women, feminism, and politics. *Time, People,* and *U.S. News and World Report* magazines, and even some international papers, carried stories highlighting the success of these female candidates. Gray Hayes was featured in a number of these articles, alongside Diane Feinstein of San Francisco; Jane Byrne of Chicago; Isabella Cannon of Raleigh, North Carolina; Carole McCellan of Austin, Texas; and Margaret Hance of Phoenix, Arizona. In 1979, *U.S. News and World Report* ran a story highlighting the recent victories of women in politics across the United States. According to this report, 750 out of 18,800 municipalities had female mayors—women were making clear inroads into politics at all levels. From 1975 to 1979, the number of women in public office increased from 4.7 percent to 10.9 percent, with the largest increase at local and state levels.[17]

In the wake of the Watergate scandal, female officeholders offered a fresh choice to voters and they had a clear advantage as candidates, because they were perceived as "clean and were outside the pockets of developers," wrote one scholar.[18] A 1974 "Survey of Voter Attitudes in the City of San José," prepared for the Janet Gray Hayes election campaign, confirmed the view that women were more honest and less corruptible than men. The majority of those polled—57 percent—stated that it made no difference whether the mayor was male or female, and 47 percent felt that more women were needed on the city council. Voter perceptions and the momentum of the women's movement, combined with the economic prosperity of the Silicon Valley, produced a favorable climate for female officeholders to improve family and community life through slow-growth

San José mayor, Janet Gray Hayes (right) with Councilwoman
Susanne Wilson, 1974. Janet Gray Hayes Papers, MSS-2002-01,
San José State University Library Special Collections and Archives.

initiatives, smart planning, environmental and public health policies, and equal rights legislation.[19]

The regional context played a significant role in the success of Gray Hayes and the women who followed her. As Matthews notes in her study, San José had a long history of feminist activism, dating back to the suffrage movement. The tradition of progressive politics laid the groundwork for modern grassroots activism, which forged coalitions between feminists, environmentalists, and labor groups. Feminist activism combusted with the environmental movement, and women became the clear leaders in promoting slow growth, public health and safety, as well as equal rights. In 1971, the formation of the Santa Clara County chapter of the National Women's Political Caucus (NWPC) provided important support to female candidates, and, within the first six months, the local branch had one thousand members. The Santa Clara County Commission on the Status of Women (CSW) was formed in 1973 to eliminate sex discrimination in all sectors of society. While the CSW worked to end sexual discrimination, the NWPC supported female candidates and provided a network of "Good Ole Gals" to counter male political culture. In 1977, San José hosted the NWPC's annual meeting, which further cultivated new female candidates, and many of these women participated in the 1977 Spirit of Houston—the first national women's conference in the United States. The second-wave feminist movement clearly strengthened female political activism in this region, and the resulting success of the Feminist Capital over three decades drives SJSU's current collecting priorities.[20]

Several scholars point to the economic conditions that transformed San José politics. Flammang remarked that the majority of these women benefited from their own affluence, high level of education, strong community and women's networks, and the "clean government" mentality of South Bay residents. While most of the female officeholders were white and middle-class, a few of these women came from the Hispanic and African American communities. For example, Blanca Alvarado, the first Latina elected to the San José City Council and to the Santa Clara County Board of Supervisors, came from the Hispanic barrio of East San José and was well versed in identity politics and involved in the labor politics in the agricultural strikes led by Cesar Chavez. Her election to higher office resulted from the convergence of district elections and grassroots activism within her community. Notwithstanding the affluence brought on by high-tech industry, San José has a diverse labor activist movement that spans industries, from the farm labor strikes to city and county worker strikes and high-tech labor disputes. Women worked on both sides of the political spectrum. Female officeholders and activists worked to support pay equity, working women went out on the picket line demanding equal pay for equal work, and electronics industry workers and environmental activists pushed corporations to protect the health of their employees and demanded local enforcement of national and state environmental standards.[21]

The political and organization records documenting South Bay feminism are rich yet undermined resources, and the scholarship and oral histories make it clear that South Bay feminists personalized and reacted to their own political milieu. The history of this region provides the context for understanding how the political, social, and economic environment shaped women's identity and activism. The South Bay/San José NOW chapter endorsed the national platform to promote the ERA, took part in the comparable worth/equal pay movement, and promoted programs to protect women and children from rape and family violence. In this way, they also navigated between liberal and radical feminism, while the Feminist Capital offered South Bay women some political clout as they pushed for radical changes in public policy. Moreover, redistricting opened up new gateways for minority participation in the political process.[22]

The South Bay Project set out to fill in the archival gaps and to document the voices of some of the second-wave feminists in the area through oral history. All of these women connected to their communities through memberships in mainstream women's organizations that included the Parent Teacher Association (PTA), the League of Women Voters, NOW, the YWCA, and other social justice organizations. They shared common goals in wanting to improve their communities and to influence policy that addressed a variety of social, economic, and environmental problems, while focusing on issues specific to women and children. Most identified with the goals of the ERA and with the feminist movement.

The resulting oral histories bring to light some of the back-end stories of the period and have inspired new collecting priorities focused on social and political organizations that specifically document the contributions of women in the region. As a result of this project, SJSU is actively collecting political women's records, as well as the records of political organizations, clubs, and other social movements.[23]

Using Regional Archival Collections

While prominent women's repositories provide leadership in documenting national organizations and movement leaders, regional repositories play an important role in building local collections that document grassroots social movements. The collected works in *No Permanent Waves* and *Feminist Coalitions* confirm the value of national and regional collections. In particular, Gilmore's study, "The Dynamics of Second-Wave Feminist Activism in Memphis, 1971–1982: Rethinking the Liberal/Radical Divide," illustrates the dynamics of grassroots activism and the need to collect at the regional level. As Gilmore notes, "regional differences allow us to rethink conventional ways of understanding social movements in the twentieth century."[24] The grassroots dynamics in Memphis illustrate the application of what Susan Freeman describes as "politics of location"—using different tactics to accomplish a variety of feminist goals, from the ERA to policies to protect women from rape and domestic abuse. Memphis women embraced both liberal and radical tactics and issues, and they were shaped by the political and cultural environment in which they lived. Moreover, Gilmore's work provides an analytical framework for the study of social movements and feminism. Her approach looks beyond the dichotomy of radical versus liberal feminism and instead shows how local-level concerns have shaped women's activism.

The growth of scholarship using regional and community archival collections has clearly deepened second-wave historical analysis. The scholarship of Matthews and Flammang on the history of Santa Clara County highlights how SJSU and other San Francisco Bay Area archives are helping scholars to discover new resources. These studies, combined with the recent edited works by Hewitt and Gilmore, confirm the saliency of regional history in developing a more accurate and inclusive narrative of the American experience.

Archivists play a pivotal role in historical discovery by collecting materials that document women's social movements. Gilmore's work underscores the reason we need to collect social movement records at the regional level. The archival field has tended to view mainstream women's collections as documenting mainly white and middle-class experiences, which has been true for national organizational records, but local chapter records remain a significant collecting source to build diverse collections focused on women and social movements. Drawing from Gilmore's research of feminist and civil rights groups in Memphis, bridge politics brought together different groups to work on specific issues such as the ERA, rape, and domestic abuse. Archivists need to consider how different groups interacted, how individuals related to specific issues within the geographic and community context, and we must build collections that represent the diversity of our communities. Gilmore reiterates this point when she writes: "analyzing the importance of situational politics and feminists' responses allows for a more accurate understanding of feminist expression." Gilmore's research underscores the importance of regional collecting and the impact that local institutions can have in broadening historical understanding of American feminism. The increased focus on regional collecting and the demand by scholars makes clear that a diversity of collecting strategies is needed. The epic work of the Arthur and Elizabeth Schlesinger Library on the History of Women in America (Harvard University) and Sophia Smith College (Smith College) to build separate women's collections, and their leadership in supporting the growth of regional collections, cannot be understated. The combination of national and regional collecting of diverse women's organization records is a work in progress, and we all share the responsibility to document the varieties of feminist expression.[25]

Historians and archivists share in preserving and making accessible the voices of second-wave feminists and beyond. By collecting regional records of individuals and organizations, combined with oral history, we are providing future generations with primary sources that detail the rich and varied experiences of American women. These same sources will lead to new analytical approaches that allow for more nuanced and diverse studies on the history of social movements and feminism in the United States.

The 1990s represented a milestone decade when activists and collectors joined hands to preserve the history of women. Several programs were endowed across the United States, and more institutions built women's collections based on new scholarship demands. In the twenty-first century, archival collecting strategies continue to evolve with technology and changes in how we capture information and record our histories. The growth of nontraditional formats such as electronic zines and emerging use of social networking sites like Facebook and Twitter to document individual and group experiences will advance documentation strategies to collect third- and fourth-wave experiences. The recent work of Lyz Bly and Kelly Wooten, *Make Your Own History: Documenting Feminist and Queer Activism in the 21st Century*, provides archivists with some new ideas on how best to document and preserve contemporary activism. Regardless of the format or changing technology, women's archives and university library archives must strive to document in areas that fill in the historical record, and we need to develop robust colleting initiatives that represent the diversity of our communities and society.[26]

As Mason and Zanish-Belcher remind us, we "must not fall into the habit of collecting only what is easy, such as the papers of middle- and upper-class white women and mainstream women's organizations." Indeed, we need diverse collecting strategies, but we should not ignore the importance of organization records, and we should fill in the gaps where they exist. Historian Kathleen A. Laughlin, in *Breaking the Wave: Women, Their Organizations and Feminism, 1945–1985*, illustrates the significance of local clubwomen's collections and reminds us of the importance of local studies that unearth the flurry of activism that cannot be captured through national organizations and policies. San Francisco Bay Area archives are rich with primary sources that document a variety of individuals, organizations, and communities. Collecting women's organization records at the regional level will advance future studies on feminist coalitions and will help shape our understanding of the diversity of the modern women's movement.[27]

NOTES

[1] Nancy A. Hewitt, ed., *No Permanent Waves: Recasting Histories of U.S. Feminism* (New Brunswick, NJ: Rutgers University Press, 2010), 1–7; Cynthia Harrison, *On Account of Sex: The Politics of Women's Issues, 1945–1968* (Berkeley: University of California Press, 1988), 96–104.

[2] Hewitt, *No Permanent Waves*, 1–7.

[3] Hewitt, *No Permanent Waves*, 6–7; Sara M. Evans, *Tidal Wave: How Women Changed America at Century's End* (New York: Free Press, 2003); Ruth Rosen, *The World Split Open: How the Modern Woman's Movement Changed America* (New York: Viking Press, 2000); Stephanie Gilmore, ed., *Feminist Coalitions: Historical Perspectives on Second-Wave Feminism in the United States* (Champaign: University of Illinois Press, 2008).

[4] Hewitt, *No Permanent Waves*, 6–8.

[5] Hewitt, *No Permanent Waves*, 8.

[6] Gilmore, *Feminist Coalitions*, 3–5; Stephanie Gilmore, "The Dynamics of Second-Wave Feminist Activism in Memphis, 1971–1982: Rethinking the Liberal/Radical Divide," *NWSA Journal* 15, no.1 (2003): 1–4.

[7] Anke Voss-Hubbard, "'No Documents—No History': Mary Ritter Beard and the Early History of Women's Archives," *American Archivist* 58 (1995): 23–30; Eva Moseley, "Sources for the New Women's History," *American Archivist* 43, no. 2 (1980): 180–90; Eva Mosely, Documenting the History of Women in America," *American Archivist* 36, no. 2 (1972): 215–22.

[8] Kären M. Mason and Tanya Zanish-Belcher, "A Room of One's Own: Women's Archives in the Year 2000," *Archival Issues* 24, no. 1 (1999): 37–54; Gerda Lerner, "U.S. Women's History: Past, Present, and Future," *Journal of Women's History* 16, no. 4 (2004): 12; Gilmore, *Feminist Coalitions*, 1–9.

[9] Mason and Zanish-Belcher, "Room of One's Own," 37–54.

[10] Sherna Gluck, "What's so Special about Women? Women's Oral History," *Frontiers: A Journal of Women Studies* 2, no. 2 (1977): 3–13; Sherna Gluck, "Women's Oral History, The Second Decade," in "Women's Oral History 2," special issue, *Frontiers* 8, no. 1 (1983): 1–2. The series was republished in 2002;

Susan H. Armitage, Patricia Hart, and Karen Weathermon, *Women's Oral History, The Frontiers Reader* (Lincoln: University of Nebraska Press, 2002).

[11] Armitage et al., *Women's Oral History*, ix–xii; Leila J. Rupp and Verta Taylor, *Survival in the Doldrums: The American Women's Rights Movement, 1945 to the 1960s* (New York: Oxford University Press, 1987), 258–60.

[12] "Conversation with Alice Paul: Woman Suffrage and the Equal Rights Amendment," an interview conducted by Amelia R. Fry (Regional Oral History Project, Bancroft Library, University of California, Berkeley, 1976), i–ii; "Connecticut Political Activities of the First Enfranchised Women," oral histories conducted by Carole Nichols and Joyce Pendery (University of Connecticut); Carole Nichols and Joyce Pendery, "Pro Bono Publico: Voices of Connecticut's Political Women, 1915–1945," *Oral History Review* 11 (1983); Nancy D. Mann, "Directory of Women's Oral History Projects and Collections," *Frontiers* 7 (1983): 114–21.

[13] Fry, "Conversations with Alice Paul," iii–xix, 598; see also Amelia R. Fry, "Suffragist Alice Paul's Memoirs: Pros and Cons of Oral History," *Frontiers* 2, no. 2 (1977): 82–86; and Fry, "The Two Searches for Alice Paul," *Frontiers* 5, no. 1 (1983): 21–24; Nichols and Pendery, "Voices of Connecticut's Political Women," 57–58; Susan Ware, "The Book I Couldn't Write: Alice Paul and the Challenge of Feminist Biography," *Journal of Women's History* 24, no. 2 (2012): 1–7.

[14] Please visit the Online Archives of California to view the finding aids to the holdings at SJSU, http://www.oac.cdlib.org/institutions/San+José+State+University, accessed 20 March 2013.

[15] Glenna Matthews, *Silicon Valley, Women, and the California Dream: Gender, Class, and Opportunity in the Twentieth Century* (Stanford, CA: Stanford University Press, 2003); Janet A. Flammang, *Women's Political Voices: How Women Are Transforming the Practice and Study of Politics* (Philadelphia: Temple University Press, 1997). See also Paul Johnston, *Success while Others Fail: Social Movement Unionism and the Public Workplace* (Ithaca, NY: ILR Press, 1994); Stephen J. Pitti, *The Devil in Silicon Valley: Northern California, Race, and Mexican Americans* (Princeton, NJ: Princeton University Press, 2004).

[16] Mason and Zanish-Belcher, "Room of One's Own," 37–54.

[17] Janet Gray Hayes Papers (SJSU), Box 1; Jim Puzzanghera, "The Bay Area's Old Girls' Network Is Thriving," *San José Mercury News*, 17 February 2002; Matthews, *Women and California Dream*, 191–202; South Bay Second Wave Feminist Project (SJSU), interview with Susanne Wilson, 2006.

[18] Terry Christensen, *Movers and Shakers: The Study of Community Power* (New York: St. Martins Press, 1982), 103–8.

[19] Flammang, *Women's Political Voices*, 53; Janet Flammang, "Female Officials in the Feminist Capital: The Case of Santa Clara County," *Women's Political Quarterly* 38, no. 1 (1985): 44–49, 94–118; Matthews, *Women and California Dream*, 102–11.

[20] Matthews, *Women and California Dream*, 183–255; Kathryn Kish Sklar and Thomas Dublin, "How Did the National Women's Conference in Houston in 1977 Shape an Agenda for the Future?," in *Women and Social Movements in the U.S., 1600-2000*, ed. Kathryn Kish Sklar and Thomas Dublin (State University of New York, 2007), 1–16, accessed from the subscription database, 20 March 2013.

[21] Flammang, "Female Officials," 44–49, 94–118; Matthews, *Women and California Dream*, 102–11; Danelle Moon, *Daily Life of Women during the Civil Rights Era* (Santa Barbara, CA: Greenwood Press, 2011), 183–86.

[22] Moon, *Daily Life of Women during the Civil Rights Era*, 183–86.

[23] Please visit the Online Archives of California to view the finding aids to the holdings at SJSU, http://www.oac.cdlib.org/institutions/San+José+State+University, accessed 20 March 2013.

[24] Gilmore, "Feminist Activism in Memphis," 1–5, 7, 12.

[25] Gilmore, "Feminist Activism in Memphis," 1–5, 7, 12.

[26] Lyz Bly and Kelly Wooten, *Make Your Own History: Documenting Feminist and Queer Activism in the 21st Century* (Los Angeles: Litwin Books, 2012).

[27] Mason and Zanish-Belcher, "Room of One's Own," 5; Kathleen A. Laughlin and Jacqueline L. Castledine, eds., *Breaking the Wave: Women, Their Organizations, and Feminism, 1945-1985* (New York: Routledge Press, 2011), 1–5, 34.

CHAPTER 16

Building Community through Self-Expression: Zines as Archival Materials

VIRGINIA CORVID

DURING THE 1980S AND 1990S, THE WIDESPREAD ACCESSIBILITY OF PHOTOCOPIERS IN AMERICA PRODUCED A FLOWERING OF THE SELF-PUBLISHING FORMAT, ZINES. Many groups outside of mainstream corporate markets utilized the format to communicate, organize, express themselves, and create art. As part of this diverse movement, women and girls created and circulated zines that developed feminist approaches to zine discourse. These direct, innovative, and thought-provoking texts offer vital primary source materials that documents the personal, cultural, and political perspectives of their creators as well as the community networks that developed in tandem with and supported the production of these texts.

Libraries rather than archives have predominantly collected zines, but this trend has led to the undercollection of zines because they are difficult and costly to manage within library systems. Moreover, when libraries do collect zines, item-level treatment severs their interconnectedness and microcommunity provenance. In contrast, archives have the systems to efficiently handle zines while preserving their interrelatedness and community context. Significantly for archives, zines and zine networks have functioned as foundational sites for the development of third-wave feminist theory, methodology, writers, artists, and activists. By collecting zines, archives can not only document this recent feminist history, but can also preserve the frank and creative perspectives of women and girls, the histories of their networks, and the third wave of feminism's expression in the zine format.

Zines are challenging to define because the format can vary greatly, but general outlines do exist. The shortest description of a zine is a self-published booklet, and the most common construction is black and white photocopied 8.5-×-11-inch paper, folded in half and stapled in the fold. Produced by individuals or groups, zines can appear serially or as single issue "one-offs." Inside, they typically contain handwritten or typewritten text, drawings, comics, and "borrowed" images often collaged or altered in some way. Although some writers use desktop publishing software or even letterpress printing, most zines are laid out with scissors and glue sticks, then photocopied. Production values are usually haphazard and messy. The text itself often actively flouts capitalization, punctuation, and spelling conventions to create added meaning. On the whole, despite a small percentage of ornate or more formal examples, production tech-niques make the format a particularly low-cost and accessible publication venue. All a zine producer really needs is a pen, paper, magazines, scis-sors, glue, time, and access to a photocopier.

Marginalized and outsider groups have historically used this acces-sible format to cultivate their communities. Nominally, zines began in the 1930s as mimeographed pamphlets called *fanzines* produced by science-fiction fans and writers to share, critique, and connect. In the 1970s, punk musicians adopted the fanzine (later contracted to *zine*) to communicate at a time when mainstream corporate musical markets disdained the genre. Through the 1980s and 1990s, as photocopiers became increasingly accessible, punk zine production expanded, remnants of the 1960s and 1970s underground press began utilizing zines, and the newly developing indie or independent culture also utilized the format. The contributions of these diverse cultures remain evident in zine production today in many ways, including extensive science-fiction and alternative musical content as well as pervasive do-it-yourself punk ethics, generally radical politics, and edgy comics.

Although used in various communities and encompassing a wide variety of styles and content, the connections between zines and free expression unite them as a format. In *The World of Zines: A Guide to the Independent Magazine Revolution*, Mike Gunderloy and Cari Goldberg, editors of the long-running and highly influential zine-review compendium *Factsheet Five*, distill zine ethos to the simple observation that zine authors create zines "for love rather than money."[1] Personal passion for self-expression disallowed or marginalized in mainstream discourse motivates zine authors to self-publish in whatever style and on whatever topic they choose. Expanding availability of self-publishing tools such as photocopiers, typewriters, and computers fuels the expansion of these forms of self-expression. Zine distribution also requires the development of small participatory networks of exchange that, in turn, encourage more production.

The informal production and distribution of zines has significant stylistic consequences, making them particularly rich as primary sources. The freedom from writing for mass-audience appeal allows zine authors to express unpopular views or uncommon interests, and the alternative distribution networks that they travel in cultivate small, interested, and supportive audiences for these works. Readers usually must go out of their way to access zines through mail-order, research, or by participation in local scenes where they are available. Authors and readers regularly correspond and, because readers are also often writers themselves, correspondents commonly make contributions to each other's zines and exchange issues. These supportive micro-audiences create a public/private indeterminacy in zine consumption and elicit writing styles that resemble diary entries and personal correspondence rather than straight political or cultural journalism.

Engaging this characteristic of zine writing, Pagan Kennedy of *Pagan's Head* explicitly lays out her intentions of informality, self-disclosure, and friendship to the reader in the first issue of this serial zine. She addresses the reader, saying, "I'll introduce you to my friends, my phobias, my jobs, my deep thoughts about life and my sinus problems."[2] This intended style contrasts with the kind of public and high-stakes writing she did at school. She explains,

> At [my graduate program], writing seemed serious, the focus of your life and the cause of your early death. But you know what I realized in Baltimore? I'm shallow. I don't want to write deathless prose. . . . And that's what self publishing is, in a way. You don't have to compare yourself to Beckett or Nabokov. You don't agonize over every word. Instead of making something for strangers, you make it for friends—who'll forgive if your cartoons are wobbly or your prose wanders.[3]

Altogether, Kennedy describes zine self-publishing as a liberating opportunity to trust the reader as a friend. This allows her to informally share her personal experiences and thoughts in contrast with professional publishing.

Ailecia Ruscin, creator of *alabama grrrl* and other zines, relates how self-expression in zines can create a supportive community of simultaneous personal exchange and self-documentation:

> I write a zine because I don't write a journal. It is my way of processing the world around me and engaging in dialogue through the mail. I feel at home in the zine community and find zines to be far better than trendy "reality television." Zines are written by real people who are writing mostly about their real lives. I find this fascinating and integral for people like us, people living on the edges and margins of society, to document their lives, feelings and experiences.[4]

In these comments, Ruscin likens her zine-writing style to diary writing and reveals that this approach occurs regularly. Indeed, she points to how mutual engagement of this style both creates a kind of correspondence through exchange mediated by the postal service and records the personal realities of cultural outsiders.

Kennedy's and Ruscin's statements about zine writing grounded in friendship and trust through self-revelation provide a foundational understanding for the frank and open discourse that female zine authors have developed. Leveraging the accessible, unrestrictive, and affiliative aspects of zines to express themselves and to forge forums for feminist and female-centered discourse, women and girl zine writers address topics, relate perspectives, and share personal experiences often absent from mainstream media markets. Prominent issues in this discourse include femininity, sexuality, body image, gender, menstruation, abortion, motherhood, sexual and physical violence, self-defense, sex work, sexism, racism, (dis)ability, and intersectionality.[5] Women and girls engaged and continue to engage these issues with candor and wit in zine writing, expressing political interpretations of these concerns connected to personal experience.

Although a full examination of zines written by women and girls is outside the scope of any article, a brief examination of a few substantial selections of this work can begin to convey the contours of expression in the format. Within this discourse, authors combine consciousness-raising with feminist testimony, analysis, activism, art, and literature using personal experience to develop, substantiate, and amplify their feminist analyses and activist responses.

For example, the collaborative zine *Free to Fight*, which was released with a double album of female-produced music and self-defense lessons, focuses on feminist self-defense, in particular the response to the rampant sexual assault that women experience. Personal self-defense stories appear alongside instructions, feminist analysis of rape myths and sexual harassment, and calls for resistance and solidarity. One of the testimonials relates,

> You Asked For Any Self Defense Story—
> I called my best friend to meet me down the street from my house. I was feeling like shit, I needed/wanted to talk to him. When he got there we talked for a little while + then he kept making advances towards me. I hugged him, I wanted to hug him. But he wanted to kiss me or fuck me or. . . . He pushed me down on the ground, it was cold and wet. I'm like 5'2" I weigh 115 or about that—just to give you some idea—he's 6'3" about 200 lbs. He was . . . on top of me his knees were on my hands. I couldn't really move, I spit on his face but then he started to unzip his pants. I kept thinking, "What the fuck? What the fuck? What the fuck?" I'm not sure but I think

> I kicked him in the head and he fell off or over. I jumped up and kicked him again, hard. He was hard and I kicked it. He instantly crumpled into a ball. I think I wanted to kill him but I was really sick so I just threw up on him instead. I threw up a lot that day and I just kept thinking, "What the fuck? This is supposed to be my best friend? What the fuck? What the fuck?"[6][7]

This personal story works on a number of levels in the zine. It provides a personal experience of an attempted sexual assault and its successful resistance with self-defense. It also contrasts the misperception that armed, deranged strangers perpetrate rape in dark alleys and alternately provides an example of the more common experience of sexual assault perpetrated without a weapon by a male the female victim knows.[8] Interpreting the personal stories in Free to Fight as simply illustrative misrepresents them, however. Instead, the sharing of personal stories weaves together with a political analysis to better critique and represent lived oppression, advocate for effective resistance, and create a new feminist space characterized by disclosure, trust, belief, resistance, and support.

Personal stories comprise almost the entirety of another zine, Mine: An Anthology of Women's Choices. The editor, Merrydeath, explains her intentions for the zine, which shares women's abortion stories, saying, "I want to provide a forum for women to tell their stories and to feel supported by other women around them . . . there is little if any outlet for women to feel comfortable talking about their decision not to carry a pregnancy to term."[9] The stories in Mine present a number of perspectives on experience with abortion and notably relate little-heard experiences with herbal abortion, alternative contraceptive practices, and detailed accounts of experiences with abortion providers, abortion waiting periods, and seeking an abortion without much money. Janet, the author of the zine Rocket Queen, which focuses on her experiences as a stripper, contributes a piece entitled "Contagion" that highlights her resistance to chemical contraceptives. It reads in part,

> The other dancers warned me, "Be careful, it's catching." One of the 12 women in the small club where I worked had gotten pregnant.

"I'll be fine. I know my body." . . . Diana, a woman who had been dancing for 10 years said, "Sugar, I'm serious. I've never seen just one woman in a club get pregnant. At least 3 dancers catch it every time." . . . All the women at the club who were not chemically regulated got pregnant. Two decided to have their babies and one miscarried. I decided on the other route and made my appointment. . . . The procedure was surprisingly easy since a friend had warned me to opt for the intra-venous pain killer they offer at the clinic. . . . I chatted with one nurse I knew for about 5 minutes and then it was over. I couldn't believe that was it.

Then came the more painful part. A doctor talked to me afterwards and filled out . . . a prescription for birth control pills. I told her I used condoms and would not be using the pill. She snidely commented, "I guess you're just not going to have sex then." Despite the nice opiate induced feeling I had, I was livid. I told her I had no intention of making my body think it was pregnant all the time, thereby feeling as crazy as I'd felt that month for the rest of my life. She said, "I'm on the pill and I'm not crazy." I told her I didn't know her well enough to verify that. She begrudgingly let me leave without the free samples. Thinking of all the other women who go there and have the pill forced on them when they're already feeling shitty made me want to scream. To be in that headspace and then to have the doctor insult you for even questioning the pill is inexcusable.[10]

The frustration and disappointment with abortion services and critique of the medical and pharmaceutical treatment of women in general that Janet expresses in "Contagion" emerges as a repeated theme throughout *Mine*. Various authors also relate feelings of conflict, relief, shame, confusion, isolation, and anger while situating the shared experience of abortion in complex individual life contexts. Taken together, the stories in the anthology do feminist work by sharing knowledge, asserting ownership, and engaging in a conversation on a taboo, contested, gendered issue around which the personal experiences of women often remain excluded from the discourse.

The anonymous contribution in *Free to Fight* and the abortion stories in *Mine* present encapsulated personal stories with more political impact and meaning in the larger narratives of their respective zines. Other zine authors, however, interweave personal experience with their political analysis. For example, the zine *Lost I.D.* brings together pieces that explore identity, nationality, race, and gender. The editor, Claudia von Volcano, explains the title and her intentions for the zine: "So i lost my i.D. and i thought to myself Lost. Identity. . . . In this zine we explore the issues that are relevant to us . . . feminist[s] of color. AND HOPEFULLY OF INTEREST TO MANY!"[11] One contributor, SelenaWhahng, critiques American and Japanese imperialism, plastic surgery, and the role of women in perpetuating sexism and presents an example of how gender, race, and nationality interlock. She writes,

> even before sexism and racism there was Other and lack and insecurity. it must have been around the forties or fifties when those amerikan movies came around and koreans saw these larger than life people—Hepburn, Taylor, Bergman. how beautiful and sophisticated and powerful they were, like amerikan imperialism. the japanese also occupied korea. the japanese invented these quick and easy operations, making folds by cutting slits on yr. eyelids so you look caucasoid, an optical illusion that makes your eyes look bigger. this is called sangkyopul. not as prevalent but still widespread is breaking yr. nose and raising that bridge, straight and tall. this is called kokosul. thay say this gives your face more character. my mother says I *really* should get sangkyopul and she wished she had done it. It would have saved a lot of time with the makeup. my cousin says that I have a pretty face but my eyes are too small. but korean amerikan girls tend not to cut up their faces.[12]

Whahng's deadpan yet scathing critique of plastic surgeries for Asian women aimed at making them appear more white and therefore more beautiful seamlessly transitions to her personal experience of receiving pressure from female family members to undergo such procedures, thereby underscoring how the personal and the political remain inseparable. The larger context of the zine positions Whahng's writing in a framework that questions how middle-class American whiteness is reproduced in zines and presents more personal experiences and analysis of how gender, race, class, and American identity interface in inseparable ways.

These brief excerpts can necessarily only begin to convey the issues, experiences, and topics women and girls have written about in zines; yet they do represent this discourse in their striking candor, their use of personal stories to forge political analysis, their work to create alternative supportive communities, and the frequent presentation of experiences and perspectives largely absent from the mainstream. Additionally, from these limited selections, the creation of third-wave feminist discourse in the zine format begins to become apparent by the authors' topical choices, interpretations, and explicit goals.

In *Girl Zines: Making Media, Doing Feminism*, the first scholarly monograph to address zines written by women and girls, author Alison Piepmeier argues for this understanding of feminist zines, asserting, "zines are sites for the articulation of a vernacular third wave feminist theory" and observing that "the theoretical contributions—the vocabulary, conceptual apparatus, and explanatory narratives—of the third wave have not been recognized by scholars because they are being developed in unexpected, nonacademic sites, like zines."[13] While scholars like Piepmeier have begun to take up zines as sites of third-wave feminist theory, the close relationship between zines and the third wave also becomes apparent from the notable crossover of feminist zines and zinesters into more mainstream roles and formats. The third-wave feminist magazines *Bitch* and *Bust*, for example, began as zines, and countless scholars, writers, musicians, activists, and artists began as zinesters or have strong ties to the zine community.[14] In sum, women and girls as creative cultural producers continue to use zines to develop their voices, create community, and name and resist the societal dynamics such as sexism, racism, and homophobia that oppress them.

The result has been a stunningly candid documentary record of the experiences of women and girls, especially related to topics or perspectives little addressed or taboo in the mainstream. In zines, women and girls give direct personal accounts of what *they* find most important and what is generally disallowed or self-edited. This material is rare and also vital to the completeness of the documentary record. Additionally, these zines document the development of the third wave of feminism, the lives and thoughts of prominent but underrecognized feminist activists and cultural workers and the histories of their communities. These zines at once present a more intimate view than organizational records and a broader view than personal papers. This history is also in danger of being lost because of undercollection.

Predominantly, library special collections, institutions devoted to zines, and public libraries collect zines.[15] Zines as a format offer many challenges to libraries that wish to house them, however, because they require all-original catalog descriptions, have fragile physical formats, are difficult to purchase, are often impossible to replace, and require specialized display equipment because they lack spine titles or room for spine labeling. Collecting zines in libraries, therefore, requires extra financial investment for equipment, purchasing, and cataloging as well as increased time investments for developing library solutions to meet these challenges. Additionally, the popular culture designation of zines, their explicit content, and direct purchasing has further discouraged their collection by academic and public libraries. As a result, comparatively few libraries collect zines. The growing body of library literature advocating for zine collection underscores these barriers because it is mostly devoted to sharing strategies for overcoming the difficulties that accompany zines, including building institutional support, negotiating purchasing procedure accommodations, cataloging, making circulation choices, displaying, making access choices, and preserving.[16]

In contrast, archives could more easily accommodate zines. Archival practices of collection-level description and acquisition, combined with preservation strategies and closed-stack access systems, circumvent the challenges zines pose to libraries. Indeed, implementing these archival practices has functioned as key to the handling of zines in institutions devoted to zines and in library collections of zines.[17] In short, archives have systems in place to deal with zines' irregularities. If archives abstain from collecting zines, much material will pass into oblivion. Given their rich documentation of third-wave feminist and women's history, the mandate for archives to incorporate zines is compelling.

Provenance, however, offers the most compelling argument for archival collection of zines. Because zines circulate in small, affiliative communities, they have myriad interconnections. Writers and readers are embedded in these microcommunities and accumulate collections that include their own work, the work of friends, and the zines of others they have never met but with whom they correspond. As part of this exchange culture, zinesters also regularly contribute to each other's work. One small example of this prevalent trend is the work of Cindy Crabb, author of the well-known and long-running illustrated feminist zine *Doris*, which relates personal stories and reflection. In addition to writing *Doris*, Crabb also compiled and edited *Support*, a zine that brings together stories, poems, letters, and comics about coping with experiences of sexual assault, supporting others who have experienced it, and highlighting the importance of consent.[18] She also contributed excerpts from *Doris* about her abortion experience to *Mine: An Anthology of Women's Choices* and advertised for submissions to *Mine* in *Doris* as well.[19] Additionally, pieces written by Janet, who also wrote the serial zine *Rocket Queen*, appear in both *Mine* and *Support*.[20] In other words, the low barriers to creating zines and the affiliative networks they travel in make zines a near-print participatory format that documents the experiences, perspectives, analyses, art, and activism of small supportive communities interested in the same issues.

Because of their investment in these communities, every active zinester with the means to physically house a zine collection over time does so, thereby organically accumulating a community record as a zine collection. Researching and reading in these collections with their rich context and coherence contrasts sharply with the experience of reading in many library collections, as libraries often collect zines individually or break up collections by mixing them into the entire library collection. Zine collections not obtained or grouped by provenance convey the sense of disjointed snippets of different conversations.

Zine communities are social, artistic, and intellectual, and zine collections encapsulate them as they were lived. Collecting zines individually and treating them to item-level handling severs and scrambles these connections, effacing or obscuring the community and intellectual histories they contain. Keeping zines together in collections organically accumulated by zine community participants effectively documents zine-community niches. In the context of feminist zines, these community niches fostered and continue to foster the development of strands of third-wave theory as well as the development of prominent academic, political, and cultural workers.

These feminist zine collectors and authors recognize the significance and value of their collections to women's and feminist history, and they also share archival values of historical preservation. Researchers would benefit from the preservation of these collections in archives as *collections*, and women's archivists will most likely find creators of these collections interested in donating them to archives. The challenge for archivists remains to make these connections before the collections are destroyed and the common lifestyle factors of zinesters—such as economic instability, extensive traveling, and relocation—make the need to reach these collections even more urgent.

Just as the widespread availability of photocopiers made the explosion of zine publishing possible, in more recent times, the increasing availability of personal computers and the Internet has made the proliferation of online self-publishing possible. This trend could suggest that the zine format has had its day and online models of self-publishing will replace zines, yet examination of feminist zine communities online demonstrates a more complicated dynamic.

Today, feminist zinesters utilize the Internet extensively to build larger and international networks, communicate inexpensively, conduct interviews, reach a wider audience with their activism, and distribute zines—but they also maintain an affinity for the print zine format. Elke Zobl's site gRRRL zine network, for example, lists over one thousand zines from over thirty countries and also posts interviews with feminist zinesters.[21] Utilizing the Internet to accomplish the same work as previous print-based zine listings like the *Action Girl Newsletter*, the site can reach more people, but notably does not try to replace the zine format itself. Instead of acting as a forum for personal feminist expression, gRRRL zine network works to facilitate the exchange and study of this expression in feminist zines.   Interviews with some of the zine authors featured on the site provide further perspective on the facilitating role of the Internet for feminist zinesters, but also stress the importance of the print zine format itself. For example, Stina B. of *(her) riot distro* comments on taking for granted the continuity of the zine format,

> The internet means a whole lot. I would never sell as many zines if
> I didn't have a web site up and I wouldn't be able to have such good
> contact with other zinesters and friends as I do now.[22]

Similarly, Nikko Snyder of *Good Girl!* stresses the significance and the utility of the Internet but leavens this perspective with her preference for print:

> The Internet is a hugely important means for communicating, espe-
> cially when money is scarce. It's really the only way to connect with
> people affordably, especially in huge countries like Canada or the
> US. I think that's why there's so much revolutionary stuff happen-
> ing online.
>
> At the same time, I can't imagine the Internet taking over real
> books, zines etc. I could never read a book online, and I barely ever
> read anything off the Internet, unless I have to. I totally appreciate
> the work of the countless awesome online zines and projects, but
> I'd way rather sit down with a real magazine or book, get it all ratty
> and worn.[23]

Olivia of *Persephone Is Pissed* expresses her loyalty to the print zine format more succinctly, stating, "The Internet is a great networking tool, but *Persephone Is Pissed* is and always will be all cut-and-paste."[24] Liouxsie of *Danger! Hole* elaborates on this perspective:

> Ah, the internet. It's interesting you bring that up, I'm torn on the
> issue of technology and the impact it's made on activism . . . the
> internet kicks ass at hooking me up with strangers. It's how I deal

with international distros, random isolated kids I never would've known existed otherwise, it's how I find/conduct interview potentials, and it's how I learned about you guys, actually. I owe the internet a thumbs up for its convenience, speed (on good days) and networking capabilities. I want to slap it in the face with a glove for making human connections so cold and . . . inhuman.[25]

Elena Stoehr of *It's not just boy's fun!*, who produces both a print zine and an online zine, further discusses how the Internet makes connecting to other people easier, but also comments on how she finds it lacking in comparison to print zines:

i mostly use the internet for communication and i guess i write about ten or more e-mails a day . . . since i have a homepage, i also got in contact with lots of different people and parts of my zines can be read online. of course the internet has changed my ideas of making zines, especially because i am not only doing a "paper-zine" anymore but also an e-zine. i still like "real" zines much more than those online-zines. they are too impersonal in my eyes.[26]

The comments of feminist zinesters on gRRRL zine network, as well as the continued production of feminist zines, suggest that feminist print zines will continue into the future and that feminist zine networks will continue to thrive. Although the Internet offers unprecedented low-cost opportunities for communication, distribution, and network building, it lacks the exchange and the tactile and intimate aspects of the paper zine format. Feminist zinesters' affinity for the print format suggests that archivists interested in documenting these communities, and the frankly expressed experiences of women and girls contained within them, will have continuing opportunities to do so. Online networks that feminist zinesters utilize can also provide contact information for connecting to zinesters interested in donating their collections.

By seeking donations and preserving feminist zines as *collections*, archives can document the perspectives and experiences of women and girls and also the development of the third wave of feminism in zine community networks. Although public libraries, special zine libraries, and special collections have thus far taken the lead in collecting zines, unique zine-format characteristics argue for the relevancy of archival zine collecting. The liminal qualities of zines between published and unpublished materials, and their resulting resemblance to collections of correspondence and journals, suggest that zines qualify as archival materials. Furthermore, the irreplaceability of zines and the difficulties zines pose to libraries argue that zines need archival preservation. Most important, the rare and dense documentation of issues, perspectives, and experiences of girls and women largely absent from other types of sources calls for collection in archives. Feminist zinesters purposefully set out to communicate what they were not supposed to talk about or think about, but that nevertheless defined their experience of the world: sexual and physical assault, sexual harassment, abortion, the continuing problem of racism, restrictive beauty standards, control of their bodies through consumption and medicalization, verbal abuse, and constructions of their inherent inferiority, as well as lack of identification with dominant constructions of femininity, heterosexuality, and motherhood. In zines, women and girls take advantage of the simultaneous openness and intimacy of the format to express these little-heard perspectives and develop activist, analytical, and creative responses to them—in part, creating the third wave of feminism in zine communities. Archives can and should collect these underdocumented perspectives and the third wave of feminism by acquiring feminist zine collections and keeping their connections intact and accessible.

NOTES

[1] Mike Gunderloy and Cari Goldberg, eds., *World of Zines* (New York: Penguin, 1992), 2.

[2] Pagan Kennedy, *Zine: How I Spent Six Years of My Life in the Underground and Finally Found Myself—I Think* (New York: St. Martin's Griffin, 1995), 13.

[3] Kennedy, *Zine*, 14.

[4] Julie Bartel, *From A to Zine: Building a Winning Zine Collection in Your Library* (Chicago: American Library Association, 2004), 10–11.

[5] See, for example, femininity, *Femme Vitale* edited by Tara Robertson; sexuality, *I ♥ Amy Carter* by Tammy Rae; body image, *I'm So Fucking Beautiful* by Nomy

Lamm; gender, *Green Zine* by Christy Road; menstruation, *This Is My Blood, This is Your Blood* by the Scarlet Tide Brigade; abortion, *Mine: An Anthology of Women's Choices* edited by Merrydeath; motherhood, *The East Village Inky* by Ayun Halliday; sexual and physical violence, *With Our Hearts, With Our Voices* edited by Sara Lindsay; self-defense, *Women's Self-Defense: Stories and Strategies of Survival* edited by Ariel; sex-work, *Rocket Queen* by Janet; sexism, any feminist zine; racism, *Evolution of a Race Riot* edited by Mimi Nguyen; (dis)ability, *Ring of Fire* by Hellery Homosex; and intersectionality, *Bamboo Girl* by Sabrina Margarita Alcantara-Tan.

[6] Feminist zinesters regularly break stylistic conventions of grammar to create added meaning. Zine excerpts included in this article reproduce original spelling, symbols, and capitalization without the use of [*sic*] which would only be distracting in this context. Shortening for excerpting purposes is represented with ellipses.

[7] Anonymous, "You Asked for Any Self-Defense Story," in *Free to Fight* (Portland: Candy Ass Records, 1995); Jody Blyele, ed., zine, Zine Archive and Publishing Project, Seattle.

[8] Patricia Tjaden and Nancy Thoennes, *Prevalence, Incidence, and Consequences of Violence against Women: Findings from the National Violence against Women Survey* (Washington, DC: National Institute of Justice, 1998), 3, 8.

[9] Introduction, *Mine: An Anthology of Women's Choices*, ed. Merrydeath (2002), zine: personal collection.

[10] Janet of *Rocket Queen*, "Contagion" in *Mine*.

[11] Introduction, *Lost I.D.*, ed. Claudia von Volcano (New York, n.d.), zine: Zine Archive and Publishing Project, Seattle.

[12] Selena Whahng, "y korean girls cut up their faces," in *Lost I.D.*

[13] Alison Piepmeier, *Girl Zines: Making Media, Doing Feminism* (New York: UP, 2009), 4,10.

[14] To name a few prominent examples, the author of the zine *Painter Lewis* and editor of the zine *Nightmare Girl* (as well as drummer for the bands the Haggard and Cadallaca) is currently program director for Portland Oregon's Rock 'n Roll Camp for Girls, which seeks to build girls' self-esteem and foster their self-expression through musical workshops. Another prominent musician, Kathleen Hannah, currently singer in the popular band Le Tigre and formerly lead singer for the band Bikini Kill, wrote the zine *Bikini Kill*, which played a foundational role in the development of Riot Grrrl feminist discourse. In addition to connections to music production, feminist zine writing has also

unsurprisingly led to careers in writing. Jennifer Blyer, for example, author of the zines *Googlebox, Roar,* and *Mazeltov Cocktail,* went on to found *Heeb* magazine and currently writes for the *New York Times;* she also teaches journalism at New York University. Feminist zine writing has also preceded careers in feminist scholarship. For example, Red Chidgey, author of the zine *Varla's Passed Out Again,* currently teaches "Zines and the Politics of Alternative Media" and "Third Wave Feminism: Theories, Praxis and Media" at the University of Salzburg in Austria; and Mimi Nguyen, author of the zines *Aim Your Dick* and *Slant* and editor of *Evolution of a Race Riot,* is currently an assistant professor of women's and gender studies and Asian American studies at the University of Illinois at Urbana-Champaign.

[15] See, for example, the New York Public Library, the Denver Zine Library, the Salt Lake City Public Library, the Zine Archive and Publishing Project, the Independent Publishing Resource Center, Barnard College Library, DePaul University Special Collections, the Sallie Bingham Center for Women's History and Culture, and Bowling Green State University Browne Popular Culture Library.

[16] See Richard Stoddart and Teresa Kiser, "Zines and the Library," *Library Resources and Technical Services* 48, no. 3 (2004): 193–96; Jerianne Thompson, "Zine, It Rhymes with Teen: How a Zine Collection Can Help You Connect with Young Adults," *Tennessee Libraries* 57, no. 1 (2007): 4–7; Chris Dodge, "Pushing the Boundaries: Zines and Libraries," *Wilson Library Bulletin* 69, no. 9 (1995) 2–3; Colleen Hubbard, "DIY in the Stacks: A Study of Three Public Library Zine Collections," *Public Libraries* 44, no. 6 (2005): 354; Jenna Freedman, "Your Zine Toolkit, a DIY Collection," *Library Journal* 131, no. 11 (2006): 36–38; Bartel, *From A to Zine,* 23–91.

[17] Bartel, *From A to Zine,* 23–91.

[18] Cindy Crabb, ed., *Support* (Portland: Microcosm, 2002), 1, zine: personal collection.

[19] Cindy Crabb, "Abortion #1," "Abortion #2," "Abortion #3," reprinted from *Doris* 12 in *Mine,* ed. Merrydeath.

[20] Janet of *Rocket Queen,* no title; and "Supporting Someone Who's Reliving Sexual Assault," in *Support,* ed. Cindy Crabb, 34–37, 43–46; Janet of *Rocket Queen,* "Contagion," in *Mine,* ed. Merrydeath.

[21] Elke Zobl, gRRRL zine network, http://grrrlzines.net, accessed 12 January 2012.

[22] Stina B., "It's a passion! (her) riot distro gives something to think about," webpost, June 2002, gRRRL zine network, http://grrrlzines.net, accessed 12 January 2012.

[23] Nikko Snyder, "Good Girl! Communication across difference and building community among Canadian Women," webpost, 2002, http://grrrlzines.net, accessed 12 January 2012.

[24] Olivia, "Do it. Sit down. Make it. That's all.," webpost, 2002, http://grrrlzines.net, accessed 12 January 2012.

[25] Liouxsie Doyle, "Danger! Hole: 'Feminism Loves You . . .'," webpost, 2008, http://grrrlzines.net, accessed12 January 2012.

[26] Elena Stoehr, "It's not just boy's fun!," webpost, 2002, http://grrrlzines.net, accessed 12 January 2012.

Conclusion

CHAPTER 17

Holistic History: Challenges and Possibilities

GERDA LERNER

In this essay I revisit a question that has occupied me since 1969: what is the significance of Women's History for the entire field of history? How will Women's History affect and change the practice of historians in the future? I wrote on this subject several times during the past decades and often addressed it in my public lectures. The longer I wrote and taught Women's History and the more I experienced the profound transformative effect it had on women students, the more I became convinced that the development of this new field of scholarship amounted to a major cultural breakthrough, a paradigm shift. Surveying the field in recent years, I was struck not only by its astonishing growth, but also by the proliferation of different approaches and specializations that seemed to splinter the field and diffuse its message. Interest in the histories of various identity groups—African American, Latina, Native American, Jewish, Asian American, and women of other ethnic groups added a new dimension to traditional knowledge about the American past. Lesbian/Gay/Transgender and Sexualities Studies added several new categories of inquiry to the focus on socially constructed identities.

Gender Studies challenged and complicated the generalizations in Women's History. Theories, such as postmodernism and cultural studies, derived from literary theories, influenced much new research that focused on representation, images, performance, and popular culture, marking a sharp turn away from social history. While I saw the proliferation of interest groupings as a sign of strength, rather than of division, I was concerned at the lack of interest contemporary historians seemed to have in social movements and the actual lives and experiences of women in the past. I was alarmed at the fact that most current work was concerned with the recent past—a trend that was overwhelmingly obvious in the topics of dissertations—and that there seemed to be very little thought given to the larger, historical meaning of what historians of women's history are doing.

In the current essay I take a somewhat different view. I stress the far-reaching influence Women's History scholarship has had on transforming the general field. Rather than drawing conclusions from current trends, I decided for once simply to project my own ideas of where I think the field should be going. I end up with a call for a new holistic history and with several fairly utopian statements. Knowing full well that historians are not supposed to predict the future, I have taken this liberty on the basis of claiming the privilege of my age. Old women and men, at the end of life, are entitled to express their vision. And so I have done here.

THE MILLENNIA-OLD OMISSION OF WOMEN FROM RECORDED HISTORY HAS RESULTED IN A SERIOUS DISTORTION OF THE RECORD OF CIVILIZATION. It has presented a world to us in which seemingly all significant events were activated and executed by men, with women relegated to marginality and cultural insignificance. Men had agency; men built civilizations and cultures; men devised theories and explanatory systems of thought; women took care of reproduction, the rearing of children, domestic production, and the maintenance of daily life. These false assertions led to the equally erroneous claim that women had no history, or at least no history worth recording.

With the growth of universities, which from their beginnings in the Middle Ages and well into the twentieth century excluded women from access to higher education, the male monopoly on formal knowledge became institutionalized. When the recording of history became a profession, all scholarship was male-centered and male-defined. Man was the measure of all that is significant; male activities, like warfare and the control of land and resources, were deemed more significant than the rearing of children, the daily maintenance of life, and the building of communities. University-trained historians, all male, asked only androcentric questions of the past. The recorded history that resulted made it appear as though women had made only marginal contributions to the building of civilization. Such findings reinforced already existing biases against women and led both men and women to view women's subordinate place in society as though it were appropriate and acceptable. Although individual women resisted such definitions and asserted women's claims for equality, their voices were ignored, distorted, or defined as deviant.

By arrogating to themselves the representation of all of humanity, men have built a conceptual error of vast proportion into all of their thought. As long as men believed the earth to be flat and at the center of the universe, they could not understand its reality, its actual relationship to other bodies in the universe. As long as men believed that their experiences, their viewpoints, and their ideas represented all of human experience and all of human thought, they were not only unable to see the connections and complexities of human interaction, they were also unable to describe reality accurately.

Traditional history accustomed both men and women to a construction of the past based on narrow slices of reality and to an acceptance of a partial story for the entire narrative. The effect of this on women was that they internalized the myth of their inferiority, their passivity, their inability to think creatively and strive for originality. Believing themselves to be persons without a history of their own, they accepted the patriarchal gender characterization of being victims of history, at best, assistants to men in the building of civilization. That this has been damaging to women's development and to their ability to improve their position in society is in retrospect quite obvious. Less obvious is the damage this patriarchal fallacy has done and is doing to men.

The assumption of male innate superiority is obviously counterintuitive and contradicts the life experience of every male. Every man has known strong and capable women in his life, just as he has known weak and incapable men. To accept the dominant mental construct of male superiority, men have had to suppress their own life experience. They have to be trained, and continue to train themselves, to live an intellectual lie. This damages not only their intellect, but their soul.

The androcentric fallacy has led to the acceptance of a record of the past that makes a false claim to universality. For traditional history has left out not only women, but the vast majority of men. Slaves, peasants, workers, colonials were made as invisible as were women. While exceptional women of elites, such as those substituting for missing male heirs as queens and rulers, were included in the historical account, traditional history has been, by and large, the history of male elites. It has been a history presented in slices of life, incapable of reviving and re-creating the organic fullness and interconnectedness of human existence.

The male-centered historical framework was decisively challenged by the Women's History movement of the 1970s. That challenge led not only to the spread of Women's History as an established field in the profession, but to a decisive transformation in historians' thought and practice.

After forty years, what has Women's History added to historical knowledge and practice?

It brought a hitherto neglected and forgotten group into historical consciousness, thereby broadening the field of historical scholarship.

Because sources on women were scattered, often unidentified in archives, and since women were subsumed under their husbands' names, and generally underrepresented, historians of women had to find new approaches to research. They soon recognized that to find data about the past of women, their approach had to be interdisciplinary. Women's History used the tools of social, economic, and demographic history to great advantage. Anthropology and psychology provided conceptual frameworks for interpreting the conditions under which women lived. Literary sources, such as diaries, memoirs, family correspondences, fiction, and poetry by women, offered information not only about the actual lives of women, but about societal strictures and gender role definitions that defined and constrained women's lives.

Church records and those of religious orders and church-affiliated groups provided rich sources on women's spiritual, religious, and welfare concerns. Testimonials of religious conversions became a valuable source for women's life histories. Many of these sources had already been in use to describe the activities of men. But for Women's History, the emphasis and the interpretations were different.

As Women's History developed, its accomplishments enriched historical research and analysis as a whole. Five of its most significant accomplishments are worth highlighting here.

1. The methods used by historians of women to find documentation on women in sources that were not organized to make such searches accessible and the search for new and unusual sources influenced and helped other historians in dealing with hitherto neglected and silenced subjects. Historians dealing with the developing fields of various ethnicities, Gay and Lesbian History, and Jewish Women's History increasingly used interdisciplinary research, oral histories, and journalistic sources, such as letters to the editor.

2. The periodization of Women's History loomed early on as a major problem. It became clear the great "events" of world history—wars and revolutions—impacted differently on the lives of men and women. Further, economic, cultural, and technological changes that decisively altered the condition of men's lives did not similarly affect women. The conditions for women, in several aspects of their lives, showed great continuity over time, in contrast to discontinuities for men. For example, while the Industrial Revolution opened employment to a small number of women workers, they and all other women continued to be mainly engaged in housework and child rearing. The double burden of working women's longer hours of labor, combining paid work outside the home with unpaid work within the home, has continued for over 150 years and has shown an amazing consistency and resistance to change, regardless of where it is being measured. It is as true for Western countries during early industrialization as it is for developing countries under twenty-first-century globalization. Similarly, women have had access only to a gender-defined labor market, regardless of where they live. Throughout the nineteenth century in the United States, most working women were to be found in two occupations: domestic work and sex work. The same pattern shows up in today's developing countries, where sweatshop industrial work and sex work are the jobs in which most women work. Globalization has

added another innovation: migratory domestic workers who leave their families, children, and home countries and work at substandard wages and often under deplorable conditions in foreign countries. Most of these are women. Recent scholarship has shown that, for women, access to education, the availability of safe contraception, and medical reforms guaranteeing a lowering of maternal and infant death rates represent more important historical turning points than do wars and revolutions.

Different periodization in regard to historical events and differences in economic access and mobility for women and men raise serious problems about generalizations and synthesis in historical writing.

3. Women's History, by uncovering the social construct of gender, has pointed the way to showing the social construction of other categories. African American scholars long ago uncovered the social construction of race. Ethnicity has similarly been destabilized as a natural concept and has been shown to be socially constructed. Biological sexuality has also been questioned under the impact of postmodernist theories. Lesbian, Gay, and Transgender History have become scholarly fields of specialization.

4. Women's History, prodded in the 1980s by challenges from African American historians of women, opened up to a more biracial and later a multiracial perspective. The discussion of "differences" among women inevitably led to the recognition that any number of categories by which people were separated one from the other were socially constructed and that these socially constructed identities served as means of keeping elites in power. These discussions were broadened and enriched by the work of postcolonial historians and by postmodern theorists. A further extension of this critical inquiry focused on the long tradition of societies to socially create deviant out-groups, who, in times of crisis, become scapegoats for persecution, thereby shielding those truly responsible from public scrutiny. Some scholars have focused their work on exposing the interconnections and interdependency of the categories

race, gender, class, ethnicity, and sexuality. This work is ongoing and very promising. If we can at last go beyond two-dimensional descriptions to a rounded picture of how societies actually function, how power is constructed and sustained, how the subordination of large populations is organized and sustained, perhaps reform and social change could be speeded up and become more effective. Meanwhile, scholarship in a broad range of fields has been inspired and enriched by these developments.

5. Another accomplishment of Women's History is the wiping out, or at least the blurring, of distinctions between the public and private in human affairs. Since patriarchal gender definitions relegated women to the private and men to the public sphere, much of women's agency in history became hidden. By focusing on women's role, Women's History scholarship called attention to "influence" on the exercise of power, thereby gendering its inquiry. The role of petition campaigns, the unseen influences that created change in public opinion, the influence reform organizations exerted on political discourse—these and many similar themes became topics for analysis. The changed angle of vision provided by Women's History scholarship deeply affected such fields as Legal, Diplomatic, and Labor History. It also decisively transformed the writing of biography. The kind of biographies written until the 1980s, in which the public lives of public figures are discussed as though their private lives had no impact on them, are today quite rare. The new biographies examine the connections between the public and the private and offer more complex, more lifelike representations than were possible with traditional history. They point a way to a future, holistic history.

If the past is a broad river flowing toward the ocean, it cannot be described in a single snapshot or in a series of snapshots taken at different spots along its way. The river has come into being out of tiny springs that at various points along the way became joined together. It has adjusted its shape; it has narrowed and deepened when the terrain demanded it; it has eroded its banks or been confined by them. The river has overcome obstacles by creating waterfalls; it has left side branches, stagnant and irrelevant, as it formed itself into a broad stream. It is not only made of water and earth, it constantly re-forms itself in an interplay of gravity, rock hardness, wind, and moving energy. If photographs cannot adequately represent it, film can do better, but it will have to include a variety of standpoints and parameters—long shot, wide-angle lens, close-up.

The unseen aspects of the broad stream hide the obstacles overcome in its flow, hide the complex history of what made it as we see it at any given moment. The river's obstacles can be likened to the failed events in history, the unseen forces underlying public events, the resistances that shaped outcomes. Did the obstacles obstruct the flow of the river; did they restrain its breadth; did they deepen its channel and increase its strength? If the obstacles remain untold and uncharted, we cannot accurately describe what a river is—what made it and why it is as it is.

Each human action occurs within a network of forces; each is in organic connection to other forces; there is constant interplay, adjustment, and flow. It is probably impossible to adequately describe even a single event of the past in a way that encompasses all its complexity. But the historian must strive for more complexity, more awareness of the connections between the event and its surroundings—for a more holistic representation.

In real life, a person is constantly engaged in multiple activities, functioning on different levels of social organization. Dailyness and extraordinary moments of significance coexist, not impeding one another or obstructing the flow of events.

How do events interconnect? What precedes a visible event—what invisible forces, accidents, unplanned and bizarre coincidences? Conscious decisions lead to unforeseen consequences. How does the event connect to what happened before it? And after?

The play of power is never merely two-dimensional. It consists of overt power, and resistance to it, and of invisible powers—the constraints on the mighty rulers exerted by the nameless, the anonymous, the collectivities of the oppressed. Somehow, historians must be aware of these complexities and represent them.

The complexities of representing past reality are discussed by the great French historian Marc Bloch in his book *The Historian's Craft*.[1] The fact that he wrote this book while living underground as a member of the Resistance in France during the Nazi occupation attests to the urgency these questions concerning the practice of history held for him. He never finished the book; he was arrested and killed by the Germans in June 1944. Here he contrasts the methods used by scientists to those of historians, whom he compares to artists:

> From the view which I have from my window, each savant/scientist selects his proper subject without troubling himself too much about the whole. The physicist explains the blue of the sky; the chemist the water of the brook; the botanist the plants. The task of reassembling the landscape as it appears to me and excites my imagination, they leave to art. . . . The fact is that the landscape as a unity exists only in my imagination. . . . For in the last analysis it is human consciousness which is the subject-matter of history. The interrelations, confusions, and infections of human consciousness are, for history, reality itself.[2]

The scientist can limit the scope of inquiry to a distinct field; the historian, like the artist, must reassemble the whole and encompass all the fields. Bloch makes the challenge even more complex by demanding that the historian include human consciousness with all its complexities in his description. Bloch asks for the writing of holistic history: "The knowledge of fragments, studied by turns, each for its own sake, will never produce the knowledge of the whole; it will not even produce that of the fragments themselves. But the work of reintegration can come only after analysis."[3]

Marc Bloch saw the need for historians to oscillate between related phenomena running over long periods and specific moments of direct experience. A holistic history, not bound by the old categories and "fields" must be true to the multicausal, multilayered, energy-flowing interplay of forces, the clash of contradictions that make up life. Each actor on the historical scene was once a living organism set within an environment, grounded in an interplay of cultures, belief systems, superstitions, customs, and trivialities. No event in life is two- or three-dimensional; no event occurs isolated in time and space. No slice of life can present reality.

How Has Women's History Affected Historical Studies?

The emergence of "gender" as a tool of analysis was an important and transformative development. Gender is the socially constructed definition of appropriate sex roles for men and women; it varies as to time and place and culture. Used early on as a cataloging category to be added to other concepts, such as race, class, and ethnicity, in locating historical actors and explaining their decisions, it soon proved to have a far wider reach. Gender moved from being a descriptive device illuminating the social relation of the sexes to being seen as a critical factor in shaping power relations in society. As such, it proved to have strong explanatory power extending from individual decision making to public policy and law making. Alice Kessler-Harris in her book *In Pursuit of Equity: Women, Men, and the Quest for Economic Citizenship in Twentieth-Century America* brilliantly demonstrates the transformative power of gender analysis.[4] In her study of the origins of supposedly gender-neutral New Deal legislation—Social Security, unemployment insurance, fair labor standards—she reveals how deeply ingrained beliefs about gender distorted the aims of these laws so as to reinforce women's economic dependency and diminish their economic citizenship rights. Government policy, based on the generally accepted idea that the primary role of women is maternal and subsuming all women under this stereotype, sought to protect women workers from exploitation by forbidding them night work and limiting their hours of employment even if that meant curtailing women's chances of gainful employment. Protective labor legislation, based on traditional ideas of social order—men in the workforce, women in the home—regulated and institutionalized a socially segmented labor force. Thus, gender became reified in the form of proscriptive laws. In a later work, *Gendering Labor History*, Kessler-Harris argues that the division between Labor History and Women's History perpetuates an outdated male-centered framework, obscures a true understanding of class, and marginalizes women.[5] Labor History, traditionally focused on men and institutions, must incorporate gender into its analysis, she argues. For Labor History to reflect accurately the changing conditions brought on by modernization and globalization, it is essential to understand how gender shapes class formation and how private and familial values determine decisions about labor migration and the sexual division of labor. Such a new Labor History, transformed by the integration of Women's History and gender analysis into the old Labor History, represents the vanguard of a future holistic history.

Other subfields of historical scholarship have already undergone transformation thanks to the impact of Women's History and gender analysis. The awareness promoted by Women's History's contesting a strict division between the private and the public spheres has led to transformative work in Diplomatic History. Scholars such as Ann Stoler and Chandra Talpade Mohanty have shown how institutionalized gender prescriptions were used by colonial powers to reinforce their rule over the colonized.[6] Regulation by the colonizers of the sexual practices of colonized men, proscription of racial intermarriage, and the pervasive myth of the need to protect white (colonizer) women from sexual attacks by native men served to strengthen colonial rule and to limit economic choices and possibilities for the upward mobility of colonized men. The same pattern of sexual and racial regulation has been abundantly documented in African American history, where it served similar aims of reinforcing dominant power. By now, similar practices and patterns of empire building have been shown at work in India, the Dutch East Indies, Algeria, and the Near East.

Diplomatic History can no longer be told as simply the contest of states by means of negotiations between diplomatic bureaucracies and political leaders. It also must consider the multiple ways in which gender definitions and the regulation of sexuality serve as instruments for gaining and consolidating power. The transformative force of questions and methods derived from Women's History have enriched historical scholarship and rendered it more complex and more interesting.

Similarly, the recent trend toward departing from a strictly Euro- or Western-centered historical narrative reflects the engagements of historians with questions derived from Women's History and Women's Studies. Transnational history is, by definition, comparative history; it contradicts hegemonic assumptions and decenters the narrative. Recognizing the complexities of periodic events, it is multicentered and manages to integrate the various brooks, rivulets, and streams that make up the river of history in its holistic narrative.

Legal and Political History have also been changed. New questions have been raised: what has been the effect of centuries of discriminatory treatment of women on the institutions of society? On its culture? How has the construction of deviant out-groups—witches, heretics, promiscuous females, homosexuals, welfare mothers—served the interests of state power? How have gendered definitions of citizenship affected social reality? Historian Linda Kerber in her most recent book, *No Constitutional Right to Be Ladies: Women and the Obligations of Citizenship*, examines the gendered obligations (rather than the rights) of citizenship, including taxation, the duty to work, eligibility for welfare, and the duties of serving on juries and in the military.[7] Offering a sophisticated and nuanced analysis of gender- and race-defined differences, Kerber rewrites legal history from a woman-centered point of view.

Where Does Women's History Need to Go?

In answering that question I will not attempt to predict where Women's History will go, but I will express where I would like it to go.

In the past forty years, Women's History has not advanced far toward constructing a model for what a new egalitarian history of women and men might be like. Feminist theory has emerged from many other fields—sociology, literature, anthropology, psychology—all of which have influenced the work of women historians. The reverse has not been the case. Women's History has not influenced the theoretical foundations of the other disciplines.

I would like to see more theoretical work concerned with the question of how knowledge of women's actual historical past is necessary for moving women's issues forward in today's society and for gaining equality for women.

Women's History needs to continue the work of finding, reviving, and recording the missing history of half the US population. This work is far from finished. Many periods, regions, and groups remain undocumented and uninterpreted. The lives of rural women, of women of ethnic immigrant groups, and of working-class women (apart from those active in unions) have not been studied systematically. The stories and life cycles of women who combined traditional housewife and mothering roles with income-producing part-time work have been mentioned but not sufficiently documented. The multiple, often sequential child-rearing responsibilities of working-class women, who took care of their own, their relatives', and often their children's children, are cited in individual biographies but have eluded historians' research interest. While we have studied women in groups and organizations and have amply documented women in leadership roles, the majority of women have lived far different lives, with different constraints and challenges than those facing educated, middle- and upper-class women. The teachers trained by Emma Willard in her Troy, New York, Female Seminary and those trained by Catherine Beecher in her seminaries and through her American Woman's Educational Association (1852), who virtually staffed the emerging public school system before the Civil War, need to be studied individually and in groups. The women speakers who criss-crossed the country in the decade before the Civil War and for thirty years after providing cultural, educational, and political challenges to their audiences, should similarly be subject to study. They lectured to vast and enthusiastic audiences; one can only assume that they exerted some influence on these audiences. The women active in the various minor parties and mass movements of the late nineteenth century—Greenbackers, Farmers Alliances, Populists— should be identified, studied, and evaluated in terms of their impact on reform and politics. In all of the cases mentioned above, primary records are extensive and available.

Sometimes historians have used easily available and voluminous records in limited and restricted ways that do not do justice to their potential. Although the vast network of women's clubs operating from 1892 on and their organizational records could provide material for dozens of dissertations and books, they have yielded only a few, which have provided merely a descriptive overview. Yet, if even a few of these dry, organizational reports of local clubs in all the states sent annually to their national headquarters were used in combination with deep and detailed research in the particular locality, a holistic and very rich description of the actual lives and activities of ordinary women would emerge. One example of the dynamic effect of women's initially moderate reform activities concerns a club of elite white women in Honolulu, Hawaii, who were active late in the twentieth century. Concerned with fostering community beautification to encourage tourism, the women undertook as a first step to remove all advertising billboards from the highway leading from the airport to the town center. The ladies were astonished when they suddenly found themselves in deep conflict with the city fathers, many of whom were their relatives or close friends. Shocked to discover that their high status and influence were of no avail against business interests, the women refused to yield. Instead, they concluded that they must work to elect more civic-minded town leaders; they transformed their beautification club into an activist political organization. Several years later, having become a force in town politics, they succeeded. If the story of their club work was located in a deep analysis of the political, social, and economic forces in their community and was then compared with one or another case study of women's club work elsewhere, we might be able to discern long-range patterns and firmer generalizations about the meaning of women's community work than we have been able to do up to now.

Women's History should answer some basic questions relating to the meanings of the field. How did women's activities and ideas affect or change political, social, and cultural trends? Some of this work has already been done in regard to reforms of the Progressive movement, women's struggle for higher education, and the temperance and woman suffrage movements. More needs to be done.

How have individual women's improvised care for the sick and elderly shaped the organizations of communities and of government policies? Thousands of women served on school boards and on library committees decades before women had the vote—what of their stories and their collective impact? Women, African American and white, were responsible for founding the first day care centers and kindergartens in the United States. Though it was through their labor that these educational innovations became part of the public school system, the significance of this work is yet to be studied. Women's cultural activities—the founding of reading circles, libraries, museums, orchestras, and centers for art and theater—need to be studied, not in isolation, but as sex-specific activities spanning centuries. By linking and comparing various case studies, we might understand how women (as a group) acted as agents in history differently from men.

Did women act just like men in the public realm? If not, how did they act differently and why? How did this affect outcomes? We already know that women organized differently from men in communities. We know that they went about the work of gathering antislavery petitions in ways different from their male relatives. We know that their priorities for communal betterment in the Progressive period were different from those of men.

Historian Charles M. Payne, in his important book *I've Got the Light of Freedom: The Organizing Tradition and the Mississippi Freedom Struggle*, studied grassroots organizing modes in the civil rights movement from the 1940s to the present.[8] Rejecting the top-down version of history with its emphasis on the leadership of great men, Payne compared male and female patterns of organizing. He found that women were frequently the most numerous and effective force in the grassroots movement, both at the local and at the national level. Payne not only provided the reader with a powerful revisionist view of the civil rights movement, but also represented a growing and emergent trend in social history.[9]

Women's History needs to keep intellectually and institutionally separate from Gender Studies. Even though the use of gender as a tool for analysis has proven to be a useful and exciting new line of inquiry, it is no substitute for Women's History. If our long-range goal is to create a history that is organic, functional, and gender neutral, then the restorative work of Women's History must be allowed to continue for a long period of time. After all, men have been defining history as a male enterprise for at least two thousand years. In view of the overwhelmingly androcentric record of the past, the work of writing the missing history of women is a prerequisite for understanding what a truly holistic history might be like. I hesitate to ask for equal time, but certainly forty years is insufficient.

Our awareness of differences among women must permeate all our thinking. Women are at least half of every population we are studying. To do justice to this fact, we must recognize that women, like men, do not constitute an undifferentiated whole. The particulars of region, religion, ethnicity, race, and sexuality are the ground on which we must test every generalization. In so doing, we will be forced to do more comparative work, which might yield unexpected insights.

Linda Gordon's *The Great Arizona Orphan Abduction* is a masterly account of an obscure local incident that powerfully illuminates Mexican and Anglo race and gender relations, along with religious and family values, in a setting of sharp class conflict.[10] In 1904, several nuns brought forty Irish orphans from the New York Foundling Hospital to Clifton-Morenci, a small western mining town, to be placed for adoption with Catholic Mexican families who had been carefully prescreened as suitable parents. On their arrival, a waiting group of Anglo women observed the transfer of the white, blond children to the waiting Mexican parents and became highly agitated, considering these adoptions an outrage that violated taboos against interracial mixing. They incited their husbands and family members to form a vigilante group and kidnapped twenty of the children, nearly lynched the nuns and the town's priest, and forced them and the remaining children to leave town. The vigilantes coerced the Mexicans to turn the children over to them, and the Anglo women took twenty of them into their homes and later adopted them, firmly convinced they were "saving" them. When the New York Foundling Hospital sued for the return of the children, three judicial instances, from the local judge to the US Supreme Court, ruled in favor of the Anglo adoptive parents on the grounds that since the original adoptive parents were Mexican Indians, they were unfit to raise white children.

Linda Gordon deliberately used a wide-angle lens to tell this story. She interwove chapters that narrated the events with background sections giving a historical account of the major themes of the conflict. She traced the economic development of the copper mines, the importation of a Mexican workforce, the long history of struggle between management and labor culminating in a bitter strike that preceded the incident with the orphans. She explored the religious conflict between Protestants and Catholics, the differing notions of child and community welfare held by Anglo and Mexican mothers, and the conflicting cultural and family values determined by race and class. Her discussion of the history of vigilantism, western expansionism, and racism provided yet another dimension that allows us to explore the construction of citizenship and law in a constant struggle of competing definitions. Using methods from several separate disciplines, Gordon endowed a local event with multilayered meanings and a rich texture that comes as close as possible to the lived experience.

Women's History must be women-focused and woman-centered, at least until the groundwork for a new holistic history is laid. Up to now we have been able mostly to tell how women lived under patriarchy and how they coped with its constraints and sometimes overcame them. We have made small beginnings into telling the stories of how women related to other women and how they supported one another. The stories and facts we know about this aspect of women's past are scattered among organizational histories, biographies, and local stories. We need to assemble them so as to make the larger patterns visible. Women have worked for hundreds of years by building sustaining networks, some based on family affiliation, some on common interests, some on specific projects. Can we discern a distinct women's culture of organizing by networking?

Another area in which more scholarship is needed is the intellectual history of women. The centuries-old struggle of women for access to education at all its levels is well documented, but its meanings are insufficiently explored. How did their indoctrination to intellectual inferiority affect women's consciousness of self? What strategies did they devise for counteracting it? How did they formulate theories and plans for their own emancipation?

We might ask some transforming questions of our theoretical research: how has the tension between reality and image in women's lives affected women's consciousness? What is the relationship between changing gender definitions and changing economic and social conditions? What are the points of change in women's historic experience by which we might accurately periodize a history of women?

The truly transformative question remains: **If women were at the center of our analysis of any period or event, how would our account be changed?**

This seems to me the most urgent long-range question that needs to be explored. It is premature to expect to get a final answer at this moment, when the compensatory aspect of Women's History is not far enough advanced to make a large body of historical materials about women available in adequate quantities to match information about men. But I think we can first of all begin to think about such a possibility and consider what steps might have to be taken to devise a model.

Finally, looking both backward and forward, I see the task of pursuing and maintaining Women's History as one of truly revolutionary significance. Not only are we restoring their history to contemporary women and those of the future, we are bringing the past of women of all kinds into the center of intellectual discourse, thereby disproving, once and for all, the distorted patriarchal version of the past that has been sold to both men and women as a true account.

I believe the work we have done in the past forty years illustrates that men and women have had a different relationship to history. They also have had a different experience of history. Even if they themselves belong to oppressed groups, men have lived with an intellectual construct called History that affirmed the agency and heroism of people like themselves, namely men. They have told and retold the story of male superiority, and many have believed it.

Women have experienced the past as a series of humiliations, defeats, and disasters. For them, living with the construct History has affirmed their inferiority, passivity, and lack of imitable heroines. I believe that the different experiences of history for men and women have created actual differences between the sexes that are more significant and determinative than are the obvious biological differences. If I am right and women and men have lived in different cultures, then the work of righting this false version of the past is more than educational and reformist, it is revolutionary and restorative. The Renaissance put Western white men in the center of history. The Enlightenment asserted the abstract rights of individuals and allowed the middle class access to political power. Now it is the turn of half of humankind, women, to understand that we have always been equal, always had a history, and always shared in the building of civilization and its mental products.

The new holistic history will at last come closer than anything that has been written up to now to presenting a rounded picture of past events, inclusive of the viewpoints and actions of those hitherto forgotten and left out. In so doing, it will ground women's claims for equality in the solid record of past achievements and make women realize their collective strength and their individual abilities. This new history, in which women and men will be at the center of power and agency will, for the first time, make equality more than an abstract goal. It will make equality a realistic possibility.

NOTES

This article was originally published in Gerda Lerner, *Living with History/Making Social Change* (Chapel Hill: University of North Carolina Press, 2009), 163–79.

[1] Marc Bloch, *The Historian's Craft: Reflections on the Nature and Uses of History and the Techniques and Methods of the Men Who Write It*, trans. Peter Putnam (New York: Alfred A.Knopf, 1953).

[2] Bloch, *The Historian's Craft*, 150, 151.

[3] Bloch, *The Historian's Craft*, 155.

[4] Alice Kessler-Harris, *In Pursuit of Equity: Women, Men, and the Quest for Economic Citizenship in Twentieth-Century America* (New York: Oxford University Press, 2001).

[5] Alice Kessler-Harris, *Gendering Labor History* (Urbana: University of Illinois Press, 2007).

[6] Ann Laura Stoler, *Carnal Knowledge and Imperial Power: Race and the Intimate in Colonial Rule* (Berkeley: University of California Press, 2002); Chandra Talpade Mohanty, *Feminist Genealogies, Colonial Legacies, Democratic Futures* (London: Routledge, 1997).

[7] Linda K. Kerber, *No Constitutional Right to Be Ladies: Women and the Obligations of Citizenship* (New York: Hill and Wang, 1998).

[8] Charles M. Payne, *I've Got the Light of Freedom: The Organizing Tradition and the Mississippi Freedom Struggle* (Berkeley: University of California Press, 1995).

[9] For another example of the new scholarship on the civil rights movement, see Barbara Ransby, *Ella Baker and the Black Freedom Movement: A Radical Democratic Vision* (Chapel Hill: University of North Carolina Press, 2003).

[10] Linda Gordon, *The Great Arizona Orphan Abduction* (Cambridge, MA: Harvard University Press, 1999).

CHAPTER 18

I Am My Sister's Keeper: Women's Archives, a Reflection

ELIZABETH A. MYERS

MOST ARCHIVISTS WOULD AGREE THAT THE CURRENT AND NECESSARY PROFESSIONAL EMPHASIS ON DIGITAL CONTENT HAS OVERSHADOWED OTHER SIGNIFICANT AND RELATED ISSUES WITHIN THE FIELD. While much reasonable concern and welcome celebration is expressed by archivists around digital culture, the conversation often drowns out other professional trends that technological advance promises. Herein is a point of contention that suggests the hubbub over technology and digital content might belie a deeper concern within the profession over its own relevance and identity. This anxiety manifests itself most clearly in the revived debates over the very purpose of archives and the role of the archivist: a division that places digital records managers (evidence values) on one side and custodians of collective memory (cultural values) on the other.[1] On the one hand, the concern is practical. All archivists should want to avoid the "impotence of virtue," especially with administrators making important funding decisions.[2] On the other hand, the concern is more existential. That archives and archivists *should* exist is not a convincing argument to ensure that they always will; neither does it help guide the form it should take. Both sides rest on the essential question: why do we do what we do? To a profession that has always struggled with its public image and experienced difficulty in defining its social and cultural value, the future may seem uncertain indeed.

Happily, the existence of these concerns has not produced professional paralysis. In fact, we see quite the opposite. Archives and archivists are more visible and vital now than ever before in our professional history. The best example of this revitalization is the multifaceted emphasis that many archivists place on access, including reference services, promotion and advocacy, social media, and institutional websites, as portals for content and information about the repository. Add to this an influx of civic- and public-minded archivists into the profession, expansive collaborative projects, and repository-level adoption of useful technologies, and the image of archivist as gateway, rather than gatekeeper, is affirmed. In this context, there are numerous examples from the field of evidence versus cultural archival ideologies that are not hotly contested; neither are these constructs treated as mutually exclusive. Yet, the struggle over professional identity persists and concerns over the future of the profession seem to grow rather than subside.

Ultimately, as the archival paradigm shift continues, it is important to remember that while archives and archivists are universally affected by technology, we are not wholly defined by it. Instead, by seeking to steer a course through anxiety over purpose, archivists should make themselves students of those models of archival tradition, evolution, and relevance where they already exist. To wit, in this seventy-fifth anniversary year of the founding of the World Center for Women's Archives, this book of essays offers a rare chance to reflect on the past, present, and future of women's archival traditions. Within its pages and from multiple perspectives, a solid feminist intellectual tradition connected to the practice of women's archives emerges. Some may believe that the (re)discovery of feminist roots within any tradition should be avoided. Yet that history is analogous to women's archives—the two cannot and should not be separated. Further, (re)discovery of the feminism within women's archives practice is an essential way to honor the past, actively engage with the intellectual tradition today, and guide women's archives into the future. Rejecting the antiquated silo model of archival practice, the traditions of women's archives also offer extraordinary lessons for the archives profession as a whole. Certainly, few other types of archives have had to suffer the questioning of their worth for as long, while an equally limited number of archives have had to struggle continually with their politically charged foundational roots.

Then and Now: (Re)discovering Traditions

One might think that archivists automatically excel at the practice of history. In the late nineteenth and early twentieth centuries, despite the warnings of Sir Hilary Jenkinson, the line between historian and archivist was thin and traversable.[3] This generally remains true today as the qualitative value of a master's degree in history for archivists persists despite steep competition from other academic disciplines. The analysis of archival history itself, though not without its dramatic twists and turns, is really a tale of consolidation and unification of professional archival practice in the early twentieth century. While the later effect of the civil rights movement on archives has also been well documented, the explosion of identity- and subject-based archives that followed tends to be where the narrative slows or even stops.

As is generally conceded, since social historians desired subject archives and subject collections—especially related to race, ethnicity, and class—in the 1960s and 1970s, they came to be. In other words, archivists found themselves responding quickly to the tectonic shifts within the history profession. By this account, archivists appear reactionary rather than visionary, which—as demonstrated by this book—is not a wholly fair characterization. At the same time, it must be recognized that archivists have not always been among the vanguard of those moving the archives profession forward. This tendency is reflected clearly in the post–civil rights market demand for subject-identity archives, but it does not reveal the older, often complicated, and fraught process by which an entire genre of archival practice came to be. More specifically, the stories of the men and women who founded women's archives after the turn of the twentieth century remain, in the contemporary professional literature, fairly opaque. We might wonder, what drove them to see the absence of women within the record and make the difficult, sometimes forsaken, attempts to rectify the problem? What lessons might their trials offer archivists today interested in working toward a more complete and diverse human record? Thanks in large part to the work represented in this book, we can conclude that the connection between feminist ideology and the feminist archival practice ebbed just as the larger feminist political movement did. What remained in the memory of archival practitioners of that legacy was, sadly, fragmentary.

A principal lesson from the collected essays of this book is the rediscovery of that long feminist tradition in women's archives. Aptly demonstrated in the chapters by Anke Voss and Eva Moseley, the early history of formal women's archives is firmly anchored in the feminist impulse of the first wave, both in terms of politics and sociopolitical ideology.[4] Though the desire to document women could be reduced to the overt and hence highly documented woman suffrage movement, the poignant truth is that the wave had crested and was diminishing with still much to be done—women were not yet equal in the fullest sense of the word. Women's archives proponents, especially women like Mary Ritter Beard, recognized that documenting women was itself an argument of and for women's equality. This concept was revolutionary; it inspired the founding collections of Radcliffe and Smith and mirrored parallel impulses in Europe.[5] This is not to claim that only women's archives collected women's papers or that women's archivists were the only practitioners who saw an absence in the records. Women have always found their way into the papers of men, institutions, and organizations in and out of the public sphere as is clearly demonstrated by Janice Ruth in her essay on the holdings of the Library of Congress. But, as noted by Moseley and others, to varying degrees, women's records were treated with disregard if not disdain.[6] The inherent value of women's collections and papers, wherever they were found, was at best diminished by the very people employed to collect the documents and use them for research. What most archivists concede now—and early women's archives proponents understood then—is that collection and appraisal are very subjective processes. A feminist critique in particular lends itself to a better understanding of how norms can consciously or unconsciously marginalize minorities and of what dire consequences exclusion has for those left outside of the norm. The generalized historical narrative that results might be easier for an audience to digest, but it is hardly accurate. So it is with women's documented history.

The 1930s feminist challenge to inequality in the records also stands out as a transition in the US feminist movement from concrete political objectives (i.e., the vote) to more localized and sociocultural-based objectives (i.e., documenting women). Perhaps, as Eva Moseley maintains, there might come a day when women's archives would be unnecessary because men and women would be equally represented in the historical record. But in the early postsuffrage years, the creation of women's archives was still an overtly political act; the creation itself functioned as a critique of the existing historical profession, a claim toward women's equality, and a way to engender consciousness among women. Though the connection has yet to be made explicitly in research, a tentative claim could be that the legacies of women's collections, well under way in the pre–World War II period, fed the imaginations of young women who grew into the vanguard of the second wave. If that connection is too tenuous, then another subtext that emerges from this book is the remarkable parallel between the growth of women's archives after World War I *and* after World War II.

Women's archives of the first wave lacked one essential element that the second wave enjoyed—namely, a radical shift in the history profession. Gerda Lerner, in particular, effectively frames the increased demand for sources usable for social history and women's history in the opening essay of this book, but other contributors remark on it as well. Also well noted is the effect of the demand for new sources on the archives profession: new collecting policies, new archives, re-evaluation of existing collections, and renewed partnership with historians in collection development are all meaningful examples. This sequence of events reveals the extent to which the archives profession was challenged by outsiders—in this case, new historians seeking to write a new kind of history. Kären Mason illustrates how meetings of feminist historians at the Organization of American Historians (OAH) conferences, including Gerda Lerner and Anne Firor Scott, shifted attention to existing women's archives and collections that had been long overdue. Though the road from those early meetings at OAH to Andrea Hinding's *Women's History Sources* is hardly a straight one, the renewed collaborative partnership struck between historians and archivists is worthy of reflection.[7]

Without a doubt, these initial demands for women's collections and the writing of women's history began with the simple recognition that the value of women's collections remained seriously diminished between the wars and after. That diminishment was true of archivists and historians alike, with some important exceptions. As such, the renewed support of women's archives and records in the 1970s remained an act as overtly political and feminist as it had been forty years earlier. Couched within the larger civil rights movement, however, women's search for women's history paralleled a larger rights-and-identity revolution, thereby giving women's equality—and the feminism on which it was based—a degree of legitimacy and power that had been absent in the 1930s. At the same time, the search for sources and the growth of women's archives also reveals the fundamental limits of both first- and second-wave women's archives initiatives.

Audrey T. McCluskey and Deborah Gray White clearly demonstrate the extent to which the political and social feminism of the 1960s and 1970s failed to address the issues of all women and their archival materials. African American women were first to cry foul to historians and archivists, both within and outside the profession. While parallel documenting projects and collecting of African American women's records emerged, in particular the Black Women in the Middle West Project (BWMW), the charge of women's collecting *as middle- and upper-class white women's collecting* persisted. That critique ultimately helped all women's archival practice: archivists gained a keen recognition of how marginalization functions at multiple levels in multiple places and is constantly changing over time. In short, "personhood" and "citizenship" meant different things to different people along different racial, ethnic, religious, and gender lines. Another consequence of the gender-racial critique was the recognition that absent records are often the result of accidental omission as well as intentional exclusion based on the ideologies of the document creator and the perceived future historic value of persons documented. Unless archivists are able to practice Jenkinsonian principles flawlessly, which is unlikely under the best of circumstances, then we have to recognize that even deliberate, well-intentioned appraisal decisions *to include* always function *to exclude* as well. This realization has resulted in a general rethinking of the boundaries of *woman* with important, even radical, ramifications for all archivists. At least in theory, by viewing history through the prism of identities, the historical profession helped complicate archival practice. Further, these new identities did not easily translate within known schemas or categories of control.

Oral histories provide a premier example of this rethinking. As noted at length by White, the strength of an oral history tradition within African American communities offered historians and archivists a different way of defining a record and prompted them to ask entirely new questions about how the record is created. What role did the format have in the value of the story it contained? Could or should archivists be cocreators of the records? What were the barriers (past and present) that kept women hidden from or hidden within the record? How could archivists document the otherwise hard-to-document? The answer is, in retrospect, simple: African American women, working-class women, immigrant women, and many others can be found within the stories of their own communities. This shift raises anew the importance of locality in the archival profession. While geography has always been a way to narrow collecting scopes and revise archival missions, oral histories capture happenings at a particular place, in a particular time, for people who might not otherwise be included in any formal historic record.

Of course, oral history is also a powerful counterpoint to the limits of a written record, which include the long-standing tradition of oral history in some communities, the function of artifact-as-story-telling, and illiteracy. The valuing of unwritten records rejects the Western Eurocentric expectation of how legitimate, authentic records are created and by whom. These insights, which emerged from the criticisms brought forth by African American women's collections in the 1980s and 1990s, gave women's archives programs new impetus and direction by inspiring archivists to rethink what *woman* means and how that history is created and captured. The lessons proved immediately helpful in the women's archives community even as the second-wave feminist impulse subsided.

Though the women's liberation movement celebrated many victories in the 1970s and 1980s, many barriers (seen and unseen) remained anachronistically in place. The shift from legal and political feminism to cultural and social feminism in the 1980s and 1990s is often seen as an ebbing within the feminist rights movement, very similar to the pattern of the 1930s. Yet it is in the fading of the overtly political feminist movement that Kären Mason and Tanya Zanish-Belcher offer a convincing argument in support of the relevance of women's archives. Noting an exponential growth of new women's archives in the 1990s, their case is made largely to refute claims that women-only archives created a ghetto of isolation for women's collections, while at the same time privileging women's collections to the detriment of other subject records. Underlying these criticisms at the time was the surge in postmodernist thinking inside both the academy and the archival profession. A rejection of positivism, the essential framework of postmodernism is to recognize the subjectivity of human experience through a deconstruction of texts—words, symbols, images—which results in the lack of any singular Truth about the lived experience.[8] Within this context, for example, there is no man and no woman; there is only the construction and/or deconstruction of masculinity and femininity. Not coincidentally, the surge in postmodern theory paralleled a much more popular discourse that feminism is unnecessary because women had proved themselves to be equal. Both arguments could be reduced to the question of whether feminism—and, by extension, women's archives—held any continued relevance. Certainly, if either argument prevailed, then women's archives and the ideology that long underpinned their operation and growth would be rendered meaningless.

What Mason and Zanish-Belcher offer in response is brilliant for its truth and simplicity: women's archives were, are, and remain a substantial symbolic representation of the value that society ascribes to the materials contained within. This harkens to French philosopher Jacques Derrida's claim that "the arkhe—the archives—appears to represent the *now* of whatever kind of power is being exercised, anywhere, in any place or time."[9] Similarly, Michel Foucault claimed that "the archives does not so much stand in for the idea of what can or cannot be said, but rather *is* 'the system that establishes statements as events and things.'"[10] Taken together, these ideas reckon the archives as an institution *and* as a symbol that represents a core value system of society. Archivists capture and keep materials perceived to hold value to the society—now and in the future. To keep any item is to render unto it meaning and importance that is automatically stripped from the discarded. Women's archives provide, and, I argue, have always provided, a politicized collecting model for sub-cultural or marginalized groups. By collecting the uncollected, archivists render those individuals and groups valuable; by keeping the materials of the previously invisible, we make them visible. Further, as the authors note, the rectification of women's absence in history is hardly complete. Women's archives, by their very existence, promote the study of women by making those records accessible. In many cases, the archives emphasize local communities and women's unique recordkeeping and storytelling methods, while also serving as a continual reminder that though some women may exist in larger collections, systemic barriers exist to limit access to them. In this broader analysis, keeping and expanding women's collections, creating new access points to the collections, and correcting metadata equates to a social valuing of women as a whole.

The substance of Mason and Zanish-Belcher's 1999 work is refined in the article "Raising the Archival Consciousness," originally published in 2007. Therein the authors reiterate the value of women's archives as a model for documenting the non- or underdocumented, including rural women, working-class women, the disabled, women's ethnic subcultures, and women on the right—to name just a few examples. They also make clear an assumption that has existed in the roots of feminist archival prac-tice since its inception: to claim a feminist archival tradition is to recog-nize that not all points of view are represented elsewhere. This idea is at the core of much of the archival tradition writ large. Archivists collect materials that are unique and original, by intent or accident documenting multiple points of view for researchers to suss out.

Danelle Moon, Susan Tucker, and Janice Ruth all explore different expressions of feminist recordkeeping and archival practice. Moon's analysis of documenting the second wave reveals powerful connections between the so-called first and second waves of women's collecting efforts. The significance of this work, however, is in her continued emphasis on locality and inclusion. Citing multiple examples of locally based women's archives projects, including the collection and cocreation of oral histories, the value of women's archives lies in their regional (or smaller) focus on local women's history. While larger institutions (such as the Library of Congress and Smith College) have always collected women's history and continue to do so, even these venerable institutions cannot collect everything. The strength in microcollecting is, as Moon argues, the ability to better document local activity, to contextualize the records through individuals and organizations only locally known, and to understand the effect of geography on the formation of history. The uniqueness of women's records is also emphasized in the work of Tucker who, in the spirit of oral history enthusiasts before her, challenges archivists of women's collections to rethink record format through a gendered lens. Women's work and sociocommunity pastimes are, in this sense, revalued in a profoundly feminist way. Quilts, scrapbooks, diaries, and oral histories all contribute to documentary diversity of women's lived experience.[11] Further, Tucker exposes the essentially gendered nature of recordkeeping itself that moves beyond the metanarrative of professional versus nonprofessional collecting habits. Instead, proximity to elders and fixed locality (family roots) result in what can only be thought of as the feminine and domestic nature of family history.

Several essays of this book give repeated evidence of a mature, if implicit, feminist tradition. These investigations are proof that contemporary supporters practice feminist inquiry and uphold a feminist archival tradition. More specifically, Taronda Spencer reveals the challenge of women's history (and archives and archivists) to reevaluate existing collections to find the previously ignored. Her primary example is that of the

Historically Black Colleges and Universities Archival Survey Project and a useful analysis of corresponding—not competing—documentation of African American women. At the root of her analysis is the smart critique of how African American women's identity has always been multidimensional, obscuring easy generalizations about race, class, and gender, especially over time.

Mary Caldera's history of the Lesbian Herstory Archives in New York City offers an essentially feminist analysis of discrimination and marginalization that is made evident in the effect of women's archival traditions as well as critique of it. Noting a pattern applicable to most marginalized groups, Caldera argues that the gay and lesbian community moved from invisible to local community building to wider, mainstream visibility over time. Though much is still required for the establishment of legal rights and equalities, LGBTQ history and archival tradition reiterate the feminist theory of multiple positionality or points of view as well as multiple points of marginalization. For example, being a woman is one aspect of marginalization that is complicated by race and sexual orientation among other identities; a Catholic Chicana lesbian has multiple points of consciousness and multiple points of potential oppression—including parallel potential for exclusion from the historical record.[12] The response to the exclusion is the ongoing founding and growth of community-based LGBTQ archives.

Though perhaps not naturally regarded as allies in other contexts, the archives of women religious experience problems similar to those of lesbian archives. Fernanda Perrone demonstrates how women religious are barely visible to the wider society and culture unless perhaps by caricature. Though the exclusion from the record is not part of any intentional campaign or controversy to exclude women from the larger record, women religious nevertheless experience grave exclusion. Existence within a strict hierarchy, such as the Catholic Church, can often strip the individual of autonomy and thus the existence of an autonomous record documenting her lived experience. Women religious have also been subject to self- and system-imposed expectations of modesty. Finally, as Perrone notes, documenting the religious always confronts the problem of documenting faith—an abstract, often intangible form of personal, often private, expression. Recalling Moon here, how must archivists of women religious or religious communities more broadly rethink documentation of the women faithful? Herein is a question for archivists: how do we document belief and nonbelief?

The challenges of women's documentation are also revealed by Tanya Zanish-Belcher in reference to reproduction. In this case, the parallel questions of how to document and in what documentary form are framed by topic instead of by a specific group of women. Yet, as Zanish-Belcher maintains, the topic affects all people and presents significant barriers to traditional records collection ideologies. Primary among them is the concern for privacy and confidentiality that sex and reproduction collections automatically carry. In addition, reproduction is a generally marginalized topic due to social taboos. Zanish-Belcher provides a long and impressive list of reproduction-related collections and archives. But, as she points out, this belies the extent to which researchers and archivists are confronted by limited or skewed metadata. She challenges archivists to rethink and revisit their own collections and engage in proactive outreach to document the issue of reproduction and sexual health, rightly admonishing those who do so to document the issue, not only one side of it.

Virginia Corvid's presentations of the feminist and uniquely woman-centered world of zines offers an interesting, if unintentional, response to the call of Zanish-Belcher, as well as the microcollecting described by Moon. Hyperlocality reigns again as many of the low-production-cost zines reflect the specific places of their creation as well as the specific points of view of the women who created them. The zines also document, in sometimes deeply personal ways, the creator's opinions, feelings, and experiences of sex and sexuality. Corvid makes explicit the developed sense of interconnectedness of the zine community through read-and-responses, local references, and consciousness raising in the dissemination of shared understanding based on a largely feminist ideology. Though her intent is to rightfully critique past collecting strategies related to zines generally, the result is the exposure of a unique woman-centered subculture and how it is fundamentally endangered by traditional collecting and classification schemas.

What this book demonstrates, in particular through sections 2 and 3, is the vast importance of inclusion and locality in collection development. Archivists must focus on finding women *where they are*, whether in HBCUs, convents, lesbian communities, reproductive health collectives, or zines, for example. The expectation that traditional records—vital, government, and institutional—will somehow capture the complexity of women's lived experience is irresponsible, if not dangerous, for archivists to maintain. In addition, archivists are fundamentally responsible for engaging all publics that their archives serve and must reevaluate those publics critically and often. Who is being collected, how, and why? Who is not being collected, how, and why? Ultimately, this is the lesson for the profession as a whole: relevance of the documents and the archives that house them does not depend upon the twists and turns of the political and social winds but rather upon the inherent value of both, transcendent of time. While archivists could persist in the 1950s model of being passive, rather than active, agents of the documentary future, all indications point to the opposite. What makes archives essential in this context is not that we collect the low-hanging fruit, but that we are agents of discovery, salvage, and preservation of the utterly unique that might otherwise be lost. That is a tremendous legacy of the feminist impulse of the first women's archives and a guide for the profession into the future.

Holistic Archives: A Feminist Vision, a Feminist Future

In her essay, "Holistic History: Challenges and Possibilities," Gerda Lerner offers some predictions on the future of women's history based "on the privilege of my age. Old women and men, at the end of life, are entitled to express their vision." Lerner is entitled to much more than that. Archivists and historians alike owe women like Lerner a great debt. Minimally, that debt comes with an obligation to recognize her role and dogged determination to turn a profession over, exposing an untidy underbelly of

exclusionary practice. Like Mary Ritter Beard before her, Lerner recognized that consciousness was born from more than just votes and laws.
Women have long internalized their own marginalization, their own minimal worth, because androcentricism was (and is) so systemic. To challenge the system meant a fundamental reordering of values, with special
respect to sexual equality. Lerner's assessment of the accomplishments of
women's history—which must be shared with archivists—is detailed, the
accomplishments far reaching. Her description of future directions for
her field is just as instructive for the future of women's archives.

One of Lerner's principal concerns is the need to keep women's history intellectually and institutionally separate from gender studies. This
is already a heated debate within women's studies and gender studies
departments, the consequences of which have yet to break out of academia and into public discourse.[13] The emergence of gender studies cou-
pled with a shift in the generational demographic of students presents a
serious challenge to the traditional structure of women's studies with its
focus on the essential woman. Scholars of color have already correctly and
successfully challenged the rigid boundaries of the definition of *Woman/
Women*, just as women's archives have.[14] But, beginning in the late 1980s
and early 1990s, and backed by the rise of postmodernism, *gender* posed
for many second-wave feminists a more significant challenge to the basic
premise of why women's studies or women's history should exist at all.
The early proponents of *gender* as a category of analysis were from different disciplines, but the main protagonists included women philosophers
and historians such as Judith Butler and Joan W. Scott, respectively.[15] The
issue was, and remains, the theoretical distance between *woman* (biologically defined) and *gender* (the social and cultural construction). Lerner's
argument—that androcentricism is not yet fully destroyed and therefore
the focus on gender is premature—is echoed by others wishing to retain
a sex-based focus on the practice of history and in other academic disciplines. But what does gender mean for women's archives?

Ultimately, archivists—and women's archivists in particular—must
recognize that there are larger shifts taking place within academia, which
may yet have a great impact on archival practice. Though archivists are

not wholly reactionary, we know that archivists have been prodded, sometimes forcefully, into new collection areas. There is little need for that pattern to repeat among contemporary practitioners. This may mean that women's archivists have to think in broader terms about the documents of gender—which may in fact be different than the records of biological sex—but also be inclusive of women's issues. One example is the question of inclusion or exclusion of transsexual persons in women's archives or individuals who cross-dress or identify as transgender. Another example includes documenting masculinity and femininity along the same thematic lines as in film, advertising, fiction, music, dress, and online and other places where gender negotiation is active. Archivists should look for the places where gender appears most inflexible and contested—where the negotiation is *in process*. Collecting in this context is less about individuals and organizations, than about documenting the exchange of ideas. A prime example within this book is the issue of sexual reproduction, but there are many others including faith, work, family, politics, and so forth. Perhaps archivists would do well to remember that a new generation of gender scholars is emerging into the field with new questions and is looking, perhaps, for new types of documents. At the same time, all women negotiate gender and its construction every day to varying degrees. On that basis alone, archivists of women's collections should pay attention to and think critically about how gender is documented and how that documentation is preserved.

From the metalevel view of women's archives, however, archivists are already documenting, even if by accident, various social and cultural negotiations around gender. Recalling the basic premise of postmodernism as the study of *texts* that create and destroy common understanding of the world, it must be conceded that archivists are practicing postmodernism whether they like it or not. The traditional and nontraditional documents of women's history are already filled with examples of women's built social roles, gendered expectations, and rebellions against or reinforcement of gender norming. As a result, by documenting women, women's archivists are already documenting gender, if in an unintentional way. While the addition of *gender* as a category of analysis offers scholars another boundary by which to deal with content, it does not follow that archivists must redefine their practices. Arguably, repositories collect regardless of the theoretical framework employed by the researcher, and so postmodernism is not a way to invalidate the worth of women's archives as much as it is another tool to be used within the archives itself. Therefore, women's archivists must be aware of and perhaps anticipate the debates within academia and work toward complimentary documenting strategies when possible, but also not be consumed by them.

Another area of concern for Lerner is the function of women's history to unearth those women still left out of the historical narrative: local women, rural women, the disabled, ethnic minorities, immigrants, working-class women, housewives, part-time workers, transient women, and mothers, to name a few. This repeats sentiment already discussed by Mason and Zanish-Belcher who add the critique that, given the feminist roots of women's archives, collecting practices can and do reflect a feminist bias that omits groups or individuals with differing opinions, such as pro-life groups and otherwise politically conservative women. I agree wholeheartedly. Though women's archives and those who collect women's records more broadly have made tremendous leaps and bounds in documenting women's history, there remains much work to be done. As in all archives, there are practical, institutional limitations to extensive outreach programs. But in considering the value of women's archives in the twenty-first century, documenting the full experience of women broadly defined must be at the top of the list even if it requires a reordering of resources with which to do it. The lessons of this book—why women's archives came into existence and how they have transformed our understanding of who and how to document—have to be reemployed by supporters of the field. The impulse to document women who might otherwise be marginalized, women whose points of view differ from the mainstream or even our own, women who are otherwise exiled to the periphery of history, have to be reclaimed. The consequence of not embracing this truly holistic type of collecting will be the stagnation of women's archives as a whole. In particular, I charge women's archives practitioners to continue to rethink *Woman/Women* and focus on the places of women's experience in a thematic framework. This practice is illustrated in part by the essays on reproduction, women religious, lesbian communities, and zines. But where else might we look? Documenting women's subcultures is not just a way to find the esoteric; it is a methodology of holding up a mirror to the dominant society and finding a complex history reflected back.

Finding women's subcultures and other marginalized locations also requires rethinking of documentation itself. As Tucker thoughtfully illustrates women's unique role within families, capturing and keeping their own history, so too must all women's archivists conceive of women's lived experience as complex and, as such, documented in multiple and perhaps unexpected ways. This practice emulates feminist scholarship that emphasizes women's own lived experiences as the best starting point from which to build knowledge.[16] Women's double consciousness—of their own lives and of the dominant systems governing it—lends to endless possibilities of documentation and study.[17] For example, what can archivists do to document gendered spaces such as hair salons, bridal shops, strip clubs, department stores, or family planning health facilities and the activities going on within? What about women's social activities such as running clubs, gyms, roller derbies, prayer groups, children's play groups, schools, book clubs, home sales parties, or women-centered social networks (online or in person)? Can archivists do more to document women at work, the reasons they leave the workforce, or barriers to returning after an absence? How are these questions essentially reframed by geography, religion, class, and race? Asking these and other questions re-inscribes the role of the archivist as active and conscious of documenting the diversity and complexity of women's lives. In this context, the standard dichotomy of documenting the powerful or powerless is less central than the more general purpose of documenting all women, in whatever ways possible.

Further, finding un- or underdocumented women also means reaching new audiences in the form of new donors and new users. Also, donor advocacy responds directly to the aforementioned "impotence of virtue" of archives and combats contemporary criticisms and the claim that "everything is online." Indeed, the proliferation of modern documents (duplication) and the relative ease of sharing records online is referenced often in the professional literature. As a consequence, the uniqueness of archival materials operating in a traditional context is seriously diminished. However, archivists must successfully argue that while there is some duplication of contemporary materials and easy access to some materials online, every effort is being made to collect in areas that are otherwise uncollected or remain nondigital. We still seek the rare and unique, even if the delivery method of those materials is radically different than it was twenty years ago. Further, there will never be an end point to which archives are able to claim a complete record on any subject, even those well represented in manuscript collections. So much remains, especially among the marginalized, to be found and protected. Women's archivists in particular are smartly placed to continue the practice of finding hidden women—this is the tradition inherited from a long, complex professional past—but all archivists should certainly follow the model. New donors and the scarcity of the documents can underscore the value of the materials for users as well.

Another question that vexes Lerner is how does knowledge of women's history actively push forward the agenda of women's equality? This question is an ideal vehicle to address how contemporary women's archives transcend collection and documentation barriers, in particular with the help of digital technologies. More generally, unbound from the physical survey and print media, technology revolutionized the playing field of big archives versus small, local versus national, subject versus broadly defined—though serious resource gaps persist between individual archives. This is especially true for women's archives. One need not look further than the many cited examples in this book—the historic impact of widespread OCLC adoption, the expansion of NUCMC, the accelerated use of EAD finding aids, as well as the network of H-Net Women, the Women's Archives Roundtable, the Women Archivists Roundtable, and leadership examples at the national level such as the Library of Congress's "American Women" web page—for proof of the transformative power of new technologies. Without question, the Internet has broken down barriers between archives, archivists, and users in very meaningful ways. The democratizing of archives through the web is often itself an opportunity for collaboration—emphasizing the value of locality but ending the physical isolation that can accompany it. In this sense, women's archives actively push the agenda of women's equality by participating in access tools that, by definition, do not privilege content but emphasize heretofore inaccessible materials. The more accessible the content, the larger the challenge to persistent critics who assume women's contributions to history have been minimal. Further, the democratic nature of the web means that there is a community of women's archives participants not easily defined as a monolithic group. Intentionally or not, some are helping to redefine traditional boundaries of both women's archives and professional archivists. In fact, one may argue that some of the new digital archives and women's history initiatives are significantly pushing boundaries of archival practice, bringing full circle the discourse around the current archival paradigm shift. Examining some examples of the neo-archival impulse bears out the roots of some professional anxiety but, more importantly, gives hope and direction to the future of archives as a whole.

One major example of this phenomenon is the Jewish Women's Archive (JWA). Launched in 1995, the JWA's mission is to "uncover, chronicle, and transmit to a broad public the rich history of American Jewish women."[18] The website, which serves as the main portal to all JWA public functions, is free and open to all users. The staff of the JWA is notably free from the markers of traditional archival training, instead boasting several PhDs and a mix of educational backgrounds, including study in literature, American civilization, English, education, and communications. The JWA markets itself as a virtual archives, which translates to serving as an interactive resource guide for primary sources related to Jewish women in North America. A kind of one-stop shop for users, the JWA offers an encyclopedia of Jewish women and issues, lesson plans for teachers, online exhibits, film guides, active blogs, and short oral histories. The oral history collections are particularly deep, created and exhibited in part via podcast by the JWA, and feature a "Community Oral History" subset that includes "Katrina's Jewish Voices," "Contemporary Activists," and "Weaving Women's Words."[19] The site also encourages user-created content through comments, questions, and suggestions. In addition, the JWA offers an "On the Map" interactive module so that users can contribute knowledge about landmarks significant to Jewish women's history. JWA also offers a very accessible "How-To" guide for preserving family papers and conducting oral history interviews with Jewish women. All the while, the site offers users a chance to follow the JWA through Twitter, Facebook, Tumblr, YouTube, Digg, StumbleUpon, and email.

Screenshot of the Jewish Women's Archive website, http://jwa.org.

From the JWA website emerges the model of a nonphysical archives functioning as a portal to an information community framed by archival materials. The cooperative and interactive nature of the website means that the content is not mediated by any one person, such as an archivist. In fact, there are no archivists present. Instead, the JWA functions as a third party in collecting content, makes referrals to brick-and-mortar archives, promotes the use of historical resources, and offers links to widely available subject-based research. The smart use of the "On the Map" feature, among other functions, allows users to contribute content, thereby building a wide body of knowledge that might otherwise be kept at the local level. The interactive nature of the website also engenders an investment on the part of contributors. While managed by the JWA, the website contains information related and relative to a much wider audience. One need not think further than *Wikipedia* for a widely popular and successful model of this approach. While the features of the JWA website could be part of a general Jewish archives and research center (such as the Spertus Institute in Chicago), the existence of the JWA continues to highlight and thereby emphasize women's unique contributions to the historical record.[20] The very existence of the JWA does not undermine any other Jewish or Jewish women's archives; rather, it is an important supplement to those traditional archives.

Screenshot of Washington Women's History Consortium, "Walking Tour " web page,
http://www.washingtonhistory.org/research/whc/WAWomen/walkingtour/.

Another example is the collaborative project, the Washington Women's History Consortium (WWHC). Created by state statute in 2005 as part of a Washington State Historical Society project, the WWHC is "dedicated to preserving and making available resources about Washington women's history."[21] Whereas the JWA functions as an agent and portal to archives and historical preservation broadly defined, the WWHC is a partnership of several representatives of public history, including the Washington State Library, the State Archives, Western Washington University, Central Washington University, Eastern Washington University, Washington State University, and the Northwest Museum of Arts and Culture. The initial goal was to launch the website and coordinate efforts around the Centennial of Women's Suffrage in Washington (1910–2010), but the outreach platform and purpose of the WWHC has expanded since.[22] Recipient of a major National Endowment for the Humanities (NEH) grant, the WWHC offers federated searching of WWHC members, as well as subject guides around relevant themes unique to women's history. Similar to other consortium search models, rather than one repository shouldering the often immense cost of such a dynamic web presence, federal grant money helps to support the access and use of materials without necessarily privileging one archives over another.[23] Significantly, the WWHC website offers a navigation bar to highlight new collection additions regardless of the repository to which they were donated.

The WWHC also offers several interactive features, such as a City of Olympia Women's History Walking Tour (see screenshot on page 453), as well as resources including biographies, digital collections, newspapers, oral histories, interactive maps and timelines, links to organizations, writings, and how-to prompts for doing women's history research. Taken as a whole, the WWHC facilitates subject-based access to collections, offers interactive features for users, promotes new collections and partner archives, and gives theme-based subject guidance from the unique perspective of women's history.

Another example of a women's documentation/women's archives partnership project is Through Women's Eyes: Southeast Asian American Women's Stories, which highlights a 1991–1992 project to document Asian American women living in the Washington, DC, area. Lisa Falk and

Screenshot of Through Women's Eyes: Southeast Asian American Women's Stories,
"Project Background" web page, http://www.u.arizona.edu/~falk/index.php

Uaporn Ang Robinson documented these women's complex lives; they
sought to create oral histories and photographs of the women "about their
dual identities as Southeast Asians and Americans and their multiple roles
as professionals, wives, mothers, daughters, tradition bearers, and community leaders."[24] A prime example of the charge to find and document
unique women's populations *where they are*, Through Women's Eyes offers
images, transcripts, and biographies of the women who participated.
Though affiliated with the University of Arizona, Through Women's Eyes
was and remains a largely private endeavor to document a very particular
group of women living in a particular place. The heavy emphasis on locality, like many of the web projects discussed so far, is both emphasized
and negated at the same time—emphasized in the sense that location and
community define the project scope, and in the uniqueness of the micro-
cosmic lived experience of the women involved; negated through a vital
and interactive web presence that is not defined or confined by any physical boundaries. Similar work is being done at Smith College in the Voices

of Feminism Oral History Project. Described as a project that "aims to bring race, class, and sexual diversity to the holdings of the Sophia Smith Collection," it consists of several parts: 1) searching for personal papers and organizational records of women of color, grassroots organizers, and others marginalized in traditional historical accounts; 2) conducting oral histories; 3) collaborating with Gloria Steinem to identify potential donors; and 4) developing plans for a video documentary series based on these new materials.[25]

In this case, the emphasis on locality is almost totally absent, but, in exchange, there is a diversity of information and content on the sixty-plus women interviewed. The Voices of Feminism Project is an example of how

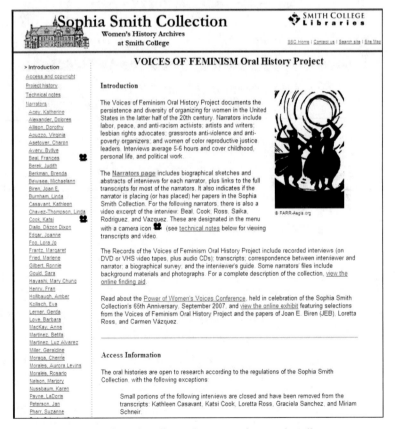

Screenshot of Smith College Libraries Sophia Smith Collection,
"Voices of Feminism Oral History Project" web page,
http://www.smith.edu/libraries/libs/ssc/vof/vof-intro.html.

archivists of women's collections perceived absences within their existing collections and actively sought to change them. In these cases, when archivists seek the marginalized, the solution is not simple, but rather involves a multifaceted approach to collection development that includes oral histories, pathfinding new donors, and developing multimedia access tools. Impressively, the Voices of Feminism is only one of several oral history and other documentation projects featured by Smith. Others include the Population and Oral History Project; An Activist Life: Student Oral History Project; and Documenting Lesbian Lives: Student Oral History Project—almost all of which offer biographies of the participants and transcripts of the interviews.

The Promise of the Archival Future

Women's archives and archivists of women's collections do not hold exclusive rights to the Internet, nor do they employ methodologies utterly divorced from other genres of archival practice.[26] At the same time, women's archives and archivists of women's collections have been active in creating an accessible documentary universe of women's records as part of social change. That universe as it exists today is dynamic for its evolving embrace of new definitions, collection scope, and technology, and its emphasis on locality and diversity of women's experiences. Indeed, all archivists can aspire to the goals proposed by Lerner, to recognize that "Each human action occurs within a network of forces; each is in organic connection to other forces; there is constant interplay, adjustment, and flow . . . [archivists] must strive for more complexity, more awareness of the connections between the event and its surroundings—for a more holistic representation." What that means within the profession is, like most things archival, unique to each institution. However, close and critical evaluation of women's archival traditions illustrates the promise, pragmatism, and pitfalls of collecting women's records over the past century—as broad, viable lessons for other archivists.

First, women's archives were and are created as a political act—as argu-ably most subject archives are. By focusing on those who are excluded, especially due to discrimination, archivists embrace a social and politi-cal responsibility. Second, the diversity of subject archives is not a given. Women's archives, even while actively challenging androcentricism, prac-ticed patterns of exclusion and omission based on race, sexuality, and class. Third, the value and authenticity of a document does not depend upon its form. The role of the archivist can be that of creator or cocreator of materials, such as oral histories or other types of documenting projects, if that results in the creation of a more diverse and complex record over all. The participation of archivists (or partnerships with historians) does not render the materials less valuable or genuine, but makes transparent the connection between those who create and those who keep. Fourth, archivists should recognize that we do not have—and never have had—sole control over the collection and preservation of the historic record. Similarly, no one archives could possibly be responsible for making it all accessible and advocating its use. Instead, the promise of the archival future rests in the continued, perhaps even reinvigorated, emphasis on local collecting and the sharing of that content online. In addition, archi-vists must welcome third-party participants into our professional dia-logue—partners in creating access and promoting the collections we all value—whether they are archivists or not. Ultimately, archival relevancy is reinforced, not diminished, by sharing resources, exposing absences, and promoting the marginalized into the mainstream narrative of his-tory. The successful model for these approaches is amply documented in women's archives and women's archival traditions.

NOTES

[1] See Mark Greene, "The Power of Meaning: The Mission of the Archives in the Postmodern World," *American Archivist* 65 (2002): 42–55; Mark Greene, "The Power of Archives: Archivists' Values and Value in the Postmodern Age," *American Archivist* 72 (2009): 17–41; Luciana Duranti, "Meeting the Challenge of Contemporary Records: Does It Require a Role Change for the Archivist?," *American Archivist* 63 (200): 7–14; Luciana Duranti, "The Concept of Appraisal

and Archival Theory," *American Archivist* 57 (1994): 328–44; and Richard Cox, "Re-Discovering the Archival Mission: The Recordkeeping Functional Requirements Project at the University of Pittsburgh, A Progress Report," *Archives and Museum Informatics* 8 (1994): 276–300. However, the roots of this debate outside of the new technology are soundly between the theories of Hilary Jenkinson/Margaret Cross Norton and T. R. Schellenberg.

[2] As quoted by Mark Greene in "The Power of Archives," 17–41; original citation: Sidney J. Levy and Albert G. Robles, "The Image of Archivists: Resource Allocators Perceptions" (paper presented at the Society of American Archivists Annual Meeting, 1984).

[3] James O'Toole and Richard J. Cox, *Understanding Archives and Manuscripts* (Chicago: Society of American Archivists, 2006), chapter 2; Hilary Jenkinson, "Reflections of an Archivist," in *Modern Archives Reader*, reprint, *Contemporary Review* 165 (1944): 15–23.

[4] There is a vast amount of scholarly literature on the first-wave women's movement with a focus on the feminist ideology that supported it. Nancy Cott wrote or edited extensively on the subject and remains a valuable access point to the topic. See Nancy Cott, *The Grounding of Modern Feminism* (New Haven: Yale University Press, 1987), *No Small Courage: a History of Women in the United States* (New York: Oxford University Press, 2000), and *The Bonds of Womanhood: Women's Sphere in New England, 1780–1835* (New Haven: Yale University Press, 1977). Similarly, Gerda Lerner's work must be cited, including *The Creation of Patriarchy* (New York: Oxford University Press, 1986), *The Creation of a Feminist Consciousness: From the Middle Ages to 1870* (New York: Oxford University Press, 1983), and *The Majority Finds its Past: Placing Women in History* (New York: Oxford University Press, 1979).

[5] See the history of the IAV/IIAV/Aletta archives for further reference.

[6] See also Eva Moseley, "Women in Archives: Documenting the History of Women in America," *American Archivist* 36 (1973): 215–22.

[7] Andrea Hinding, ed., *Women's History Sources*, 2 vols. (New York: R. R. Bowker Company, 1979).

[8] Essential reading for postmodernism is Michele Foucault, *Discipline and Punish: The Birth of the Prison* (New York: Pantheon Books, 1977) and *History of Sexuality* (New York: Pantheon Books, 1978).

[9] Jacques Derrida, "'To Do Justice to Freud': The History of Madness in the Age of Psychoanalysis," in *Foucault and His Interlocutors*, ed. Arnold I. Davidson (Chicago: University of Chicago Press, 1997), as quoted in Carolyn Steedman,

Dust: The Archive and Cultural History (New Brunswick, NJ: Rutgers University Press, 2002), 2.

[10] Derrida, "'To Do Justice to Freud.'"

[11] See also Folk Life in Louisiana, "Louisiana Quilt Documentation Project," http://www.louisianafolklife.org/quilts/homemaster.shtm for specific reference to quilting projects.

[12] The concepts of *double-consciousness* and *positionality* are explored at length by Sharlene Nagy Hesse-Biber and Michelle L. Yaiser, *Feminist Perspectives on Social Research* (New York: Oxford University Press, 2004); and Joey Sprague, *Feminist Methodologies for Critical Researchers* (Walnut Creek, CA: Altamira Press, 2005).

[13] There are several good books and collected essays dealing with this subject, including Elizabeth Lapovaski Kennedy and Agatha Beins, eds., *Women's Studies for the Future: Foundations, Interrogations, Politics* (New Brunswick, NJ: Rutgers University Press, 2005); and Marilyn Boxer, *When Women Ask the Questions: Creating Women's Studies in America* (Baltimore: Johns Hopkins University Press, 1998).

[14] See Gloria T. Hull, Patricia Bell-Scott, and Barbara Smith, eds., *All the Women Are White, All the Blacks Are Men, but Some of Us Are Brave: Black Women's Studies* (Old Westbury, NY: Feminist Press, 1982).

[15] In addition to Michel Foucault, see Judith Butler, *Gender Trouble: Feminism and the Subversion of Identity* (New York: Routledge, 1990), *Bodies that Matter: On the Discursive Limits of Sex* (New York: Routledge, 1993), and *Undoing Gender* (New York: Routledge, 2004); as well as Joan W. Scott, *Gender and the Politics of History* (New York: Columbia University Press, 1988), *Feminism and History* (Oxford: Oxford University Press, 1996), and "Gender: A Useful Category of Analysis," *American Historical Review* 91 (1986): 1053–75.

[16] Abigail Brooks, "Feminist Standpoint Epistemology: Building Knowledge and Empowerment through Women's Lived Experience" in *Feminist Research Practice: A Primer*, ed. Sharlene Nagy Hesse-Biber and Patricia Leavy (Thousand Oaks, CA: Sage Publications, 2007), 56.

[17] Brooks, "Feminist Standpoint Epistemology," 63–64.

[18] Jewish Women's Archive, "About," http://jwa.org/aboutjwa, accessed 12 February 2012.

[19] Jewish Women's Archive, "Community Oral History Projects," http://jwa.org/oralhistory, accessed 12 February 2012.

[20] Spertus, "Library and Collections," http://www.spertus.edu/library, accessed 12 February 2012.

[21] Washington Women's History Consortium, "Interactive Web Resources," http://washingtonwomenshistory.org/, accessed 12 February 2012.

[22] Washington Women's History Consortium, "Interactive Web Resources," http://washingtonwomenshistory.org/, accessed 12 February 2012.

[23] See the Black Metropolis Research Consortium, http://bmrcsurvey.uchicago .edu, and the Catholic Research Resource Alliance "About," http://www .catholicresearch.net/cms/index.php/about-crra/. The success of larger, more comprehensive collaborative web portals (like the Online Archives of California) at highlighting women's collections depends heavily upon the metadata that controls the access to collection-level information. In other words, web portals need not be solely dedicated to women's issues to be successful at promoting women's collections, but the points of access have to be meticulously managed to ensure that women are not rendered invisible in the larger catalog.

[24] Through Women's Eyes: Southeast Asian American Women's Stories, "Project Background," http://www.u.arizona.edu/~falk/background.php, accessed 12 February 2012.

[25] Smith College Libraries Sophia Smith Collection, "Voices of Feminism Oral History Project," http://www.smith.edu/libraries/libs/ssc/vof/vof-intro.html, accessed 12 February 2012.

[26] For explorations of the role of the participatory/activist archivist, see Andrew Flinn, "The Impact of Independent and Community Archives on Professional Archival Thinking and Practice," in *The Future of Archives and Recordkeeping: A Reader*, ed. Jennie Hill (London: Facet Publishing, 2011); Max Evans, "Archives of the People, By the People, for the People," *American Archivist* 70 (2007): 387–400; Lyle Dick, "The 1942 Same-Sex Trials in Edmonton: On the State's Repression of Sexual Minorities, Archives, and Human Rights in Canada," *Archivaria* 68 (2009): 183–219; Verne Harris, "Knowing Right from Wrong: The Archivist and the Protection of People's Rights," in *Archives and Justice: A South African Perspective* (Chicago: Society of American Archivists, 2007), 203–15; Randall Jimerson, "Archives for All: Professional Responsibility and Social Justice," *American Archivist* 70 (Fall/Winter 2007): 252–81; Rodney Carter, "Of Things Said and Unsaid: Power, Archival Silences, and Power in Silence," *Archivaria* 61 (2006): 215–33.

Author Biographies

 **Mary A. Caldera** is the head of arrangement and description in Manuscripts and Archives, Yale University Library. She received her BA and MLS from Texas Woman's University. She is actively documenting the lesbian, gay, bisexual, and transgender communities of southern Connecticut. Caldera's research interests include representation of sexual minorities in archives, and diversity and inclusion in the archives profession. She is the former cochair of the Society of American Archivists Lesbian and Gay Roundtable, Yale University Library Diversity Council, and the Yale University LGBTQ Affinity Group.

 **Virginia Corvid** is a recent graduate of the University of Wisconsin–Madison's Library and Information Studies Program where she specialized in archival administration and records management. She received her BA in history from the University of Washington, and her honors undergraduate thesis examined antisexual violence discourse in Riot Grrrl Zines. She is a long-time volunteer at the Zine Archive and Publishing Project located in Seattle, Washington, and is currently the records management assistant at Espresso Vivace.

Gerda Lerner, historian, educator, and author, was born in Vienna, Austria, on 30 April 1920. She escaped to the United States in 1939 where she worked first as a translator and writer. She received her AB from the New School for Social Research (1963) and MA (1965) and PhD (1966) from Columbia University. Lerner served as a professor at Long Island University and Sarah Lawrence College prior to being appointed Robinson-Edwards Professor of History and Wisconsin Alumni Research Foundation (WARF) Senior Distinguished Research Professor at the University of Wisconsin–Madison in 1980. She became emerita in 1990. One of the earliest proponents of women's history as a field of study, Lerner made lasting contributions to the development of the discipline by her distinguished research and writing, by developing curricular materials in women's history, by preservation and publicizing of women's history sources, and by upgrading the status of women in the historical profession. Her research explored abolitionism, slavery, African American women's history, and nineteenth-century women's history. Her writings include *The Woman in American History* (1971), *Black Women in White America: A Documentary History* (1972), *The Majority Finds Its Past: Placing Women in History* (1979), and *Why History Matters* (1997). The Gerda Lerner Papers are located at the Schlesinger Library, Radcliffe Institute for Advanced Study, Harvard University. Dr. Lerner passed away in January 2013.

Kären M. Mason is curator of the Louise Noun–Mary Louise Smith Iowa Women's Archives at the University of Iowa Libraries in Iowa City, a position she has held since the establishment of the archives in 1992. She earned a master's degree in history from the University of Minnesota and a PhD in history with a cognate in archival administration from the University of Michigan; her dissertation explored women's political activism and gender roles in Progressive-era Chicago. Her involvement with women's history dates to the late 1970s, when she worked on the *Women's History Sources* survey at the University of Minnesota and co-authored *A Women's History Tour of the Twin Cities*. She is the author or coauthor of several articles on women's history and on women's archives.

Audrey Thomas McCluskey, PhD, is professor and director of graduate studies in the Department of African American and African Diaspora Studies, and adjunct professor of American studies and African studies at Indiana University. She is imme-diate past director of the Neal-Marshall Black Culture Center. Before that, she served for seven years as director of the Black Film Center/Archive at IU. Her research and publications focus on issues of gender and history in education and racial representation in popular culture, including film. Her scholarly works appear in several noted journals, and her books on black educa-tors, film, and popular culture have been published by Indiana University Press and the University of Illinois Press. They include *Mary McLeod Bethune: To Make a Better World* (with Elaine M. Smith); *Race and Racial Representation in Film Poster Art*; *Richard Pryor: The Life and Legacy of a "Crazy" Black Man*; *The Devil You Dance With: Film Culture in the New South Africa*; and *Frame by Frame III: A Filmography of the Black Diasporan Image*. Her forthcoming book, *A Sisterhood Like No Other: Black Women School Founders of the Early 20th Century*, is due to be pub-lished in 2013 by Rowman-Littlefield Publishers.

Danelle Moon is a full professor/librarian and director of San José State University Special Collections and Archives. She holds an MLIS from Southern Connecticut State University and an MA in history from California State University–Fullerton. Her areas of expertise include women and politics, social reform during the Progressive Era, California and the West, and archival management. She has published numerous articles and presented research focused on women's social movements and politics. She is the author of *Women and the Civil Rights Movement* (ABC-CLIO, 2011), a general history of women's social movements from suffrage to feminism. She is currently working on another book, *Bridge Leadership in the Civil Rights Movement: Lobbying for Social Justice and Human Rights in Mid-Century America.*

Eva (Steiner) Moseley was curator of manuscripts at Radcliffe College's Arthur and Elizabeth Schlesinger Library on the History of Women in America, the country's, and perhaps the world's, largest library/archives devoted to women's history—or, as a former director put it, to *social* history "but we look at the women first." Her BA in philosophy from Mount Holyoke College (1953) and MA in Sanskrit and Indian studies from Radcliffe (1955) provided no technical knowhow for archival work, but that humanities background helped her to see actual collections and potential acquisitions in a wider context. After some minor assignments, Moseley cut her archival teeth by processing the papers of Charlotte Perkins Gilman (1860–1935), a writer and lecturer considered the philosopher of the first-wave women's movement. Reading Gilman's letters and notebooks, Moseley says, made her a feminist. Retiring in 1999, she launched an oral history project at a senior citizens' home; helped revive the Cambridge (MA) Archives Committee, made up of archivists and curators at the city's numerous repositories; and planned and implemented the exhibition *Growing Up Is Hard To Do: Harvard's Special Collections Document Some Trials of Our First 22 Years.* She is now sorting family papers and beginning to sort (and weed) her own papers for deposit at the Schlesinger Library.

Elizabeth Myers, PhD, CA, is the director of the Walter P. Reuther Library of Labor and Urban Affairs. She received her MA and PhD from Loyola University Chicago where she studied twentieth-century US history with a concentration on culture, gender, and politics. She came to the Reuther

Library and Wayne State University by way of Chicago, where she served as the director of the Women and Leadership Archives at Loyola University, a position she held for more than five years. In total, she has more than twelve years of experience in archives and special collections with active research interests in professional ethics, outreach, and collection development. Her most recent publication, "Juggling Act: Negotiating Third Party Collaboration in the Collection Development of Second Wave Feminist Materials," in *Make Your Own History: Documenting Feminist and Queer Activism in the 21ˢᵗ Century,* reflects her longtime interest in the intersection of history, archives, and identity.

Fernanda Perrone is archivist and head of the Exhibitions Program at Special Collections and University Archives at Rutgers University. She holds an MLS from Rutgers University, a DPhil in modern history from Oxford University, and a BA in history and English literature from McGill University. Previously, she worked as a project archivist at Rutgers, specializing in women's manuscript collections. Her research focuses on the history and archives of women religious communities and women's colleges. Articles include "Vanished Worlds: In Search of the Archives of Closed Catholic Women's Colleges," *Archival Issues* (2006); and "Whose History Is It? Doing Research in the Archives of Women's Religious Communities," *Catholic Library World* (2009). Her current interests include oral history and material culture as a way of understanding the history of women's religious communities.

Janice E. Ruth is the assistant chief of the Library of Congress Manuscript Division, where she previously held positions as a processing technician, reference librarian, writer-editor, and manuscript specialist in American women's history. She is one of the authors of *American Women: A Library of Congress Guide for the Study of Women's History and Culture in the United States* (2001), *Women Who Dare: Women of the*

Suffrage Movement (2006), and three Library of Congress websites relating to women's history, including Women of Protest. She was one of the organizers of the 2003 symposium "Resourceful Women: Researching and Interpreting American Women's History" and cofounded the Library of Congress Women's History Discussion Group, which brings together staff and researchers. She is a Fellow of the Society of American Archivists, served on the committee that developed the Encoded Archival Description (EAD) standard for electronic finding aids, and helped write the *EAD Tag Library* (version 1.0) and the *EAD Application Guidelines*. She holds an MLS and an MA in American history from the University of Maryland.

 **Taronda Spencer** was director of the Spelman College Archives and college historian. A second-generation archivist, she followed her mother, Emanuella Spencer, archivist at the Amistad Research Center in New Orleans (now retired), into the profession. Spencer earned a BA in history from Spelman College and an MA in history from the University of New Orleans. Professionally, she worked at a number of institutions including the Amistad Research Center, the Historic New Orleans Collection, and the Walter P. Reuther Archives of Labor and Urban Affairs at Wayne State University in Detroit. Spencer passed away suddenly in May 2013.

 **Susan Tucker** holds degrees from Tulane University, the University of Denver, and the University of Amsterdam. She has worked as an archivist at the Newcomb Archives since 1988, where she has written about the history of Newcomb College and various collections in the repository. She has also authored and edited such books as *Telling Memories Among Southern Women* (LSU Press, 1988), *The Scrapbook in American Life* (Temple University Press, 2006), *New Orleans Cuisine* (University of Mississippi Press, 2009), and *Women Pioneers of the Louisiana Environmental Movement* (University Press of Mississippi, 2013).

Anke Voss is the director of the Champaign County Historical Archives, the Urbana Free Library, in Urbana, Illinois. She is an adjunct faculty member in the Graduate School of Library and Information Science at the University of Illinois at Urbana-Champaign. She is active in both national and regional professional associations and most recently served as treasurer of the Midwest Archives Conference. Voss has a BA and an MA in history from the University of Massachusetts, Amherst, and an MSLS from the University at Albany, State University of New York.

Deborah Gray White is Board of Governors Professor of History at Rutgers University, New Brunswick, New Jersey. She is the author of *Ar'n't I a Woman? Female Slaves in the Plantation South* (1985 and 1999); *Too Heavy a Load: Black Women in Defense of Themselves, 1894–1994* (1999); *Let My People Go, African Americans 1804–1860* (1999); and coauthor of several K–12 textbooks on US history, and the African American textbook, *Freedom On My Mind: A History of African Americans with Documents*. As a recent fellow at the Woodrow Wilson International Center for Scholars in Washington, DC, and as a John Simon Guggenheim Fellow, White conducted research for her forthcoming monograph, *Lost in the USA: American Identity at the Turn of the Millennium.*

Tanya Zanish-Belcher is the director, Special Collections, and university archivist for Wake Forest University, after previously serving as the head of Special Collections and University Archives at Iowa State University (1998–2013). She received her BA (1983) in history from Ohio Wesleyan University and an MA (1990) in historical and archival administration from Wright State University in Dayton, Ohio. She has published articles about women's archives, women in science and engineering, and other aspects of archival management. Zanish-Belcher has given numerous presentations to local and regional groups, as well as professional organizations such as the Midwest Archives Conference (MAC) and the Society of American Archivists (SAA). She is a past president of MAC and currently serves on the Council of SAA. She is an SAA Fellow.

Index

Figures are indicated by (f).
Illustrations are indicated by (i).